London to Kabul

Grateful Steps Foundation
333A Merrimon Avenue
Asheville, North Carolina 28801

Cox, Wayne G.
London to Kabul: the journey that led me to her

Cover photograph by Özgür Çakır
Cover design by Miriam L. Cox
All photographs in the book interior are from the author's personal collection.
All maps are modified from CIA maps in the public domain.

THIS IS IT
Words and Music by KENNY LOGGINS and MICHAEL McDONALD
© 1979 MILK MONEY MUSIC and TAURIPIN TUNES
All Rights Reserved
pages 377-378

All Scripture references are from the King James Version of the Bible.

ISBN 978-1-935130-70-3 Paperback
Library of Congress Control Number 2015903832
Printed in the United States of America
Versa Press, East Peoria, Illinois
FIRST EDITION

PUBLISHER'S CATALOGING-IN-PUBLICATION DATA
Cox, Wayne G.
London to Kabul : the journey that led me to her / Wayne G. Cox. -- First edition.

pages : illustrations, maps ; cm

Issued also as an ebook.
ISBN: 978-1-935130-70-3 (paperback)

1. Cox, Wayne G.--Relations with women. 2. Children of God (Organization)
3. Interfaith dating. 4. Man-woman relationships. 5. Women, Arab.
6. Missionaries--Arab countries. 7. Hippies--Travel--Arab countries. I. Title.
HQ801.8 .C69 2015
306.84/3   2015903832

www.gratefulsteps.org

*To my dear wife, to our four loving
children and to God*

Contents

MAPS

Near the pier at Huntington Beach, California, 1968, a preacher gave peanut butter sandwiches to hungry hippies and invited them to a coffeehouse to talk and to listen to rock music. More disillusioned youth of this affluent city came, and some began living communally in the home of the preacher and his wife. They became a movement of young people called the Children of God. Here is the story of one of them.

London to Kabul
THE JOURNEY THAT LED ME TO HER

WAYNE G. COX

GRATEFUL STEPS
ASHEVILLE, NORTH CAROLINA

PART ONE

London to Istanbul . . .

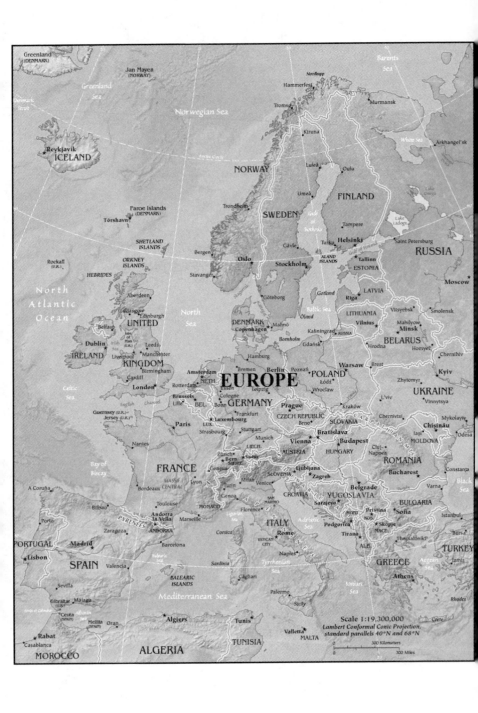

Chapter 1
⟨ *The Journey Begins* ⟩

"LOOK HOW GREEN it is down there!" I said to the girl sitting next to me. She leaned over to peer with me out the window of the Boeing 747 jumbo jet that had just broken through a low ceiling of clouds on its final approach to London's Heathrow Airport. The typically overcast sky of England was enhancing the lush greenery below, leaving me, at 22 years old, soothed and refreshed to be arriving in this new and foreign land, away from America, embarking on a spiritual calling to the rest of the world. Nineteen others and I aboard this flight from New York were part of the Children of God—a Bible-based group that started in 1968 in Huntington Beach, California, and now consisted of hundreds of mostly young people from diverse backgrounds. None of us owned anything either, except maybe a passport and whatever might fit into a suitcase or backpack. Each one of us, somewhere in the world, probably on some street, had experienced such an abrupt spiritual awakening we were willing to give up all our worldly goods, drop whatever we were doing in life and join this group. And, like the twenty of us aboard this airplane, members were now traveling to distant lands to share this new love with others. It was August 1972.

An old, red, double-decker bus belonging to the London branch of the group awaited us at the airport. It was a typical British city bus except both sides blazed with huge letters that read:

THE JESUS REVOLUTION.

I recognized next to the letters a painting of our group's logo—a bearded, long-haired doomsday prophet wearing sackcloth, a wooden yoke around his neck like an ox, and holding a foreboding wooden rod.

About 20 members of the London colony had come along to greet us and soon after we pulled away from the airport, the whole inside of the bus filled with the sounds of live acoustic guitars and singing. We headed southeast to our new home outside of London—a huge warehouse in the middle of the town of Bromley, Kent. Donated by a British millionaire, the warehouse had become the main London home for over one hundred members of the group. I didn't know it, but I would be taking over as "Head of Building Maintenance"—a nightmare of endless, dirty, physical responsibility.

I was about to see my beloved brother, Gary, also part of the group and living somewhere here in England. Gary and I had established an exceptional bond of brotherhood back in the States in recent years, living together in our perfectly kept rented home with a circular organic garden in the large backyard near downtown Orlando, Florida. We had both dropped out of college, done plenty of drugs, shared expenses and unrelentingly backed one another through the turbulent sixties of America.

Both of us at the same time, at the end of 1971 in Orlando, were approached by the Children of God.

It began inside the Warren Stanley shoe store on Colonial drive in East Orlando nine months back, when two girls came up to us and started talking about God. After a while, the girl talking to me looked me straight in the eyes and told me she loved me—not *me* exactly, but my *soul*. It blew my mind really. No girl had told me she actually loved my *soul*. She wasn't one bit pretty, but the Light of God shone in her eyes! The girls talked to us separately for 15 minutes or more in the store—despite some older couple in a car outside waiting for them and the owner of the store curiously looking on. The one girl asked me if I would pray with her, right then and there in the shoe store, to receive God's Holy Spirit. I did, holding her hands and bowing my head.

Gary and I both already believed in Jesus, taught through our loving Mom all our lives, but the Holy Spirit changed everything. When I asked the girl about the older couple waiting for her, she responded, "The only important thing right now is *you*."

The girls told us they lived communally with some people up in Atlanta, Georgia, and handed us a pamphlet with their address on it.

"Come and see for yourselves the *real* love there," the one talking to me said.

Two days after meeting the girls, we drove to Atlanta in fairly heavy snow and pulled straight up to the address on the pamphlet: a huge, white, two-story, wood-framed house at 971 Piedmont Avenue, N.E. And sure enough, we were given the same sincere love and attention as the "shoe store girls" by those inside—25 to 30 young men and women, mostly in their twenties, like us. They had each forsaken all they had in life and were now living together, concentrating on reaching souls in the streets—or shoe stores—or wherever, with the love of God. Gary prayed with someone in the evening to receive the Holy Spirit. We spent the night and left the next day. "We'll be back to join you once we get rid of our Orlando possessions," I told the leaders.

Gary and I were not employed at the time, although we'd made and saved good money working full-time planting the grass, flowers and trees of Walt Disney World before its October 1971 opening. In fact, I ended up with quite an excellent job of trimming and shaping the newly planted trees throughout the Park. Disney Company's Landscape Division then offered me a permanent tree-trimmer position. But when the Park opened to the public, the management demanded that all male employees cut their hair really short and even shave off their moustaches . . . so Gary and I quit. Never mind, there were plenty of jobs in the Orlando area.

We had suddenly found a purposeful calling in our lives and began to sell or give away all our furniture, records, stereos, appliances, everything. I gave away Kitty, my Siamese cat, to some girls across the street. After all, joining the Children of God required we get rid of everything we had, according to verse 14.33 in Luke: "So likewise, whosoever he be of you that forsaketh not all that he hath, he cannot be my disciple." We would then have to trust in God, like the rest of the group, for our daily needs and money.

That December, once we'd decided to join the group in Atlanta, a couple rather shocking incidents occurred. One was when we took our more valuable goods—furniture, appliances, stereos—to a flea market outside of Orlando where we met a vendor called "Brother John," an older, congenial guy with a long, white beard. We explained to John *why* we were selling everything, and he offered to sell it all for us and give us the money. So, we returned a week later, looked him up, and he said he had misplaced our stuff. "Come back after Christmas," he said. We returned after Christmas, tried to find him and learned he had died of a heart attack on Christmas Eve! Gary and I looked at each other with gaping mouths. *Had God taken this guy's life for stealing from us?* I wondered. We departed the market without so much as a dollar for our things but with plenty of *awe* and fear of God!

Near the end of December after we counted our money and were getting closer to leaving our "old life" behind, Gary started having last-minute doubts and said, "Hey. Maybe we should keep back half the money here with Mom and Dad . . . in case things don't work out with the group."

"No. It's all or nothing," I said. "This is it. If it doesn't work out, that's tough."

That same evening, we opened our new Bibles to the beginning of Acts, Chapter 5 in the New Testament. It is the story from verses one to eleven of two people—Ananias and his wife Sapphira—who came to join St. Peter and the apostles but had kept back part of the price of the land they had sold. Peter knew it, confronted Ananias with it, and the latter "gave up the ghost"—died right there. Sapphira came three hours later, not knowing what had happened, was similarly confronted, and she too died right there. *Oh God!*

We said goodbye to friends and spent one last good Christmas with our parents in Orlando. I remember Mom saying before we finally left, "Are you sure you know what you're doing? You both had good jobs out at Disney. Bill can get you both back in out there if you want." Bill, who had originally hired us, was Disney's director of landscape architecture. He was good friends with Dad.

"Mom," I said. "Anybody can work at a regular job all day. That's not hard. But *this* is going to be a challenge. It might not be easy, but we're gonna give it a try. We love you, Mom."

We drove back up to Atlanta at the end of December 1971 and moved into the home on Piedmont Avenue. We handed over every dollar of the $1,800 we had, along with the keys to our immaculate, burgundy 1969 Volkswagen Kharman Ghia, and jumped into this new life.

We remained at the Atlanta home for only two weeks before the group sent me to a colony at 1016 Cumberland Avenue in Knoxville, Tennessee. They sent Gary to Charleston, South Carolina, and then on to England.

Now, seven months later, I was within a few hours and a few short miles from once again meeting up with him.

The day after my arrival at the Bromley colony, I was driven a few miles away to the "Chinbrook" home—a large, quaint house Gary maintained on Chinbrook Road where the group conducted a Montessori school for children. A perfect setting for the reunion. Gary was in an upstairs room of the home, and as I entered the room, he stood looking out the window, admiring the garden below, unaware anyone had entered. I silently walked over and put my hand on his shoulder. Not even knowing I was in England, Gary turned to look into my eyes, and we both wept while hugging each other. After all, we'd been adjusting separately to this odd new spiritual life with the Children of God now for seven months. It was time to catch up.

"What the hell are you doing here, you weirdo?" Gary said. "I didn't even know you were *coming* to England."

Typical of me—living day to day and rarely planning too far into the future, not bothered enough about what I might do in life to give my brother advance notice of my coming.

Gary dropped what he was doing and devoted his attention to me. Exhilarated with his new life here in the English countryside, he gave me a tour of the domain he now maintained. One of his favorite areas, the backyard of the school/home, had a white-gravel path winding through lush green grass and around a small center garden of fragrant pink, red, white and yellow roses, normal for England.

But it was at the warehouse back in Bromley where I would spend the next four months as maintenance supervisor—a position of tremendous burden. I took over the job from Gary so he could now concentrate on building Montessori equipment for the school. The huge warehouse had been converted into two floors of living space with various office rooms throughout and separate dormitory rooms upstairs equipped with metal bunk beds for the single men and women. Both floors had tremendous open space for meetings and get-togethers—too much space, because the home soon became a *blob* of members funneling through from the States to Europe and countries farther east.

There I was, conscientious and dedicated to always do my best at whatever job I had, in charge of maintaining this massive building, keeping it properly heated, driving a Bedford van to the dump with barrels of horrible, wet, food-garbage from the over one hundred people, cleaning, fixing . . . always something to be done. All for free, too, all volunteer work, no salary.

The warehouse job was a strain but not the major contributing factor that led me to Italy and countries farther east. For one thing, after living with my parents in Paris and Turkey when my dad was in the military, and visiting the Holy Lands once, I remained drawn to Europe and the

Middle East—felt the grass was greener or something. But what also compelled me to head east was a revelation by one of the Bromley colony members who said one night during a prayer meeting, "*Go! Go to the untouched fields of the East, where the spirit is real, where there is a spirit behind every rock. Go where the spirits are alive. Go!*"

So, I didn't have to think twice when an opportunity arose for me to split the wet and cold of England—and my warehouse job—and transfer to Italy to join others in the Work there. Arrangements were quickly made by the Bromley leaders for my immediate departure, along with another volunteer named Bob. Also, accompanying Bob and me to Italy would be—*the trunk*—a large, black chest packed by the Bromley leaders to be delivered to those in charge in Rome. "Sure," we said, even though we had no idea what was inside it. We were just dumb sheep.

Gary remained busy these days remodeling the "Hollingbourne" mansion—another home the group had a few miles southeast near the town of Maidstone. Gary was also quite busy courting his British wife-to-be, Rebekah. The saddest thing about my leaving for Italy, though, was the quick goodbye note of a few scratched-out lines on a small piece of paper I left for Gary. He broke out in tears when he read it after finding it on his Bromley bunk bed. In the haste of the leaders deciding to send Bob and me south, and upon us accepting the transfer without hesitation, I had no time to say goodbye.

Bob and I, like most group members, were always packed and ready to leave with our entire worldly possessions in one backpack each and an attached sleeping bag for a bed. *Praise God.*

After receiving last-minute instructions, train tickets and enough money for the journey, we were driven in the group's van on a sunny but cold morning to the bustling, organized line-up of trains at Victoria Station in London, for the train to France.

Bob was a fantastic "brother." He looked a bit like Frankenstein, standing well over six-feet tall, lanky, American, blond, with blue, sunken eyes. Kinda handsome and kinda strange-looking at the same time, he was bold, strong and trustworthy—a great person to have as a partner.

In fact, when it came to shuffling that trunk on and off French trains and between the legs of French people standing on Paris subways, only someone as courageous as Bob could do it without care or bother. What a scene: two idiot Americans bending over with dumb-looking backpacks strapped to their backs, dragging this huge, black trunk through crowds of intolerant French commuters.

Why were we in the Paris *subway* at all, when we were supposed to be taking the *train* to Rome? I soon saw train travel was not so easy in Europe, especially if not fluent in the language spoken over the loudspeakers. We had boarded this train at the Paris junction, settled in (trunk and all), backpacks finally off our shoulders, when a fellow passenger told us, "You're headed in the wrong direction."

Great. Fortunately, we hadn't traveled too far. We disembarked and took the subway back to Paris—along with the trunk of course—arriving at what must have been the Paris workers' rush hour. The next train to Italy departed several hours later, so we sat on our trunk and enjoyed some fresh, hot French bread with Gruyere cheese followed by some fancy French pastries.

Chugging into Northwestern Italy the next night, I said to Bob, "Look!"

"Oh, they're beautiful!" he said.

Through a huge aisle window of the train, we gazed upon the Italian Alps glistening blue and white in the moonlight, their peaks jutting into that cold December sky. The beauty of the snow outside our warm train rewarded us for stepping out to travel and change.

The next day we reached our destination—the main train station of Rome. We made a phone call to the Rome colony and two brothers came to retrieve and welcome us. One had a guitar with him. Both were Americans, but one had been here in Italy for a while and spoke pretty good Italian. We boarded a not-too-crowded city bus with them, trunk and all, and before long the two brothers broke out singing in Italian in the middle of the bus, one playing the guitar while Bob and I just sort of clapped, went along with it all and helped pass out tracts in Italian to the people sitting there and looking at us in wonder. Okay, obviously the "Work" was strong here in Italy, and the group not one bit inhibited about getting the "Words" out anywhere, anytime.

I was a bit embarrassed.

We ended up at the Rome "art gallery" colony. The group thanked us immensely for bringing the much-needed contents of . . . the trunk . . . from the London Work. It felt good to finally dump such a load, to have accomplished a mission and to have satisfied others with needed items.

The colony was quite homey. Located on a typical, cobblestoned, Rome side street just around the corner from the Piazza Navona, the dwelling itself indeed had been a small art gallery the group had converted into both a home and a sort of coffeeshop. Entering the place from the street, we came into a large room set up with chairs at little round tables. Passing through a stone archway, we found ourselves in a small dining room. From there, another similar archway led into a small kitchen in the rear of the gallery. In a corner of the dining room, a staircase of wrought iron steps led upstairs to a cozy, low-ceilinged room the length of the coffeeshop below, where 15 or more members could sleep. This is where Bob and I stretched out our sleeping bags for the sleep we didn't get much of on the train.

The next day was Christmas Eve and all Children of God members in Rome and nearby cities were to spend two days near Florence at Certaldo on the farm of an Italian duke—a friend and newly joined member of the group. All made their way to the Certaldo farm . . . except Bob and me. We had stepped out for a walk and returned to find the gallery locked and with a phone number taped on the door. We called the number to learn we'd somehow "missed the boat" and were given directions to the Certaldo farm by a girl on the other end who finally said, "Try to get here on your own, you guys. We love you!"

No problem, I thought. *We'll hitchhike to Florence.* Well, we never got the slightest *hint* of a ride after sticking our thumbs out from the same spot on the outskirts of Rome from noon until dark. One of our first lessons: don't *ever*, if a male, expect to hitchhike successfully from Rome, Italy!

We had no money, but fortunately, Bob spoke some French, and after we prayed, he convinced a kind restaurant owner nearby to give us each a plate of hot spaghetti and meatballs. We then walked the cold streets of Rome and tried to convince the manager of each of three hotels to give us a room for the night. Nothing. Feeling bedraggled, we ended up at the main Rome train station along with various other vagrants, sleeping on cardboard and newspapers over grates issuing warm, under-city updrafts. From *that* discomfort, we went into the train station where we attempted to sleep, sitting in the cushioned waiting chairs until about dawn. Train officials, convinced we were bums, not ticket-paying passengers, kindly asked us to leave.

Merry Christmas, Wayne and Bob. Oh boy.

We never considered ourselves as bums begging for food, but rather as emissaries who had been called to preach the gospel, recalling from a verse in the Bible that "the labourer is worthy of his hire" (Luke 10.7). We spent much of that Christmas Day on a hill of grass, across the street from the half-crumpled Coliseum, and were fortunately given a good, free lunch by another kind-hearted restaurant manager.

That night, after a desperate prayer, we were given a nice, warm, three-star hotel room about a block from the Coliseum. The manager of the place, a beautiful Indian woman, provided the two of us with the room, a good meal and breakfast the next morning. *God bless her.*

The next afternoon, now our third day, we returned to the art gallery to find the others who had finally returned from *their* Christmas holiday in Tuscany.

After only a few days at the art gallery, I transferred across town to Trastevere where I spent the next three months at the river-front apartment of "the Duke." I had somehow been selected to move into the Duke's apartment to keep the place clean and tidy and to be one of his drivers.

The Duke was indeed an Italian duke who actually joined the group in 1972. A lawyer, disillusioned by the Italian system, he leaned toward involvement with the Communist Party of Rome. One day, on the Spanish Steps of Rome, he heard one of our music groups called the "Italian Band" playing music, with lyrics proclaiming the answer to life's inadequacies was through God's love. The Duke grasped it all wholeheartedly and before long fell in love with and married one of the group's original members, Queen Diane—a beautiful, long-haired, open-minded California girl of the sixties and one of the leaders of the Children of God.

I got along well with the Duke and Diane and the select few who lived off and on in the Duke's Rome apartment. Meanwhile, I kept the place clean and always remained ready to drive and run errands.

Various leaders of the worldwide family visited Rome and stayed at the Duke's apartment. One—a Jewish-American guy, turned born-again Christian, named Arthur—arrived at the apartment one day with stories from farther East, particularly Istanbul, Turkey.

Arthur—outspoken, short, fairly bald-headed, with black hair and black eyes—was precious and lovable. He'd been put in charge of the Middle East area, kinda like how the Catholic Church assigned bishops over certain areas. He was now in Rome to commission others to this domain of his.

On the night of his arrival, when a group of us gathered in the Duke's kitchen, Arthur jumped up and down with excitement about the Work in Istanbul, Turkey, where his associates ministered predominantly to the transient foreign travelers there. Story after story filled the kitchen—stories like one of the brothers praying for a young German heroin addict in a crowded Istanbul café, which caused the German kid laid out on the floor to miraculously spring up, praising God.

Well, Arthur needed more laborers there "in the field" to further the fruitful work beginning to bud in the Middle East. I was again ripe for a change, and Arthur knew it. Not that I was completely gullible to his sales pitch. I remembered the revelation back in London of a "spirit behind every rock." I had now been in Rome about three months, *loved* this fabulous land of Italy, but once again felt bored and uninspired with my mundane maintenance job. So, after a bit more planning than I'd done back in London when I abruptly left there with Bob and the trunk, and after contemplating whether or not I really did want to go to Turkey, I readied my backpack for adventures farther east with Arthur.

Chapter 2
⇾ *Istanbul* ⇽

IN MARCH 1973, Arthur and I boarded a flight from Rome to Athens, Greece—paid for by the Duke. *Greece! Yes!* We landed before sunset at the Athens airport in time to see the dry, small, barren-but-beautiful mountains and, in the distance to the west, the glistening of the turquoise-blue Mediterranean waters, with islands sprouting out of them. Exiting the plane, I was pleased to feel the warm-yet-dry climate in this new country.

Arthur introduced me to the handful of "pioneers" of the Athens family who lived in a clean, small, first-floor apartment in a lower-middle-class neighborhood. There were only eight of them in the little family, with a married couple heading them.

Greece definitely felt Middle East. Perhaps something mythical about the region and the Mediterranean itself explained why the Greeks seemed more Middle Eastern than European. For instance, whereas Italians, and surely the French and British, could commonly take or leave Westerners singing on street corners with guitars, the Greeks—men and boys, that is—would immediately mass, gawk and quickly become a blob of confusion. This could get unpleasant, but generally, I liked the nonchalant, third-world atmosphere that permeated everyday life in Greece—the open markets, siestas in the afternoon, leisurely nightlife strolls and general simplicity of the people.

I lived in Athens less than two months before Arthur asked me by letter to continue east to Turkey. Too bad, really. I was starting to enjoy the warm, welcoming atmosphere of Greece. Hopefully, I would return to savor it some time, but I accepted the calling to Turkey. Over a year ago, when asked by the leadership back at the Knoxville colony where I would choose to go if I went overseas, I said Turkey. I had lived in Izmir, Turkey, for two years with my parents when I was 12 and 13 years old, and something about the Middle East enchanted me from that time on. Some of that enchantment might well have come when my family (father, mother, brother, two sisters and I) traveled by car from Izmir to Jerusalem and the Holy

Lands in Easter of 1962. At the age of 12, to walk around on the same streets and lands that Jesus and the prophets had walked—as so well explained to me by my precious mother and father—was an experience not easily forgotten.

Gathering my meager backpack-belongings and a bit of money and instructions, I headed to the Athens train station for the trip to Istanbul. On this journey, I would be partners with a husky, homely German sister named Harriet. We departed Athens late evening, the train so crowded the only seats Harriet and I had were our own backpacks in the *aisle*.

The *moon* hung full and high overhead on that clear spring night, its brightness against the dark sky a comfort, as if it were reflecting the blessings of God on us.

By the time the train reached the large city of Thessalonica in the north of Greece, Harriet and I finally found real bench seats in a normal train compartment. But more travelers boarded at Thessalonica and the aisles filled up again.

Some time in late morning the following day, we reached the Greek-Turkish border where checking passports took at least an hour before the train could chug on into the Western Turkey countryside.

Had we arrived in Turkey? Yes. How did I know? When I saw Turkish men *squatting* along the concrete platform of train depots we whizzed past. The men were whiling away time, in what I called the "Turkish squat"—a position not easily performed by a Westerner. Our train finally wound its way to the final stop of Istanbul.

"Ahhh, it feels good to get off that train," I said to Harriet. But the mass of people on the platform confused us. And our assignment— another sudden one—meant no one at the Istanbul colony knew exactly when we would arrive.

We squeezed through crowds of Istanbul Turks—a substantial number staring at us—to the closest main street from the train station. Up it we walked with our goofy backpacks and checked into the New Istanbul Hotel—a class or two above flea bag.

Opening the door to our room, we took our backpacks off, put them on the wooden floor and immediately threw ourselves onto the single beds. What bliss to stretch out again! As for sharing a room alone together, we were pretty greatly unmatched mentally and physically for anything sexual to happen, Harriet taller than me, definitely heavier and "German-muscular" enough to probably beat me up if she wanted. Having separate single beds in the room helped. The toilet—down the hall and shared with other guests—was a small room with a hole in the floor one had to squat over, Turkish style. The toilet room itself was completely clean, but there is no way around the distinctive odor that can emanate from such an old hole in the floor when the ceramic plumbing beneath its opening has become *porous* with corrosion, thereby retaining such odors from the decades of human waste passing through it. There was no toilet paper in sight either. Instead, we found a spigot with a tin can under it to fill up with water to . . . somehow clean with—a good idea really since the rather ancient sewer system wasn't up to processing much toilet paper.

Okay. Checked in. Settled. Washed up and feeling great. Regardless of the class of hotel, just having our own beds in our own room was a reward. I felt I had accomplished something.

"Shall we go find something to eat?" I asked Harriet.

"Yeah, I'm so hungry!" she replied. We walked down the street to snoop around for available food—*cheap* food, since we had little money. And cheap food is what we ended up with. I actually remembered some of the Turkish language—though mostly cuss words—from the time I had lived in Izmir from 1961 to 1963. At least I could count, ask prices and understand the response.

Like idiots, we ended up eating *tripe* soup, made from the stomachs of ruminants such as lamb. *Oh, my God.* Not until about three months later would I discover what it was we had eaten. Actually though, except for a strange, never-experienced-before taste, it wasn't too bad. Besides, with that always-present quarter loaf of fresh-baked Turkish bread at every person's place setting—along with freshly-cut lemons, and certain spices to mix in with it—it went down well. Ridiculously cheap of course. Probably half a U.S. dollar to stuff ourselves.

The corner place where we consumed the soup was undoubtedly a Turkish workers' restaurant. Crude, simple and cheap. Metal chairs with turquoise Naugahyde cushions sat at metal tables with Formica tabletops in a large room lit up by fluorescent lights overhead. A few tables away from us, Turkish men nonchalantly picked at or devoured whole, cooked sheep heads—brains, eyes and all. Several restaurants in the area displayed these sheep delicacies in their windows. I didn't gawk at the men eating these heads, but it was a phenomenon I wouldn't forget. It reminded me of the Old Testament verse that came to me back at the huge meat and produce market outside of Rome when I saw lambs being led to butchers there. Some say the verse, Isaiah 53.7, is a prophecy of Jesus—". . . he is brought as a lamb to the slaughter, and as a sheep before her shearers is dumb, so he openeth not his mouth."

In a way, I considered some of these people, and even some of the rough Italian meat market merchants, as the butchers of today who would likewise take present day Christians and believers, like myself, to slaughter, like lambs, no problem.

The next responsibility for Harriet and me, after unwinding for a day by ourselves, was to contact the brethren of Istanbul. Now, the family of six living here had been informed by letter that we were coming from Greece, but no one knew the day, nor were we given any address or telephone number. All we had was a post office box number at the main Sirkeci, Istanbul, post office.

After a strong prayer the following morning, Harriet and I found our way to the post office, wrote a quick note and delivered it to the PO Box of our colleagues. We then sat down on the long stretch of gray marble steps outside the building, hoping one of the family members would come for their mail . . . and they did.

Patrick, head of the Istanbul team, and a girl named Judy came to check their post box and to mail some letters. No one of the four of us had ever met the other, and despite there being several other Westerners in this city, something led the four of us to approach one another.

"Hi! I'm Wayne. Are you Patrick?" I asked.

"Yeah," he said. "And this is Judy. I heard you guys might be coming, but no one said for sure."

There was no shaking of hands. Instead we hugged each other like lost relatives.

"Judy just joined recently," Patrick announced.

"That's great!" I said. She looked sweet and humble and seemed encouraged to see new faces like ours come to town. But I felt a slight coldness from Patrick.

"Where are your things?" Patrick asked.

"We have a little hotel up the street. Shall we go there?" I suggested.

"Yeah. Lead the way, Wayne." We four walked up the street to our humble room, chatted awhile and then checked out of the hotel.

"Let's get you guys home," Patrick said. He knew his way around this town, so the four of us boarded a city bus up to the Sultan Ahmet area. We changed buses and went on to the area of Laleli where the home was located.

The home was a first-floor apartment—one floor above ground floor—in a building of only eight apartments. Once inside we were again warmly welcomed, this time by sweet Sam—the real brother of Judy.

In the following days, Patrick and I ran errands, boarded buses together, purchased and ate Turkish *halva*—a sesame-oil-based sweet—probably the best in the world, while he explained how the group here focused on speaking to Western foreign travelers passing through the city. Something I didn't realize though was that I had actually been sent to Istanbul, by Arthur, to possibly *replace* Patrick as head of this Istanbul colony. The reason was so that Arthur could send Patrick to France where his old girlfriend, Samantha, from back in New York, choreographed for a dance troupe of the group. Patrick had received a letter that she wanted to marry him, and leaders of the group were encouraging the union.

Well, Patrick was *into* Turkey and into being the leader of the Work here and wasn't ready to hook up with Samantha. Not when there were pretty Turkish girls everywhere!

So, while I didn't have the slightest idea of all this intrigue, Patrick insisted on defending his post: to fight this intruder . . . me . . . who might ultimately force him into one of the world's highest commitments—marriage.

Currently, the two real leaders of the Work in this region, Matthew and Edward, were out of the country on a "visa trip"—a trip to renew their visitor visas by exiting Turkey to another country and re-entering, usually 24 hours later. In the meantime, Patrick saw Harriet and me as a threat to "his" Istanbul Work and made up his mind that she and I were being led by . . . the devil! *Imagine!*

Five days after Harriet and I arrived in Istanbul, Patrick, in cohoots with Sam, his assistant, came to me and said, "Wayne, I hate to say it, brother, but you and Harriet are just not fitting in here."

"What do you mean?"

"I mean, I don't know where your hearts are, but they're not here. Sam and I discussed it, and we think we're going to have to *isolate* you both to the other room for now, away from Judy."

Oh, my God! What's happened? I wondered. As *shepherd*, or leader, of this Istanbul colony, Patrick was supposed to be "anointed" and led by God. Harriet and I momentarily accepted his decision and moved into one of the bedrooms. And there we stayed, the pathetic two of us for nearly three days, so we wouldn't affect the new disciple, Judy. We were fed regularly and had use of the bathroom but had to remain in the room.

Why didn't we fight back? Well, I was never the belligerent type, and Patrick had become so in love with Turkey and his authority over the Work here he actually convinced Sam, Harriet and me to buy into his actions. Our personalities clashed. While Patrick exemplified the gung-ho, dive-in-without-thought follower of what he believed, I remained the cautious, slow, not-easily-excited worker. The devil used my lack of excitement in convincing both Patrick and me I just wasn't cut out for this forsake-all, discipleship ministry. *Hey*, I didn't smile all day long unless moved to.

One of those tortuous days, Patrick had me sit with him and Sam in the kitchen, and he asked me, "Wayne, where is your heart?" implying my *heart* was not really *into* this sacrificial movement of young people.

I contemplated the question for a few seconds, and, mostly to appease my "interrogator," I responded, "I guess it's sitting on a beach in Florida." In truthfulness, I guess—outside of this new spiritual life with the Children of God—I missed surfing back at Satellite Beach, Florida. But, the metaphorical question reeked. Imagine, my own poor heart—bloody valves and all—sitting all lonely on a sandy beach! God *damn!*

As for Harriet, I don't know how they portrayed her. Was her stoical, German composure used to judge her? Poor thing.

All I know is that the devil got heavy on me in that isolated room. After two days in there, I saw with clarity for the first time in my 23 years . . . the devil's *mercy*—that he has *no* mercy whatsoever and will condemn you to death if he can by insanity, suicide or any way possible. He will magnify any doubt that might enter the heart or mind. And through some human on earth to help him, he will not let up until one of God's people breaks the spell or the victim himself shakes it with realization of the truth.

But Patrick fought on for what he thought was right. He told Harriet and me that we would have to leave—be *excommunicated*.

Never mind. My older sister Diane currently lived in Izmir, Turkey, a bit farther south, with her husband, a general in the U.S. Army. We could stay with her. So, with bus tickets and a bit of money from Patrick, Harriet and I made the 20-or-so-hour trip to the charming coastal city of Izmir. Before going, mind you, Patrick and Sam *prayed* over us—apparently to rebuke the devil out of us! *Oh, brother.* And then he prayed for us to ask Jesus into our hearts—for the *second* time in our lives, which, according to my interpretation of scripture is impossible since once you're saved, you're saved. In addition, a truly saved person cannot be *possessed* of the devil. Perhaps influenced—often easily—and even *obsessed* by the devil, yes, but not possessed. *Damn.* It was freaky, though, how someone like Patrick, supposedly doing God's work, could connive in his mind such a judgment against Harriet and me as we served God the best we knew how.

Traveling out in the world on a bus with the Turks was great—especially when were free from the Istanbul colony and our "dungeon." Sure, Harriet and I were both bewildered about what had actually transpired in Istanbul, but by the time we arrived in Izmir, we had shaken the horror off us. We felt we could be a blessing once again to those we met, like the Turkish businessman on the bus, who insisted we join him for lunch in Izmir. At a small restaurant next to the Izmir bus depot, the guy treated us to a lunch of sheep's brain, served in slices on a small ceramic plate. The brain didn't taste too bad, but sinking my teeth into its white sponginess was weird.

I had no phone number or address for Diane. Izmir is not a big city, and I actually knew my way around, having lived here when in the sixth and seventh grade. The U.S. Army Officers Club seemed the best place to try, so we headed there by taxi. The club was still there—on a ground-floor corner, with its same tinted windows overlooking Izmir Bay.

We didn't get far into the club before a military officer stopped us. Nice enough, the guy accepted I was Diane's brother and looked up her number. He dialed it himself.

"Wayne! How are you? I'll be right there." She showed up in minutes with a driver.

"What are you doing here in Izmir?" she asked, after a squeezing hug.

Without any details, I said, "Well, I'm living in Istanbul now and thought I'd come down to see you. Hope you don't mind."

"Sure! Let's get to my place."

The military driver drove us eastward along the waterfront to her home. She and husband Jack lived in a U.S. Army-paid-for, sixth-floor penthouse apartment. Like the Officers Club, it also overlooked Izmir Bay. The apartment, with Jack's antiques and Oriental rugs, was so plush and the view across the shimmering water so stunning, Harriet hardly knew what to make of it all. And Diane simply overwhelmed us with her love. When Jack came home from work, he too made us feel totally at home. *God bless him. Such a great person!*

Diane and Jack remained busy with their lives, while Harriet and I became a team in Izmir. During the day, we walked around the quaint city—a city I knew from earlier days. Strolling through Culture Park, we met young Turks and ministered Bible passages to some of them. Our extradition from the Children of God had left us alone and confused, but we had the same convictions as ever to share God's love with others. We achieved that by befriending strangers we met, gaining their trust, learning if they believed in God and telling them how He had changed our lives. He had given us a purpose for living and had strengthened our faith through His daily provisions.

Amazingly, on our third day in Izmir, I received two hundred dollars from my parents for my birthday. Mom and Dad must have mailed the money through the military for it to have arrived so quickly. On this same day, after counseling together, Harriet and I decided *she* would return to her homeland of Germany.

But how to get there? By bus, overland, alone? No. With most of the two hundred dollars, I bought her a one-way airline ticket and felt the satisfaction of "giving" when I delivered her to the airline office the following day.

"I love you, Wayne," she said, in front of the Turkish Airline ticket office, from where a bus would take her to the rather distant airport.

"I love you, too." I gave her a good hug and kiss on the cheek. She boarded the Turkish Airline bus. And when she waved back at me from the window as the bus pulled away, tears came to my eyes. I could tell by her smile from behind the glass of the window how the luxury of an airplane ticket home comforted her. The two of us had endured humiliation, spiritual torture, condemnation and horror and had come through it all, shining brightly in God's saving, loving grace.

During the confusion, back in Istanbul, something had told Harriet the two of us were matched for one another, and she almost said it once. But I sensed she felt that way. Knew it in her face. And when it nearly exited from her lips, I threw cold water on it. *Damn.* However far this misery had confounded us, I knew damn well Harriet and I were opposites and as far apart as any two people of the opposite sex could be. Was the devil trying to further freak us out? God bless her, though; I'll never forget her hand wave of gratitude and her happy face through the window of that bus.

Meanwhile, Jack's mother and another lady came from the States to visit Diane and Jack, and the four of them went on a Mediterranean cruise together, leaving me alone at the apartment. I actually enjoyed being alone. I had not experienced solitude for nearly a year and a half since joining the group. But . . . *that* is when the devil can strike best at God's children, or anyone, when there is no one to pick them up from the blasts. The ole boy wasn't finished with me yet. In fact, that first night alone, about midnight while I was deep in sleep, that evil bastard gave his last shot at snuffing me out—a vivid and frightening nightmare. I dreamed I lay on my back, tied to a table. One of those huge pendulums with a tremendously large cutting blade swung over my stomach, just like in a horror movie. And each time it completed a swing, it moved a bit lower, toward me, until it nearly reached my stomach to slice me up, finish me off! And then . . .

Bang, bang, bang! Bang, bang, bang! A knocking on the front door of the apartment startled me awake. *Oh my God.* I had escaped the nightmare only to awaken to something nearly as frightening— someone trying to get in on me in the physical world. *Lord.* I was so scared!

"Wayne! Wayne!" Two voices whispered intensely through the door. They belonged to the leaders of the Turkey/Mid-East region of the Children of God—Matthew and Edward. Still in fright from the dream, I opened the door. There they stood, with smiles beaming across their faces. They both reached out and hugged me. "God *bless* you!" they said. I let them in.

"How *are* you, Wayne?" they asked.

"Shit, I guess I'm all right," I said, still shaken by the nightmare. I wondered, had I not been *physically* awakened and delivered from the dream, could I have actually been *snuffed* out? By being so frightened by the reality of it that I had a heart attack or something and died in my sleep? In other words, could a person's soul be taken in his sleep through fear? Perhaps if he had some kind of an illness or weakened condition at the time. Who knows?

"What are you doing here in Izmir?" I asked.

"We came to bring you back to your family," one of them said.

I couldn't determine which guy was over the other in seniority. They both seemed about equal, at least, in their disgust, shame and apologies for Patrick and Sam with whom they had, days before, left the running of the colony back in Istanbul. They had returned to Istanbul only to find what had happened to the two unfortunate arrivals—Harriet and me—at the hands of the temporary leaders. Matthew and Edward utterly freaked on Patrick, jumped on a bus and made it to Izmir. Luckily, days earlier, I had written a letter to those in Istanbul with Diane's address on it.

I had never met these guys, but when they learned from Arthur and others of my proven loyalty and faithfulness, the two of them were compelled to retrieve me and bring me home.

Exhausted from their trip, they were relieved to find me and now to have a comfortable place to rest. I served them milk and cookies. After I got to know them, Matthew asked, "Wayne, did it seem to you the strange events that happened to you and Harriet were of the devil? Did you feel Patrick and Sam completely oppressed you both and gave you no chance to defend yourselves?"

Still fresh from the ordeal and not really able to counsel with anyone of the world on so spiritual a matter, except of course with my codefendant Harriet, I replied, "I don't know. You know, maybe I wasn't inspired enough or as wild and fanatic as Patrick and Sam. Maybe I shouldn't have come to Istanbul." I proceeded to defend Patrick and blame myself, suggesting that maybe my subdued outlook on everyday affairs led Patrick to believe I was not sold enough on the Revolution for Jesus/Children of God. But I learned that Matthew and Edward believed that Patrick's intent on being the leader of the Turkey Work remained the underlying cause of the near annihilation of two good and faithful servants of God.

"We've dealt with Patrick and Sam about it, and we only pray and ask that you forgive us for leaving the Work in their hands. God bless you, brother. We love you."

Praise His Name. We all slept comfortably that night, the two now my guests. The three of us spent much of the next sunny and cool morning on the balcony of the penthouse, watching ferry boats shuttle smoothly across the bay of Izmir. Matthew and Edward felt like kings in the place and, God bless them, I felt they deserved a reward of some kind for their expedience and sacrifice in rushing down to Izmir to retrieve me.

But no one wanted to leave Patrick and Sam in charge back in Istanbul. So we purchased three, one-way bus tickets to Istanbul. I wrote a note of sincere thanks to Diane for all she'd done for me. She and I had spent good hours together these past days. I had explained to her how Gary and I had met the Children of God and, now fulfilled in our new spiritual lives, were sharing God's love with others. She had been amazed at how I had changed from being a rather strung-out hippie, when I last saw her two years before, to an encouraging brother, now quoting Bible scriptures to her hungry spirit. She had nearly cried with joy. The unplanned visit at least had that reward.

We boarded the bus to Istanbul the following day. On the trip, I swear, Edward nearly died of some kind of illness. *The devil again, upset at my rescue?*

"Oh, God, help me," Edward moaned. "Pray for me, please!"

Matthew and I prayed intensely for him, and God only knows what might have happened if we hadn't. I mean, he broke out in a heavy sweat, fought not to spill his guts all over the bus and exhibited near-terror. He came through it, and we arrived the next day in Istanbul.

Reuniting with everyone back at the Laleli home was awkward for me. But a certain love and forgiveness overcame everything. After all, we were young people trying to serve God the best we knew how. We'd given our lives wholly to this cause and had now become susceptible to spiritual battles with an enemy we couldn't see. We were attempting to "know" the voice of God and His will. As for Patrick, I think he saw himself as the "chosen one for Turkey," so when Harriet and I came on the scene and, by our presence, threatened his position, he ostracized us.

When I saw Patrick and Sam again, they seemed to be "eating humble pie" after Edward and Matthew had thoroughly rebuked them. "We're sorry for the judgment leveled against you," Patrick said to me.

I saw good intentions in Patrick. Despite what he had done to me, I respected him, a strong follower of the cause.

Still, I had spiritual wounds from the ordeal. I found that walking the streets of Istanbul now brought back memories of the horrors I had gone through a little over a week ago. *Man! Is the devil now trying to indicate that the spirit of Istanbul itself bred all the wickedness?*

No. I would have no more of this foolishness and instead became enthralled with Istanbul. It is so *Eastern*. Turkey itself will always be the East, once one crosses the Bosphorus or the Dardanelles that geographically separate it from Europe. I felt the vibrations as soon as I arrived here.

Istanbul is busy, with every kind of individual, every kind of store, market and geographical delight—mountains, bays, rivers and seas. The huge, famous Blue Mosque and the Topkapi Museum together look upon the Bosphorus and the glistening Sea of Marmara; endless markets weave through sloping, hillside streets, selling brass, copper, rugs, gold, spices and everything else; and undoubtedly some of the world's best and cheapest food is here. Then there's the Turkish glass of *tea*. I doubt better black tea is served anywhere in the world. First of all, the tea *glass* itself is ingenious—*clear*, so one can *see* and appreciate the rich, reddish-gold color. Then, since the glass is in the shape of a tulip, the tea tends to remain *steaming* hot while retaining any residual *loose* tea leaves from which it's brewed (no teabags used, ever!) so the very last drop of tea can be swallowed. On the small saucer sits a small spoon and plenty of sugar cubes. Rather strong, the tea is served a single glass at a time, which usually suffices and is presented just like this throughout the far corners of this wonderful country.

So, nine of us, all Americans, attempted to spread some of God's words of love and care as told in the Bible to those we could reach in Istanbul—without getting thrown out of the country. Those souls proved to be non-Turks—travelers. "World travelers" they were called—Germans, British, Americans, Canadians, Australians, French, Italians, Spaniards (a few), Dutch, Swedish, Swiss, South Americans (a few), New Zealanders, Japanese (rare, but some) and scatterings of people from other mostly industrialized nations. Usually young people in their 20s, they were here for adventure and for filling the spiritual void within their lives. Never reached spiritually by churches in their lands, many of these folks were headed for India. Yep, India, where they sought spiritual enlightenment.

Istanbul was a major crossroads for these travelers coming and going, and they nearly all sojourned at the Sultan Ahmet area—the location of the Blue Mosque and Topkapi Museum—just a mile or two from our Laleli home. Most of them stayed in cheap hotels in the area, while a few lived in their own mobile homes like Volkswagen minivan buses.

They met at the Pudding Shop, a known-worldwide rendezvous point—"I'll meet you at the Pudding Shop in Istanbul on so-and-so date." Unfortunately, certain Turks of Istanbul would also gather there and try to deal highly illegal drugs to these travelers, finagle money from them or flirt with the pretty Western girls. These weary travelers needed this meeting spot, so they had no choice but to cope with these guys. I wondered if anyone had actually been murdered there. I had a knife pulled on me once by a Turk inside and saw fights out front of this miserable outpost. Yes, they *did* sell *pudding* there, although of all the fabulous foods produced and prepared in Turkey, pudding is not one of them, in my opinion. Inside the joint, a rather gruff, all-male staff of waiters and cashiers offered food and drink in a cafeteria-style manner.

In spite of the surroundings, we tried to concentrate on souls. Most were receptive, while some were antagonistic toward us. Not to mind, the Work went well and many received the good news with glad tidings and went their ways—except for the American guy Ray who interrupted his journey and joined us. After completing five years of college in Nevada, he was now on that road to India.

Somehow, travelers like Ray knew that VW minibuses were cheap and plentiful in Amsterdam, so he had bought one there for the trip to New Delhi. His destiny led him to the new convert, Judy, during the time I was in Izmir. And, as with all members who joined the group, wherever that might be, he forsook all to follow. That included his VW bus, his money and anything else he had. He was athletic and fit, but more importantly, humble.

Now, how did all of us eat and pay the rent since we had no visible means of support? Music helped. For instance, here in Istanbul, two or three of us would enter a restaurant with a guitar and sing a song or two in Turkish with some godly message. The owner or manager of the restaurant then compensated us with a delicious, hot Turkish meal right then and there. Patrick spoke a good bit of Turkish in his short time here and led such ventures. He really was a devoted and adventurous servant of God, despite his pushiness.

New members helped our subsistence because they ". . . sold their possessions and goods, and parted them to all men, as every man had need" (Acts 2.45). Some had practically nothing but the shirts on their backs, while others had cars and money—or castles, vineyards and farms, like the Duke back in Italy.

We also went "provisioning"—a sort of sophisticated form of begging. With plenty of money and goods in the world to be shared, and since we were daily in the streets trying to reach souls, why couldn't businessmen of the community help?

We applied this idea to Turkish businessmen and merchants. Especially at Istanbul's main food and vegetable market—a huge, partially enclosed area of every sort of foodstuff, from fresh vegetables and fruits to nuts, teas, rice, grains, spices and endless other grocery items. And, as the saying goes, "When faith goes to market, it brings a *basket* along." Which is exactly what Patrick and I did when we needed vegetables and staples for the home.

He and I would take a taxi, along with two large straw baskets— nearly two feet deep—to this great Istanbul market on an early morning. When we reached the market, we each strapped a basket to our backs and started the process. With Patrick leading, we entered certain grocery stores or stalls and asked for the *patrone*—manager or owner of the place.

"Good morning! God bless you! We help kids get off drugs. Can you assist us with a donation?" Patrick said to them in Turkish.

If the patrone agreed, he charitably bagged up apples, bananas, rice, nuts or whatever we might have specifically asked for or pointed at in his particular store and dropped them right into one of the baskets on our backs. Patrick knew a good many of these guys and made his way to them, as long as he hadn't visited them too recently. By lunch time we commonly had both baskets nearly full—all donated by these generous Turks, not one lira spent. In fact, Matthew's wife, Clara, made a list of needs the night before. We then sought God's blessings to fill that list.

But I think the *list* indirectly led to the disfigurement of Patrick's face! After several trips to the market, certain regular merchants became our friends, so we talked with them about our social work. We voiced our sincere gratitude to these guys with the simple Turkish phrase, *Allah-o-bereket*, offering God's blessing. It seemed to truly touch their hearts, too.

My partner felt he should go a bit further in ministering to some of these merchant-helpers, so one day he brought a small pamphlet of the Gospel of St. John in Turkish. We had nearly completed our provisioning for the morning when Patrick came across a group of Turkish shopkeepers he knew, sitting on wooden chairs under a shop's awning, and congenially opened the pamphlet to one of them. And which verse did he point out? Indeed, John 3.16—the one verse that intensely contradicts the most basic Muslim belief, that God had no son, while presenting the main cornerstone of Christian faith, that simply believing in the only begotten Son of God brings salvation and everlasting life. Ahmed, the *patrone* Patrick knew, didn't mind it, but the guy passed it around at the request of curious, idle shopkeepers nearby, pointing also to the John 3.16 verse. No small stir developed. In fact, quite an uproar soon arose on that cobblestone alley as one burly Turk from the group began to grumble about the words.

By now, Patrick and I were down another alley, attempting to provision some rice—one of the last items on the list. I soon heard a ruckus ensuing from the area where the Turks had the pamphlet, so I advised Patrick we should split the scene—*right now*. But Patrick, possibly due to his pride of not having had the faith to fulfill . . . *the list*, insisted on trying to get the rice anyway.

Nobody knows how many verses the group of Turks read *after* verse John 3.16, but the four verses following it could enrage any Muslim, such as verse 18 that says, ". . . but he that believeth not is condemned already, because he hath not believed in the name of the only begotten Son of God." And sure enough, the burly Turk stormed into the rice store, huffing and puffing, screaming and yelling in his own religious fervor.

Whoosh! He pushed me violently in my chest, and I flew against a wall, fortunately stacked high with large burlap bags of rice that cushioned the impact along with the big straw basket still strapped to my back. This giant of a man then found Patrick and began screaming in his face. It was too late now. The rice man/friend had no idea what was going on, but soon the whole street of shop owners and onlookers realized the reason for the outbreak as the Turkish guy kept screaming about these two Christian blasphemers.

Now, in this instance (and later in my life), I determined that my thin frame, shortness of stature—about five feet, seven inches—and kind of young-looking face saved me from the onslaught of belligerent, vicious attacks from human bullies. Strange, but at a point of violence toward another human being, it seems that a good fighter or bully will often have enough last-minute self-respect to direct his onslaught on the bigger or more matched opponent for his vicious punches instead of cowardly wiping out the smaller companion. Patrick stood easily five-feet-ten-inches tall, if not taller, and whether or not the beast knew who originally produced the epistle of St. John, he chose *Patrick* as his rival. He looked like a monster next to Patrick, though.

"Police! Police!" Patrick shouted as this guy grabbed him by his shirt and dragged him up the street to the cluster of shops where John 3.16 was introduced. The man wanted to show his wrath right at the spot where the little pamphlet now remained. He wanted to scream out his religious zeal and his disgust with the words he'd just read. He'd been pierced to the heart by these few verses, as in Hebrews 4.12, "For the word of God is quick, and powerful, and sharper than any two-edged sword, piercing even to the dividing asunder of soul and spirit, and of the joints and marrow, and is a discerner of the thoughts and intents of the heart."

The Turk pointed to the pamphlet, picked it up, shook it around at the onlookers, briefly explained its contents in his crude way and threw it down. Then he pushed Patrick. Patrick pushed him back. Once. And then . . . whack! One heavy punch directly into Patrick's face. It knocked poor Patrick to the ground, spilling half the contents of the basket strapped to his back. He fell face down in the cobblestones, hands cupping his face. The Turk even started kicking him, and that's when I entered in with pissed-off adrenaline and, amazingly enough, pushed the giant away from my partner. Others then somehow restrained the big oaf.

Patrick must have passed out because it took him some seconds to even stir—like a prize-fighting boxer briefly knocked out on the mat. After a few more seconds of bent-over moans and groans and with my assistance, Patrick rose to his feet, still cupping his face, leaving a small pool of bright red blood on the cobblestones. His nose was broken and bleeding; blood covered his hands and he was groaning in pain. *Poor Patrick. Damn!*

I gathered the spilled foodstuffs back into Patrick's basket with the help of some of the on-looking Turks, and the two of us hobbled off. I guided Patrick, who had his head tilted back trying to stop the bleeding. Along the way, some sweet people assisted us, giving Patrick a cloth for his nose and fresh water to clean his face and hands. Meanwhile, between moans, Patrick continued to threaten to call the police.

But *me?* I wanted to get the hell out of there and not look back. I did not want to involve the police—especially with a religion-related matter. That wouldn't have fixed Patrick's nose anyway. We walked on out of the market and away from gawking onlookers until we found a bridge and went beneath it for privacy. I then prayed fervently for the healing of Patrick's wound and even his nose if it was broken. With all due respect to my prayer though, I doubt God sticks his hand down from heaven and resets broken bones. I believe it's performed rather through practicing doctors here on earth.

With the bleeding hardly stopped, we hailed a cab home. Walking from the cab to our apartment, with both baskets nearly full of supplies, we passed the curious, ever-present neighborhood kids, dusting around in the lots and streets. But they stared more today than usual at foreigner Patrick who held a bloody rag to his nose, his head cocked back. We finally made it into the serenity of our home. When Judy and the others saw poor Patrick, they needed no explanation. Judy and Clara immediately ministered to him, dressed his wound and had him lie down most of the afternoon. Everyone appreciated the provisions. But we soon realized we had better find more *common* ground in the Word if we were going to reach Turks.

Our work in Istanbul remained "underground," especially since proselytizing was against the law in Turkey. So we spoke to Turkish people with discretion. Hungry souls could be shown God's love without blatantly forcing Jesus "down their throats."

More instances showed us the futility of trying to share spiritual love in the streets of Istanbul. At a garden one night, across town near busy Taxim Square, five of us with one guitar along had to break apart and hide. A guitar and one or two foreigners, especially females, can attract masses of curious Turks in a matter of minutes. In such a crowd, there may be a few spiritually hungry souls touched in their hearts by a song, a word or even a friendly look, but the majority are going to be . . . hecklers. And, depending on the country where this crowd is gathered, it can become a riot. Wisdom used in a timely manner might avoid it.

I hated mass witnessing and knew it was fruitless, particularly in a place like Istanbul. And at night? But there stood the five of us, three guys and two girls, at the entrance to this park in the dark, at about 9 p.m., singing songs. Almost instantly, male Turks gathered around us, some curious and interested, but most just obnoxious. They edged in closer until, at the end of one of our songs, I got a message across to the others: "Okay. That's it. We're outta here. Let's split up."

With each sister holding onto a guy, we scurried off into the park. Somehow we found one another, consumed some Turkish sandwiches and caught a late bus back to the sanctuary of our Laleli home. *Praise His Name!*

Across town at the Roman Catholic Church, we communed with the priests and members of the congregation. Sure, differences of doctrine developed, but instead of dwelling on those, we stuck to positive ways to reach the world with God's love.

We also befriended the phenomenal Little Sisters of Jesus. Though similar to nuns, they chose not to live in monasteries but rather among people who didn't have access to church ministration. The Sisters seemed to be associated with the Roman Catholic Church but lived throughout the world in their own little homes, held menial jobs and considered themselves women of prayer. Once, I visited one of their abodes in Istanbul and everything in it was little—little tables, little chairs, little rugs, little candles, little everything. Always smiling, they just wanted to be a "sign of love" to others. *They were precious, God bless them.*

We made friends with Turkish hotel owners, restaurateurs, business-men and students, but we spoke mainly with non-Turks—foreigners, of whom there was always a turn-over, preventing us from stagnation.

But on a hot summer day, someone would say, "Hey! Let's go to one of the Princes' Islands." By a cheap (roughly $3 roundtrip) ferryboat ride from the closest bay, we easily reached these nearby Turkish gems, nine of them out in the Sea of Marmara. Even walking to the ferry was a treat, past the famous Covered Bazaar quite near Sultan Ahmet, past the fish and meat markets and over the Galata Bridge where we bought cold, crisp slices of cucumber off the cucumber man. Aboard the ferry, we enjoyed glasses of steaming Turkish *chai* (tea).

We usually took tents and sleeping bags and spent the night on one of the islands. *Fantastic.* We'd camp either in the middle of the island in a secluded spot of forest or on a small overlook by the sea itself. Such a relief from crowded, bustling Istanbul.

The islands were sparsely inhabited but had delightful little villages. They were hilly and partially forested with coastlines of rocks and cliffs great for diving into the clear water. Many of the islands' pleasant coves and beaches—usually of smooth, round rocks—could only be reached on foot or by boat.

On one island visit, Edward and his beautiful bride of one month, Amber, accompanied the group. Edward, jokingly, complained once when his amorous wife was off collecting berries, "Man! She's insatiable. She's wiping me out!" The girl was slender and attractive with long, dark hair down her back, fairly tall and Jewish-American—like Edward.

We swam and dove into the refreshing water and sunbathed on the largely secluded beaches. But I'll always remember one day, watching slim, trim, new-bride Amber swimming *completely* naked in front of us all. *Goodness.* What a sight, that wonderful creature, definitely God's crowning creation—the woman!—wild, young and free, jumping off rocks and slithering gracefully through the clear waters, her uncommonly white body offset only by the small, triangular patch of black pubic hair nestled between her exquisite thighs. I think I was the first to notice the guy on the ridge though. "Look. Up there," I said to Matthew. There, on the cliff above, a lucky Turkish islander also filled his eyes with this rare treat, causing Amber to leave her sensuous swim and don her bathing suit.

The islands renewed our spirits for any battles ahead back in the city. A weird contrast for the human soul—to wallow in God's calm, beautiful nature and then expose that same soul to man's creation of a noisy, dangerous city. Delights to *eat* existed though in most cities if you knew how to find them. I found such a treat one day—a fresh fish with scales straight out of the Sea of Marmara near the main Galata Bridge, which crossed the bay. A Turkish fisherman, who caught it that day from his small wooden rowboat, expertly fileted the fish right there on the pavement next to where his boat was tied.

Then, he grilled the filets to perfection on a rickety, hibachi charcoal grill and served them on quarter loaves of fresh-baked Turkish bread all for some ridiculous third-world price. *Superb.* I would grab one whenever I passed that way hungry and the fisherman was there serving it.

Three months had passed rather quickly since I entered Turkey. The time arrived for my visa-renewal trip. Patrick, too, neared the end of his three months, so the two of us made the trip to the border together.

We boarded the bus west to the Turkish town of Edirne, a town that bordered Greece. We had hardly a lira in our pockets except for bus fare. These visa trips gave us a great break, almost like a vacation, except we never had much money along for any material luxury, that's for sure. The plush, Mercedes-Benz buses had high-backed cloth seats, each person in his own seat, with generally no one standing or "camping out" in the aisles. These coaches appeared spotlessly clean, inside and out. The Turks took pride in these forms of travel and had perfected the comfort of them through the years. Designated stops along each route allowed for "watering"—eating, peeing, washing up, drinking tea. And when the ride resumed, an assistant to the driver made his way down the aisle with a liter-size, opaque plastic jug shaped like a vase with a handle. He squirted a few drops of lemon-scented water into our hands for us to splash on our faces to help freshen us up. Unfortunately though, the drivers often drove fast and daringly—trying to pass slower vehicles. Indeed, these huge, often-full buses, with drivers trying to make or break schedules, too frequently caused horrific collisions throughout Turkey, often *head-on* with other vehicles, resulting in enough deaths and injuries to make international news. It required much prayer.

Reaching Edirne, Patrick and I began the walk to the border. The sunny August day was hot, yet dry and pleasant in this hilly part of Western Turkey. The stringent smell of animal dung permeated the air of Edirne. To me, these odors were a pleasant contrast to the smells of Istanbul. But the little burr-headed Turkish kids bothered us as we walked through the center of town. For some reason, these scalawags just had to throw rocks at us and otherwise torment us any way they could. We couldn't throw rocks back at them. It would be playing into their hands. Besides being expert rock throwers, they knew all the best hiding places and could run to safety instantly. We learned we could frighten them with stern looks, and eventually they'd give up or become like friendly puppies.

We walked through vast fields of vegetables and sunflowers on the road to the border until dark. We were tired from our journey. With our backpacks and sleeping bags along, when we spotted a clump of small trees on the edge of the road, we rolled our beds out and fell asleep under the clear—*thank God, no rain!*—sky.

Morning came early with the sweet voices of five little gypsy girls and their baby brother. Probably ranging from 4 to 10 years old, the girls offered us some freshly picked tomatoes and berries. Imagine, *gypsies* offering something to two Americans rather than begging off us. It was great. We started to get up out of our sleeping bags and the kids eased back a bit in caution but still smiled. Not a person in sight except them and us. We spoke some of our broken Turkish to the girls. They seemed to understand only bits of it, but the trusting rapport between us seemed communication enough. Patrick had some beads in his backpack and I had some trinkets, which we gave to the girls. Luckily we had our pants on inside the sleeping bags, but the girls still watched and giggled when we emerged out of the bags to put our shirts on. We rolled our bags up, attached them to our backpacks, got back on the road and waved goodbye to the little gypsies, who just stood there staring at us with their smudged faces.

Another bright, sunny day. We soon reached the Turkish side of the border. There, the Turkish immigration officials checked us out of Turkey with no problems since we hadn't let our current three-month visas run out. We then walked the half-mile or so of lush, green no man's land between the two countries until we reached the Greek border station. Entering into Greece wasn't so easy since immigration officials are never too thrilled to grant visitor visas to penniless people like the two of us.

"What are you doing in Greece?" they asked us.

"We only want to stay a day and then return to Turkey. We live in Turkey," we told them. Fortunately, they kindly stamped visitor visas into our passports. It would have been a drag, for sure, to come all this way and not be able to renew our visas.

It is amazing how only a fraction of a mile of no man's land can separate entire nations and cultures from one another. Entire spirits change. As for me, I rather loved the Greek neatness and relaxed atmosphere compared to that of Turkey. We were now in the *West*. Indeed, old Constantinople—Istanbul of the Ottoman Empire in history—actually did and, to this day, does divide East from West. Not that this particular little Greek border town was any Paris, but there was something about that vivid, thick spirit of the East back in Istanbul.

Walking through the quiet town, we happened upon a small Greek Orthodox church that overlooked a serene meadow of grazing cattle. We went inside and ran into the presiding priest. I remembered some Greek and the priest knew some English, so we explained to him our trip, our work back in Istanbul and . . . our need for a meal.

"*Katheestay, katheestay, sas padakalo,*" the guy said to us. "Sit down, sit down, please." The guy generously brought us fresh Greek bread and plates of cheese and olives from the church kitchen. We sliced up the tomatoes from the gypsy girls, added them to the cheese and olives and stuffed ourselves. While we were eating, the priest returned to the kitchen to prepare two steaming-hot Greek coffees, which he brought back and humbly served to us on a silver tray in little demitasse cups. We talked with the guy about God, and though not quite ready to let us sleep in the church, he showed us a safe corner inside the stone building where we could leave our backpacks.

Back at the bus station in Edirne, we had learned that buses departed back to Istanbul at 11 a.m. and 4 p.m. daily except Sundays. We felt tempted to cut short our stay in Greece and chance catching that four o'clock bus back to Istanbul. Maybe the Turkish border guards had changed posts and new ones wouldn't hassle us about jumping across the border and then jumping right back into their country. *Nah. Why rush it when we can sit back, and relax here in this pleasant Greek town?* And, given our little home base now of this Greek church surrounded by shady deciduous trees on the edge of a lush green meadow of mellowed-out livestock, we decided not to deny ourselves such a needed break from bustling Istanbul. So we grabbed our sleeping bags, did some reading just inside the tree line at the edge of the meadow and slept the night right there.

Rising the next morning, we went to the church to wash up at the outside faucet, found our friend the priest, who let us use the bathroom, and said our goodbyes with hugs. We committed his name to memory and told him other brethren would look him up if they came on similar visa-renewal trips.

Off we walked, first back to the Greek police and guards who yesterday hassled us some about having no money and who probably doubted we would really keep our word that we didn't intend to travel farther into Greece. Then on through the no man's land, again passing ox-driven carts—this day piled high with straw—with Greek or Turkish peasants smiling and waving at us. Then on into the Turkish border station. Now, not that it is determined by the hour or minute necessarily, but it is wise to appease these visa requirements by staying away at least a full 24 hours. It makes it easier to get that new visa stamp, which we did receive after a few aptly spoken Turkish phrases that seemed to warm the hearts of the presiding officials. After all, we didn't present ourselves as typical, nervous backpackers these officials usually saw. But intimidation at these border stations can get thick and scary, making it important to maintain some kind of composure in order to cut through it all—and win!

Thankful for our three-month visas, we walked back into Turkey, past the lone clump of small trees where we'd slept and had the great gypsy encounter. We walked into Edirne with its gawking children, some of them the same ones. Only *this* time one of the leaders of the kids decided to be our friend and companion and proudly walked alongside us with an ever-present stick in hand. Patrick went right along with the kid's new role of escort, imparting to him in Turkish as much love and concern as possible in the few minutes we walked together to the bus station/tea house.

We purchased bus tickets with Turkish lira we'd reserved for the return trip and boarded the 11 a.m. bus to Istanbul. One last luxury of this two-or-three day visa trip was to sit back in our own high-backed cloth seat on a Turkish, Mercedes tour bus, absorbing rolling fields of sunflowers and wheat blowing in the wind.

Vacation in the countryside over, it was time to once again face the mass of crowds, horrible traffic, honking horns . . . and deal with the cheapest taxi or minibus back to Laleli. At least we had the peace and serenity of our cozy home.

Chapter 3
⤠ *Busted! in Istanbul* ⤠

MEETING THAT INFLUX of foreign wanderers, singing in restaurants, mingling with members of the Roman Catholic church and sharing provisioned food with needy travelers, kept us busy in Istanbul. And then a letter from the London headquarters arrived in the mail.

The letter was titled *Shiners?—Or Shamers!* The letter spoke of passing out literature in the streets of the world and receiving donations for it, determining each member to be . . . shiners, who distributed a good amount of literature, or . . . shamers, who distributed little. It caused a tremendous change in the Children of God Work. Get out and "litness" (a combination of literature and witness): get words of faith into people's hands but also try to get a donation for it at the same time.

But could this . . . should this . . . be done in every country? Even Turkey?

Our Istanbul colony read it together the day it arrived. We figured at least two of us would go into the streets the next day to obey and fulfill it. *Be careful*, I thought. *Blind faith and blind obedience can be unwise.*

"Yeah. We'll obey it for the Work's sake," the others said. "Get out and do what *Shiners?—Or Shamers!* says to do. Right now."

So the next day, the two "sacrificial lambs" ended up being Sam and me. We gathered up a stack each of 8½-by-11-inch pamphlets in English, French and German and headed out the door, caught a bus to the Sultan Ahmet area, made a rendezvous time of 5 p.m. in front of the Pudding Shop and split up. Foreign world travelers remained our targets. Sam turned out to be the shiner, and I, the shamer. Always conscious of the uptight spirit in this land, I kept an eye out for any irate Turkish religionists or police. I walked from van to van, traveler to traveler, getting a few pieces of literature out and receiving a small amount of money in exchange. Meanwhile, Sam obeyed the letter more literally without regard to any laws of the land and blatantly passed out several pieces, receiving a good amount of lira in return for it.

Unaware of Sam's method, I continued litnessing on my own until the appointed time, 5 p.m., when I showed up in front of the Pudding Shop to meet him. There stood Sam, accompanied by whom? *Oh, please, not a Turkish policeman!* The distraught look on Sam's face confirmed it, even before the policeman—one of those fairly uneducated types and, most sickening of all, one in plain clothes—flashed his hideous police badge at me. He opened one side of his light brown sports jacket with his other hand just so I could see his concealed revolver in its leather holster. And there I stood with my leather pouch of pamphlets over my shoulder and a small stack of the incriminating literature under my arm. *Damn.*

I immediately tried to talk our way out of it. But this guy was one of those hardliners, rather young, intent on climbing the police-officer ladder and, at the same time, sporting a shallow mentality behind a set of merciless eyes. The horror of it. And I walked right into it, not even caught passing anything out. Just Sam's accomplice. The creepy cop arrested us right then and there and escorted us off—handcuffed together—through several world travelers (who surely figured it a drug bust) to the police station. The station was not more than a block around the corner from "misery's" Pudding Shop.

Busted! In Istanbul, Turkey. Hardly a day after reading the *Shiners?— Or Shamers!* letter. *Wisdom, dammit!* God gave us brains to *use,* instead of necessarily obeying the letter of the law. Consider the laws of the land you're living in, I say.

The plainclothesman led us, common criminals now, up a decrepit wooden staircase to the first floor, where we faced the next-higher-up officer in a room with a view of the Sultan Ahmet and Blue Mosque area. With our accusations rattled off in Turkish, we understood nothing while the higher-up guy—a mean sucker in a real policeman's uniform— pondered it all as he sorted through the confiscated literature and our leather satchels. We stood with two Turkish prisoners. The officer got up nonchalantly and walked around the room. Out of the corner of my eye, I saw Sam smacked to the floor by this brute.

Whack! The cop's opened hand landed on the side of Sam's face to both our surprise. Somehow, I escaped such a blow. Poor Sam, though not seriously hurt, appeared visibly shaken, and the gravity of the matter suddenly became evident. *Now what?* The guy spouted some obviously humiliating remarks at us in Turkish before returning us to the original, arresting policeman who led us back downstairs to a room on the ground floor.

Here sat a fat, middle-aged Turk sound asleep at a desk in the far corner of the room, the side of his face nestled in the open palm of his right hand. A badge pinned to his shirt identified him as some kind of plainclothes policeman. We sat down in this rather dark room (dark so this guy could sleep) while the original cop made some phone calls. After a few minutes, the fat guy woke up and, upon hearing the charges from our accuser, looked both of us over with that horrible, self-righteous disdain cops love to give to newly caught criminals. But that wasn't enough. This crumb had to pull out his pocketknife with its four-inch blade, wave it in front of us and, with the meanest look he could conjure up, pass the knife in front of his own throat, insinuating he planned to cut our throats. *Shit.* This devil might have actually slashed us if it hadn't been for the original straight cop rebuking him for his foolhardiness.

But these two, plainclothes cops didn't really know what to do with us, it seemed, until finally a regular, uniformed policeman came in. This new guy put handcuffs back on us and led us back outside, into the world, away from that dungeon-like room with the knife-wielding maniacal cop. Again, we were paraded through the area busy with the world travelers who looked on us with a sort of sympathy as we passed handcuffed together and led by a Turkish policeman. These on-lookers no doubt assumed we'd been arrested for the same illegal drugs they risked buying here in Turkey and were likely high on right then.

And how did we reach the jail across Istanbul? By city *bus.* Yep. This new, nervous cop simply waited with us at the bus stop for the next bus. The three of us boarded it, and there Sam and I stood, handcuffed together, alone in the aisle with the cop behind us, amid a busload of people in their seats. Embarrassing really. It's horrible being a prisoner, a reject of society, with no more rights, a dirty feeling, looked down on as not much better than an animal. You've done something wrong, condemnation raises its ugly head, you've got no *freedom*—this whether you're guilty or not.

We soon arrived on the other side of the bay near the Istanbul Hilton and Taxim Square, where officials booked and jailed us in a pretty decent prison, which sat on a hillside. Our cell was downstairs one floor, quite clean and for just the two of us.

No sooner had we settled into this high-class cell and bought some yogurt to eat (seemed we had to *buy* food if we wanted to eat) when a somewhat civilized cop came down and opened our cell. *Heck, that wasn't too bad,* we thought. But we soon found ourselves in the back of a little Turkish, *civilian* car riding *back* to the first Sultan Ahmet police station. A policeman then drove us downhill toward the bay to the Sirkeci prison—the *real* prison. *Oh, Lord.*

Oddly, the huge, black, metal door to the place faced a normal city street of stores and markets.

Apparently official booking took place at the nice "civilized" police station across town, and now we'd be held like common criminals here. We were led directly toward the main "holding tank" to a huge police sergeant—the guy who "welcomed" all new prisoners with a long, black, rubber whacking stick that hung from a special holder on his waist. Our escorting cop spoke a few words and walked off. The sergeant then took our belts and frisked us while mumbling demeaning Turkish the whole time from his cruel face.

We could see the bars of a large holding cell not six feet away, and inside two young foreigners walked toward us. Most everyone else inside had their eyes on us as well. After being searched and our personal possessions taken, the sergeant grabbed Sam and me each by our hair and banged our heads together. *Ha.* We felt lucky that was the *only* abuse we received for entrance into the big cell—that, and simultaneously grabbing us by the backs of our collars to throw us inside.

There were about 35 prisoners inside. The large cell had no furniture other than a long bunk bed made of plywood and two-by-fours across the far wall. Two small windows with bars, too high up to look from unless we stood on someone's back on the top rack, granted a view of some alley in the city outside. A doorway led to a large bathroom that had three sinks, a large urinal and five holes in the cement floor for squatting over—no stalls whatsoever, not even those footstool-type toilet encasements over the holes. Amazingly though, both rooms were absolutely clean. The prisoners themselves shared in keeping it so.

As we entered, the two white foreigners immediately approached us with desperate, yet hopeful, looks. Swedish and in their twenties, they'd been caught with some kind of pills. "We didn't have any illegal drugs on us, only some prescription medicine," one told us. "We've been here for three weeks now, with no word from our embassy, even though our arrest was in the local newspaper. You have to inform our embassy, please, if you get out of here before us."

They didn't waste any time telling us their names. "My name is Elof Norgen," the tall one said.

"And my name is Bjorne Hanssen," the other said.

"Again?" we asked. We then concentrated a little better on their names in order to memorize them.

They saw a ray of hope in us, so immediately put us in their care. "Come, you'll be on the top rack, next to us," Bjorne said.

When we sat down on the upper rack, one of the guys unfolded from his pocket the disheartening newspaper clipping of their arrest with photos of the two of them. Then they filled us in on the prison's procedures, certain prisoners' accusations and every other particular about our new world enclosed by four walls.

Like all holding cells, this one held every sort of criminal—*accused* anyway. Sam and I—though we didn't know it at the time—were in here for "Christian propaganda." Next to me on the upper rack sat a Turkish guy in his early thirties with spots of his wife's blood still on his white, disheveled, long-sleeve shirt. He had caught her with another man and felt it within his rights to kill her—like men had done for years in some Muslim countries. I felt sorry for the guy. Now staring at the floor in a daze, he looked bewildered, in shock and with obvious remorse at what he had done. On the other side of this guy sat a kid who had been caught stealing—a crime strictly looked down upon in Turkey. Any thief can expect beatings. The kid—a sharp-looking lad of about 17 years old, with a courageous spirit—was a friend with the Swedes. They wanted him to lift up his shirt and show us the welts and marks on his back from past beatings. They said the police called the kid out of the cell on occasion, took him to some room and whipped him periodically. Who knows what else they did with him? We declined the offer to see the stripes, but assured them we believed it to be true.

Other prisoners paced the floor below. Back and forth. One end to the other and back, usually in pairs talking to each other.

"How do you eat around here?" I asked Bjorne.

"You have to buy your own food. You guys have any money?" Apparently, any food, cigarettes or drinks had to be bought. I now felt fortunate that Sam was a *shiner*. He had made enough lira for us to buy some pretty good soup and bread. Had we not had any money, we could see the other prisoners would never have let a fellow prisoner go hungry. Those with money willingly shared it with those without. *Far out.* These down-trodden of society possessed a bond among themselves. Looking at them, I saw them as sheep having no shepherd. Some no doubt deserved jail, but many just seemed like society's rejects, people who didn't fit in, maybe even political opponents. But they were precious in God's eyes, broken individuals whom He loves—"The Lord is nigh unto them that are of a broken heart . . ." (Psalm 34.18)—broken men, broken hearts.

The lights, of course, never went out, but we lay down on our beds—cardboard on top of the plywood—and slept a few hours.

Morning brought the same scene as the evening before—pairs of men pacing the cell, others sitting around. That depressing caged feeling crept into all of us, especially the newest ones. That feeling of *Oh my God, I really am in prison. Busted. No visible way out. Helpless and at the complete mercy of the prison system. Hellish.*

All day long, those of us inside witnessed new arrivals on the other side of the bars, each systematically frisked and their personal possessions except money taken and put into the crummy metal desk of the sergeant. All of them got the palms of their hands beaten by the sergeant's black truncheon. He would order them to hold their hands out, and with some verbal, degrading abuse, would whack their palms a few times. Yeah, some might say, "Oh, it's the guy's *job* to do that." Well, he seemed to love this abuse of humans too much, and I doubt there was a prisoner who ever passed the man who didn't fantasize about personally beating the living hell out of him. *May God deal with him.*

Certain detainees were called by name and released all day long, either for transfer to other cells, to go to trial or for whatever. In the meantime, Sam and I conversed with one another and with the Swedes, who again made sure we had memorized their names since no one had pens or pencils in here.

Glory to God. Sam and I heard our names called out some time early that afternoon. Immediately the Swedes looked at us with forlorn faces. Once again, persons other than themselves might leave the prison. At the same time, the two guys had a glimmer of hope that Sam and I might just be instrumental in getting them released.

In our short time together, the four of us had spoken about our lives and about faith in God. We four jumped down from the upper loft, hugged each other and said goodbye with tears in our eyes.

"Don't forget us," they pleaded.

"Don't worry. We'll go to your embassy as soon as we get out." The Swedes believed us and seemed comforted.

A cop received us on the other side of the bars while the sergeant handed us our belts. We transferred to the Sultan Ahmet police station where we were originally booked. Meanwhile, Patrick and the others had been praying and working nonstop for our release. The police never offered us the opportunity to make a phone call— our Laleli home had no phone anyway—but when Sam and I didn't return the evening before, our colleagues pretty much knew we'd been nailed for passing out literature.

Patrick telephoned the U.S. embassy that evening to report us missing. Then he and a newly-arrived brother, George, went straight to the Sultan Ahmet police station, knowing Sam and I had headed near there to try out the new "litnessing" technique.

"Yes, two Americans were arrested here yesterday—for propaganda," a policeman told them.

The police, also, after obtaining the address from Sam and me, had made a surprise, early-morning visit to the Laleli home to snoop around—to uncover any weirdness, subversive activity, communist threat, religious fervor, anti-government activity or anything else among these foreigners. But inside the small apartment, they found nothing but the cooperative smiling faces of our seven friends, some guitars and our neat, clean home. Not even a picture of Jesus on any wall. The police were likely concerned with any pro-communist activity, but finding none, returned to their superiors with a clean report.

Our friends decided they would use all possible means to secure Sam's and my release without leaving it totally in the hands of the U.S. embassy. So, Patrick and George—the latter a superb musician who had just arrived from Athens—and sweet-faced Judy ventured down to the police station, guitars in hand, George with his melodious 12-string Gibson. Guitars? At the Turkish police station? Yes, and they were *not* intended for the knife-wielding guy on the ground floor, or the straight arresting officer or the first-floor green meany—green because the Turkish police always wore perfectly fitted, slightly bell-bottomed, dark-green slacks along with form-fitting dark-green shirts—who had slapped Sam to the floor. No. You've got to go to the *top*. To the chief of police of that district, two flights up the rickety wooden staircase on the uppermost floor. For *him* they sang. Sang? Yes, sang. Some heart-piercing songs in both Turkish and English that reached this guy. He melted. Thank God, he had an open heart. It's amazing how, in this crazy, mixed-up world of ungodly men, it's often the man at the *top* who is the most open to change, the only one who will bend, who can deal with and welcome a diversion from the status quo. Perhaps it is because he has been to the top and knows it's still nowhere—that it doesn't satisfy—and is searching still for that special something to fill the void of his heart.

This guy—with authority over arrests in his precinct—turned out to be pretty sweet. Touched by the sincerity of the odd minstrels, he loved the songs. Patrick speaking Turkish helped immensely. The trio would not give up until the Turks freed Sam and me, but we were *damn* lucky this police chief was a nice guy.

As the minstrels sat with the chief, a consular official from the U.S. embassy arrived to go over our case. Spontaneously, the chief *imagined* what might have caused our arrest. He explained in Turkish to the U.S. official: "I think what happened was while these people were playing their guitars in the nearby square, curious onlookers gathered, and one of my officers, in his misunderstanding of the situation, arrested these two who happened to have these pamphlets on them at the time."

The chief deemed the whole affair a *false arrest* and contentedly dropped the whole case! During the negotiating upstairs, Sam and I stood handcuffed downstairs in a large coat closet on the ground floor, *for God's sake*. We didn't know what took place, although we *had* caught a glimpse of our three colleagues when we entered the station earlier.

"You think they can do anything for us?" I asked Sam.

"Maybe," he replied.

A cop finally unlocked our metal handcuffs and took us upstairs where we embraced Patrick, George and Judy.

"You guys! God bless you! What's going on?" I said.

Patrick introduced the consul to us.

"The charge of Christian propaganda against both of you has been dropped," the consul explained. "The chief here has considered it all a false arrest."

I noticed that the outcome appeared to have stunned the consul, but he dealt solemnly with the affair. Looking through some of the incriminating evidence of our pamphlets, he had discovered they weren't normal tracts on salvation. Instead, they were full of interesting drawings of political and current events, interspersed with Bible passages. Whatever, he took any arrest of a U.S. citizen with intense seriousness. Looking at Sam and me, he said, "I strongly advise you guys to leave Turkey as soon as possible, in case the chief changes his mind." He said this because he knew we could spend a lot more than 24 hours in a Turkish prison if we got caught again trying to get these words out. Our passports weren't even stamped with any record of arrest as was normally done in Turkey.

Now, to retrieve our passports from the "nice" prison across town, we had to provide our own transportation. So, using the VW van Ray had donated months earlier, we drove across town, along with a fairly mindless policeman who still had Sam and me under his authority until official agreement released us. Pretty crude, I thought, to transport a policeman in *our* car to do *his* work, but that's the economics of developing countries. The others in the van—not Sam and I as we were still officially criminals and dirt, so to speak—befriended this young cop, asked him about his family and mentioned Allah's love.

But I regretted not ripping off my choice, 3-inch-by-5-inch, complete, little Collins Bible from the cop while riding in the van—our *own* van. The guy would have never missed it. It contained valuable, handwritten notes, leaving me disturbed for letting it remain with the evidence. Oh well, who knows? Maybe it fell into someone's hands who could use it.

The next day, following our glorious release, Sam and I headed immediately for the Swedish embassy. We informed the consular general of the names of the two Swedes in the jail, location of the prison and the desperation of the poor lads. Expressing genuine gratitude, the consul assured Sam and me he would take action. I felt we accomplished something for two fellowmen.

I loved Turkey. It had mystery and challenge. The fact that it was "the East" had struck a chord with me, and Istanbul itself teemed with everything Eastern. The Turks, could seem somewhat barbarous, but I saw them as simple, friendly, earthy. But due to the events of the last two days and the realization that remaining in Istanbul might even jeopardize the Laleli family, I figured I'd better leave this interesting land, at least for now.

Sam and I accepted the consul's advice. Three days later, we left for Athens, Greece.

Chapter 4
⸎ *Greece* ⸎

FIVE OF US—out of the nine here at the Istanbul home—gathered our belongings, bid farewell to friends we had in the city and prepared the Volkswagen van for the trip to Greece. Besides Sam and me, Matthew, Clara—Matthew's pregnant wife—and Ray made the trip. Ray needed a new visa and could stand a change from Turkey while Matthew and Clara had been invited for a leadership meeting in Athens. After last hugs with the remaining members of the Laleli family on this sunny August morning, we headed westward toward the border of Greece.

About five hours of pleasant driving through the rolling hills of Western Turkey brought us to the town of Ipsala, then a few miles farther to the border station where we exited Turkey and entered Greece. Now, owning a decent vehicle like this VW bus satisfied the Greek officials that we weren't vagrants, so they didn't hesitate granting us three-month visitor visas each. *Thank God, no hassle.* They did make a quick look through the van for any contraband (drugs from Turkey) before we drove into their country.

Beautiful already—Greece! Greener than adjacent Western Turkey and freer in spirit. For sure, Sam and I were relieved to be safely out of Turkey. We soon reached the first Greek city of Alexandroupolis where homes, signs on stores, everything seemed to be painted in Greece's colors—blue and white. Now three o'clock in the afternoon on this hot summer day, the place was like a ghost town. It was siesta time—hardly anyone in the streets, stores completely shut down. Even restaurants were empty. It was *sleeping* time in Greece—after that huge midday lunch—until about five in the afternoon.

We drove through the "closed" city without stopping. On the outskirts stood two foreign hitchhikers—a French guy and girl—whom we picked up. The couple flipped out to have a ride with us to their same destination of Athens.

Cruising through this new country among friends in our own transportation was the way to go. The mountainous, rugged terrain looked quite different from Western Turkey. Here, bright, white rock formations jutted up everywhere in magnificent contrast to the green hills they sprang from. The climate, although rather hot, was pleasantly *dry*, sending our spirits soaring. Along this northeastern region of Greece grew lush fields of Greek tobacco. I saw huge, already-harvested leaves being hung out to dry on wooden racks at small outcroppings of civilization along our route. A variety of fruit and nut trees grew here as well, though most not in season.

Our main purpose—that of the five of us—was still to preach the gospel to every creature. And now, here in the back of this well-running Volkswagen minibus, cruising through all this splendid scenery, we had two captive French creatures. Ray drove and Matthew navigated while Clara, Sam and I spoke with the couple in the back.

"What part of France are you both from?" Clara asked them.

"A small town outside of Paris," the girl, Michele, responded. "Where are *you* all from?"

"We are from America. Different parts," Clara answered.

"Where did you all meet?" the girl asked.

"We just came from Istanbul where we live together. We are part of a group called *Les Enfants de Dieu*. Have you heard of them in France? We have many there."

"Yes, I think so," Michele said.

"Do you believe in Jesus?" Clara asked.

"Yes," Michele said.

Soon, with all this talk of Jesus, the guy, Maurice, seemed ready to get out and take his chances for another ride. The girl was a "sheep," a term we used for those who want to hear about God, while the guy was a "goat" and didn't want to hear. Sensing the conflicting views, we all soon enough just sat back and enjoyed the trip to Athens.

Matthew, Ray and I switched driving through the night, and we arrived in Athens early the next morning. The French couple went their way while we located the Athens family who were well established by now—much more so than when I had been here four months earlier.

The five of us moved temporarily into a new, first-floor apartment—crowded with girls, boys, singles, married couples and babies—that they had rented in a decent part of town. Everyone did the same work of getting the Word out and being a sample of God's love as much as possible by witnessing to people in the streets about our belief in God.

The members here in Athens were eager to hear news about the Work in Turkey, but we were just too tired, so we rested.

We used various methods to reach souls, but "litnessing" now dominated all else. As for Greece, Athens was, of course, the main target area, and local Greeks and friends had already begun vigorously translating the literature into Greek. Like the Istanbul brethren, the group here in Greece had just received *Shiners?—Or Shamers!* and were experimenting with it. Mind you, with Greece being a Christian nation and a *world* apart from uptight Turkey, it was as different as clear skies and cloudy storms in getting the papers into the hands of the public. It could actually be fun and a great way to make some cash at the same time.

"Mibos boris na mas voy thesis mai lega pseelah?" That's about all we had to say to someone to make some money after handing them a piece of the literature. "Perhaps you can help us with a little change?"

It was a revolution—a total change—and what everybody in the Children of God was abruptly doing, overnight. "So you'd better get used to it," we were told. Other aspects of our work included childcare, singing, translating and winning disciples, but litnessing was the ticket.

Mind you, litnessing became a great way to get us off our butts and right into the streets among souls, especially if we practically depended on it to make a living. But I would *never* be a good litnesser, no matter how much I prayed, no matter how much I tried, no matter how many different techniques I attempted. Nevertheless, I had to bear it, suffer through it, get out there and do it.

Get out there I did, too. I was still young—23 years old—single, ready for adventure and change. So, when teams were sent out on road trips—going out on the road by faith, with little or no money, the *meat* of adventure—I was ready. That's how the lot of litnessing once again fell upon me. Actually, my first such trip would serve two purposes: the chance to put litnessing to the test and to help my partner, Christina, get a new visitor visa by going into Turkey.

Christina was slightly heavy, not gorgeous, but had a sexy mane of long, straight, dark-brown hair to the middle of her back. She had attributes better than physical ones though. Unlike most of the sisters of the group, Christina was hilariously funny and rarely took herself too seriously. Already a great litnesser—a shiner—she possessed a strong love for the Greeks and spoke Greek quite well. Although American, she could easily have passed for Greek. I was most thankful to be matched with her, so fantastic a partner to have on any such road trip.

It never took us too long to ready ourselves for the road—pack some clothes, our Bibles, sleeping bags, and, most importantly . . . literature, which by now came off the presses in excellent quality and variety. Christina and I set out one morning in the middle of August 1973 from Athens and hitchhiked northward on the main E75 highway toward the closest Turkish border.

Hitchhiking with a girl is the key to success, so it took us only three rides throughout the day to reach all the way up to Alexandroupolis, the coastal northeasternmost city of Greece. Although late evening, we attempted to reach the border station and cross into Turkey. But a car from Alexandroupolis dropped us a few miles shy of the Turkish border at a fork in the road where the driver had to continue north on the E85 instead of straight into Turkey.

The place was desolate. Not a car, truck or even a person in sight—except for some farmers way off in the distance. What the heck, we were tired, it was getting dark and it made no sense to push this day any further. So we wandered off from the road into an adjacent, vast and barren crop field where we stretched out our sleeping bags in one of the long, deep furrows of the field. A bit scary since one of us was a girl. We feared some weirdo might see us out here in this huge flat expanse in the middle of nowhere. But actually, the furrows between the hills of this particular field were so deep (and so cozy), lying down flush to the ground completely hid us and our backpacks—at night anyway. Perfect quietness set in out there under the stars and yellow crescent moon in the typical, cloudless Greek sky.

The angel of the Lord encampeth round about them that fear him, and delivereth them, we claimed together in prayer from Psalm 34.7, before falling off to sleep.

Awakening the next morning in the middle of the open field of dirt left us feeling rather exposed since the same hills and furrows hid nothing and no one in the daylight. Not only was it embarrassing, but the heat of the bright rising sun quickly became uncomfortable. Greek farmers in the distance noticed us but kept to themselves making nothing of us. We emerged from our sleeping bags, packed up and slipped on out to the main road again to catch a ride to the border, with that lousy feeling of not being able to wash our faces, brush our teeth or do anything else.

When no cars or trucks passed by, we began walking eastward toward Turkey. Finally, an old truck with a wooden flatbed rambled by, picked us up and dropped us at the Greek border station. Inside the station, Christina spoke some affable Greek phrases to the fairly friendly Greek police, brightening their morning with her sincere and loving smile. *God bless her.* We then walked across the no-man's-land bridge over the Evros River on into Turkey . . . another world.

Turkish border police hemmed and hawed when they noticed the accumulation of entry and exit stamps in *my* passport, but I looked them in the eye, taking no guff. *"Teshekurederem,"* I said, thanking the guy who stamped entry visas into both our passports. I grabbed them from him and we made our way out of the building. I glanced at Christina and noticed she'd become apprehensive, perhaps from Turkey's spirit. But I knew this land and even some Turkish, so I tried to stay nonchalant and confident to keep my partner's uncertain air from getting the best of her.

Back in Athens, the colony leader had given us enough money to cross into Turkey, rent a hotel room, eat and return to Greece. No sense messing up with visas expiring or not having the means to expediently fulfill such legal, worldly obligations. Play this silly visa renewal game and be done with it. So we caught a ride with a friendly Turkish farmer from the border station, headed toward the closest town of Ipsala and checked into one of the town's only hotels. *Oh, yes! A hotel room.* You could never appreciate a hotel room, even a crummy one, until you had to sleep out in an open dirt field like we did last night. This hotel was adequate and an extreme blessing. Christina, still wary of Turkey, however, immediately prayed over our high-ceilinged room to rebuke any evil spirits (not a bad idea whenever bedding down or moving into a new room, house, apartment or structure—especially ancient ones). The prayer seemed to help ease her anxiety for the moment.

Now, had the two of us not been concentrating on spiritual things in our as yet fresh, young, "changed" lives, this quaint little hotel room could have allowed us to indulge in some great and wild sex the remainder of that day and night. But, believe it or not, that temptation didn't even raise its head between us. Although free-spirited and radical, Christina remained dedicated to her walk with her Lord and until now, sex had no part in her new spiritual life. I too was still cruising along on some kind of supernatural deliverance from being constantly compelled—as before *my* spiritually renewed life of one and a half years now—to *try* to pick up and go to bed with girls. I found this a miracle. Neither of us even considered groping one another's body here in our Turkish hotel room, despite the fact we would be sleeping side by side in the one and only sagging double bed of the room.

So we whiled away the day reading our Bibles and other spiritual writings—renewing and strengthening ourselves for journeys ahead.

Ipsala reminded me of an old, western ghost town—small, few inhabitants, old, dusty. It took only minutes to walk around it after eating a cheap, tasty, Turkish lunch from a restaurant near our hotel.

As if on vacation, we relaxed and thoroughly enjoyed having no obligations and yet ample money not to worry about our next meal or where we'd sleep this night. Furthermore, any litnessing or open preaching here in Turkey was forbidden for us—not worth risking arrest during our brief stay.

The previous day of hitchhiking through Greece and sleeping out in the exposed field, left us plenty tired. After a fine dinner at the tried-and-proven, nearby restaurant, we retired to our room, read for awhile individually and crawled into bed for an early night's sleep. Christina, not being naïve to sexual drives of men—having experienced plenty of sex in America *before* her spiritual calling— put forth an obvious disinterest toward any remote chance of sex play to me with a quick, "Goodnight," as she turned her back to me on her side of the bed. This would be all it took, too, to give me the hint for the remaining nights we would share hotel rooms on this trip together. Not until later would I learn that sweet Christina was also "saving herself" for Bill—her boyfriend back in Athens—and was therefore taking necessary precautions to keep their relationship warm, *bless her heart.*

We slept soundly and awoke together with the same friendship as the day before. There had to be some degree of supernatural grace from above for us to wake up in the same bed like this without offending one another but rather with mutual respect and understanding to . . . keep moving and please our God.

After a simple breakfast of fresh bread, feta cheese and hot Turkish tea, we checked out of our Ipsala hotel at about check-out time. We made arrangements with the hotel for a taxi ride to the border station, got stamped out of Turkey—Christina quite happy to be leaving this odd land—and walked across the same no-man's-land bridge back into Greece.

"*Kali mera! Pos eesthases?*" she said with exuberance to the same two Greek police from yesterday, bidding them good morning and asking how they were. She was back in her realm and noticeably relieved. We had fulfilled the 24-hour requirement, and the Greeks, once again cheered by Christina's bubbly smile and amazed at the excellent Greek she spoke, stamped three-month visas in our passports. After a short wait, we caught a ride into the port city of Alexandroupolis, free now to embark on our road adventures of Northeastern Greece.

Alexandroupolis is quite a large city, so we had no difficulty finding a suitable hotel in the center of it, and with money still left over from inexpensive Turkey, we hunkered down to a warm Greek lunch overlooking the Aegean Sea. Although things like food are similar in Greece and Turkey, the two countries remain practically opposites, to the point of being hateful toward one another. Sweet and chunky Christina, although a little embarrassed at her weight, never hid her craving for good food and plenty of it, another tremendous plus in the matching of us as a good road team. I definitely required regular meals and could get edgy if too much time passed between my . . . feedings! And I found the Greek and Turkish cuisine right up my alley—anyone's alley, for sure—cheap and always delicious.

After lunch we wandered along the waterfront to scope out the town and found it nearly empty of people. Siesta time. So, back in our hotel room, we too rested, read and prepared for our first evening of litnessing. Christina was eager.

"Oh! I can't wait to hit the streets again!" she said, counting her literature.

"Uh-huh," I responded, not revealing my lack of enthusiasm for this battle I had to accept and the end of our little vacation. We did have to earn some money, though, in order to survive, now at the last of what we'd brought from Athens. And we met success, thank God. The crowds on this cool, summer evening were receptive and generous, pleased to confront two smiling Americans, who spoke some Greek to them while handing them Greek literature. *Glorious.* We were so uplifted to have delivered several pieces of literature to responsive souls for two or three hours and in turn to have more than enough drachmas to pay for our present hotel room and good meals well into the next day or two. We also felt we obeyed a calling to "go out into the highways and hedges, and compel them to come in . . ." (Luke 14.23). The literature—when accompanied by a good smile—had the potential to reach hungry souls with a ray of hope and a glimmer of God's love. Each piece also had an Athens address on it if anyone wished to further contact us. Alexandroupolis, like all port towns, had plenty of foreigners roaming its streets, so we did not look completely odd to the people here except for being an American man and woman . . . with definitely different spirits from, say, the merchant sailors roaming the streets.

We spent two more nights in Alexandroupolis, enjoying meals, passing out literature in the evenings and relaxing during the day. One afternoon we met a Filipino merchant sailor and went aboard his freighter— docked at the harbor outside the city—to eat a fabulous ship-cooked meal and meet some of his shipmates. Christina and I explained how we and others had forsaken all our worldly possessions, lived together in small communities and traveled all over the world, sharing God's love. Running across English-speaking people was a bonus since we could converse in depth with them. We asked the sailors about their lives, their families and what it was like working on these ships. The Filipinos poured out their hearts to us. We exchanged addresses, and before we left the ship, the original guy prayed a heavy prayer with us, almost asking Jesus into his heart.

No sense wearing out our welcome in Alexandroupolis, though, so the following morning we hitched a ride to the next largest town of Komotini. It was election time in Greece, as we couldn't help but notice, especially at the entrances to the cities. Large blue and white arches erected across the main highways plainly broadcasted the name of the current president—George Papadopoulos. In fact, by the time we made it completely out of Alexandroupolis, I had this guy's name, "Papadopoulos," stuck firmly in my brain.

We reached Komotini by late morning and headed straight for a coffee shop on the main square where we ordered two Greek *kafés*. We found the Greek restaurant owners in such remote towns hospitable and eager to speak to outsiders. We could rarely pay for our own coffee or any other drink. The Greeks stumbled through their English and we stumbled through our Greek. And then we met on the common ground of *O Theos* and our mutual love for Him. Wisdom taught us, however, to save handing the restaurant guy any literature until *after* we had distributed some to the populace. We didn't want our newly found restaurant friend to feel responsible as our instant "host" or to report us for distributing the stuff in the streets.

We established a trusting bond with these guys who allowed us to "park" our backpacks in their coffee shops before we headed into the town, each with a stack of literature in hand. Although remote, Komotini was busy with people this weekday morning. We distributed plenty of papers and received a decent amount of donations in return—enough to enjoy another fabulous hot Greek lunch. This time it was baked eggplant, potatoes and minced beef, all swimming in onions, spices, tomato sauce and olive oil and topped with some harmonious white sauce of cheese and yogurt, the whole dish called *mousakka*. We then retired to a shaded park to read and rest while Komotini, like *all* Greek cities and indeed the whole Mediterranean, shut down to nothingness for the remainder of the hot afternoon.

Determining Komotini to have a substantial population for its size, we checked into a hotel room and, at about 6 p.m., hit the main square and streets of evening walkers. Komotini, being one of Greece's northernmost cities and near Turkey, uniquely had a small Muslim population of Turks and some mosques. I actually felt some kind of inexplicable bond when I saw the Turks, perhaps because here they were a minority, or underdogs, or simply that I still related to and liked them. The evening went well, and we again distributed several papers and received fairly good donations, rewarding ourselves at the end to more scrumptious, olive-oily Greek food, salads and rich baklava sweets.

The following morning was another story. We were nearly chased right out of town by the local police. *Yep.* In her now confident, zealous attitude, Christina had moved too rapidly in distributing the literature down a small side street. She ended up offending a Greek shop owner who tried to alert police about "two foreign panhandlers" after he saw a lady in front of his shop window hand some money to Christina. I was distributing literature across the street when I heard the guy shouting at Christina. *"Ti ena ofto?"* he demanded, asking Christina what she had.

When I saw him head for the corner to inform a policeman, I went over and grabbed Christina, now quite shaken up by the shop guy's verbal assault. Somehow, we slipped away from the whole scene.

Small cities like Komotini were like timid, untouched damsels with whom it was necessary to be slower and more sensitive in one's lovemaking. We snuck out of this place and hitched from its outskirts toward another small town. I would later realize political tension permeated the air of Komotini—as it did throughout Greece.

I don't know if those generous Greeks who picked us up appreciated their country as I did, but the green, rolling, rocky hills of Northern Greece soothed me. Such beautiful land! The countryside of tiny villages, vineyards, peach orchards, almond trees, tobacco and other farms appeared primitive, yet civilized, and traveling through it calmed us from Komotini's threats.

But when we arrived in the next, fairly large town of Xanthi, Christina remained paranoid. She thought detectives had followed us all the way from Komotini. Needless to say, it dampened our enthusiasm to accomplish much in Xanthi. The stronger litnesser of us, Christina, was in too much of a fright to be much use. "I just can't go out in the streets right now, Wayne. I'm too freaked out."

"For sure," I said. "Let's get some coffee." We found the upstairs of a fancy, uncrowded coffee shop and proceeded to kick back, unwind, count literature, count money, write letters and reorganize over coffee and Greek sweets. We decided to skip Xanthi entirely. In late afternoon we hitched a ride to Greece's "Miami"—Kavala—a fairly large, attractive city on the Northern Coast.

Christina had been here once before on a similar road trip and upon arrival, blossomed into a new creature. "I love this city," she said with a grin all over her face.

Late evening and time to eat, we headed for a restaurant near the main square whose owner, a lady named Alexa, Christina had met on her previous trip. The lady—a jolly, overweight Greek woman dressed all in black—was so happy to see her chunky acquaintance, Christina. "Christina! *Pos paté? Kala?*"

"*Kala emay, kala,*" Christina responded, and the two of them carried on awhile together in Greek, *God bless her*—Christina—learning the language and loving this land.

The lady's restaurant was unique in that we stepped from street level, *down* into its cozy, compact atmosphere. Madame Alexa sat with us at a table while Christina spilled out excellent Greek phrases of love and godly encouragement to her. And without us even knowing, the lady summoned us a lavish, three-course Greek dinner.

Financially, we weren't doing too badly. We had high hopes for Kavala, so we checked into a fairly decent hotel room in a nice area of the city. And we prospered in the three days we spent here, getting much literature into the Kavala crowds. We also swam and sunbathed on one of Kavala's clean, public white-sand beaches a bit west of the city, along the magnificent Aegean Sea. Christina wore a modest, black one-piece.

Kavala was like a breath of fresh air compared to the two cities of Komotini and Xanthi. The two towns had their own special charm, as probably every city of Greece, but there's just something different about beachside, coastal cities—worldwide. It seems to me that no matter how backward or traditional the interior of a country might be, its coastal cities feel more free. The people are natural and more open-minded. They let inhibitions fall off—even the nationals of the same country— when they reach the coast. It must be the open expanse of water and beach surroundings that enhance people to subconsciously blend into the natural air.

Had we stayed longer, we might have experienced another bonus of Kavala—the close-by island of Thassos. As it was, we walked all along the coast of this fine, modern city until leaving it. On our third morning here, we departed for the long trip back to Athens, hitchhiking— possible, again I say, with a *girl*, but nigh unto impossible without.

We made it quite easily back to "home base" with our new three-month visas. We had money left and, most importantly, a bit more faith-on- the-road experience. Not to mention a delightful taste of Northeastern Greece and its people. I had learned much Greek from Christina by the time we went our separate ways in Athens, having established a loving friendship between us.

Chapter 5
∽ *The Greek Islands* ∽

"WE SHOULD GO out to the islands," someone suggested. "It's too hot here in Athens right now."

"Definitely!" I said. It was now August, the hottest month.

Reams of 8 ½-by-11-inch papers in Greek, English, French and German came off the presses and teams began departing Athens to the islands.

Teamed up with a young Dutch guy named Ruben, I rolled up my sleeping bag tightly and stuffed my backpack with some clothes, a swimsuit and masses of literature. As usual, we would take along almost *no money*. Indeed, all of us continued to live with no visible means of support, no sure flow of money. Yet there was no day when we went without food and shelter. Not many luxuries, but somehow all our needs were met. We sort of lived by a creed: the simple Old Testament verse of Habakkuk 2.4, ". . . but the just shall live by his faith." We lived by faith. "Ask, and it shall be given you; seek, and ye shall find; knock, and it shall be opened unto you" (Matthew 7.7). Or, ". . . prove me now herewith, saith the Lord of hosts, if I will not open you the windows of heaven, and pour you out a blessing, that there shall not be room enough to receive it" (Malachi 3.10). We took these promises from the Bible—literally and spiritually—and put them to the test, holding God to His promises.

Ruben and I and another team of two guys, Bill and Mark, left Athens on a hot, sunny August day by train and subway to the nearby port city of Piraeus, to the southwest. It's almost always sunny in Greece during the summer, rarely a cloud in the sky, unless at night when it sometimes rains. We had enough money to pay one-way fares to our first two island destinations. The Athens leadership organized the island-hopping itinerary—who would go to which islands—with both our teams scheduled to meet on the distant, southeast island of Rhodes.

Ruben and I purchased third-class, one-way tickets to Limnos and Lesvos—two fairly large islands northeast of Athens. Nobody wanted to waste time on islands too small or too unpopulated. Not on this first trip anyway.

After a two-hour wait in the city of Piraeus, Ruben and I boarded our ship, having earlier wished Bill and Mark godspeed on *their* mission. These ships ferrying tourists and islanders were those huge, white, multi-decked luxury-liners. Different classes of tickets accommodated passengers accordingly on the boat. As for us, we had no private first-class cabin down below, of course. Bare essentials—backpacking, roughing it, sleeping where you can—our class of ticket! But with these lowest, tourist-class tickets *so* cheap and reasonable, we really couldn't complain. After all, we could wander about freely. We could sit for free inside an enclosed area that had several rows of airline-type seats or use any of the many lounge chairs and seating on different decks outside, weather permitting.

Cheap tickets or not, it was great to be out of Athens, clipping along on a cruise ship at sunset, looking down into the blue Mediterranean Sea. I recalled my dad saying when he brought us to this part of the world: "Oh! The blue Mediterranean!" He loved this sea. How its deep blue color could instantly take him from the harshness of his engineering career to the comfort of God's nature.

Fresh breeze on our faces, we were headed toward our first island: Limnos. When darkness fell, Ruben and I, along with other tourist-class passengers and backpackers, set out to find our beds for the night—just about anywhere on one of the outside teakwood decks. Kind of cozy, really, sailing along under the stars. But man! . . . in the middle of night, even though it was August, it got so cold out there on the top deck where Ruben and I had found what we thought a good spot near the ship's hot, rumbling smokestack. Indeed, a chilly rain, mixed with cold, salt-water spray from winds that had kicked up in the night, rendered this otherwise comfortable, open-air sleeping lousy and sleepless.

About mid-morning the next day, after stops at some other ports-of-call, we reached and disembarked onto one of Greece's many beautiful islands, Limnos. Like most Greek islands, this one too had its quaint little village of shops and restaurants strung along the waterfront where the ships dock. We explored the village, Mirina, until on a hillslope outside of town, we discovered a lone restaurant/café looking back onto the whole scene of the town and the calm, blue bay.

"We need to go up there and make friends with the owner," I said to Ruben. We ambled up to it.

"*Apo poo isthasis?*" asked the restaurant guy.

"*Ego, apo Ameriki,*" I responded of myself. "*Aftos apo Olanthia,*" I said of Ruben. I struggled in Greek with him, asking if he wouldn't mind if we left our backpacks inside his restaurant, in a corner somewhere—something these gracious, Greek restaurant men rarely denied a backpacker. And off we strode up a hill behind his place along a shaded road through a neighborhood of villas with pink, red and purple bougainvillea flowers cascading over stucco walls everywhere. Beautiful! Not a care in the world. So peaceful. Everything I'd expect a Greek island to have, on this sunny, not-too-hot, afternoon.

Although we would enjoy our time here, we weren't really on vacation, but on a "pioneering" mission to get as much literature as possible into the hands of the people without getting kicked off an island as nuisances. After our walk, we relaxed at some outside chairs of the restaurant/café until it looked like people had emerged from their siestas and were promenading along the harbor. Not a bad slew of people for such a small town.

We each grabbed a stack of literature, prayed together and—still leaving our backpacks at the restaurant—made a discretionary dive into the unaware islanders. Not only was *I* a horrible litnesser, but it turned out my Dutch partner wasn't too good either. *Uh-oh.* But we made attempts that first evening, got a few pieces out and scrapings of drachmas—although not enough for a good meal. *Darn.* The crowds were complacent, but we were probably, also, too cautious. *No sense wearing out our welcome the first night,* I figured.

After an hour or two of passes up and down the seaside promenade, we called it quits. Forlorn and hungry, we entered a mediocre-class restaurant at the east end of town and handed a piece of literature to the owner. In my broken Greek, I asked him if he could provide us a meal. I was thinking "for the labourer is worthy of his hire" (Luke 10.7). The owner agreed—not as enthusiastically as some I had provisioned from—and returned soon from the kitchen with two hot meals of spaghetti and meat balls. We thanked him immensely, then returned to the original café where the owner brightened to see us claiming our backpacks, relieving him of the tinge of responsibility for them. Grateful for his original assistance toward us, I still didn't feel too embarrassed to ask if he had any suggestions on where we could sleep for the night. After all, his unique restaurant, secluded from the town on a little hill and by itself, proved ideal for Ruben and me to spend the night close by.

"*Mibos eki?*" I asked him, pointing to a flat clearing under the trees a short distance from his restaurant.

The owner, somewhat reluctantly, consented to it but only for the night. "*Mono apopsay, endoxi?*" he said.

He didn't want some bums moving in on him for the rest of the summer now, did he? We thanked him, stretched out our sleeping bags under the trees and slept the night.

In the morning we washed up at a faucet on a wall outside the place, used the toilet inside and ordered—*paid for* from our earnings the evening before—a Greek coffee with some bread and cheese. On this calm, sunny and cool morning we wistfully overlooked the glass-smooth bay and quaint town of Mirina. But we didn't want to overstay our welcome at the café so strapped on our packs and said some grateful goodbyes to the owner. "*Efharistoomay podipoli. O Theos mazisoo,*" I said, thanking him.

Although probably glad to see us leave, at the same time, it seemed God had blessed him with a slight, warm glow for the hospitality he had shown us. Jesus had said, "Inasmuch as ye have done it unto one of the least of these my brethren, ye have done it unto me" (Matthew 25.40). This man had risked letting us stay on his property. We were little more than bums. He took us in. That makes points with Jesus, as though the man had befriended Him.

We decided to explore this wonderful island and walked northward through the west edge of town and up a paved road, past the few houses outside the town limits. The terrain was hilly and rocky, though fairly green, with guava trees scattered along the roadside. Nice, this island, but both the small number of people and the difficulty in making enough money to endure dampened prospects of staying very long. As for lunch today, we resorted to what I would later in my travels refer to as "Traveler's Delight"—yogurt and bread, a fairly healthy combination of protein, vitamins and minerals. Filling, and most importantly, one of the cheapest ways for a *poor* person to survive. Depending on the grade of bread and yogurt, it could taste pretty good, too.

This island was too small for us to remain longer than tomorrow, when we'd be able to catch the boat to the next larger island of Lesvos to the south. At least we had already purchased tickets for that trip.

So we spent the day just enjoying Limnos. That night our distribution of literature proved successful, and the villagers seemed happy to receive the words. But in such serenity along this quiet little harbor, two intruders like us from the real world, could hardly expect to break through the aged complacency, at least not with our limited time and in the fashion dictated in *Shiners?—Or Shamers!* The letter suggested to pretty much force the papers into people's hands, get some change in return and move on. We gave it our best though—back and forth along the dock, up and down side streets, in and out of shops—and got a fair amount of the words out with decent drachmas in return. Enough to pay for a good, hot Greek meal, relax and look out across the Limnos harbor—like normal people.

We camped outside of town in a safe, secluded spot and awoke the next morning in preparation to leave on the ship before noon. We had accomplished something in Limnos, and now we could sit back and enjoy the six-hour cruise to the island of Lesvos.

Lesvos was more like it. More potential for existence. The port of Mitillini where we docked was a bustling city, not half asleep like Limnos. It actually had *buses* on it to transport the larger number of people. Prospects looked good to us as we walked down the gangplank into the crowded dockside street.

As litnessers, we had to strike with the words and then kinda disappear. And on an island, there's not much place to escape to after vigorously bombarding people with strange, foreign papers. In our brief history of litnessing in the Mediterranean, we had also learned almost the only time to succeed at getting the "lit" out was in the evening, when people walked in the coolness. So we acted on that knowledge. We chose a restaurant—never a high-class snobbish place, mind you, but rather a humble one worthy of a blessing—whose owner/manager allowed us to leave our backpacks behind the counter. We sipped a hot Greek coffee there, grabbed a stack of literature each, prayed and delved into the walking crowds. *Fair* success only—typical for Ruben and me. Perhaps I was too conscious of upsetting the status quo of the island comfort. No sense getting kicked off the island the first night.

Ruben and I had only been in Greece about two months each so neither of us knew much of the Greek language, making it nigh unto impossible to explain our work and thereby provision something like a hotel room and meals . . . until we met Dimitri, the owner of a modest, two-story hotel, just off the main street from the bay. Entering the hotel, I handed him a paper across the reception desk.

"Where are you guys from?" he asked in perfect English with even a Texas accent.

"I'm from America, and Ruben here is from Holland," I told him.

"Where in America?" he continued.

"Florida, mostly," I replied.

"I lived in Texas for eight years," he said.

"No wonder you speak such good English." I looked through my pouch for a pamphlet in English.

"Yeah. I loved it there. It's a great place, America," he said. "So, what is this?" he asked, looking down at the paper.

"We live in Athens with some others," I told him, "and we distribute these papers all over the place." I fished out an English paper on current events that might best match this guy's intellect and handed it to him, on top of the Greek one in his hands. "We believe in God and try to help others any way we can. Do you believe in God?"

"Of course I do, I'm Greek," he answered.

We enjoyed conversing in English with someone.

"Where are you guys staying on the island?" he asked.

"We don't know," I replied. "We just arrived today. We don't have much money."

"I've got a room upstairs for you, if you want . . . on me," he said.

"That would be great!" I said.

Dimitri turned around and grabbed a skeleton-type key out of one of the scores of little wooden boxes along the wall behind him, came around from the counter and led us upstairs to room 219. He unlocked the door, showed us into the room and handed me the key that had "219" engraved and painted white on a small piece of wood dangling from it.

"You guys enjoy it. Sorry it's the only night I can give you though. I'm booked full with reservations through August. Come see me in the morning. We'll talk," he said, and left.

Although Ruben spoke excellent English—as do most Dutch people—he didn't quite hear or grasp, that Dimitri was donating the room to us free for the night until after Dimitri left.

"What?" Ruben exclaimed. "He's giving it to us for free?"

"Yes. God bless him, huh? What a precious guy," I said. Ruben beamed. At 19 years old, he had joined the group only six months before, so little miracles like this helped a lot. "It's only for tonight, though," I said. "He's booked through August."

"No problem," Ruben said, smiling.

We cherished the room, the shower, the comfort—real beds, real sheets! A chance to regroup our bodies with our minds and spirits. Renewal, until check-out time at 11 a.m. tomorrow morning.

The following morning, Dimitri informed us all about the island. He suggested we visit the northern, coastal, hilltop village of Mithimna and even donated drachma for the bus ride there. Ready for adventure, we set out with our backpacks to the main bus station on the west side of town and bought two roundtrip tickets to Mithimna—this northernmost village of the island.

These islands! They're heavenly. And Mithimna? Magical. Arriving mid-afternoon, we climbed a fairly wide, zigzag stone pathway to this town perched on a hilltop overlooking the misty, blue Aegean Sea to the north and east and a beautiful stretch of sandy tourist beach below and westward. *Nice.*

Everything appeared clean and *white* since the populous white-washes most buildings of Greek villages yearly. The cobblestone streets seemed shadier than those in most towns. Donkeys traipsed around and quite a few tourists shopped and walked about. For now, we leisurely explored the whole place, ending up on a grassy bluff among some old ruins, east of town.

Except for its beauty and quaintness, we made a mistake venturing to Mithimna—with so little money. As we soon discovered, by the end of that evening of litnessing, prospects for making a living here dimmed— yogurt and bread for dinner. *Darn it!*

We made our way down from the village toward the stretch of swimming beach to the west. Adjacent to it, surrounded by soothing shade trees—not always so common on Greek islands—sat a funky kind of restaurant and simple hotel. We met the manager of the place but felt too little reception to ask for a free place to sleep, so we eased out through the shady pine trees to a nearby grove of fig trees where we stretched out our sleeping bags on the dry ground for a decent night's sleep beneath the stars.

The next morning we enjoyed a swim at the beach, provisioned a good seafood lunch from the restaurant manager—despite his unfriendliness—and generally relaxed the whole day. Then, a second try on the small streets of Mithimna that night proved as futile as the night before. *Oh well.* Dimitri probably had no idea how poor we really were when he sent us here, figuring we'd absorb the beauty of this place like anyone else.

At evening time, we descended this hilltop town for the last time and made our way to a dirt road we had spotted down below and to the east. The road led to a pine forest that looked to us from atop Mithimna as perhaps a good place for us to camp for the night. Well, inside this forest is where Ruben—still young, in both body and new spiritual life—would break and freak. Our lack of funds, and so far rather unsuccessful adventures, no doubt attributed to the poor guy's hysteria. This night, I would also surmise that Greece and particularly its islands were . . . *mystical*: many leftover spirits—ancient ones—inhabiting and enchanting these lands.

If it hadn't been for a nearly full moon in the clear sky, casting a soothing blue light over the landscape, it would have been fully dark by the time we reached the edge of the forest. It was scary entering the dense forest of towering trees, but beams of light from the moon guided us nicely through the woods until we came upon a flat clearing, actually lit up as if the moon was a spotlight on it.

"This looks like a good spot," I said. "What do you think, Ruben?"

"Yeah," he responded. We took off our backpacks, then raked up a bunch of pine needles with our hands to make a bed big enough for both of us and stretched out our sleeping bags on top of it. *Pretty cozy. But, oh!* Some of those Mediterranean spirits must have actually inhabited this very forest and Ruben must have been sensitive to them because as we drifted off to sleep, he started shivering intensely into a groan and moan and an eerie whimpering cry. He freaked for some reason. Then some donkeys in the distance started braying on top of it all. *Shit!* Those donkeys, I just knew, must be possessed by demons, seeing them, or at least obeying them as they continued to scream out their obnoxious noise.

By this time Ruben actually cried in fear. So, being Ruben's elder, and seeing the seriousness of the situation, I shuffled my sleeping bag closer to him, put my arms around him and held him to my chest, even grasping his head as one would a baby. I prayed over my shivering partner, rebuking the goddamn devil and any unclean spirit that might be in that forest, causing this commotion of horror. Ruben soon fell off into a sound sleep, nestled next to me like a child, while I stayed awake contemplating this spiritual experience, communing with my Lord until I too drifted into a deep sleep. *A spirit behind every rock.*

Next morning we made the walk along the same dirt road back toward Mithimna, picking up dried figs from under fig trees along the way, and caught the bus back to Mitillini and . . . civilization. Arriving in Mitillini, the largest city of the island, we felt what must compel country/village people worldwide to move to big cities—the chance to make a living, get some money, get our heads above water. Prospects for survival.

We went to Dimitri, spoke with him about Mithimna—how great it was and how *right* he was, but not about the wild spirits and misery there! We left our packs behind his front desk.

In the following days we struggled at making a living with the literature while also wallowing in the pleasures of this island's charm. One trip by city bus to the northern outskirts of Mitillini brought us to a secluded beach of smooth, round pebbles, crystal clear water and diving rocks. *Fabulous.* Other foreigners sunbathed there, carob trees stood along a hilly bank for shade, and a well with a working hand pump gave forth cold, drinkable water. Back on a side street in the middle of town, we met the owner of a fruit and vegetable market who happily provided daily—for free—any produce we desired from his shop. We earned some money from the literature but not enough for a hotel room of any sort.

Desperate for a place to sleep, but not desiring to scratch off too far from the city, we wandered to a jetty on the far, southeastern side of the Mitillini harbor. Along the jetty, with its narrow stretch of pebbly beach, we noticed a rather large, white, wooden Greek fishing boat dry-docked near the water's edge. The boat, although clean inside, looked as if it hadn't been used in quite a while. Its bow had a deck, which made a cozy little covered cabin beneath it—just enough room for both of us to stretch out in our sleeping bags for a fairly good night's sleep.

Slap! Slap! Slap! We awakened the next morning to the sound of Greek fishermen slapping their fresh catch of octopi against the nearby seawall. *Damn.* The process apparently tenderizes the meat of these unfortunate, bottom-dwelling invertebrates. The fishermen seemed surprised when they saw Ruben and me emerge, somewhat embarrassed, from within the boat. But throughout the country, Greeks accepted hobo, back-packing Westerners—so no big deal to see the two of us living in this boat. And with stealing rarely a problem with the Greeks, we hid our packs deep inside the boat for now.

Across the street from our "boat home" on a point overlooking the sea sat what must have been the island's classiest hotel. With plenty of finesse, hair combed and shirts tucked in and looking as neat and clean as possible, we walked into the front door, through the lobby and to the men's bathroom—me leading the way. By now, in my street travels, I had acquired an instinct to be able to walk into a hotel lobby, preferably that of a luxury hotel, as if I belonged there, and head, unwaveringly, directly to its men's room to use their facilities. As long as I could *look* as neat and sharp as possible—not like the bum I was—it was amazing what I could get away with. In this case, we were able to comfortably wash up and even shave. We purchased a small breakfast from the hotel, strolled across town to our vegetable store contact for some fresh tomatoes and apples and, as it began to get hot out, returned to our boat to get our towels and bathing suits. We then went back to the hotel, walked in as if we were guests, changed in the bathroom and jumped into the luxury of its freshwater swimming pool for a swim. Not a very big pool, but so refreshing, and we had it all to ourselves, not a hotel guest in sight. We swam for half an hour, never noticed, and eased on out, grateful to this establishment for not catching on to us.

Ruben and I had spent five days now eking out a living here on Lesvos, and today was one of those days when, if it hadn't been for our faith that God would always supply, we would have despaired with our unsuccessful attempts at surviving with the literature.

Meanwhile, those back in Athens with our island-hopping itinerary, knew Ruben and I would be at this well-inhabited island of Lesvos for approximately a week, so they forwarded any mail addressed to us to the "Poste Restante" section—that section of post offices where anyone can present identification, especially passport, and receive mail in their name.

Now, my mother—one of God's precious sheep—faithfully sent letters of love and encouragement to me wherever I traveled. On this morning of despair, we found such a letter at the Mitillini post office, forwarded to me from Athens. I opened it and what did I find inside? A U.S. twenty-dollar bill! *Oh.* Mom would *often* enclose a twenty in her letters, that I would spend wisely, but *this* twenty was like winning the lottery. Ruben and I about flipped out at its crisp look and feel. Imagine. Just twenty dollars! We were such bad litnessers, or this was the wrong island to pioneer. Whatever the case, we carefully sliced up that Andrew Jackson. We *feasted* on it like rats on a fresh carcass. Our lunch today—paid for from our own money—was a hot, meaty, Greek dish, preempted by one of those Greek salads of tomatoes, cucumbers, feta cheese, olives and oregano, all swimming in local olive oil. You can never appreciate money as much until you've been without it. That twenty-dollar bill stretched into the next two days, since even the Greek islands, especially for eating, can be fantastically cheap.

After two nights spent in the boat, our abode became a hillside of grass and pine trees across the bay, just outside the northeast corner of the city. An ideal setting near the ruins of some old castle overlooking the sea. But we were ready, *more* than ready, to leave Lesvos for our rendezvous with Bill and Mark on the island of Rhodes. But how? We had beat the streets of Mitillini and Mithimna, and still had no money for the fare and hardly enough to eat on.

When I awoke on the northeast side of the Mitillini harbor and looked down through the trees, I noticed a small freighter docked below. Apparently this side of the harbor serviced cargo ships while the center of the harbor processed the fancy cruise ships. I had mixed feelings about the fancy *cruise* ships, feelings that first came to me back on a grassy hillside of our first island of Limnos. Gazing into and admiring the peaceful solitude of the Mirina harbor there, I heard all of a sudden, out of the blue Aegean Sea: Honk! . . . Honk! A monstrous, white cruise ship would come dieseling its way into the quiet harbor, ugly black smoke trailing from its smokestacks, while announcing itself with its annoying fog horn. Although sleek and attractive, these ocean liners seemed out of place to me as they intruded into such tranquil settings like something from another age. I imagined how appealing it would be to the spirit of the islands to have, instead, a magnificent *clipper* ship cutting quietly into the glassy water of the bay by only the force of the wind on its canvas sails. *Maybe in another time . . .*

Now, as the one freighter I'd seen docked on this side of the harbor loaded and unloaded cargo, I got an inspiration.

"Ruben, let's go down and see what's going on at that dock." We walked down the hill with our backpacks on and, upon reaching the dock, chatted with some workers there until I noticed a guy up on the bridge, overlooking the loading-unloading process, both his elbows on the wooden rail. He must have been the captain of the vessel. I took my backpack off and, in between all the loading, made my way up the gangplank, looking like a normal human being and not the destitute, broke preacher I was and approached the man on the bridge who carefully watched me board his ship.

"*Yasus. Pos eesthasay? Emay Wayne,*" I said to him with a beaming smile and my hand outstretched.

"Hello, Wayne. I am Stavros. What can I do for you?"

Thank God, he speaks good English. I explained our noble work of reaching lost souls of the world with the gospel. Now earlier on the dock, I had learned the freighter would soon be on its way to Rhodes! So, after my spiel, I asked him if he would take the two of us there. No doubt aware of why I bothered to board his ship in the first place, he was entirely open to us and didn't hesitate to warmly invite us aboard his ship.

"Yes, of course you can come with us to Rhodes. You are welcome," he said, with the generosity of a saint. "Tell your friend to come aboard. We leave in two hours."

"Thank you! I will tell my friend," I said, and then walked back down to the dock with a smile stretched across my face.

Joy! Thank God! And goodbye Lesvos! If I see you again, it will be with money in my pocket!

Ruben flipped. "All the way to Rhodes? For free? Fantastic!" It so encouraged him.

Backpacks on, we boarded this friendly ship, now completing its loading. Then, from inside the bridge, I looked out upon the ship and saw some of its main cargo: *live* sheep, goats and cows, over one hundred of them staged all over the outside decks of the freighter, calmly awaiting transportation to the island of Rhodes, kind of like a Noah's ark. The animals looked pretty sweet out there too, bleating and mooing, giving the whole ship a down-to-earth feeling. The crew had strewn plenty of straw across the decks for them all to eat and had tied each animal so as not to fall overboard. Apparently, common freighters often supplied these islands with farm animals. Most economical on the part of these shippers was to haul regular freight down below and utilize the vacant decks for these other passengers.

Ruben and my living quarters would be inside the bridge in a dining area near the captain's room. Here, red-leather, booth-type seats, wrapped "L-shaped" around a Formica dining table, became our comfortable beds at night. But first, after pulling out of the harbor of Mitillini at sunset and heading south toward the island of Chios, we were served, by order of the captain, one of those satisfying, hot ship meals, which we thoroughly enjoyed in his company and that of some of his deckhands. Feeling like kings, stomachs full, enjoying the sea air—oddly mixed with down-home, farm-animal smells—we were praising our God Who never fails. *Just be ready and expect Him to do things contrary to normal expectations—out of the ordinary and radical. Like this free ride with animals all the way to Rhodes!*

After a somewhat-rocking goodnight's sleep and some breakfast, we wrote letters to loved ones and to the colony back in Athens. Believe it or not, in sending teams out to the field—in this case these islands— the organization hoped for enough success to reap dividends in the way of funds sent back. Right. Not from *my* team. But I communicated to them nonetheless. I also wrote a letter to Sheila—a beautiful American girl, now in England, who was both a singer-guitarist and sought- after childcare worker of the group. Having crossed paths back in New Orleans, New York City and London, we appealed to one another. But I, as usual, continued gallivanting around, never settling down long enough in one locale to allow a relationship to grow. So for now, she and I kept in touch through letters.

At noon, the freighter docked at Chios, an island so close to the mainland of Turkey I could quite easily see Turkey from the port where we docked. It brought back childhood memories of living in Izmir at 12 and 13 years old. I thought I saw my old stomping grounds of Izmir when I spotted land directly eastward, but my geography was wrong. Instead, a long stretch of jagged land extends out from Izmir as if trying to touch Chios, but just misses it. Through the haze, I probably saw the beach town of Cesme, east from Chios. Cesme, I pondered, must by now be a dynamic tourist resort area because, as a 13-year-old (back in 1963), I could vividly remember its *idyllic* coastline of deserted, white sandy beaches, rocky coves, diving rocks, crystal clear waters and colorful, untouched reefs. A skin-diver's paradise back then.

From "our freighter," I noticed Turkish ferry boats flying the red Turkish flag with its white crescent and star in the middle, shuttling passengers back and forth between Chios and Turkey. It was a phenomenon, in my mind, how jumping onto one of those ferryboats could catapult an unsuspecting foreigner in a matter of minutes, across those few short miles, into another world . . . the East—Turkey. Sure, ancient spirits intermingled in the region, but Turkish culture, religion, way of life, language and history are vastly different from Greek.

The freighter unloaded some cargo and continued on toward the island of Samos. More beautiful blue Aegean waters to cut through, while looking over the deck from the bridge at the dumb, sweet animals. During the cruise, I spoke with the captain from time to time, and when I opened the Bible to him, some amazing verses appeared that I had never seen before, one so fitting to shippers like the captain. The verses were 23 to 30 in Psalm 107, which read, "They that go down to the sea in ships, that do business in great waters; these see the works of the Lord, and his wonders in the deep. . . ." The captain and I both marveled at the words. He took the Bible from me and read on to the end of Psalm 107.

Upon docking at the Samos harbor at sunset, the crew busily loaded and unloaded cargo. All the animals remained for the trip to Rhodes, and we soon sailed off for the last leg of our journey. On the way we passed Cos, popular among young foreigners, who actually took up habitation in caves at one end of this island. A neat place to visit. Maybe someday.

On into Greece's island of Rhodes where, at mid-morning, Ruben and I stood before the captain on the bridge.

"Thank you so much, Stavros," I said. "God bless you."

"Yes, thank you." Ruben added.

"You are both welcome," Stavros replied. "O Theos mazisoo."

I looked into his eyes, and he seemed to know he had opened his arms—taken the risk of letting strangers onto his ship like this—for two of God's children.

We said our goodbyes to him with a hug each, then strapped on our packs and walked down the plank of this far-out freighter, turning around for one more wave goodbye to our shipmate friends before making the walk along a stone seawall northward toward Mandraki Harbor, the center of town. What a difference from the previous two islands we had "pioneered." A *world* apart, this one. Total luxury dripped all over the waterfront here in the form of super yachts owned by Americans, Europeans and whomever else. Glistening white paint on their hulls, with trim and ornaments of shining brass and richly-shellacked teak and mahogany wood, oozed over these boats moored at the harbor. The *other* life. On the decks, owners, captains, crew and guests lazed in lounge chairs shaded from the bright Greek sun by canvas canopies, just sipping drinks, kicked back—no problems.

Not that I was envious. Admiring, but not envious. I knew I had grasped hold of the true riches a year and a half ago—true peace with my God and a calling to serve Him, a spiritual experience at age 21 that changed my life and satisfied my soul and mind unto this day. And now, the pleasant journey on the freighter from Lesvos had left Ruben and me relaxed and renewed, ready for the next challenge—this fresh new ground.

I observed the yachts through the stone archways of a covered arcade with fancy stores and coffee shops here at Mandraki Harbor. Then Ruben and I sat down in the midst of the whole scene at an outdoor café to ponder the situation over Greek coffee. Spirits up, but pockets nearly empty, we saw the place as promising with so many people, side streets, main streets—a *huge city* compared to our last two islands. Actually, this *particular* promenade of wealth and luxury intimidated us "begging" litnessers. But I knew it had to be done, someone had to reach them, break their normal routine of shopping and strolling . . . and make some survival funds at the same time.

No sooner had we paid for our coffees, gone to a nearby shady park to count out a stack of literature each, found a coffee shop for our backpacks and entered the covered arcade to "dive" into this Rhodes crowd, than Bill and Mark came up behind us.

"Hey! I'll take one of those," Bill said with a smile from ear to ear. The four of us hugged one another.

"When did you guys get here?" Bill asked.

"Oh," looking at my watch, "about two hours ago."

"How'd you get here?" inquired Bill. "We've been going to the docks whenever ships from Mitillini are expected to arrive, looking for you. We gave up though."

"Yeah, I guess you did. We came by a freighter. Thank God, we met a precious guy, the captain, back at Lesvos who gave us a free ride all the way here," I answered. And, getting to the point, "We didn't have enough money for the fare here from Lesvos. We've been struggling at *our* two islands. How've you guys been doing?" I asked this, although their breezy attitude, mixed with brand new clothes indicated they had been doing quite well.

"Have you been sending any funds back to Athens?" Bill insensitively asked.

"Send funds to Athens?" I responded. This horrid question pissed me off pretty bad. I mean, some people can be so blunt. *Couldn't that question have been disregarded or reserved for later?* I had to restrain myself from responding too harshly so as not to cause anyone of the three to stumble spiritually or to make it sound like murmuring and speaking doubt, like the children of Israel did when they were hungry and complained to Moses and Aaron for freeing them from Egypt and taking them out into the wilderness (Exodus 16.2-3).

Eyebrows up, eyes wide open, looking straight into Bill's eyes and without the slightest start of a smile, my expression in those few seconds more than answered Bill's dumb question. He looked away from my stare, quickly realizing he wasn't dealing with the normal, praise-God-everything's-just-great brother but someone forthright and opinionated.

"Do you realize how we've been living for the past week or so? Needless to say, we haven't done too well. And no, we definitely haven't been sending any money to Athens. Right, Ruben?"

Ruben, looking down, more embarrassed than pissed off, said, "Yeah," almost ashamedly.

Bill bubbled up and broke the gloomy atmosphere now developing with, "Praise God! Let's get you guys moved in with us at our hotel. We'll show you around this place. This is not the right area for litnessing anyway. Where're your backpacks?"

Bill really was a humble and precious brother, though, chubby, baby-faced, no more than twenty years old. He was Christina's boyfriend and a "shiner," obviously.

The four of us made a quick stop at the post office—a building adjacent to the arcade, where Bill and Mark were headed before they ran into us—to mail letters and check the Poste Restante. Ruben and I retrieved our backpacks from the coffee shop, and we all headed back toward the Old Town, where Bill and Mark lived. Beautiful, this island. Flowers of all colors bloomed in flowerbeds and cascaded from baskets hanging on lightposts, shade trees lined the streets, and gravel-strewn parks spread throughout the town. Strolling through all of this, we soon reached a wide, curving, stone walkway leading to the Old Town—an actual city within the walls of a castle overlooking the picturesque harbor below. The castle, built in the 1300s during the Crusades by the Knights of St. John of Jerusalem, gave off a comforting feeling of oldness when I got closer to it.

The last stretch into the Old Town crossed over what would have been a typical moat with water in it around the castle. I looked down and, instead of water, saw a small forest of trees, plants and meadows created specifically for the live deer, grazing throughout it below. *Nice.*

Inside the castle walls, we walked the ancient cobblestone streets between old apartments, past lively shops and restaurants and through narrow alleyways. All this history. The cheapest hotels were also located here, one of which Bill led us to on the edge of this Old Town, near the sole Turkish area with a mosque. The little hotel would be our home here in Rhodes. Like a hostel—although not an official youth hostel under government control—everyone slept in a large room full of single beds and shared the same bathrooms, showers, laundry rooms, dining and recreational rooms. Nothing private. In fact, unless girls paid extra for a "girls-only room," they also slept in the same large room full of beds with everyone else—which got interesting when they dressed and undressed. But the main feature about these places was their *price*—the cheapest possible way to have a bed, a roof over our head and access to plumbing. And worth every drachma if not particular, as in the case of the four of us, especially Ruben and me to whom this represented near *luxury* compared to what recent days had brought us.

Fortunately, there were two vacant beds in this nearly-full hotel for Ruben and me, and Bill paid the night for us.

As we discovered on the walk here, Bill and Mark had done well on three islands before even coming to Rhodes, had bought new clothes—even *blue jeans*, which in these parts were prestigiously expensive—and had, yes, sent money back to Athens. Sure, I felt some sense of failure, but a comforting feeling pervaded that no one else had done any better on Limnos and Lesvos since no one else had ever been there. Anyway, we were all now together in Rhodes with one common mind, mission and . . . purse. I would always give litnessing my earnest attempts, but if someone like Bill could bring in the drachmas, *fantastic.*

"Rhodes is great, you guys," Bill said. "You'll like it here. It's good for litnessing even. A lot of Greeks live here year round. And so many tourists right now. They get package deals, or something, with round-trip airfare, hotel and meals. Direct from Europe, a lot of them. Watch out for the Scandinavian girls—they're beautiful!"

"And generous, too," Mark added.

Ruben and I did pretty well with the literature here on Rhodes. With the many interconnecting streets always busy with Greeks and tourists, our two teams together never wore out the place or became too noticeable. Like everywhere, some folks liked the words and others despised them—or couldn't be bothered while on vacation. Good donations helped, and yes, the Scandinavian and European women were particularly gracious, God bless them. A bonus too was conversing with so many English-speaking visitors.

Apart from litnessing, we stopped in at the home of a Greek couple whom Bill and Mark had met and who donated a few hundred drachmas to the Work. We attended a festive Greek wedding on a bluff overlooking the sea, and, with his name and address given to Bill by a clergyman back in Athens, we looked up the bishop of the Greek Orthodox Church of Rhodes at his church on the coast next to Mandraki Harbor.

We ate well, slept well and played well—all of which I tried to do wherever I traveled. Also, knowing I would likely *never* visit Rhodes again, as remote as it was, I made sure to make the best of it.

One day, we swam in the clear waters at the main tourist beach on the northeasternmost tip of the island. On another day, we took a local bus along the eastern coast to an uncrowded cove of sandy beach where we sunbathed and swam in the calm Mediterranean water. From this cove, we traipsed off on a dirt road, away from the tourists, to have lunch in the shade of a secluded grove of olive trees. Along the dirt road to the olive trees stood fig trees teeming with fruit, both on the trees and fallen beneath them. I always looked for the tree-ripened figs on the ground—naturally sun-dried and yummy—as long as I checked them inside first to make sure I saw none of those vicious, tiny, black "fig bugs" scampering madly throughout the meat. Nobody wanted them in their stomachs. And, unlike back in the States where a person could be fined as much as fifty dollars for picking *one* orange, in places like Rhodes and indeed the third world in general, owners of orchards would never deprive a passerby the delights from their trees. Nevertheless, more than enough figs lay scattered on the ground, going to waste.

So, with refreshing swims, delicious Greek-restaurant meals, leisurely waterfront strolls, sidewalk café coffees and decent sleeping quarters in the Old Town within the castle walls—all balanced out with our *work* and purpose—the four of us completed our island-hopping, summer escape from Athens, with Rhodes the crowning success of islands visited. The most fun and the most people reached. We purchased third-class, cruise-ship "deck tickets" to Piraeus and departed this distant island of Greece's string of treasures, which, like them all, reflected her respect for non-oppressive living. Martial law—uneducated soldiers patrolling the streets with rifles, like in Turkey sometimes—did not exist in her lands, thank God.

But when we sailed out of the peaceful paradise of Rhodes, we were reminded that curses still exist and there is *no* heaven on earth anywhere. Since the night before, Bill had something in one of his eyes, causing him severe discomfort. Well, once out on the open blue sea and in the light of the afternoon sun, I peered into Bill's eye to see if I could see anything in it. And, disregarding any stares from other passengers, there at the extreme stern of the ship, I watched an almost microscopic *worm* wriggle across the outer circumference of Bill's sad, blood-shot eyeball!

"Huh?" I questioned. Staring intently into the eyeball, my mouth dropped open in amazement, I paused a few seconds in order to gather the right words with which to break this horrible observation to Bill. "I saw something run across your eyeball," I said.

"What was it? A bug?" asked Bill.

"I'm not sure," I responded, looking fixedly into the eye.

"Huh!" I gasped, inhaling a breath of air. "There goes another one. Looks like a tiny worm."

This didn't comfort Bill at all. Worms? Living in his eyeball since the night before? "Get 'em out, can't you?" Bill pleaded.

There must have been eight or more of these cursed creatures in Bill's eye. I rolled tissues into tiny points and hand picked every single worm right out of that eyeball. A worm, each one about an eighth of an inch long, would start at the edge of the eye and slither across to the other side. With tissue tips, I intercepted the worms' attempts—their coming or going across the eye—extracted them, squished them and made sure I saw no more of them. *Damn them! So strange.* What were they? Some kind of physical manifestation of some creepy Mediterranean island spirit? Or could they be explained scientifically? Perhaps some weird bug—either from the air or from Bill's bed—laying eggs in the poor guy's eye while sleeping back in the hostel. Nothing is perfect, not even these Greek islands. Bill was most grateful for the doctoring, and we made a patch for the terrorized eye in order to rest it.

I considered the remainder of the cruise back to Piraeus one more reward for stepping out by faith to pioneer these islands. Besides having the money to treat ourselves to snacks, meals and drinks aboard the ship, the sea remained calm (with the approach of September, these seas can be unpleasantly rough) and the boat itself, uncrowded. One special, spiritual experience happened when, sometime in the night, we sailed quietly into the secluded moonlit bay of the island of Patmos, not a sound around except for our ship cutting through the still water—so easy to imagine how John the Revelator, exiled here some nineteen hundred years ago, received and wrote the Book of Revelation. I could visualize how this isolated island may have remained pretty much unchanged all these years. The ship loaded and unloaded only a few passengers and exited out of this spiritual cove. I absorbed every second of the stop.

We slept comfortably in our sleeping bags, stretched out on benches and lounge chairs beneath the shelter of an upper deck. The cruise continued with smooth sailing and pulled into the port of Piraeus the following day, early afternoon.

"Gross, huh?" I said to Bill as we stepped onto the Piraeus dock.

"What's gross?" Bill asked.

"Arriving back in the city," I said.

"Yeah, no kidding," he replied.

After the tranquility of the islands, Piraeus gave us that shock of transforming one's spirit from nature's perfect peace to man's hard, blunt metropolitan creation. We hopped the quick subway/train to Athens, and fortunately, now the middle of the afternoon—siesta time—the streets remained bare, shops closed, hardly a soul in sight. Otherwise, with its masses of people and traffic, Athens would have been a worse shock to us. During normal hours, it must be one of the easiest cities in which to get run over by a car while attempting to cross its streets—something about how close the cars (especially taxis) come to the curb when they make their turns.

Sisters warmly greeted us on our arrival at the colony home outside of downtown. Since we were the first of the Athens members to go island hopping by faith, we shared how God supplied our needs. It refreshed my soul to be out on the limb with nothing but faith and the clothes on my back, watching the Creator supply as he used us to deliver his words to his hungry sheep. But it was also nice to be back in a stable home environment, with home-cooked meals, activities organized and my pack and sleeping bag waiting for me at the end of the night in the same place I left them—my own personal resting place—even if just on a floor with other single guys.

Chapter 6
Bed of Hay and Yugoslav Monastery

So far I loved Greece. Who wouldn't? Even the capital, Athens, was clean, cheap and organized. Although summer in the city is hot, its dry climate makes it bearable. And it seems there's hardly a cloud in its blue skies throughout the entire summer. These factors attract tourists and sun seekers—especially Europeans and Scandinavians whose countries (rather expensive and often rainy) contrast with this nearby Mediterranean corner of Europe. Also, even though Greece is geographically joined to Europe, the similarity of its culture and people to the Middle East adds to its attraction. Young travelers to and from Athens found transportation a bargain, especially by "magic buses"—chartered, hippie-like "freak buses," usually originating from Amsterdam or London and driven mostly by young people. Reliable, economical and more often than not . . . fun because of the camaraderie, these buses.

In the fall of 1973, our numbers increased in this fine city, and we began concentrating on reaching Greek *nationals* with our message. High-school-age boys and girls visited our home regularly for Bible classes, and I became a teacher for these kids, enjoying growing them spiritually in the Word. Two young Greek guys helped us translate the original English literature into Greek. We printed it and distributed it throughout Athens and, eventually, throughout Greece. In the next-largest city of Thessalonica to the north—home to a large university—we established another colony.

In Athens, boredom never set in. We rose early in the mornings—about 7 a.m.—did chores, ran errands, read, hit the streets with literature, taught new members, cooked, cared for children of the group, met businessmen who contributed to our endeavors, and we even worked with the Greek Orthodox Church. I enjoyed this "home base" activity—security for the body.

Fortunately, the cards I drew led me to road trip adventures; otherwise, being a homebody recluse, my life may have turned out quite dull. As for now though, my old friend Arthur—who now ran the Athens Work—recognized secretarial-type talents I possessed and offered me the job as his right-hand man and office worker. And, after spending the past two months on the road, out on "God's tree limbs," living day-to-day and meal-to-meal, I jumped on that sit-back-do-your-job, don't-worry-about-where-the-next-meal-is-coming-from position at headquarters. A jovial, chunky, little guy, Arthur often took himself and his position too seriously, so I simply *had* to lighten him up from time to time—to keep him amused at himself. "Arthur! Don't worry about it," I might say. "God is going to supply the money for a typewriter in His time, no matter how much you worry about it."

Another brother, Andrew, a superb guitarist, Jewish-American and close friend of Arthur, lived in the same apartment along with Arthur, Arthur's wife, Rachel, two or three other singles and me. The group considered both Andrew and I "leadership material." About the same physical and spiritual age and with similar drug-filled, hippie-like pasts back in the States, Andrew and I got along well.

On one occasion, Andrew and I traveled to the Thessalonica colony to check it out and visit with the parents of a close Greek friend of the group. We went there with a single girl who would remain at the Thessalonica home. Consequently, our hitchhiking *up* there succeeded, but on the return trip to Athens, we reconfirmed that two males don't successfully hitch rides! Even though it's probably rare that any *sexual* contact is ever made between the driver and the female companion of one or more male hitchhikers, perhaps just the remote chance of sexual play with her compels a man to stop his car and offer a ride. Or . . . they are simply magical creatures, females.

Anyway, Andrew and I fulfilled our Thessalonica mission in two days and needed to get back to business in Athens. We had some literature, but no money, of course. Andrew had his guitar in its smart case, and we had the choice to either pass out some literature—which we *both* hated to do—and thereby earn some money to pay for train fare back to Athens, or, hitchhike. The two of us. And, scorning the *work* and difficulty of litnessing in the hot sun in front of the Thessalonica train station, we opted for the simpler choice of hitching. Couldn't be *that* difficult . . .

We got a ride from the train station rather quickly, but a short one to just outside the city limits on a two-lane road toward Athens. It was noontime and we remained in the *same* spot the remainder of that day—

thumbs out, no success. The only offer of the day occurred when a semi truck stopped. We ran to it with high hopes, but the pervert driver said he'd only take one of us. *Oh brother.*

Night fell, and across the road from where we'd stood all day, a good-size, roadside restaurant had its lights on. Entering it, we met the owner of the place, explained to him our work of helping young people, and without hesitation, the guy sat us down to a full-course Greek dinner of meat-and-cheese-covered pasta, fresh salad and a half-carafe of white wine. In return, Andrew, by request of the owner, happily proceeded to serenade the diners of the restaurant, table to table, with eloquent Greek songs. I awkwardly accompanied him by clapping and trying to follow along singing, at least to make us a unified team. The live, soft music made the diners better clients to the owner as they ordered more wine, ouzo and food to prolong the merriment.

Fortunately, not a crowded night at the restaurant, our serenading obligations soon eased off. After a long day on the road—the same exact *spot* of road—and extended entertaining, we needed sleep. But *where*, Mr. Owner, are our two wayfarers going to sleep? These two who are not really bums, but have no money, and yet *seem* to be sent from God. With our countenances trustworthy and our words godly, the owner *knew* he had to provide us with a place to sleep before we even hinted or asked for it. He had no place for us though in the small adjoining living quarters of the restaurant where he and his family slept.

He led us outside around the side and back of the restaurant, along a grass pathway to what would be the most comfortable, unforgettable bed I had ever had—a thick bed of *hay* on the floor of a small stable. We both were overly gracious to the guy since he kept apologizing to us, which we understood him to be doing, no matter how little Greek we knew.

In the stall next to us a couple of noiseless cows stood, asleep, I guess. Andrew and I strewed some loose straw about in a manner prescribed by the owner, stretched out our sleeping bags and hunkered into our natural beds for the night. Being late September, the night got cold, but the straw insulated us perfectly. When we arose in the morning, the imprint of our bodies remained in the bed of hay that had caressed us. Neither too soft, nor too firm. Just right.

The heavenly bed made up for the previous day's failure to get a ride anywhere. Finally, after eating fresh little apples from the restaurant's orchard, an "angel" truck driver stopped, picked us up and delivered us to Athens.

Andrew and I took another trip together. This time, fortunately, that great sister Christina accompanied us. *Nothing like a female companion.*

Near the end of October 1973, the three of us needed new visas. This time we would experience a quick taste of the communist block country of Yugoslavia. From Athens it was a shorter distance than to Turkey, and a main highway led straight north into the border town of Gevgelija.

We had enough money for return train fare, and this time we took a small pup tent, along with sleeping bags and backpacks, in order to be self-sufficient, since we were three in number. No surprise, we successfully hitchhiked into Yugoslavia in a day and passed on through the quiet border town, remaining as unnoticed by the authorities as possible. Late afternoon, we wandered from the road to a remote grassy cliff overlooking the edge of Gevgelija where we pitched our tent. We'd made it safely into Yugoslavia, found this knoll on which to sleep, and now we needed . . . dinner.

The spirit of the little suburban village below seemed pleasant, so we left most of our belongings in the tent—except, of course, our pouches of passports, Bibles and literature—and walked down to the town. With the weather chilly under an overcast sky and getting dark, almost no one was out. Somehow, we found ourselves at the waist-high, wrought iron gate of a quaint, little, gray-stone church. And no sooner had we entered through the gate to see if someone was around, than the priest himself approached us from his parsonage adjacent to the church. Seeing we were Americans and, moreover, that we carried Bibles and had decent spirits, the priest, in his broken English, warmly welcomed us. When he discovered we were actually missionaries of a sort, who had dropped in from Greece for the day, he immediately invited us into his home for dinner before we even had a chance to beg . . . uh . . . ask for something to eat.

Goodness, what a warm, little cozy cottage of love this guy shared with his wife and two young children. His wife equally welcomed us, despite the no-doubt sudden inconvenience the three of us had posed. For sure, the family sacrificed much of their portions of the already-cooked dinner, but they seemed pleased to serve us and savor this unexpected encounter with Western, God-fearing youths.

The meal must have been a typical "communist" one—warm and gratifying on a brisk night, even though only an inexpensive bowl of bean soup with some potatoes, carrots and bits of meat inside. On the table lay ample chunks of freshly-baked bread, along with raw radishes and leaves of lettuce for salad, and fresh fruit for afterwards. The priest served us some of his probably cherished red wine as well. We communicated altogether in our broken Greek and English for a good part of the night, and we handed the family some appropriate pieces of our literature, which topped off this delightful union and proved to the priest we really were who we said we were.

"Where will you sleep this night?" the priest asked us, no doubt by instigation of his sweet wife. And when we told him of our dumb idea of sleeping out in the cold rain in our small tent, he came to our rescue again. "No. It is raining," he said. "I have a place for you. We'll go in my car."

Andrew, Christina and I gave loving farewells to the wife and children. The priest then put us in his humble, little car, drove us to the site of our tent to gather our belongings and headed south toward Greece.

"There's an old monastery down this road," he said. "I'm friends with the owner. No one lives there anymore. You'll like it, I think."

Before long, he drove us through the stone archway of the monastery and parked in front of a small building. "Wait here," he said, and he went inside. Soon, from the doorway of the building, he motioned for us to come in. "Bring your things."

Stepping inside, our three mouths dropped open at the soothing ambiance of a large room. Everything seemed made of hand-carved wood, bathed now by the flickering light of oil lamps lit by the priest. *Cozy.*

"This is the dining and meeting room of the monastery," the priest explained. He apologized that he couldn't provide us with actual mattresses and beds since he didn't have keys to the adjoining wings of the monastery's living quarters. Needless to say, we assured him how grateful we were. He bid us a good night's sleep and left. We looked at each other in utter amazement at how God had provided us the hot meal, the precious priest and now this magical, furnished shelter.

"Hallelujah! Thank You, Lord!" we exclaimed out loud. We hugged each other, realizing how *warm* it was inside the room, compared to that small cliff outside in the rain! We arranged a sturdy, wooden dining table and two wooden benches in a manner suitable for beds, spread our sleeping bags on them and fell asleep. *Glory.*

Early the next morning, gazing through the bay window of our room, we found ourselves atop a knoll overlooking a magnificent expanse of rolling hills and valleys of the Yugoslavian countryside. Not lush green, but still a beautiful site. We cleaned ourselves up, returned the furniture to its original position and went outside into the crisp, sunny morning to drink in the rest of the wonderful setting.

The monastery had apparently closed down due to either a lack of interested monks or too much pressure from the Yugoslavian government against Christianity. Or any religion. Or both.

While we were exploring, a shepherd came up the hill with his tiny flock of sheep. Just then, the priest arrived with breakfast of fresh bread, cheese and olives. Too much, this priest!

"*Gunaydin,* Mustafa," the priest said, greeting the shepherd in Turkish. Well acquainted with the shepherd—the caretaker of the now-run-down monastery grounds—the priest explained to him how the three of us were his friends and how he had allowed us to sleep in the place.

"Thank you so much, Yeorgos," we said to the priest. "We will be returning to Greece today, so we will not need the place anymore. God bless you."

"You are an angel," Christina added and hugged him.

When the priest left, I made small talk with the Turkish shepherd—*real* small talk, since I didn't know a lot of Turkish and the shepherd spoke some kind of odd Yugoslavian dialect of the language. Nevertheless, as with any third-country national, he loved having an American know at least *some* of his language. It helped smother his apprehension of us—and perhaps jealousy that we were allowed to sleep *inside* the monastery.

Next to the monastery, someone had planted a small garden of hot peppers, and, after biting into one, I will never forget how hot a hot pepper can be. *Wow.* Sweat, hiccups, fire in the mouth. Fantastically hot.

Like on other visa trips, we relaxed and used the day to discover this new and different land of Yugoslavia. Once more I found myself amazed at how a country could be a *world* apart from the adjacent country across the border. Of course, we hadn't traveled far enough into Yugoslavia to make a fair judgment of it. Still, there were obvious differences. We walked down the hill to a train depot and simply watched some of the Yugoslav workers loading and unloading freight. No one seemed to have a smile on their faces anywhere—not that citizens in *any* country run around laughing, joking and jumping around in joy. But an obvious air of oppression hung over this land that couldn't have been more evident than when we boarded the train that evening for the Greece border. Yugoslavs packed the train car we entered, many of them young people returning home from work or schools. The seats all faced one way, similar to a school bus, and not a sound or smile existed inside. For sure, we three Westerners, with our backpacks and especially our smiles, stood out when we stepped inside.

We wanted to break the icy spirit of this train by passing out literature or maybe even singing to the sad passengers—until we saw the cause of this oppressive Yugoslavian spirit: two stern-faced, Yugoslavian *policemen* walking up and down the center aisle, looking for anyone disrupting the system or creating any anti-government sentiment. And the reason for all that man-made fear and unhappiness seemed to emanate from one place, the symbol of which stood out so ominously from the front and center of these policemen's hats—the red star of communism! To me, it was like East meets West, communism versus democracy, freedom versus imprisonment—to be face to face with that red star. Not a word need be said. Those few minutes in that packed train of fresh young souls governed by the dread of those two policemen represented what must be the situation of the whole country of Yugoslavia. *Sad.*

After a long wait for passport checks at the border, we continued on into Greece and, finally, into Athens, with new, three-month visas, a taste of Yugoslavia and more testimonies of how God provides for his own. *Thank you, Lord.*

Chapter 7
Athens Revolution 1973

ATHENS GETS QUITE cold in the winter and often it snows. So, my role inside headquarters, as secretary, gofer and general right-hand man to Arthur, pleased me. Now mid-November 1973, the political tension I sensed three months ago in Northern Greece began exploding—literally—in Athens.

Greece's dictator, George Papadapoulos, had ruled the country with his iron fist for too long. The freedom-loving Greeks wanted their hard-fought democracy back and took to the streets demanding it.

At 23 years old, I would see a realm of life I never knew. Most of the revolution began at the Polytechnic University on Patission Street. The students staged a sit-down strike in front of the university, demanding a change of government, which spread throughout the city.

Andrew and I ventured down to the university to see the protest firsthand. Streets near the university overflowed with on-lookers like us, and students and police mingled everywhere. The only way to get closer to the university—the vortex of the revolution itself—was by a city bus that passed directly in front of it. Andrew and I boarded it.

With the revolution still in its early days, the students were inspired and vigorous. When the bus stopped in front of the campus, Greek students rushed it. They had already spray-painted the poor bus with anti-American, anti-Nixon graffiti—since, as usual, they blamed America for backing Greece's now-ruling dictator Papadapoulos. As soon as the bus doors opened, the students outside nearly forced those inside to get off immediately to join their revolution.

"Come! Come! Join us!" they kept shouting in Greek. And sure enough, a fair number of easily persuaded Greek girls in their late teens, thrilled by this radical disruption of the Greek status quo, allowed themselves to be grabbed right off the bus into the uprising. The confusion and the intensity of persuasion frightened me. These screaming, worked-up students were so overpowering that they controlled the movement of the bus and, in fact, the traffic along the entire, broad Patission Street. Fortunately, after winning some flighty female supporters from the bus, the students allowed us to proceed. I felt relieved to have survived such a confrontation, especially one with such anti-American sentiment.

The existing Greek government "seemed" to be tolerating the protests and general uprisings. But in reality, secret police filtered throughout Athens, observing the evolving situation, planning and organizing. One day, near the university, I observed plainclothes police grab two university-age young people, question them and then beat them—behind a car and out of sight. I learned from friends such incidents regularly occurred.

On another occasion, Arthur and I got a bit too close to a group of protesters and got our first taste of tear gas—fired by the Greek police. Along with several Greeks, we found shelter in a coffee shop. Although we were on the extreme outskirts of the gassed area, it still stung our eyes considerably. The gas was an effective weapon to get someone out of an area, leaving him not too anxious to experience it again. We hailed a taxi and went home, still gasping and eyes watering.

Automatic-weapon fire from the university area sounded in the night, about a mile from our apartment. Another first for me— hearing government guns killing its citizens.

We kept tuned to events by listening to radio broadcasts, translated by Greek friends. The government imposed a curfew between 7 p.m. and 7 a.m. From the news, we learned students at the Polytechnic University had planned their revolution well. Deep within a university building, they had set up elaborate radio equipment broadcasting their demands.

Around midnight came a strange rumbling sound in the distance. It steadily increased. I would later learn the ominous rumble that night, was ... tanks! Coming from some military base on the outskirts of the city, they headed for the university. The existing government would no longer tolerate the anarchy.

Student radio broadcasts stopped. Probably only those people living in apartments surrounding the Polytechnic University of Athens could accurately give account of the horrific events that transpired that night as they peeked from their windows at the confrontation. News media had no access to the raw, university killing fields, leaving the world unaware of the full extent of the horror.

Although not confirmed, I heard that the Greek students, so sincere and adamant about their cause, resisted even the tanks. According to rumors, the students refused to surrender their siege of the university. Boldly and defiantly they ripped open their shirts and bared their chests while the tanks broke through the surrounding walls and machine-gunned them down. The siege of the Polytechnic University and heart of the revolution, quickly crushed, left untold numbers of young Greek students dead.

But a momentum of rebellion continued in Greece. Greek workers sympathetic to the students organized rallies and street protests in hopes of upsetting the existing regime.

Days after the Polytechnic massacre, tanks and armored personnel carriers positioned themselves throughout Athens to maintain the status quo. I found it strange to see military machines take over a city against its own people. Weird. Nighttime curfews remained as the regime continued its suppression of change by fear and actual torture. More than one acquaintance reported seeing Greek youths who were innocently walking past a military machine, being grabbed by soldiers and beaten behind the thing.

Anxieties increased until it was now too risky to continue with the literature. Prior to the revolution, some of our group had been taken in by police, interrogated and even threatened to have their fingers cut off if caught passing it out again. It was not a "lovely day in the neighborhood." We scattered to other countries, leaving the Greeks to fight and work it out among themselves.

Arthur assigned me, one of the more fortunate, to the fabulous island of Cyprus. I would go with Arthur's wife, Rachel, while Arthur stayed back in Athens.

Rachel and Arthur previously lived in Cyprus. For some reason, immigration authorities there had kindly asked Arthur to leave. With only four people of the group now in Cyprus, the Work needed more laborers.

In discussing Cyprus with me, Rachel said, in a rather sexy overtone, "I think the girls in Cyprus would really like you, Wayne."

I wonder what that actually means? If nothing else, it enticed me, and, despite my growing love for Greece, I became eager to embark on this new adventure to a new country.

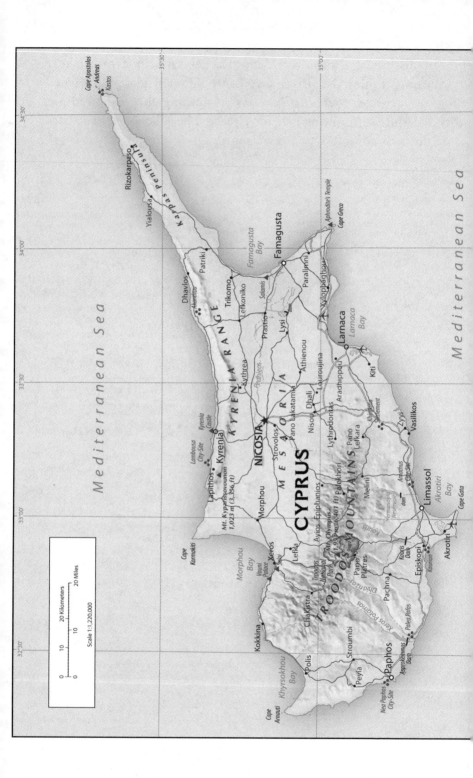

Chapter 8

～ *To Cyprus* ～

SINCE THE GROUP "had all things common" (Acts 4.32), and "neither was there any among them that lacked" (Acts 4.34), and "distribution was made unto every man according as he had need" (Acts 4.35), the fare to Cyprus for Rachel and me just appeared, as always. But now December of 1973, the price of oil had *quadrupled* from $3 a barrel the year before, to nearly $12! So, when Arthur, Rachel and I went to Piraeus to inquire about ship fares to Cyprus, the seriousness of the current Arab oil embargo hit us. Greek and European liners were not sailing at all. Not leaving the harbor. They couldn't afford the fuel even with ships full of passengers. We intended to go by ship because Rachel didn't want to *fly* into Cyprus and chance confronting any of the same immigration officials at the Nicosia airport who might remember Arthur and recognize her, refusing her re-entry into the country.

"What's with that ship over there?" Arthur asked. "Looks like *they're* busy."

Docked at the other end of the harbor sat the *M/S Adjara*—a sleek, white Russian liner.

"Of course!" Arthur exclaimed. "Russia's got their *own* oil. They're not dependent on Middle East oil."

Sure enough, that was the only ship sailing. Arthur bought Rachel and me tickets on it. We packed our things the next day, said our goodbyes, and on December 10, 1973, Rachel and I boarded the *Adjara*.

Taking a cruise ship instead of flying also created a "guise" for Rachel and me. Cyprus, such a gem of a country, made officials at her borders touchy about who entered. Arriving by ocean-liner on a three-day cruise would hopefully make the two of us appear as normal tourists coming to Cyprus to spend lots of money.

Although never liking ships and highly prone to seasickness, I found the three-day cruise fantastic. Just clipping through the Mediterranean Sea and gazing down into its deep blue color enthralled me. And it so happened this beautiful sea remained calm the entire three days.

A steward led us to our moderate cabin below deck—nothing fancy, bunk beds and rather small. I guess it entered my mind when I saw the beds, as to what might ensue between two healthy people of the opposite sex like us, living together in these small quarters out on the open sea for three days . . .

"Which bunk do you prefer, Rachel?"

"I'd like to be on the bottom," she responded, slightly blushing from the words she used. "Okay, I'll be on top," I said. *Whoa.* We both smiled.

Rachel, not gorgeous maybe, mainly because she didn't do much for herself, was short—five feet two inches or so—a bit plump, yet shapely and well built. Part American Indian with beautiful, thick, wavy, black hair nearly to her waist, big black eyes and fairly light skin, she wore no makeup, didn't think herself attractive and didn't try to make herself so. She was hands-off to me anyway. *What am I talking about here?* Considered a leader of the group along with husband Arthur, she accepted her responsibility and remained faithful in her role. Like most of the girls I worked with in this family of young people, Rachel—now in her early twenties and a California girl of the sixties—had done her share of psychedelic drugs, experienced plenty of sex and felt content to now be spiritually minded and free of that constant concentration on sexual obligation. She didn't tease or encourage me to make any advances on her married body anyway during our pleasant Mediterranean cruise.

Aboard the uncrowded ship, the two of us behaved like brother and sister or shepherd and sheep—me being the sheep, still, at this stage. Neither bothered the other. I might sit out on the sun deck of the ship, while Rachel stayed inside reading or writing. To others, we probably appeared as a couple, eating meals together and daily enjoying one another's company.

"Isn't it strange, being around all these Russians?" I asked Rachel.

"Yeah, kinda is," she answered. "We've been so brainwashed about them back in the States."

Besides the all-Russian crew—who certainly hadn't gone through any capitalistic charm courses on how to pamper and butter up good-paying customers—most of the passengers were also Russian. They seemed a sullen lot, although in all fairness, we hardly talked to anyone. We didn't want someone telling the Cypriot authorities upon arrival that we were weird evangelists or something. So we remained "incognito" the whole three days, appearing as a normal, tourist couple visiting Cyprus.

We did laugh a couple times at this "ship from the other world." Once, while walking along a main corridor, I grabbed Rachel by the arm. "Check this out," I said, pointing inside some glass display cases. "It's their duty-free shop of cigarettes, liquor and perfumes, and everything's priced in 'wicked' U.S. dollars."

Then, while dining together for lunch, "Listen," Rachel said. "Do you hear that?" Loud and clear over the speaker system came the Beatles' song, "Back in the U.S.S.R." We couldn't tell if the Russians aboard loved it. Rachel and I sure did.

The cruise included a stop in Alexandria, Egypt, which is why it took three days to reach Cyprus. Another country, another continent. I absorbed the country from the rear sundeck of our ship as we steamed slowly into Alexandria's harbor, past a fair amount of anchored, U.S.-flagged military vessels. I felt a bit odd wondering if any U.S. intelligence personnel honed in on the *Adjara* and those aboard it, like myself.

Leaning on the wooden rails of the ship as it pulled alongside the dock, Rachel and I pondered the confusion below. Throngs of Egyptian merchants looked up at those of us aboard, ready to pitch to us everything from trinkets to giant five-foot-high stuffed camels.

"Oo-oo, no thanks," Rachel said. "I'm staying right here!"

"For sure," I responded. It would only be a brief six-hour stop. No sense subjecting ourselves to the onslaught of those guys down there and chancing never getting back on the ship. And just to say we'd set foot in Egypt? No thanks, not today. Instead, we took up lounge chairs in the sunshine, wrote letters and enjoyed the security of our rented space aboard this floating, luxury hotel.

Pulling out of the harbor at mid-afternoon, after delivering some passengers and taking on a few more, the ship sailed parallel to the coast for a while. Seeing the city of Alexandria stretch on and on for miles, I wondered if I would ever have the faith to delve—with a mission of reaching lost souls with the love of God—into such wild territory.

The coast of Egypt disappeared around sunset, somewhere near the entrance to the Suez Canal and Port Said, as our ship sailed north toward Cyprus. Rachel and I savored our last evening and night on the ship, and around noon the next day, we arrived at the sunny, eastern and main port of Cyprus—Famagusta.

Back in Athens, we both had secured three-month visas for the island, but apprehension set in heavy on Rachel. With previous Cyprus stamps in her passport, she feared the immigration officers might wonder why she had returned to the island. She couldn't say, "Well, I'm a disciple of Jesus." That didn't fit any criterion for granting visas. But, acting upon the verse "man looketh on the outward appearance, but the Lord looketh on the heart" (1 Samuel 16.7), we both at least had dressed neatly and fashionably, if not professionally. "Nothing succeeds like success" was our motto. No country wants bums within its borders if they can help it.

Looking up at the officials with her big, black, puppy-dog eyes, Rachel responded well to their rather thorough questioning about her previous stay on the island. A handsome Greek Cypriot guy stamped her on in. I, of course, had never been to Cyprus, but because I appeared to have money, an official stamped me on in too. We made it. Rachel seemed quite relieved now to finally sit down in a taxi and drive away from the port and immigration officers.

The taxi drove us south through the city of Famagusta—population about 41,000, nearly a third of the population of Cyprus—to its southern suburbs and a small, two-story apartment building. We climbed the stairs to the top, second floor where Rachel knocked on apartment #5.

Bryan, a young, single Canadian brother, opened the door. "Rachel! You made it!" He hugged her.

"Bryan, this is Wayne," Rachel said.

"Hi, Bryan," I said and went to shake his hand, but he grabbed and hugged me too.

"C'mon in. Welcome to Cyprus. How's Greece doing?"

"Not that great," Rachel answered. "They're demonstrating everywhere still."

Bryan had been left alone in Famagusta weeks earlier, when Arthur and Rachel flew to Athens, so he was pretty happy to see us. The rest of the Cyprus team—American couple, William and Cindy, and their three-year-old daughter, Sophia—lived in the capital, Nicosia, 35 miles inland.

In charge of the Children of God's Middle East countries, Bryan had made Cyprus the headquarters. Bryan wasn't the only one who saw Cyprus as geographically strategic. Indeed, the eyes of many world leaders lusted over Cyprus, desiring to put their military bases on her—for better access to the Middle East.

Bryan spent his time reporting on Cyprus and the region. And when he wasn't doing that, he was sunbathing in his stupid-looking, black, bikini bathing suit—or boring everybody to death talking about himself. I knew I wouldn't last long in this apartment, but I endured it for now. I relaxed and unwound in this new country and did my part as gofer and confidant for both Rachel and Bryan.

My first taste of Cyprus—Famagusta here—was right up my alley. *Yeah.* The apartment itself sat less than two blocks from the Mediterranean Sea, which I could see glistening between some of the buildings from the back window. Living at Cocoa Beach along Florida's Central East Coast had made a beach-bum-surfer out of me, I guess. Famagusta's beach didn't have waves, but its broad expanse of clean, whitish sand stretching from fabulous restaurants, modern hotels and apartments, far out into shallow, clear, Mediterranean water, made it a tourist's playground and destination of many Scandinavians and Europeans. Women sunbathed in their tiny bikinis everywhere. But with December not the height of the tourist season, Famagusta remained an easy-going city of Greek-Cypriot inhabitants.

Rachel and Bryan knew owners of local pubs and restaurants and introduced me to them. A very decent guitarist, Rachel brought her acoustic music into these places and, on her last stay, had already touched many hearts with songs of love and salvation. Locals here liked Westerners and were particularly interested in how we'd come here on a mission, not as pleasure-seeking tourists.

For now, Rachel, Bryan and I enjoyed each other's company, and I myself relished this paradise island and the security of the headquarters apartment. The island mixed Middle Eastern and European cultures. While small restaurants served Middle Eastern "doner kebab"—slices of meat cut off huge, rotating, grilled slabs of pressed lamb and stuffed into pita, or "pocket" bread along with fresh, finely-cut lettuce, parsley and tomatoes—perfectly-modern grocery stores sold any Western item imaginable.

This Christmas proved a great step up for me over last year. Rachel and Arthur had met a Greek Cypriot named Petros, whose family lived on the extreme opposite end of the island from Famagusta, near the tiny town of Ayia Marina. Petros invited our whole clan of William,

Cindy and their daughter, Sophia, Rachel, Bryan and me for a typical Cypriot Christmas at his family's home.

We had no car, but transportation on Cyprus was cheap, and the Cypriot people so friendly we easily crisscrossed the island by hitchhiking. However, group taxis, or "service taxis" as they were called, proved the best way to hire a ride. Usually Mercedes-Benz limousines, they comfortably carried seven or eight passengers per haul at a reasonable rate. Rachel, Bryan and I took one of these to Nicosia the day before Christmas Eve, where we met up with William, Cindy, Sophia and Petros. From Nicosia we hired the even-more-reasonable means of transportation—a mini-bus, or van, which took us through the Cyprus countryside westward to the foothills of the Troodos Mountains, from where we hired a different mini-bus. This last stretch of the journey was the tricky one. After almost no rain on the island for five years, recent downpours washed out many dirt roads, like the barely two-lane one that kept crumbling beneath our vehicle on the way to Petros' town of Ayia Marina. Treacherous. Rachel remained a nervous wreck until we reached paved roads on the other side. Our descent past quaint villages, looking out into the Mediterranean Sea, calmed us.

The humble one-story home of Petros' family sat on its own piece of land about 50 yards from the coast here in Northwest Cyprus. The family ran a sort of wholesale grocery and grains store, which adjoined the home. They served us sweets and coffee as soon as we arrived, and Rachel broke out her guitar and we sang to them. Except for a tiny grocery store, the small town had closed for Christmas. A beautiful warm and sunny day, we lazed on green hillsides of newly planted wheat sprouts and strolled along the strange coastline. From the house, the coastline couldn't be seen, just the inspiring glitter of the sea. But when we walked to the water's edge, we found no beach whatsoever but instead, a long, gray shelf of mud, rock and sand stretching along and then abruptly dropping two feet off into the sea. *Strange.*

Between the house and the water's edge sat an enclosure for pigs. I happened to be near the enclosure when suddenly, "Eee-e-e-e-e! Eee-e-e-e-e!" The most horrible, squealing sound I'd ever heard. Looking toward the shed of pigs, I saw Petros' older brother holding up a male pig by its hind legs, and, with a normal, double-edged razor blade, neatly castrating the poor thing! Unfamiliar with pig-raising, I learned right then from Petros that the family traditionally castrated one of their male pigs at Christmastime in order to fatten him up for next Christmas—so he'd lust only after food and not sows the rest of his pig life.

Indeed, a large, roasted, hog-of-a-pig highlighted *this* Christmas. Everyone feasted on it Christmas Eve night and Christmas Day. Never in my life had I seen such a tremendous beast laid out on a table, smoked and roasted to perfection. Truly one of the most succulent chunks of fresh-cooked meat *any* of us Western guests could remember. An abundance of meat still remained there on the table, after upwards of 25 of us feasted and gorged ourselves on it all day and night. *Amazing.*

The highlight of this Christmas for me came when the chilly night set in and I ended up sitting with Petros and his grandmother in front of the blazing fire in the cozy, upstairs room of the adjoining cottage. Sitting with the grandmother—a shepherdess of a fairly large flock of the family's sheep—was like being with an angel. She had a perfect figure and an attractive face, and only pleasantness emanated from her. Born and raised in this same cottage, she had shepherded sheep only a few miles into the surrounding hills of Ayia Marina. Her continuous smile and calm nature—a contrast to city dwellers— spoke highly of the age-old profession of shepherding. If this woman's excellent health, trim stature and enlightened countenance typified tending sheep, perhaps more of us should consider such a humble job out in God's nature. As translated by Petros, though, the lady had many questions about life in America. *The eye of man is never satisfied.*

The guys and I slept soundly by the fire that night, the grandmother in her room downstairs. The next day involved more feasting on the dead pig, fresh fruits, vegetables, bread and Turkish coffees. We poured out our gratitude to this precious family for treating us to such a memorable, Greek-Cypriot, seaside Christmas and departed, back to Nicosia and Famagusta.

I continued living in the Famagusta apartment with Rachel and Bryan, generally just helping out, cooking, doing the shopping, running errands, cleaning and managing "survival" supplies. Highly skeptical of the world's economy and pervading instability, every home of the group set aside essential survival foods and supplies like grains—wheat, rice, barley, oats and cracked wheat—flour, sugar, powdered milk, canned foods, candles, baby needs (diapers, Q-tips) and especially water. Who knows when some disaster might occur and you suddenly need a few-days'-supply of essentials?

Famagusta had a fabulous, covered farmer's market where Rachel and I would shop on Saturdays. My first time there amazed me how one island could have such a variety and abundance of fresh foods— meat, fish, endless varieties of fruits and vegetables like oranges, pomegranates, artichokes, almonds and walnuts, and then kinda heavy, round loaves of the best, freshly-baked whole-grain breads I ever put in my mouth. Rachel had contacts at the market so we moved quickly through the place, choosing the best products at the best prices.

As for the weather in Famagusta, it could change drastically from warm enough to swim—here in December and January—to rain, sleet and even snow!

But I was not being used to the best of my ability. I knew it, and Rachel and Bryan knew it. After all, someone had to reach the 650,000 inhabitants of Cyprus with words of faith, and with only five of us now on the island, I became a prime candidate. Time to hit the free and open road again. It meant breaking away from the security of the beachside apartment, but it also meant challenges and action. Besides, I'd heard enough of Bryan's stories about himself whenever I sat down with the guy.

So, I transferred to the main Nicosia home, 35 miles to the west, where I would make my base and eventually visit nearly every stretch of this beautiful country.

Chapter 9
—◇ *Hitting the Streets* ◇—

WE RENTED A home on the eastern outskirts of Nicosia in a quiet Greek-Cypriot neighborhood of mostly one-story, single-family homes. By the end of January 1974, the "Cyprus team," including Rachel and Bryan in Famagusta, had grown to eight adults—all of us Americans in our twenties—with little Sophia making nine. The seven of us who shared the Nicosia home were William, Cindy and Sophia; Aaron, a single guy who did all the printing and had recently returned from a visa trip; another couple, Devon and Amy, who recently arrived on the island and were expecting their first baby; and me. The single-story house had three bedrooms and a bath, a large attic and a small backyard. Aaron had stocked the attic with survival supplies and non-perishable foods that he regularly recycled, or "turned over."

William and Cindy, both with dark hair, dark eyes and dark complexions, could pass for just about any Middle Eastern race. William was tallish and good looking, and Cindy, although slightly overweight, with her straight, waist-length dark hair, big brown eyes and full, pouting lips, was a sexy woman. Conscious of her weight, Cindy didn't grasp herself as that attractive, which to me, made her more attractive.

Cindy and William, with the love and pride they had for Sophia, could hardly prove themselves better parents. Although William took his job as head of the Nicosia home a bit too seriously, he remained humble and fairly easy-going.

Aaron came from New Jersey and, like me, was 24 years old. Having lived in Greece a while, he was familiar with the Middle Eastern mind and Mediterranean way of life. He'd been in Cyprus three months now and, with his congeniality, good outlook on life and always-smiling countenance, had made many Cypriot friends, some quite influential. Aaron did all the printing of . . . the literature. And *that* is what had to be distributed throughout the island, by someone.

Devon and Amy flew in fresh from the States. Not much bad could be said of the two of them. Amy, eight-and-a-half months pregnant, and, except for her tummy, stood tall and trim. Had she worn makeup, she'd have been a knockout. *Lord.* Husband Devon—a normal-looking guy sporting the first flat-top haircut I had seen in a long time—proved to be a great person.

But I remained the one to hit the roads of Cyprus. *Off to the front lines.* Single, no certain skills committing me to home base and now speaking some Greek, I fit the calling. If nothing else, I could get the literature into the hands of the people and, with the same phrase used back in Athens, ask for a donation in return: "*Mibos boris na mas voi thesis, mai lega pselah?*" These few words, politely asking for help with a little change, were practically all we needed to know when handing a piece of Greek literature to the locals. That phrase and a good smile, could meet living expenses on the road and even send money back to home base.

By the middle of January 1974, I embarked on my purpose and calling in Cyprus—relentlessly traveling the far reaches of this country, passing out godly literature with political information to the so-politically-conscious Cypriot people. For sure, the continuous domination of Cyprus by outside conquerors had left the Cypriots extremely politically conscious and aware of world affairs. Yet they remained simple and friendly. They were island people. The most pleasant race of people I had ever encountered.

Devon and Amy wrote down and memorized some Greek phrases from me, and the three of us headed for the city of Larnaca. One of Cyprus' five main cities, Larnaca had a population of about 22,000 people. Located on Larnaca Bay, on the southeastern coast, and with a long promenade of palm trees, it had the appearance of a European Riviera town yet with the carefree mood of a fishing village. Simple bars, cafés and restaurants stretched along the waterfront where, that cold day, only a few local menfolk sipped Turkish coffees.

The three of us came to Larnaca to get a feel for litnessing in Cyprus, and, unlike most road teams, we actually brought along some money. Yet, even with few people around, we received good donations with the literature. Who made most of it? Amy. An unbelievable woman! She amazed the Cypriots and me with her cheerful attitude in passing out the literature—her huge tummy sticking out ready to bring forth child any minute. The islanders couldn't help but grasp in wonderment anything she might be handing them, if not just to make contact with so pregnant a woman in the streets. They presumed she must have something to say.

That night we rented two separate hotel rooms, at 500 mils apiece—exchange rate being one Cypriot pound equal to about $2.73 U.S. dollars, making our stay $1.37 per room. Sure, we soon discovered the hotel doubled as a brothel, but the rooms, despite the sagging beds, sufficed. The manager and staff loved seeing Amy walking around in the hotel. She brought a certain light to them, pleased to uplift the one or two prostitutes she encountered in the hotel's hallways, *God bless her.*

The following day, Saturday, we passed out a fair bit of literature to the shoppers and half-day workers, deemed the trip a success and returned to Nicosia that afternoon. In 24 hours we'd been hooked on our mission and purpose for being in Cyprus, by the Cypriot people themselves.

This started my adventures in this fabulous land. We believed the literature, intended for the general public and, when possible, for influential high officials, could change people's lives. The papers contained currently relevant world economics and politics with the answer that only God Himself and His love could possibly fix the mess human beings had thus far caused on this planet.

On January 21 in Nicosia, one such high official on that cold, snowy night—the first snow in nearly 25 years—received two significant pieces of literature from me: Princess Margaret of England, the first member of the British Crown to visit Cyprus since the country's independence in 1960.

The Republic of Cyprus formally came into being on August 16, 1960, and became a member of the British Commonwealth. William, always conscious of public relations and influence, caught wind of the Princess' arrival to Cyprus, so he and I attempted to meet her and her entourage at the Lydra Palace Hotel. Somehow, in the lobby of the hotel and standing by all the photographers when she came in, someone pushed me around the corner to the end of a line of well-wishers. When she came around that corner, she only saw me. "God bless you, Princess Margaret," I said, and handed her two pieces of our literature, one concerning what the future might hold for England and the other about the history and economic outlook of Europe. Both shared the importance of not forgetting God in these matters.

Looking right at me, she said, "Thank you very much." Her bodyguards checked out the papers, she grabbed hold of the two pieces of literature—one called *The Crash* and the other *The Meek*—and she went her way. She no doubt thought it all part of her reception. Whatever, it increased my faith that our little mission had been accomplished.

My key partner for saturating the island with literature arrived January 24. Chris, a young American guy, 20 years old, from San Luis Obispo Beach, California, had lived in Italy as an accomplished litnesser. He possessed almost no other talent except litnessing, but he did it so well, it didn't matter.

One of those superbly intelligent types, Chris earned nothing but straight As in high school. Besides valedictorian of his senior class, he held probably every scholastic aptitude honor available. And yet, one week before graduating his senior year, he quit and never received his high school diploma. He'd met society's criteria for success and achievement, but found himself not cut out for it all. He didn't even do drugs. But in rebellion, he threw it back at them: "Sorry, that stuff is just not for me." Instead, he joined the Children of God. "I'm going to pursue more meaning in my life and hopefully help others along the way."

Chris had a sweet face, curly hair, a perpetual smile of perfect white teeth and blue eyes that, no kidding, actually sparkled. When he approached people with the literature, they found it nearly impossible to reject his love and warmth.

He and I made a good team. Chris had an uncanny devotion to getting the words out to the point of being obnoxiously dedicated to hitting the streets anytime, anywhere, under any circumstances. As an *air* sign—Aries—he *floated* through the streets on a timeless cloud. I, on the other hand, an earthly Taurus, nearly disdained the somewhat spiritually demanding feat of litnessing. I had to make Chris *stop* to even *eat* or to sleep and take free time. But, lucky for me, as with all road teams, there was *one purse*—all income shared. Despite my whole-hearted attempts and use of various tactics, I could never match Chris' success on the streets. Again though, we were a great match. Chris always brought in plenty of pounds, while I made sure we ate properly and slept enough.

Accompanying Chris on his arrival from Italy, January 24, 1974, was a short, shapely sister named Doris. She might have been Jewish-American. Like the other sisters, had she worn makeup, she could have been attractive. A close confidant of Rachel and used to doing secretarial work at headquarters, she now opted for road-team challenge and adventure. And . . . she was a horny little thing.

I didn't care much for her, but William asked me to take her, a day after her arrival, to Limassol, the third largest city of the island with a population of 52,000 on the central southern coast. I had visited there with Devon for a three-day stay, so I knew the streets somewhat and where to stay and eat.

Hitchhiking there, Doris and I were picked up by the owner of a Limassol gas station, a guy named Stelios—married and with three kids—who would remain a good friend of ours. He wanted to get into Doris' pants, but despite that, he was a congenial guy, had money and sincerely liked our mission.

We reached downtown Limassol and headed for a back-roads restaurant I knew about. The Greek Cypriot owner of the place, Fotis, had donated free meals to Devon and me a week ago. The two of us came back and paid our own way a couple times after that. A cheap lunch I loved was a white, ceramic bowl of hot, white navy beans swimming in their own sauce and doused with plenty of Cyprus olive oil, with raw onions thrown in to taste. Like in Turkey and Greece, bread came with every meal. But in Cyprus, the bread—derived from the island's own strains of high-quality wheat—was extraordinarily more tasteful. I felt I could easily have lived on just chunks of that heavy whole wheat bread, olive oil and wine!

Fotis treated Doris and me this January day to one of his finest meals, *God bless him*. We then hit the streets with the literature. In an hour and a half, I handed out nineteen "letters," as we called the pieces of literature, and received 800 mils ($2.18) in donations. I don't know how many Doris delivered, but I could see in her face she enjoyed it. We talked with the owner of a men's boutique and with an interested Greek Cypriot soldier, both of whom I noticed Doris discreetly batting her eyes at.

On my recent trip to Limassol, I discovered a *really* cheap—but clean—hotel near the Turkish section at 300 mils ($.82) a room. The mosque right outside the rooms—with calls to prayer from loud speakers blasting at pre-dawn hours of the morning—no doubt influenced the lower price of the hotel. As with the 500-mil rooms at the Larnaca hotel, we shared bathrooms with guests on the same floor.

At the end of our eventful day, Doris and I checked into one of the rooms. Never did the question of our marital status arise.

It wouldn't be the first hotel room I shared with a sister; yet I was still naïve and just into my second-year spiritual walk with my God. Doris, on the other hand, was older in her walk with her Lord, and, since she had always been around the leadership and elders as a secretary, she thought herself "spiritual enough" to lightly delve back into fleshy pleasures. From California, she was no vestal virgin, either.

There were two single beds in the room. Not attracted to Doris in the first place, and respecting her years of spiritual life over me, I had not at all geared myself up for her subtle, sexual innuendo. After we both somehow managed in the dark to climb into our separate beds without seeing the other undress, she whispered from her bed, "Wayne. I sometimes get this terrible pain in my legs in the middle of the night that you might have to come over here and massage for me. Okay?"

Uh-oh. "Okay. Good night," I said.

Well, it must not have been God's will, or so tired from the day's events, Doris was never aroused by any pain. We both slept soundly through the night and awoke with no odd feelings.

We spent two more days and nights in Limassol before hitchhiking back to Nicosia. Apparently Doris caught on quickly that either I wasn't interested in her, or I just wasn't "liberated" enough for her to try to further entice me into her hot pants.

Meanwhile, Amy, in an extraordinary show of faith and calm, delivered a baby boy in a Nicosia hospital. Using the Lamaze breathing techniques, Amy quietly endured the pain. Devon "coached" her while Cypriot nurses looked on in amazement—and gratitude—as this American couple brought forth their firstborn child *without* the horrible wailing they often heard in their maternity wards.

And the new baby, Troy, was a delight to have in the house. Aaron came up with a wonderfully teasing song on the guitar for the baby—an appropriate song for most newborns:

> *I've got no hair*
> *I've got no teeth*
> *I've got no neck*
> *I've got no shoulders*

I've got no eyebrows
I've got no eyelashes
I've got no knuckles

. . . and so on. It was great, even if Mom and Dad didn't appreciate it too much.

Sundays were usually a free day for us, so on the first one of February, Aaron and I ventured out to the Troodos Mountains southwest of Nicosia. Unlike most countries, two *guys* could successfully hitchhike throughout Cyprus. Firstly, far-flung and isolated, Cyprus isn't that easy to reach for the normal bum or ne'er-do-well traveler; therefore the Cypriot driver wasn't afraid of being either murdered or robbed. Secondly, their isolation from the world left the Cypriots inquisitive enough to want to pick up and talk to outsiders. And thirdly, the Cypriots were just downright pleasant people.

Like most excursions away from home base, Aaron and I headed out with no money. We easily reached the town of Troodos, about 35 miles from Nicosia. From there we caught rides up a scenic road through snow-covered forest to the highest point of Cyprus—Mount Olympus, at 6,410 feet. I stepped out of our last ride and looked across a valley. "No way!" I said to Aaron. "Skiers? They're skiing up here?"

"Oh yes," Aaron responded, glad to see my shock. He'd been up here before and was proud to now show me another aspect of this amazing country. "That last driver told me there's a two-and-a-half-foot-deep snow base up here."

The white winter scene of a nearby wooden ski lodge and distant slopes busy with skiers sat now like ice cream on top of this already-fabulous island.

Aaron had been in Cyprus four months and knew many people. In fact way up here he ran into an older lady he knew, the owner of a Nicosia café. We spent some time with her and she treated us to Greek sandwiches at the ski lodge.

The two of us then walked up not far from the skiers to the observatory—the actual highest point of the island—to see the magnificent 360-degree view over the whole country. But still we had no money, and as the sun began to set, we soon discovered most people had already descended the mountain, leaving almost no cars to take us back down. After much prayer, we began walking. Despite our destitution, it enthralled us to be strolling among the towering, snow-laden pine trees along this mountain road. And to think a month ago, in December, I sunbathed on a beach of this same island, at Famagusta. *Not bad.*

Somehow, we walked down an entirely different road than we'd come up, and as night fell, we chanced upon . . . God's inn. It appeared out of nowhere. Inside seemed as magical as outside, especially when the little old Cypriot couple who ran the place cheerfully bestowed on us an upstairs room along with a nice hot meal—all for free. *Glory to God.* We both were so grateful. And the upstairs room of the wood-frame inn, with the glistening, snow-covered forest outside its frosty windows, was out of a storybook. The ceilings had exposed wooden beams, everything spotlessly clean, the furniture quaint and old. The room felt cold on this winter night, but it made the little wooden beds with their abundance of thick, warm quilts that much cozier for snuggling into.

Before retiring to the delightful room—seemingly dropped out of heaven—here in the middle of the Troodos Mountains, Aaron and I went downstairs to the lobby to share with anyone there a taste of the love of God, Who had once again touched our lives, providing our every need. But there were no people sitting in the oversized living room of comfortable old couches and chairs arranged around a large Oriental rug in front of a blazing log fire of the stone fireplace.

But we had work to do. Words to get out. And, as we learned before bedding down, a 6 a.m. bus to Nicosia left the following Monday morning. We caught it, somehow for free, and arrived back in Nicosia by 9:15 a.m.

Not long after arriving, partners and I began serious excursions to all parts of Cyprus with only stacks of literature, a few changes of clothes in our backpacks and "no scrip, no bread, no money in their purse" (Mark 6.8).

Chapter 10
∽ *Coffee with the Locals* ∽

CHRIS HAD READIED the literature and himself for the first straight week on the road for both of us, away from the Nicosia base. On the distant, southwestern coast of the island, we hit our first city, Paphos, where Apostle Paul had confronted and blinded some sorcerer for a season (Acts 13.4-13).

We hitchhiked and caught a ride for the entire 100-mile distance with a speeding truck driver. Immediately we passed out papers for two hours in downtown Paphos and then checked into a youth hostel. These places, as the name indicated, were strictly for youths, or student types, and we—especially as foreigners—fit right in. Spotlessly clean, nearly empty of guests, and at 400 mils (about $1.10) each a night, we couldn't beat this lodging. One problem with these places though was they had *rules,* like a time for lights out, a curfew and no mixing of boys and girls. But they had a secure, "organized" feeling, imparted by the worldwide standard they were managed under.

The next day—in and around the streets of this remote, fairly large city—proved successful for Chris and me with receptive people everywhere buying our literature. In five hours, I sold 115 letters and gave away 28. In the afternoon we walked a mile and a half or so, down to the town of *Kato* Paphos (*Lower* Paphos). It was by the sea and beautiful. The avenue leading from Paphos to Kato Paphos—Apostolos Pavlos Avenue—had inviting shops, restaurants and outdoor cafés scattered along it. We sipped Greek coffees and read at one of the outdoor cafés.

I found it a bit difficult to work in the calm beauty of Kato Paphos amid probably my favorite realm of nature—the beach and sea. A classy promenade of tile wound along its shoreline next to a small, stone seawall, while clear, Mediterranean waters gently lapped against rocks below. Only a *small* port city, the waters and atmosphere of Kato Paphos remained crisp and clean.

Like most Mediterranean cities, evening time brought the locals out for strolls along this waterway, although, being February, it was a bit too cool for most people. Nevertheless, those who came out at sunset and into the evening were warmly receptive to us. By the end of this night, I felt there *had* to be something special about Paphos and Kato Paphos. If nothing else, these folks had fully encouraged Chris and me on this first of such faith trips throughout this country.

Rather than wear out our welcome here, we passed out some papers to school kids the next day and left it for "another time." By noon, we started hitching back eastward when a young Cypriot guy picked us up and drove us to the next main city of Yeroskipos—a village known for producing some kind of candy. The guy insisted we join him at his home for lunch. "*Endoxi. Efharistoomay,*" I said, accepting the invitation, both of us hungry anyway. And sure enough his mother prepared us a fine meal right then and there at their farmhouse, not far from the main road. We then hitched to the next town of Kouklia, location of the Temple of Aphrodite.

Pioneers of this flooding of literature into the hands of the Cypriots, Chris and I had to discover the best tactics for each locale. In hitch-hiker-friendly Cyprus, farmers with pick-up trucks often drove us to the next town of considerable size. The closest such town today was Pissouri—not too friendly, but we managed to get a few pieces of literature out in exchange for some fils.

We broke ground in such towns the same way I did in Greece—walk into an open café, as if commissioned by the Maker of the Universe to do so and, most of all . . . smile. A happy countenance could break the somber atmosphere of backgammon-playing, local men (and anyone else hanging around inside) and immediately assure them we were friendly. But the best thing going for any of us was our unmistakable appearance as Westerners. Especially in the smaller, remote towns. The Cypriots were so open and ready to welcome foreigners, talk with us, learn from us and genuinely make us feel at home.

I doubt we *ever* had to order our own coffee or cold drink. Within seconds of entering a place, one or more of the patrons in the café would invite us to sit down, "*Katheestay, katheestay,*" and ask us what we wanted to drink, "*Ti thelatay pino?*" To which we eagerly complied, sat down and ordered our drinks. We simply had to accept this hospitality, and then, know what to order. Usually, I'd order the distinctive Greek "mud" coffee—the predominant hot drink of Cyprus. But in ordering this coffee, I knew to be ready for their next, imminent question, "*Kafé leegy, i medzo?*" A little sugar, or medium sugar? They could then brew it accordingly. I ordered tea once or twice to find it was a drink the Cypriots didn't care for one bit. They couldn't really make it correctly and considered me out of place to want to drink it at all. But the *mud* coffee was what we were *supposed* to want. It's what the Cypriots drank; they knew how to brew it up— sometimes with a twist of lemon peel—and we "fit in" when we drank it among them. I informed Chris though, "Just don't get so carried away with its good taste that you sip into the 'mud'—the fine grains of coffee settled at the bottom of the cup. It can sit pretty heavy on your stomach. I know. Like an idiot, I did it a few times."

Or, we asked for a Nescafé. Now, a Nescafé in Greece or Cyprus is a phenomenon. I learned partially how to do it since it blew my mind so. They'd put a teaspoonful or so of instant Nescafé coffee from its can or jar into a ceramic mug, sugar to taste, and just enough canned milk or water to make a *paste* out of the mixture. And for the next few minutes they'd whip, grind and beat by hand with the teaspoon the stuff in the bottom of the mug until it turned from a darkish brown to a fairly light beige. Then they slowly poured boiled water into it, creating from simple instant coffee, a drink somewhat similar to a cappuccino—with foam on the surface, even. Delicious. I watched the process in numerous restaurants and tried it at home, but these guys had some special touch I could never master. Nescafé, incidentally, is a *zinger* for caffeine and to be taken seriously.

If we wanted a *cold* drink, the best one to order was a Cypriot *lemonade*, which they too preferred and made superbly. Both drinks—the Greek coffee and the lemonade—were also the reasonably-priced ones, contrary to ordering an imported, more expensive, Coca-Cola or Pepsi, like a spoiled Westerner might do, insensitive to the customs of the land.

But it was the *brandy* of Cyprus and the foods served with it that I learned to savor on escapades throughout this island. The brandy was the real stuff, to be sipped straight up. A British airman stationed in Cyprus once said to me in a pool hall, "The only problem with Cyprus is the brandy's too cheap."

Perfect. What a country. The *food* of Cyprus was another highlight, and I lost count how many times I was "forced" to accept banquets of it from the friendly Cypriots.

Indeed, if someone came up with a "top-ten list" of this life's pleasures, one would be to have a meal with a Greek Cypriot family in a small village on the island of Cyprus—unannounced, unexpected.

First of all, the sincere desire of the Cypriot people to serve and please—expecting nothing in return but the company of the traveler—envelops the entire atmosphere at a table spread with a white linen tablecloth in the open, fresh air. About the only things *cooked* at the meal are the meat, fish, beans, bread and coffee. All else is eaten fresh and raw. Artichoke hearts even. And everything is from the island itself—olives and their oil, wheat for the bread, grapes for the wine, vegetables, legumes, succulent oranges. As Hazel Thurston said in her book, *The Travelers' Guide to Cyprus*, "There is hardly a fruit in the whole world which cannot be cultivated in Cyprus' varied climate." Hopefully, the guest is enough of a drinker to sip on the brandy being served throughout the meal in small, shot-like glasses. It wasn't there to get the visitor drunk, but rather to increase the appetite for the array of fresh food served on small, white, ceramic plates. Perhaps the only *import* was the coffee, served steaming hot in a demitasse after the hour or so it took to complete the meal.

Back in the States, in my hippie days, conscientious about fresh foods, I became a vegetarian for a year, cooking mainly from a Yoga cookbook. But the Cypriots, in their everyday life, blew apart anything American vegetarians like myself could dream up in the way of healthy eating. The Cyprus *bread* alone was a meal in itself. Made from the island's own wheat, oats and barley, it came as round, three-to-four-inch-thick loaves so hearty they were heavy in weight. Certain cheeses were unique to Cyprus as well, like "halloumi," made from sheep's milk and best eaten fried.

After Pissouri, Chris and I soon reached the British base of Episkopi, where young British soldiers gave us a cot each in their barracks for the night. In the morning, the soldiers walked us over to the Royal Air Force (RAF) cookhouse/cafeteria for a breakfast of sausage and eggs. Before leaving the base, we passed simple English literature on salvation to school kids and then split to Limassol—Cyprus' second-largest city. Once there, we took buses to nearby Polemedia and Ypsonas, villages receptive to our message. That night we slept in the only youth hostel in Limassol. All in a day's work, out on the road by faith—"Nor scrip for your journey, neither two coats . . . nor yet staves" (Matthew 10.10). Plus, we sent a letter back to the Nicosia base with 20 Cypriot pounds ($55) enclosed. Not bad, considering we left Nicosia three days ago with *nothing*, a tribute not only to steady work, but to the delightful Cypriots.

We spent the next three days—February 8, 9 and 10—distributing literature throughout Limassol before returning by bus to Nicosia. And thus was Chris' and my first week-long trip in Cyprus with nothing but a few changes of clothes and some stacks of literature. The first of several such trips we'd make.

At a large, commercial printshop in Nicosia, Aaron taught me how to print our literature on a small, offset, portable printing press we owned. In the brief time I was afforded this luxury, I saw how Aaron had it made, doing the printing each day. First, we'd ride our bicycles through peaceful housing areas of Nicosia's outskirts, through the Turkish section, on into the Greek side to the printshop. Then, for lunch, at a restaurant a block away from the printshop, we ate some sort of flavorful, worker-class mush of beans, meat and fresh vegetables with Cyprus bread on the side.

But I spent very little time in Nicosia, around home base. I was a "front-liner"—almost constantly on the road, usually with Chris. But I also ventured out with William and Cindy, Devon, Amy and baby, or with Aaron.

I liked traveling the island with Aaron though. The two of us took litnessing much less seriously than the others, and Aaron was practically in love with Cyprus and the Cypriots. He also knew the best places to go, like the far southeastern tip of the island where he and I lazed one day in the serene beauty of an untouched sandy beach near the town of Ayia Napa, on our way to the adjacent Ayia Napa Monastery. Aaron always brought a guitar along with us, so when we went inside the monastery, he played several songs to the residing priest there, whom he knew from previous visits. A guitar had become the best, laid-back way of sharing God's message of love and freedom with others.

Another time, Aaron and I took a trip together to the extreme northeastern arm of Cyprus, where we passed out papers all the way to the remote town of Rizokarpaso and slept that night for free at the Apostollos Andreas Monastery. The next day, after *un*successful distribution in a small town of the area, Aaron said, "Forget this. Let's go swimming. I know this coastline pretty good."

So we walked to a secluded cove of white, sandy beach and crystal-clear, barely waist-deep water that continued probably one hundred feet out from shore, with high rocky cliffs on three sides. *Heavenly*. We had no bathing suits with us, so we swam butt-naked, not a soul in sight. Again, Aaron—the real pioneer of Cyprus—knew and loved this fine land and never failed to enjoy it.

Going on the road with William was like a vacation. Knowing how seriously he took his position as leader of the Nicosia home, I made sure to give him his space to lead the way. William mainly went on the road to be part of the crowd and to fill the role of general in the saying: The troops are only going to be as good as the general. But in his attempts to lead the way, he often caused us to waste time in either the wrong town or on the wrong people. He would drag onto the road with us, his predominant desire to meet and kowtow to notable folks, consequently failing in the main purpose of being on the road.

Cindy would also do her part as the general's wife and join up on road teams, usually with spoiled baby Sophia. I always appreciated Cindy's womanliness. *Oh, yes*. Whether spiritually accepted in the group or not, I found myself slowly drifting again to the allure of God's "crowning creation" . . . women.

It was in the fabulous town of Kiti, near Larnaca to the south, that Cindy and I, out on a short road trip together, were given a place to stay—at the end of a full day of passing out papers in four other towns— by one of Kiti's locals. This older Cypriot gentleman made a cozy area for us to sleep, on the living room floor of his home, with plenty of bedding and blankets. The floor area was so small though, between the furniture in the room, that Cindy and I were forced to lie pretty much . . . right next to each other, with Sophia on the couch.

Well, I don't know how spiritual I was supposed to be, but the voluptuousness of this woman, with her straight, dark hair falling everywhere, made it rather difficult not to be attracted to her in those cramped quarters. *She* may not have been moved by it, but I, in my now over two years without sex—although still floating on a spiritual cloud of supernatural celibacy, free from that "obligation" of the single male to "score"—was aroused like a virgin teenager when merely my *butt* rubbed against her beautiful, plump rear end before either of us drifted off to sleep. *Good Lord.* Our two butts compressed together like that, could have caused *someone* to turn right around, join lips and carry that accidental nudge a bit further. *Here I go again. What am I talking about?* She's a married woman and the loving, faithful wife of William. *Go to sleep, Wayne.*

. . .

Joining up with Devon, Amy and baby Troy wasn't too bad either. Delightful, good sports, Devon and Amy never complained, or at least not openly, about being sent on road teams, sometimes for days at a time, with the baby only a few weeks old. And Amy, like Chris, could deliver literature with effortless success! On more than one occasion, I saw her, along with baby Troy strapped to her in an infant backpack, distribute as much as 100 pieces throughout a town with several pounds of donations in return—bubbling and smiling the whole time. And she did it while Devon and I were "obliged" by locals of such friendly towns as Athna in the Southeast to partake of a brandy or two with them—a great woman, a loving wife to Devon, a sensational woman of God.

Then there was Debbie, another American girl, who came to Cyprus the first week of June. Beautiful! She looked like Olivia Newton-John. A real fox. She wore a bit of makeup, this one, and had blondish hair well past her shoulders in a fashionable, layer cut that accentuated her blue eyes and pretty face. When a few of us went swimming at a Famagusta beach one hot June day, she wore a yellow-flower bikini, revealing her near-perfect body. Yet she was modest, didn't flaunt her beauty and considered herself a humble servant to the cause. Another superb woman with whom I must *try* and work without getting too tripped-off, despite not having seen any sister in this family so attractive.

But Debbie would eventually become Aaron's wife. Which is why she came to Cyprus—to see if she and Aaron truly loved each other. They had been boyfriend and girlfriend, back in New Jersey somewhere, before their simultaneous spiritual enlightenment and consequent dedication caused them to follow the rest of us to all corners of the world, preaching and teaching God's love. For now though, the two of them remained discreet about their love for one another, never hung on each other, but instead went their separate ways just like the rest of the single brethren.

I was never coupled *alone* with Debbie out on the road. That might have been too much. In the group, only married couples were supposed to have sex. But if I had ever been out in the middle of this enchanting island alone with this girl . . .

The closest call occurred when William, Chris, Debbie and I traveled to the east of Cyprus—with married, straight William no doubt on *that* road team as Debbie's bodyguard! The four of us spent several successful

hours passing out literature in the village of Trikomo, when, at the end
of the night, a villager gave us two upper rooms of a large home to sleep
in. We were all exhausted, but my mind still wandered to lovely Debbie,
lying alone in the other room that night. It never happened. But I would
have been right there to massage any cramps in *her* legs!

Debbie flew to Cyprus with a Turkish sister named Nesrin. The latter
had met some brothers of the group in Ankara and, rare as it was, joined
up. A black sheep from a fairly wealthy Turkish family, she'd been into
drugs, slept around—at least with a boyfriend or two, not that common
in Turkey—and was ripe fruit for rescue from her wilding. I'd seen
prettier Turkish girls, but her dark eyes had a loving sparkle in them, and
she looked rather nice in the black, one-piece bathing suit she wore on
that same Famagusta beach outing.

Nesrin had been invited to Cyprus to help reach the Turkish people,
about 18% of the population. The Turks lived throughout Cyprus in
small villages and in their own sections of the larger cities. Although
the Turks conquered Cyprus back in 1571, Cyprus' long history of
domination by various empires had left it more a *Greek* country than
a Turkish one, in my opinion anyway. As far back as 1400 BC, the
Mycenaeans—generally from the peninsula of present day Greece—
migrated to and colonized Cyprus, introducing Greek culture to
the island. The language, art and religion of mainland Greece were
thereafter transmitted to Cyprus. Furthermore, the Byzantine
empire—AD 300 to 1192—included within its domain both Cyprus
and mainland Greece, creating a cultural union between the two
countries, despite 600 miles separating them.

Whatever the history, we aimed to reach the Turks as well as the Greeks
so we printed literature in Turkish, Nesrin translating it. Nicosia and
Famagusta both had Turkish sections in them with police checkpoints
monitoring who went in and out. But we, as Americans, flowed freely
through, easily making friends with Turks inside. Yet, unexplainable
tension permeated the Turkish sections. For sure, Turks in the Turkish
section of Nicosia, except for the youths, were a paranoid people—
particularly when it came to any kind of literature distribution. They just
couldn't handle it. And, sure enough, as soon as William and I one day in
June distributed some freshly printed pamphlets, an undercover Turkish
cop nabbed us and took us to the chief of police of the area. Fortunately,
we talked our way out of it with smiles and an air of complete innocence.

"Hey! What's wrong? What's the problem? You gotta problem, or what?" The guy, while sitting at his desk, thoroughly read the pamphlet, and even appeared to like it. It portrayed John F. Kennedy as a benevolent president with a heart for third-world peoples and, due to his tolerance of communism, was possibly targeted by the CIA or some other group within the U.S. This letter, *Kennedy,* was an extremely popular one in Cyprus, since just mention of his name had Cypriots recalling how he had, for some reason, distributed *milk* to them during his presidency.

William and I walked out of the Turkish police station, even parting on fairly good terms with this police chief, with the understanding of course that literature distribution, at least in the Turkish part of Nicosia, was not welcome. Obviously, the Turks—in *all* of Cyprus—lived warily. Tension between Greek and Turkish Cypriots had existed since Britain annexed the island in 1914. The two just couldn't share this fabulous land with one another, and a movement among the Greek Cypriot population—ENOSIS, an acronym based on Greek words meaning "union" with Greece—fueled this tension. In 1955, a prejudiced, military fanatic named Colonel George Grivas further aggravated the situation by creating his Greek-Cypriot, outlaw organization called EOKA (*Ethniki Organosis Kyprion Agoniston*). This Greek Cypriot Underground Organization terrorized not only Turks on the island, but the established Greek-Cypriot government as well. Grivas and his cohorts caused the Turks to demand partition of the island. But when negotiations between Britain, Greece and Turkey broke down around 1955, a settlement in 1960 eventually provided for Cyprus' independence and terms of a constitution, with treaties preventing either ENOSIS *or* partition. Archbishop Makarios III was elected the new, independent nation's first president, with a Turkish vice president, Fazil Kutchuk, and in 1961, Cyprus joined the Commonwealth of Nations and United Nations.

Large-scale fighting between Greek and Turkish Cypriots erupted several times in the 1960s with a Greco-Turkish war narrowly averted, causing UN peacekeeping forces to be sent to the island in 1965. President Makarios meanwhile, in his wise and humane leadership, considered the Turkish Cypriots as equals, and consequently an attempt was made on his life in March of 1970—not by Turks, but by radical Greek Cypriots. Immediately the government feared a possible coup, led by the same Grivas character who still pushed ENOSIS. Turkish Cypriots, on the other hand, demanded more recognition and insisted

Turkish troops be sent to the island to offset the influence of the Cypriot National Guard dominated by officers from Greece. Greek Cypriots immediately interpreted such a proposal as amounting to partition, causing the mistrust between these peoples to increase. And then the "Grievous Grivas," having been deported earlier from Cyprus, returned to the island in 1971 to rekindle his belligerent EOKA movement, causing acts of violence against the existing peace-seeking government headed by godly, efficient Makarios—first elected in 1959 and reelected nearly unanimously in 1968 and 1973 by the people who loved him.

Makarios didn't take the antagonism by Colonel Grivas lying down. Instead, he formed a national police force to suppress continuing guerilla movements of Grivas and the EOKAs. In fact, about the only evidence I saw of any disturbance of the status quo here was the various walls spray-painted with "EOKA" graffiti.

"What's these people's problem?" I asked William one day. "Cyprus seems to be running just fine with Makarios."

"Yeah," William replied. "But some people are never satisfied."

Then in January 1974, Grivas died. But the EOKA movement continued, became "EOKA-B," and remained dominated by officers from mainland Greece.

Apprehension among Turks with all this EOKA/ENOSIS business showed. I noted the Turkish sections and towns of Cyprus were more run down than the Greek areas since the Turks were uncertain of their future on the island, especially with maniacs around like Grivas. The Turks saw little reason to invest even in their homes for fear of one day being run out. So, realizing the paranoia pervading Turkish areas, we treaded lightly when there, especially with the literature.

Disregarding prejudice, we made friends equally of Turks and Greeks, inviting both, sometimes at the same time, to our Nicosia home. I remember a night when a Turkish friend came to the house to find a Greek soldier-friend of ours present—in uniform—and by the end of the night, the two of them embraced as fellow human beings.

Chapter 11
∽ *The War of Cyprus 1974* ∽

DESPITE THE MISERY conjured up by political insurgents, Cyprus was a paradise island. And mainly Chris and I went out by faith, beat its streets, distributed the literature and brought in the funds. As front-line soldiers we learned how best to do it—take a guitar along. To ease the uncertainty of small-town folks, great big smiles helped too. Or have a girl along. A congenial woman could turn the key to any man's heart.

Now the Cypriots were not only politically conscious but religiously conscious. And guess who'd been here passing out literature years before we arrived? Yep, the Jehovah's Witnesses. Chris and I abruptly discovered this when we passed out a piece or two of *our* literature on a city bus in the town of Paralimni in Southeastern Cyprus. An extremely irate Greek Orthodox priest of the village, in his traditional black robe, long beard and black hat rushed the two of us, grabbed Chris' literature—since he was the gung-ho one trying to reach even the bus riders—and threw the whole stack into the air. He pointed his finger and shouted furiously at Chris, "Yehovah! Yehovah!"

To this, Chris responded, "*Oxi Yehovah! Oxi Yehovah!*" insisting we were *not* Jehovah's Witnesses.

I stood up and spoke some Greek to the guy, attempting to persuade him we were not Jehovah's Witnesses haunting him, while most of the passengers, sympathetic to Chris and me, helped us humbly gather up the pamphlets now strewn all over the bus. The tense situation left the villagers rather speechless. I mean this guy could not withhold himself. He had a definite disgust toward Jehovahs, and, I had to hand it to him, he wasn't afraid to take action. He was still mumbling and grumbling when Chris and I sheepishly exited the bus at the next stop.

It seems the Jehovah's Witnesses had established themselves in this southeastern peninsula of the island, because in the cluster of villages of Paralimni, Dherinia and Xylophagou, which Chris and I visited the following day, we continued to be accused of being Jehovah's Witnesses. One town even had an actual Kingdom Hall.

It was time to brush up on the guitar. I had learned to play as far back as my junior year in high school, at least the main chords, and now, in my spare time, had learned some decent songs in Greek. But I hated the thought of dragging a guitar along on road trips, and worse yet, the need to break it out and use it in front of anyone . . . and to sing. *The horror.* I was *not* an inspirationalist, despite adolescent fantasies I had of banging out heavy leads as part of some rock group.

But Chris was not even *remotely* an alternate choice. He'd hardly even picked up a guitar in his life. Besides, he didn't *need* to play the guitar—he was already *way* too valuable getting the literature out.

The guitar, though, became necessary equipment on all road teams. Aaron played well and learned all the songs in Greek, William humbly did his part to learn, with Devon the most adept, owning and playing an acoustic twelve-string.

When Chris and I ventured out to parts unknown on the island, we often introduced ourselves with a song on the guitar, no matter how amateur, usually in *cafenions.* No better way to break the ice than with music. Not loud, not soft, not rock, not jazz. Just pleasant songs with spiritual undertones always in Greek—or Turkish, if singing to Turks. Villagers beamed and gave us a "key" to their town, allowing us to freely distribute the literature.

The music had more impact than we realized because, before we knew it, Chris and I, on a two-week journey in May at the western end of Cyprus, found ourselves in the town of Polemi, singing at the main elementary school in front of its four hundred students upon invitation from the headmaster. And then, four days later in the city of Polis, we did the same in front of six hundred kids. To the kids out here in this remote part of the island, Chris and I might well have been famous American rock stars. It didn't matter how well I played the guitar or how we both sang. They screamed, clapped and enjoyed it.

We had started from Paphos and headed northward to the two schools, then eastward, making a loop that touched the foothills of the Troodos Mountains. Through rolling, picturesque valleys of vineyards, rivers and pine forests, we sang and distributed pamphlets for two weeks in a total of 22 good-size villages. One day, we came almost close enough outside of Paphos to hand a pamphlet to President Archbishop Makarios, who often mingled—though well protected—among his people. Chris had already shaken hands with Makarios and handed him a pamphlet back in Nicosia a month earlier when the archbishop visited a small church there.

Chris and I got so into distributing the stuff, jumping from town to town, explaining to the inquisitive islanders what the heck we were doing, we'd often find ourselves at the end of the night in some village with no hotel in it whatsoever. And, sure enough, villagers would take us—total strangers—into their homes for the night, give us beds and meals and treat us like honored quests, sending a pitcher of water on a tray with two glasses to our room when we slept. In the mornings, they'd feed us a breakfast of fresh bread, cheese, olives and coffee.

"*Efharistoomay, podi poli! O Theos mazisas,*" we would say to them. "Thank you so much! God be with you." We were then off again singing, talking and distributing in probably three to five villages a day.

People in seven villages housed and fed us on this trip. We also stayed for free one night in a hotel-like room of the ancient Monastery of Ayia Moni, sitting over three thousand feet up in some of the most spectacular scenery of Cyprus. Another night, we slept comfortably on the hay floor of a tin shack near Paphos, followed the next morning by a refreshing swim in the cordoned off, crystal-clear municipal bath of the Mediterranean Sea at the eastern edge of Kato Paphos.

As for donations from the literature, they became more than enough to support any road team *and* to financially assist base operations. So, we pumped the papers out continuously. Aaron would print it in Nicosia, and if we needed more while out on the road, we telephoned in and someone from the base could easily re-supply us with freshly printed stacks via service taxis. We would simply go to the specified taxi office, retrieve the package and carry on.

Had this island not been so continuously rewarding with its natural beauty, perfect climate, superb foods, relaxing little drinks and friendly people, "frontliners" like Chris and I might have felt used and abused. After all, we—and all road teams—were main supporters of the two home bases of Nicosia and Famagusta, the latter housing Rachel and Doris, who hunkered in their beachside apartment, reporting on *something* all day long. But in the end, those like Chris and I, who nearly relentlessly hit the road, received the most compensation. We were the ones who learned the language. We were the ones who got to know the people, customs, traditions, foods and drinks of this fabulous land. We were the ones who stayed trim and healthy, walking in the fresh outdoors. We were the ones whose faith was strengthened as God answered our prayers for a ride to the next town, a meal or a place to stay for the night—since we sent most earned funds to home base, rarely spending any cash on ourselves. We were the ones who, while resting on a hillside under an olive tree, with a cool breeze on our faces, enjoyed village kids bringing us freshly-made halloumi cheese and freshly-baked bread in appreciation for visiting their village with our songs and words about Jesus. So, *we* were the ones who fell in love with this magnificent island and its people. The "homebasers" may have worked equally hard on *something*, their needs comfortably supplied—but *they* didn't have a love affair with Cyprus.

Cyprus has six or seven main cities whose areas are uniquely different one from the other. Nicosia, the main and capital city in more or less the center of the island, with a population of about 112,000 (1970), is the most crowded area of the island. "Watch out," I told newcomers to Cyprus. "There're too many cars here, especially in Nicosia. It's easy to get hit by one if you're not careful."

There's no spectacular geography—mountains, seaside or even hills—around Nicosia, but admirable evidence of ancient history exists in the way of well-preserved castle walls and ruins in the center *hub* of the city. During our time here, no towering skyscrapers of office and bank buildings loomed ominously overhead in Nicosia, nor did horrible four-lane highways run through the center of town, yet plenty of business went on and governmental affairs were conducted most efficiently. Exclusive stores and coffee shops lined its streets, with the international airport just outside the city. The *Turkish* section of Nicosia was the largest and most established on the island.

Eastward from Nicosia, two, fast, forty-mile stretches of road lead to the beach resort of Famagusta. Between Nicosia and Famagusta the countryside is flat, and, depending on rainfall, ideal for agriculture. Along the southernmost of the two roads are the sizeable, worthy towns of Asha, Vatili and Lysi.

In Lysi once, I said to Chris, as we sat at an outdoor lunch served to us by a Cypriot family: "Can you believe we're eating *raw* artichokes."

Famagusta is the tourist capital of the island, catering largely to Scandinavians and Europeans. Like many beachside cities, it is the most cosmopolitan of Cyprus, with fancy bars, restaurants, nightclubs, plush hotels and high-rise apartment buildings. Yet it is still Cypriot—without obvious decadence like some Western cities. People were here to have fun and to enjoy the beach atmosphere that a coastal metropolis imparts, yet in a noticeably civilized manner. The Cypriot police, adept at keeping the peace anywhere on the island, might attribute their success to a supernatural respect people seemed to give to this island—out here in the Eastern Mediterranean—that had gone from domination by one empire to another yet remained a unique country open to new ideas from all nationalities, especially in Famagusta.

The city is the main port of the island for both passenger and cargo ships, but its highlight, south of the port, is an extraordinary stretch of clean, sandy beach and calm, clear, shallow waters. And along this beach, especially in tourist season, lay sunbathers, largely from cold, European climates, the women clad in tiny bikinis, some topless. A lot of the tourists here seemed to be married couples with kids, but a substantial number of single, Scandinavian women visited the city. And, had I not actually seen it for myself, *been* to some of the discotheques they frequented, on top of having heard it from reliable sources, I'd have never believed such beautiful women in their mostly early twenties came to Famagusta—and indeed other Mediterranean countries—strictly to be *romanced* by the locals. No doubt about it, this ideal island, stuck out here all by itself, was romantic. And with the local, good-looking, dark-haired, dark-eyed—usually with distinctly long eyelashes for some reason—light-skinned Cypriot guys, these women had no problem letting themselves be captivated during their week-or-two vacation by these amorous islanders. Sure, these women were not *all* beautiful, but a lot of them looked like models.

Northeast from Famagusta, a long, narrow arm of the island extends several miles into the sea. On a map, what looks like an interesting stretch of geography, turned out—to me anyway—to be quite a letdown, its very tip past the city of Rizokarpaso to Cape Apostolos Andreas, rocky and unappealing. Even the villages along the stretch of road to this tip didn't seem too friendly to Aaron and me.

South of Famagusta lies the lovely beach town of Ayia Napa and the friendly Ayia Napa Monastery. And, unlike the northeastern arm, a warm, pleasant atmosphere permeated this southeasternmost tip of the island.

. . .

Traveling clockwise around the coast from Ayia Napa is the island's fourth largest city of Larnaca on Larnaca Bay. Its decent beach and palm tree-lined promenade along its waterfront of cafés, hotels and shops, made Larnaca most appealing. Back eastward from the city, about 12 miles away and on the coast, is the British military base of Dhekelia. And the villages surrounding Larnaca, like Aradhippou, Livadhia, Kalokhorio, Dhromolaxia and Klavdhia were some of the most cordial places I remember.

Limassol, the island's second largest city, population 52,000, lies on the central, southern coast, about 45 miles west of Larnaca. I didn't see any spectacular beaches here, though I never looked too hard for them. The one beach I did swim at east of the city had small, dark pebbles, instead of sand, with water not particularly clear, nor pleasurably shallow for any distance out. Since Limassol was a district administration center like Larnaca, some of us extended our visitor visas here. To get a three-month extension, we'd walk into the immigration office, holding in our pockets about $300 in Cyprus pounds borrowed from one of our Limassol friends in case we had to prove to officials we weren't stone-broke stragglers bumming off the land.

Chris and I spent more time in and around Limassol than anywhere else on the island. We easily reached it by Mercedes-Benz taxis from Nicosia, and it was so large we didn't wear out our welcome distributing pamphlets here. We also spent good time talking with locals.

Like Larnaca, villages surrounding Limassol such as Mesayitonia, Yermasoyia, Ayia Phyla, Ypsonas and Kato Polemidhia all graciously received Chris and me, some treating us to those feasts of Cypriot food and brandy. Also in close proximity to Limassol, less than 10 miles to the west and southwest, are the British Air Force bases of Episkopi and Akrotiri. The bases were just . . . there . . . in the distance, unobtrusive, yet efficient—as the British are—and totally in tune with the traditions, customs, likes and dislikes of the Cypriot people. On visits we had at both the Episkopi base and the Dhekalia base back near Larnaca, British forces never hesitated to generously provide us with food and overnight accommodations.

In Limassol, a Greek-Cypriot girl named Margarita, one night in March of 1974, broke my two-year-or-so *celibacy*, if you can call a passionate kiss on the lips as doing that, which, in my case you probably could.

While Chris and I passed out papers on the outskirts of the city at the "Bye-Pass area" of Limassol, Margarita called me over to the Paris Café where she was sitting with friends under the umbrella of an outdoor table.

"What is that?" she asked, with a flirty smile.

"Here," I said, and handed her a pamphlet.

"What is it about?" she inquired. "Sit down."

Chris and I took up chairs from a nearby empty table and sat next to her.

"Where are you from?" she asked.

"America."

"What are you doing in Cyprus?"

"We live with some others in Nicosia and pass these papers around. We go to different parts of the world, meeting people. The papers are about faith . . . in God."

"Oh, I'd like to do that!" she said, in all sincerity. "We are having a small party tonight. Can you come?"

"Sure," I said. "Where is it?"

She drew a map. "Be there at eight o'clock, if you can."

"Okay, thanks. See you."

Chris and I showed up around eight o'clock at the party held in someone's home. Now, in Cyprus, where things are a few paces behind Europe and the West, the party was an extremely innocent gathering of mostly kids in their last year of high school and thereabouts. Margarita was 18 years old, cute and affectionate.

"Hi!" she said. "You came!"

She and I talked together until some soft music began playing over the stereo system.

"Dance with me," Margarita said.

The room we were in had been cleared to make a dance floor with the lights turned down low. I took her, held her close to me, and we slow danced together among several other couples. A few minutes into the dance, she backed away a bit and looked up at me with her dreamy eyes not six inches away from my own eyes. Well, there was no way I was going to refuse to respond to her when her eyes slowly closed, her head gently fell sideways and her moist little lips slightly parted to meet mine. We kissed, our tongues touching lightly for a few delightful seconds.

I was *so* appreciative of that little kiss and impressed by this young Cypriot girl not a bit afraid to break traditions. Meanwhile, Chris on the sidelines caught a glance at the two of us, which kinda shocked him, I guess. Margarita's sister Martina danced with Chris, but he was a bit too straight to plant any kisses on her just yet.

I remained in contact with Margarita through letters, and Chris and I, when visiting Limassol, spent time with the two sisters and swam at the beach with them. I never failed to give Margarita affectionate touches and assurances of my love for her, but that magical kiss on the dance floor was as far as it went with us. Like an added bonus, she kept me encouraged and self-confident. But she was young, and I was too busy traveling all over Cyprus to be able to spend much time with her there in Limassol. She was so cool and precious though, *God bless her.*

Continuing westward (clockwise) from wonderful Limassol, the road passes an enchanting beach—the birthplace of Aphrodite, where fable says she walked out of the sea onto the land—leading on to Paphos at the southwestern tip of the island, nearly 40 miles from Limassol. Paphos and this whole western area of the island are another realm of Cyprus. Paphos itself, a small city of about 11,000, used to be both the capital of Cyprus in the Hellenistic period until the time of Constantine and an important seaport. To me, it seemed extremely *Greek.*

I said to Chris on a visit here once: "Did you ever see the movie *Zorba the Greek*? This place could have been where Anthony Quinn got up from his rickety, seaside café table and danced his Greek dance."

"Yeah, I remember that scene," Chris responded. "You're right. This little harbor *does* look like that same place."

On some quick trips northward along the coast from Paphos, I saw endless, untouched coves and beaches along clear Mediterranean waters. Traveling inward from the sea leads to the lush Troodos Mountain scenes I enjoyed on past road trips. Paphos itself was too small for us to hang around with literature for very long so when in this western area, we also traveled to nearby villages and towns. Chris and I only came out to this land once or twice anyway, as it was rather far removed from the Nicosia base—which kept it unique and exceptional.

Traveling straight north and then along the northwestern coast, still clockwise, eventually leads to the small city of Morphou. Only 24 miles from Nicosia, "homebasers" like William, Cindy and Aaron could frequent it on short trips. Other than Nicosia, Morphou is Cyprus' only fairly main city not on a coast, although it sits only about five miles from the Sea. Instead, flat, agricultural land and citrus groves surround it. William had some great friends here, making it always a pleasure to visit this friendly town.

And then there was . . . Kyrenia. *Oh.* I never spent enough time in this little city. It sat at the "twelve-o'clock" mark on the central northern coast of the island, about 15 miles straight north from Nicosia and had a small population of about 4,000, making it more a place to vacation than to bombard with the literature. The main action of Kyrenia centered around its calm, little harbor of pleasure yachts and small, wooden fishing boats. Surrounding the quaint harbor, small hotels, restaurants, shops and outdoor cafés stretched along its ancient cobblestone streets and walkways. At the east end of the harbor stands a well-preserved castle, built sometime in the Middle Ages. Farther east from the harbor lies the inviting, sandy, partly rock-and-cliff Six Mile Beach, stretching out along clear, swimming waters. And if that's not enough, in either direction east or west from Kyrenia along this northern coast stands the magnificent, fortress-like stretch of green and rocky Pentadaktylos, or Kyrenia Mountain range. The contrast of these mountains, so close and clearly visible from the beaches adds just another splendor to this geographically ideal island. It's like the mountains are there to be admired from the coast since they don't abruptly, dangerously drop off into the sea but instead, gradually, elegantly slope from their peaks—some over three thousand feet high and about two miles from the shoreline—into the green fields below. Along the foothills on either side of the range, several small villages have sprouted, and throughout the mountains themselves are numerous, old, appealing castles and monasteries.

The Troodos Mountains are the other larger mountain range of Cyprus, covering much of the area between Nicosia and Paphos. Unfortunately, I spent little time in these remarkable mountains other than my February visit during the snowy season and a Sunday afternoon picnic with our whole Nicosia family in the spring. It's an area that, like mountain climbing, requires devotion and reverence. Instead, since we tried to cover as much territory as possible on each road trip, we couldn't be slowed down with the winding, rather treacherous roads in and around these mountains. We just didn't have time to leisure out in the magnificence of the rock formations, waterfalls, crystal-clear rivers, dense forests and heavenly little villages.

By July, I had been here in Cyprus nearly seven months, and besides numerous visits to the main cities of Famagusta, Larnaca, Limassol and of course Nicosia, I had stopped in, sometimes slept in, ate in or sang in and always distributed literature in one hundred villages I had counted throughout the island, returning to some of the larger ones two, three or four times. We were captivated, like most people who visit Cyprus, by the beauty of the island, its ideal climate and mostly the gracious Cypriot people themselves.

What then could disrupt this near perfect place? Human beings of course. And, not unusual for the history of Cyprus—outsiders. But this time, outsiders from pretty much their own kind—military officers from Greece. Although the Grivas character had died in January 1974, apparently this union with Greece (ENOSIS and EOKA) still dominated these guys' thoughts. Like empires before, outsiders could not leave Cyprus alone. It was too perfect, too rich in resources—copper mines, tourism—too beautiful, too strategically located. Greed. Again.

Tragedy manifested itself on July 15, 1974, and would have repercussions unimagined by the thoughtless perpetrators of it—these Greek military officers and their Greek-Cypriot partisans. They had kept ENOSIS alive, feeling it feasible that Cyprus and Greece could be unified. So, the first step was to overthrow the existing government of Makarios by staging a coup against him. Sadly, hundreds of thoughtless Greek-Cypriot collaborators—people are so often *ungrateful* for what they have—joined in against Makarios, pitting Greek Cypriots against each other.

I happened to be in the Famagusta apartment with Rachel, Bryan, Doris, Chris, Aaron and Debbie when the coup began. The takeover by these thugs was swift, directing their first assault on the *palace* of Makarios in Nicosia, intending to kill him off immediately in the early morning hours. But Makarios was no man's fool. He had escaped unharmed by way of underground passageways and was then somehow escorted—by helicopter perhaps—to the British base of Akrotiri near Limassol and flown to safety in England.

Now the use of *propaganda* by takeover governments is phenomenal. Immediately, they commandeer communications systems—radio, television and newspapers—and fill it all with lies. Like these guys. They broadcasted on the radio right away and printed in all the newspapers—which also reached the *world*—that Makarios was dead. *Amazing.* The lie, intended to lower morale, might also persuade citizens to give up any hope of resistance. Even if they heard later he was *not* dead, they wouldn't know what to believe.

On the first day, the new regime imposed a 24-hour curfew, and the next day it began at 2 p.m. So we timed our food shopping carefully. The National Guard, which carried out the coup, quickly seized power and spread throughout the island. Young, radical lunatics brandishing automatic rifles and machine guns, cruised the streets in Jeeps and generally took over. Man, it didn't take more than a day to have two or three of these freaks already in the nearby little supermarket—where I went to purchase some quick food supplies—manning the cash registers and dressed in some kind of military garb, authoritative weapons ready. *Disgusting, really.*

We took time off from beating the streets with the words to read, relax and write letters, and we even swam once before the 2 p.m. curfew. Actually, here on the second day, everyday life *seemed* to function fairly normally. After all, this new government remained Greek Cypriot. Only now, a renegade Greek-Cypriot newspaper publisher by the name of Nikos Sampson headed it.

On the third day of the takeover, they lifted the curfew to 6 p.m., and that afternoon, July 18, Aaron, Debbie and I left Famagusta for our home in Nicosia. Roadblocks had now sprouted everywhere with gun-toting loyalists running them. These guys, some in civilian clothes, were nervous and insecure. With suspicion and uncertainty in their eyes, they were intent on instilling fear into everyone as they checked identification. Tension thickened the air as the Cypriots now realized the absurdity of this maniacal coup against their perfectly peaceful, previously well-functioning and well-liked, Makarios-run government. Throughout the island, Greek Cypriots who opposed the new regime began retaliating against it. Hundreds of these precious Greek Cypriots were now killing each other. *Crazy.*

On the fourth day—still rather ignorant of the seriousness of a government coup like this—we ventured out into downtown Nicosia to mail letters and check things out. But by noontime, the city had become a snarl of traffic and frantic citizens. Rumors spread that the Turks had invaded. And that *did* instill fear in everyone. There we were in the middle of Nicosia with the *real* police now gone—since they had been branded "the enemy" by the new regime. The main police station had even been blown up—where, incidentally, my passport was sitting, awaiting a visa extension. So now, these inexperienced cohorts of the new, criminal regime, many in their late teens and early twenties, controlled the traffic and everything else. And man, if I thought the guys at yesterday's roadblocks were nervous and anxious about their new role, these Nicosia recruits were *neurotic*. On my bicycle and headed home, I came face to face with one of them on a corner, but learned quickly— *don't make eye contact with a crazed person, especially when he's holding a carbine rifle! Avoid him and kindly go your way.*

Aaron, Debbie and I returned that day to our Nicosia home to discover a military tank of the new regime had just blasted several large holes into a home not one hundred yards from ours. The blasts killed eight occupants—who had strongly opposed the coup. Meanwhile, gun battles continued throughout the day and night, some near enough to keep the three of us hunkered several times onto the floor. *Stay well below windows through which stray bullets can whiz into you!* Though risky, I spent some of that day up in the attic, straightening our survival supplies and foods. Suddenly they had become quite handy and valuable.

The following day, Saturday, July 20, 1974, marked the beginning of the end of the serene, little paradise of an independent nation that Cyprus had become. At 5:15 a.m., lovely Debbie awakened Aaron and me to listen to the sound of intense machine gun battles she'd been hearing less than a mile away. It was getting freaky. Then our dear and close Greek-Cypriot friend Tasos called us at 6 a.m. "The Turks have invaded!" he said over the phone. "You have to get out of Nicosia! I'm coming now to pick you up."

Understandably, the Turks felt obligated to protect the Turkish Cypriots here in Cyprus. But they were pushing it a bit far, I thought, with their screaming Air Force fighter jets against the virtually defenseless Cypriot forces. Although the government of *Makarios* was fair—the one that had established a peaceful coexistence with the Turkish minority of the island and had included them in the government and had even appointed a Turkish vice-president of Cyprus—it had been swiftly overthrown. Things had changed. Now, for the past five days, the country was being run by a bunch of ominous Greek military officers from Greece—junta-type, right-wing hard-liners who were prejudiced against non-Greeks and influenced by the late General Grivas. They were expecting to make Cyprus part of Greece ... and be damned with the Turks living in Cyprus. So, whether that's a fair judgment of the perpetrators of the coup or not, their poorly-thought-out shenanigan now gave Turkey an *excuse* to invade and take over at least part of what they felt was theirs.

Tasos showed up at our home in his VW minibus only moments after his phone call, insisting on taking the three of us to the safety of the mountains. So we grabbed essentials—passports, other identification, toothbrushes, Bibles, several boxes of canned and other foods from our survival supply—intending to, yes, go to the mountains for an afternoon or so of *picnicking*. Not until I stepped out the front door of the house, though, did I realize the seriousness of the situation. That's when I saw, up and down the street, the fear-stricken faces of our Greek-Cypriot neighbors. Without hesitation, entire families were piling into their cars, abandoning the most cherished material possession they owned—their homes. They were fleeing Nicosia. They had experienced before what the Turks were capable of doing when fighting broke out between Greek and Turkish Cypriots back in the 1960s. The horrors crept again into their minds.

I learned another lesson here—to take heed of any upset in the status quo and expect the worst. Stock up on water, essential foods (like rice, grains, milk powder), toiletries (tissues, toilet paper, deodorants, toothpaste, shaving cream, shaving blades), and batteries. And keep a vehicle at least half full with gas. And most importantly, gather together in one good carrying bag or briefcase, irreplaceable, essential documents—passports, birth certificates, degrees, diplomas, marriage licenses. Here were four or five full days of a warning. The government had abruptly changed hands, the status quo had been drastically altered. Yet shops, gas stations and banks still functioned somewhat normally. And it's not necessarily that supplies are going to run out even after confusion sets in, but it's no fun to venture out into the chaos of jam-packed food stores and gas stations—like everyone else—and wait in long lines just for something like, say, toilet paper. Expect the worst before it happens. As for me, I left the house that morning unprepared and expecting a picnic, with nothing but a crummy, small plastic bag containing my toothbrush, "alien card"—in place of my passport that had been blown up along with the police/immigration building—Bible, and the clothes on my back. I would never again see my backpack of possessions, sleeping bag and small suitcase of books.

The four of us headed south, away from the onslaught by the Turks to the north, without—unwisely again—any planned escape route. Even Cypriot Tasos was disoriented. We drove until we reached the dead end of a curving road that led us into the foothills of the Troodos Mountains and up to the village of Ayios Epiphanios. Looking on a map of Cyprus, if one could conclude there was a center of this oddly shaped island, it might have been here at this village of Ayios Epiphanios.

It was about nine o'clock in the morning, and already heading down the mountain from the village, rumbled an open, flatbed truckload with 25 or so young Greek-Cypriot men standing within the wooden-fenced back of the truck. They were all excited and shouting.

"What were they saying?" Debbie asked Tasos as the truck passed.

"They are shouting against the Turks," said Tasos. They had gathered themselves from this small village and surrounding areas as volunteers to confront the invaders of their beloved homeland. To me, the poor guys in the back of that truck looked like sheep going to slaughter, against the overwhelming military might of the Turks.

The main cafenion of Ayios Epiphanios bustled with men of the village sitting in the morning sun at outdoor tables. None of them seemed overly shocked the Turks had invaded. Besides their peaceful composure, Cypriots are extremely politically conscious and well aware of world events. They know they *have* to be, sitting atop this exotic Aphrodite rock formation in the middle of the volatile Middle East.

Not one eye from the open-air tables missed our white VW van pulling up. Ever-smiling Aaron, the chosen and best emissary, explained to them we were refugees from Nicosia; and having a female with us—especially a blonde fox like Debbie—helped considerably in our approach to the increasingly uneasy crowd of coffee drinkers. After all, for the past five days, these normally hospitable Cypriots had been totally jerked around by the absurd coup down below their village and were now facing another morning not knowing which Greek Cypriot might kill the other or who the heck to trust. And now this morning they were sending their sons and grandsons to fight the behemoth Turkish military.

Before we knew it, the "angel" of the village, who grasped our godly sincerity, boldly stepped up to us and insisted we come to his home. He was a Greek Orthodox priest, married and with four daughters. And if anyone had authority and respect here, it was he. Like sheep, we followed the man to his quaint hillside home nestled among shady trees about a quarter of a mile from the café at the end of town. He and Aaron walked the distance together, while Tasos, Debbie and I drove ahead in the van.

Aaron, in what Greek he knew, further convinced the man that we were not tourists in Cyprus but were here, like in other parts of the world, to share with other souls the simple love of God. When the two of them reached Debbie, Tasos and me, it further comforted this guy's heart when he saw our smiles, that he had made the right decision inviting us into his home.

Cypriot Tasos had latched onto us and our message months earlier and was now an extremely devoted friend. Fluent in Greek and English, he expounded on our mission and continued through the day as a dedicated translator.

The priest's four daughters ranged from about 13 to their early 20s, the oldest having recently married. The daughters, the priest's wife and the one daughter's husband all warmly welcomed us and lavishly fed us before we were led to a cozy roof-like extension of the small villa. "You will stay here for as long as you need," Father Gabriel said.

We offered to share our meager possessions, the canned foods, but the family refused. It impressed Father Gabriel though, considering recent events, that we had prepared for such emergencies with survival foods and supplies. It also prompted him to lead us away from his home to a round piece of metal in the ground, painted green to match the grass. "This is my emergency refrigerator," he said proudly as he unlocked the metal cover of a well about a foot in diameter and probably 15 feet deep. He then hoisted up a plastic jug from the bottom of it. "Here. Try it," he said as he poured water from the jug into paper cups he'd brought along.

"Mmm! *Poli krio eenay!*" I said, remarking how refreshingly cold the water was here in the middle of the July heat.

"Yes. And if no electricity, I can keep food fresh even in summer."

But what no one should ever be without in such times is a short-wave radio. This family and everyone else in Cyprus stayed tuned all day long to BBC and VOA (Voice of America) broadcasts for updates on the current situation. As conscious of world events and prepared with survival supplies as we tried to be, it was quite ignorant of us not to have a short-wave radio. The BBC can tell listeners something that's happening right down their street they are not even aware of. At least Tasos had one. According to the broadcasts, Turkey had indeed invaded the north of Cyprus, meeting heavy resistance from the Greek-Cypriot factions. Overnight, the animosity between the Greek-Cypriot factions created by the coup had vanished and, despite bitterness among these people, they were now joined as a nation once again in a desperate attempt to push back the Turkish invaders.

The daughter's husband, Costas, took Aaron, Tasos and me to a hillside a short distance from the house. Ayios Epiphanios, at several hundred feet up in the northeastern foothills of the Troodos Mountains, looked down onto the capital Nicosia, 20 miles away in the valley below. I felt weird perched on a peaceful island hillside like this, full of beautiful wild flowers—even capers grew wild here today, hanging off low-growing bushes—while looking down and seeing a war going on in the city we'd been in only hours earlier. Clouds of black smoke rose up and distant explosions echoed in the hills. Every now and then we actually saw gray Turkish fighter jets strafing and bombing the city.

Since early morning, the radio kept urging Greek-Cypriot males between the ages of 18 and 30 to join the valiant fight against the Turks. Newlywed Costas felt compelled and indirectly pressured by the village folks to volunteer. He had missed the sending off of the first batch in the morning, but by late afternoon he had prepared himself.

Aaron played some good Greek songs on the guitar to the family, and all of us soon saw the importance of faith in such trying times. Aaron also told them in Greek that we believed we were living in the time of the end of the world, now evidenced in the valley below and with fulfillment of the scripture: "And ye shall hear of wars and rumours of wars" (Matthew 24.6). Father Gabriel perked up at mention of prophecies and questioned us about other insights.

But our *simple* faith, not heavy prophecies, compelled the older daughter and mother to request of us, "Please, can you say a prayer for Costas as he goes to this war?"

And we did. The four of us and the entire family held hands together in a circle, while Aaron prayed in Greek—"Please Lord, keep Costas safe while he is away and return him soon, unharmed." The family believed the prayer. Costas departed sadly.

By late afternoon fires burned throughout distant, northern hills, created by napalm from Turkish jets. Those fortress-like Pentadaktylos Mountains above Kyrenia might have been able to stop northern invaders in the past, but they were no obstacle to modern-day jet fighters.

When night fell, no one was supposed to burn any lights whatsoever, so Turkish jets would have difficulty locating targets. One home didn't quite get the word on this rule here in Ayios Epiphanios, left a light or two on, and they caught verbal hell from shouting villagers until they finally got the message and turned them off.

News from the radio grew dismal. Northern Cyprus was quickly falling to the Turks. Evidently, the world would not go to war over Cyprus. Not even Greece. Cyprus was too far away for Greek jets to successfully pull off raids to the island, face the Turks and return to mainland Greece with enough fuel. The Greek military junta apparently didn't need Cyprus *that* bad to become involved in a full-scale war with Turkey.

Before we all went to sleep this eventful day, something positive developed. Costas returned from his voluntary induction into the liberation army because there weren't enough guns to go around for everyone. He was sent home. A stroke of luck? Maybe. But this little family believed it was a *miracle*—an answer to their prayers, and that perhaps ". . . a prophet hath been among them" (Ezekiel 33.33). A "prophet" to whom they had opened their home, earlier today.

Debbie slept in a room with the girls while Aaron, Tasos and I slept in the open air on the flat, walled roof—a customary place to sleep in third-world countries during summer or suitable weather. Debbie had slept roughly—timid and like a frightened bird—and woke us at 5:30 a.m. We conversed most of the morning with dear Father Gabriel on world events as related to Bible prophecy. The heavy stuff. And the radio stayed on, with the Voice of America and the BBC both suggesting that expatriates, non-Cypriots, evacuate the island. Suggestions became orders for foreigners to leave. Once again, we saw the pertinence of a short-wave radio. It acted like a barometer or thermometer in a crisis. Somehow, news people—with good pay—report from the midst of the mess.

As for Aaron and me, the "orders" through the radio began to *pierce* us. Neither of us wanted to leave this heavenly island. We were learning the language, the people were so friendly, the climate ideal, the food superb, the brandy and wine cheap and plentiful. Not much was *wrong* with the place. The Turks knew all this *long* ago and were here today to grab as much of this heaven on earth as possible.

But, as events unfolded this 21st day of July 1974, hourly broadcasts stressed more urgently that foreigners leave. Meanwhile, suspicion grew throughout this tiny village of Ayios Epiphanios concerning Tasos and his reluctance to volunteer to fight. But perhaps most influential was the prudence and womanly intuition of Debbie. She knew it was time to forsake this "jewel" of Cyprus and flee to safety, heed the advice on the radio and get on with life. Why hang around in the middle of a serious war when there is a chance to get out?

Reluctantly, Aaron and I consented to Debbie's and the radio's demands. "We must leave," we told Father Gabriel. "Our embassy wants us to."

Father Gabriel and his wife looked sad.

But we made the decision, and use of daylight hours was critical. The rule of no lights after dark included vehicle lights. So, about 3 p.m., hardly 24 hours since the Father had boldly taken the four of us into his home, the whole family walked us to our van. Debbie and some of the family shed tears. War was quickly severing loving bonds, leaving hearts broken in its path. We would evacuate the island for more peaceful lands of the earth, while we could only hope and pray God would protect and keep this sweet family safe. In gratitude for their hospitality, we felt privileged giving them all the canned foods, grains and other stuff we had gathered from our survival supplies the morning before. But more appreciated than foodstuffs from us was the parting prayer we made with the family, all of us standing by the van, huddled together, heads bowed, smoke rising in the distance from the war below.

We parted still with tears, past suspicious villagers. They had already voiced concerns to the family. "Who *are* these Westerners? Do they have something to do with what is happening to our country? And isn't that one a Greek Cypriot? Was he a Grivas follower? And why didn't he volunteer to go down and fight?" Small minds can conjure up intrigue. Unlike the family, these townsfolk conceded to untrue rumors instead of worrying about the *real* problem—that the *real* enemy, the Turks, had invaded their country.

Radio broadcasts instructed expatriates to contact their embassies and/or proceed to the southeastern British Air Force base of Dhekalia. On the way down the winding road from Ayios Epiphanios, we considered returning to our Nicosia home to gather personal belongings. But, by the time we reached the southern outskirts of Nicosia, that notion was snuffed out. Heavy artillery shells exploded throughout the city and the popping of rifle and machine gun fire never stopped. The reality hit me that people no different from myself were surely being injured and killed at the ends of those thunderous bombs and at the impact of the hundreds of bullets. It unsettled me to be that close to humans killing each other.

We headed straight for the U.S. embassy. Fortunately it was on the south side of town where we were coming from, outside the battle zones and direct lines of fire. Nevertheless, the explosions and rat-a-tat clicking of rifle fire intensified as we approached the embassy.

The staff at the embassy served us wonderfully. Besides giving us instructions, advice and maps, a lady consul actually came outside to our van, carrying something.

"Here, drape these over your van," she said. She handed us two, large American flags. "They will indicate you are Americans so you won't be fired upon, bombed from the sky or stopped at checkpoints. "You need to get to the Dhekalia base before dark. You don't have much time." She started helping us attach the flags.

"No, no. We'll do it. Thank you so much for everything. God bless you!"

She went inside; we attached the two cloth flags and drove off. Nobody wanted to remain the night amid the bombs and guns. Fortunately, Tasos had another van parked at his home not far from the embassy, from which we siphoned needed gas. We headed south, never to see Nicosia again—or our home or possessions.

The Larnaca road was desolate, with fields on both sides of the highway burnt out by fires from bombs or napalm. So much evidence of war, here on only the second day, left us awestruck and saddened.

Further seriousness of the situation struck us when we arrived at the Dhekalia base at sunset. Approximately four thousand refugees had thus far gathered here camped out in tents and vehicles across an open grassy field. Somehow, the amazing British Air Force was feeding everyone in the base's cafeteria, while embassies processed papers inside. Me with no passport, since the poor thing had blown up along with the Nicosia police station four days earlier.

We went to sleep in the van at 1:00 a.m. But Tasos awakened us only three hours later. "Aaron! Wayne! Wake up!" he urged. "You have to get ready to go!" He had learned the aircraft carriers offshore were filling up too fast to take many more refugees, and England would be cutting back soon on opening *her* doors to further foreigners.

Wiping what little sleep we had from our eyes, we walked over to the cafeteria, waited in line with other refugees and to our amazement were given papers by 5:30 a.m. to proceed on, me with only my Cyprus alien card for identification. Over a free breakfast in the mess hall, we said our last goodbyes to precious Tasos without whom we may still have been stuck in the middle of the Cyprus war.

"We love you, Tasos. God bless you. Thanks for all you did for us! Stay in prayer."

"I love you guys. Contact me when you reach England."

"Of course we will," Aaron assured him. We would learn later that Tasos returned as we had asked, to our Nicosia home to gather our belongings, which he might well have to this day, safely stored in his home. *What a friend.*

Kisses and hugs, and we boarded a bus at 7:30 a.m. to a Hercules airplane, and at 8:30 a.m. flew from Dhekalia to the larger British airbase of Akrotiri, about 55 miles to the west, southwest of Limassol, arriving at 9:05 a.m. This is where we confirmed the disheartening news as Tasos had said, that England was about to stop the further acceptance of non-British refugees. Miraculously, we just made it through before this cut-off. A little after 11 a.m. we were escorted by "angelic" British Air Force officers to the same Hercules C-130 aircraft and flew off from Cyprus at 12 noon, July 22, 1974.

How extraordinary—unflustered and efficient—the British military were in handling the thousands of refugees in Cyprus. Even humorous in the uneasiness. They did the job they were asked to do in processing, feeding and comforting desperate people of different nations with no compensation. They did it professionally and generously because it was their calling to do it. *God bless them.*

The interior of the C-130 was like any military transport. No soft, cushioned reclining seats with fold-down dinner trays. Instead, the British seated all of us evacuees side by side on a long, canvas bench that stretched along both sides of the fuselage, and on another two rows back-to-back along a wall of woven canvas straps down the center length of the aircraft. This was definitely a no frills flight. But no one complained. Or got off either.

People in various states of preparedness gratefully accepted their share of canvas seating by the Britishers. One girl, it was said, on another flight, had been sunbathing somewhere and arrived at the refugee camp with nothing but her bikini and a towel.

The Britishers joked and did their best to make everyone comfortable as they passed out little spongy ear plugs to muffle the rumbling sound of the four, propeller engines. Not much "whisper-jet" soundproofing here. We took our seats side by side with smiles.

One out-of-place person on the plane happened to be seated right next to Debbie—a CBS TV reporter. Soon into the flight, he asked us, and particularly Debbie, "Would you mind if I interview you?"

"Sure!" Debbie consented. She graciously answered his questions, even though the three of us were not *normal* expatriates or tourists.

"What were you doing in Cyprus?" the reporter asked.

"We're missionaries."

"How do you feel about having to evacuate so quickly?"

"Well, years earlier the three of us wilfully forsook all our material possessions," Debbie explained, "so leaving behind what meager belongings we had, doesn't bother us much."

The reporter seemed surprised.

"But we will miss Cyprus," she added.

The plane landed in England at 7:50 p.m. London time at some Air Force base, delivering us into the helpful arms of more British. Even immigration officials were nice. It must be a special character the British possess—taking care of their worldwide colonies, as well as refugees in general. The weather in England was quite chilly, even on this 22nd day of July; therefore, since most of the refugees had little or none of their belongings, the British were ready right there with free sweaters for anyone needing them.

I had no passport, no identification other than a flimsy Cyprus alien card, and still they gave me a six-month visa with almost *no* questions asked. Luckily, I had the address and phone number of someone we could contact—my brother, Gary, now living just outside the city in the exclusive area of Hampstead at No. 50 Hampstead Lane. So, being Americans with a good address, officials gave us train fare and assigned two British Army soldiers to personally escort us all the way to Gary's front door.

Knock, knock. Guess who opens the door at 9:30 p.m. that night? Gary, of course, totally unaware of my whereabouts except that I was in—now-invaded—Cyprus.

"What the hell are you doing here?" he said, with a smart-ass greeting to hide his complete surprise. "Get in here you idiot," he added, in jest.

Everyone hugged.

"Come in, you guys," Gary said to the British soldiers.

"No. Got to get back," they said, satisfied to have delivered three Cyprus refugees to a home.

"Thanks for everything. God bless you guys," we said.

"Cheers. Only doing our job." The soldiers were off.

Gary lived here in a three-story mansion in one of the best parts of the London outskirts with his British wife, Rebekah, their six-month-old baby boy and about 30 other Children of God members. The home's main purpose was schooling young children using the Montessori Method of teaching. Rebekah was one of the main teachers. And around the corner from this house were two more three-story mansions housing yet more of the group. One house boasted a tennis court in its extensive backyard and both had large circular driveways along what was known as, "Millionaires' Row." The group did not own the homes nor pay a shilling of rent for them. We had "squatted" the three mansions—as allowed by a strange and ridiculous British law that states someone can move into an empty, abandoned property if it is unlocked or has an open or broken window anywhere. You can't *break* a window and enter one. *Sure.* Of course the *owners* of the properties—often companies or banks holding the mortgages—genuinely freak out when they learn that strangers have entered their property and taken up residence.

Our group here in England, aware of this freaky law, had taken advantage of it before in other fine properties—like a townhouse in the posh Mayfair district of London—yet nothing matched these three homes. Upon entering such places and establishing squatters' rights, someone from the group immediately contacted the owners of the real estate, explained how we were young people on a mission to help other young people socially worldwide, that we would assume all maintenance responsibilities of the home, and all we asked was that the owner give us a 30-day notice of when they would be selling, renting or requiring the property. We left the premises in better shape than we had found them, often with upgrades, repairs, new paint and always spotlessly clean. If the new, freaked-out owners found all this extremely difficult to believe, we had prominent businessmen and companies as references, whose properties we had previously occupied, who personally knew us and our work, and who could assure the newly-frustrated owners that they were in fact fortunate to have such occupants residing in their residences. The new owners would indeed contact such references and usually be calmed down. And when the owners came over—usually immediately—to *meet* their new "tenants," they were further relieved to learn we were indeed a civilized, hard-working group . . . though with no visible means of support.

Gary led us to comfortable beds. The following night, after resting under the July sun in the lush, green, English backyard garden of this old mansion, we spoke about adventures in Cyprus at the Poor Boy—a sort of disco/club the group ran in London. Scores of brethren, many we knew, eagerly listened.

A more significant sharing session of events in Cyprus came the following day, July 24. We telephoned and invited to the house two sons of a prominent Cypriot lawyer-friend of ours. Debbie had been given their telephone number back in Cyprus to look them up if she was ever in London. The two came immediately to the Hampstead home to hear from eye-witnesses the horrors taking place in their country. The brothers, greatly comforted to hear real news about Cyprus, also had their faith encouraged to learn about our safe escape from the war zone. They met again with us and became close, sincere friends.

When I arrived at Gary's doorstep, it had been a year and a half since I "abandoned" him with nothing but the scribbled note I left on his bunk bed back at Bromley, Kent. He was now happily married with his slim, British wife and enthralled with their six-month-old son. We stuck to each other like glue, taking full advantage of this unexpected union. Gary ran the maintenance here with particular emphasis on the plush, ground-floor schoolroom. In the coming days, he and I sanded and varnished to perfection the entire wooden floor of the schoolroom and painted every square foot of the showplace room at the entrance of this fine home.

When not improving something for the school, the two of us distributed literature all over greater London. If *any* American knew London, it was Gary. With his haircut, clothes and love of British rock music, he fit right into the British scene—except for the cold winters. Not to mention his craving for British chocolate, British draught beer and British bakery goods. A freak on these, he never traveled too far while out on the streets without dropping shillings into the abundant little English bakeries, candy shops and pubs along the way. The two of us did our part getting literature out to the Londoners and thoroughly enjoyed being together while doing it.

Actually, I was excused from *severe* litnessing—still crummy at it anyway—since I had no passport. A foreigner here in England, I didn't need to be apprehended for passing out literature. Finally, I located my original birth certificate and soon received a passport from the U.S. embassy for $12.

Timothy, the head of the colony, assigned me to the cellar of the home, which I didn't mind. In the cellar, three of us—Gary, another guy and I—established elaborate shelves for survival supplies in readiness for the worst—specifically atomic war. The shelves held canned goods, dried foods and grains, non-perishable supplies and, in separate, special plastic bags, two hundred gallons of water. *Drinkable* water. Critical in a disaster. But really, this "survival" trip was a fluky idea inspired by paranoid, overzealous spiritualists believing they—we—knew more than anyone else of future events. Survival supplies require too much initial effort and cost, and then constant updating, "turning over" and renewing, like aerating or changing the water every now and then. But, it can't hurt to be prepared. If not an atomic bomb, they could be used for a tornado, hurricane or some other natural disaster, not to mention unforeseen economic hardship.

A great blessing Gary and I received at this time was a visit from our parents on September 6. The two of us hadn't seen them for at least two years. Our supportive, loving parents were interested in our spiritual mission even if they didn't quite grasp it.

They had never met Gary's new wife, Rebekah, or seen their first grandchild, Jonah, so the chance to visit the four of us in one place seemed opportune. Who knew when I might return to strange lands of the East?

Sure enough, near the end of Mom and Dad's three-week visit with Gary and me and their tour of England and Scotland, I received a call from Bryan—the same organizer "general" who drove me nuts in Cyprus.

"Wayne, how about getting back to the East?" he asked, calling from the mansion next door. "We've got a team in Tehran, Iran. They could use you out there."

"I don't know, Bryan."

"They're doing good," he continued. "They've got ten thousand dollars in the bank already. Let me know."

"Okay. Thanks."

Hello? Ten thousand dollars? That gave me a boost. Especially since most homes of the group rarely had more than that day's needs. So, in all honesty, the ten thousand pried me off my dormant butt and out of comfortable England.

I made the decision the following morning and broke the news to Mom and Dad. "I'm going to Tehran, Iran," I told them.

"Oh, no!" Mom said. "Why?"

"I've been asked to by one of the leaders of the group," I said. "There's some of us out there already and they're doing well. I'm not needed here, really."

"I visited Iran," Dad said, "when I was in the Army. It's an interesting place." An officer in the U.S. Army for 30 years, he seemed fascinated I was going out east again.

"When are you going?" Mom asked.

"As soon as possible. Tomorrow, maybe."

We checked train schedules to Tehran. Mom gave me her nice, light-blue, American Tourister carry-on bag, and they bought me supplies, took me for immunizations—smallpox and cholera—and counseled me.

Mom and Dad left the following day, September 27, 1974—a heart-wrenching day. They had spent three good weeks in Britain, mostly with us, and now Gary and I took them to the Pan Am terminal for tearful goodbyes. It was difficult. Gary and I had drawn closer to them these past weeks, realizing more than ever how precious they were.

I departed the same day. Gary gathered my belongings back at Hampstead while I sat with Bryan for instructions, prayer, funds and encouragement to head back into oblivion—the East and Iran.

But I would not be traveling alone since "two are better than one" (Ecclesiastes 4.9). I was teamed up this time with a Swedish girl—a *large* Swedish girl. No model, Britta, but *so* special.

Standing six-feet tall, Britta was strong physically, spiritually and emotionally. She took crap from no one and was always cheerful and happy. She was eager to drop her hackneyed childcare job here at one of the homes and was thrilled to now be venturing out to parts unknown. Besides her native Swedish, she spoke fluent English, French and German. And she loved to talk to others, unlike me who did it because it was my job.

The day became a supernatural haze. By mid-afternoon, I had painfully sent off my parents at the airport, attempted to purchase needed shoes somewhere in London, frantically gathered personal belongings, sustained an instructions/vision session with Bryan, met the jolly, giant Swedish girl who would now appear to others as my girlfriend and was about to once again leave my loving brother.

Bryan and Gary took Britta and me by taxi to Victoria Station late this same Friday afternoon to catch the Dover, Paris, Istanbul Simplon-Orient Express, quite nearly as it began pulling out of the station. *Damn.* Our disrespect for departure times was out of hand—to be catching such a significant coach that would catapult us into another world, another chapter of our life, and barely board it. I had no time to look into Gary's sad, dark eyes and tell him how much I enjoyed every minute I spent with him. We actually had to *run* to catch this train. Gary practically pushed the two of us aboard it. *Absurd.* No time for tears even.

Chapter 12
∽ *Back to the East* ∾

To the East again. It was good it happened so fast. Otherwise I might have talked myself out of it. It was time. England didn't need me—stuck down in the survival shelter half the time and blobbed together with more than enough workers in the comfortable homes of Hampstead Heath.

"What's wrong?" Britta asked me, as the train pulled away.

"Nothing, I'm fine," I replied, trying to smile. The bonds developed in the last days between Mom, Dad, Gary and me were so real. Suddenly severing them had now left my heart sore and wounded. God's grace would have to see me through.

At Dover, England, everyone disembarked and walked onto a designated ferry to cross the crummy, rough waters of the English Channel to Calais, France. French authorities stamped our passports, and we boarded another train. We purchased a sleeper compartment for $20—a lot of money for Britta and me at the time. *But, oh, man, was it worth it.* We did have some apprehension, after hearing stories of people stealing money or valuables, while their victims slept aboard trains. And this was no private sleeper compartment, but rather one whose beds neatly folded out from the walls, accommodating five. Britta and I shared this one with two British guys and a beautiful Yugoslavian girl.

I fell asleep, exhausted from the day, as the train sped its way through France, Switzerland, the Simplon tunnel and into Domodossola, Northern Italy. That's where I awoke in the middle of the night to look out the window—as I had done nearly two years earlier on the train to Rome, with Bob and "the trunk." Snow-covered Alps once again glistened wonderfully blue for me.

We reached the border of another world—Yugoslavia. I soon realized I must not have learned my lesson on European train travel. We hadn't brought along enough food and water for the journey. A Swiss guy we'd been talking to gave us one thousand Italian lira. I purchased some apples and cheese through the window of our train now parked in the station at the bordertown of Trieste, Italy. I knew one thing though: I didn't want to get off the train and haggle over changing currency with some kid on the platform and have the train start pulling out. *No, sir.*

That's how I developed a taste for *carbonated* water. As a child, carbonated water—especially the natural, spring-fed type—tasted horrible to me. But here on this train, completely unprepared as we were and practically dehydrated—no drinkable water flowing from any faucet—a loving passenger handed me a blue, half-liter, glass bottle of cold, naturally carbonated water. *Wow. Bubbly, exhilarating, cold and wet. Nothing quite like it.* To this day, my most-respected, thirst-quenching drink.

The train pulled out, and we continued on into Yugoslavia. Of course, nobody breezes into Yugoslavia easily—not with Marshal Tito running the place. Officials spent an hour checking and stamping visas of everyone aboard. Passengers without visas were given 48-hour transit visas—long enough to travel through and get out of the country. After loading and unloading passengers along the way from London, the train was full of mostly Americans, Greeks, Turks, Yugoslavians and Bulgarians.

After getting our visas, I was about to drift off to sleep, still in our sleeper car, when in stroll two Yugoslavian police—bearing the red star of communism on the front of their hats. They were checking visas throughout the train. Sharing our compartment now was a friendly Yugoslavian couple in their early twenties. The police treated Britta and me nicely when they discovered we were Scandinavian and American. But when they came to their *own* countrymen—the young people—they began slapping and actually pushing them around the compartment. *What the hell?* Britta and I looked on with our eyes and mouths wide open.

Shouting in Yugoslavian, the cops grabbed the couple's bags from the upper rack, ready to search them. But their intuition, from mere seconds of interrogation, told them the couple were not smugglers.

The police walked out, leaving me further amazed to see that the young couple appeared unbothered by the abuse. Just another aspect of life in a totalitarian country. I flashed back on my Greece/Yugoslavia visa trip a year ago and the packed train of fashionably dressed Yugoslavian commuters sitting like minimum-security prisoners, while similar, Gestapo-like police strolled up and down the aisles monitoring them.

"They are stupid," the girl said. "What can we do?"

It troubled me to see these two, who appeared so much more intelligent than the authorities, being badgered like that.

"They were checking to see if we had blue jeans from Italy," the young guy said.

"Blue jeans?" I asked.

"Yes, people smuggle them in and sell them at much higher prices here in Yugoslavia."

Either Yugoslavia didn't make very good jeans or jeans were seen as too American or Western to permit the manufacture of them at all. *Oh boy.*

I fell asleep again as the train chugged through Northern Yugoslavia, along the Sava River until we reached the capital, Belgrade, at 10 a.m. This was the young couple's stop.

"Have a nice trip," the girl, Natalia, said. "The train will stay here for an hour and 45 minutes. You have time to get off and buy something if you want."

"Thank you. God bless you both," we said.

With Natalia's trusted information, Britta and I gathered our things and disembarked. We were hungry. Britta stayed by our stuff just outside the train while I went to the station and bought some bread, cheese and a big bottle of water. I did it! It was about time. I returned to Britta and we boarded the train, finding a better compartment with two long bench seats for us.

From Belgrade, the train followed the Danube River east to where it divides Yugoslavia from Rumania. We traveled south along the Danube until the train stopped at the border of Bulgaria. To enter Bulgaria, those needing visas, like Britta and me, paid $8 each for a 48-hour transit visa, similar to the one for Yugoslavia.

The train continued on into Bulgaria, following the Iskur River south to the capital, Sofia. From the train station, the spirit of Sofia seemed dismal and gray, much like Belgrade. Although geographically beautiful like Europe, both Bulgaria and Yugoslavia seemed backward to me—cheap, crummy cars; broken-down buses; lots of peasants using horse-drawn carts. Was it the effect of communism? From Sofia, the train found the Maritsa River as it headed toward Turkey through picturesque mountains, valleys and fields of roses.

The train breezed easily into Turkey. Finally, those checking visas—Turks—were friendly and smiling. After all, they had a country they were proud of and weren't in fear of.

The northwestern part of Turkey our train just entered—that section west of the Bosphorus and the Dardanelles—appears to be part of Europe. But no part of Turkey is European or ever *will* be. Turkey is too Eastern.

At 1:45 in the afternoon on September 30, 1974, after our three, tiring days of train travel, we arrived in Istanbul. *What am I doing here in the East again?* I didn't know. Something about this land, I guessed. I doubt I would have left it if not for the Cyprus war.

Still, I had a bitter taste in my mouth with Turkey—especially here in Sirkeci, Istanbul, where the train had come to its stop. Besides the heavy Eastern spirits of Istanbul, it was not far from this train station in Sirkeci where cops threw me in prison 16 months earlier. At least the bustling streets of busy, working Turks felt familiar to me, enabling me to comfort poor Britta. I confidently led her up the hill from the train station toward the Sultan Ahmet area of world travelers. Hopefully I would then be able to locate the handful of our colleagues supposedly residing at some Bahar Hotel.

Indeed, Britta had thus far cruised along fine in familiar European surroundings, smiling and excited. But when she stepped off that Orient Express into Istanbul's mass confusion, I could see the fright on the face of this huge, usually together Swede. Young Turkish kids shouted in tourist English, German or French; older Turks sometimes gawked. The noise of endless merchants pushing their wares along dusty, crowded alleys and from crumbling, tattered stores added to the clamor. That's when I had to take the offensive and plunge through the whole mess.

A visitor should look nonchalant, not make eye contact and definitely not appear bewildered, even if overcome by it all. The locals sense fear fast, especially at such a major, international train station where they prey on new arrivals. *But wait a minute. What are we talking about here?* It's not that evil or life-threatening. It's just the obnoxious factor—young kids sent by owners of restaurants or hotels to advertise to new arrivals about where to stay or eat and to physically lead the way to such a place. In fact, these little guys can be quite beneficial in leading new arrivals to a reasonable hotel or restaurant, their guidance free of charge. Proprietors reward them accordingly. It made me reflect on how a *Turkish* couple might describe *their* arrival at a main, downtown train station of some major U.S. city for the first time as foreigners? Now *that* could be justifiably frightening *and* life-threatening!

One of these young Turkish kids became instrumental in leading Britta and me, within minutes of our arrival, to Rachel—the same Rachel with whom I went to Cyprus on the Russian ship, nearly a year ago. I had been instructed to phone her at the Bahar Hotel, and since phones didn't work at the train station—typical—this Turkish kid led us right to a working phone outside the Sirkeci Post Office. On the phone, the guy at the Bahar Hotel said, "No. There's no longer any such Americans at this hotel." *Great.* And right then and there, out walks Rachel from the post office, along with Turkish sister Nesrin.

"Wayne!" Rachel shouted. "Bryan told me you were coming."

"Here we are," I said. "This is Britta."

"God bless you guys," Rachel said, then kissed and hugged us separately.

"Hi, Wayne," Nesrin said, smiling. We hugged each other.

Of course the Turkish boy was still standing by, observing these events unfold. The kid, putting two and two together, felt he should get the credit for this magical reunion of friends, since *he* led us to this phone in the first place. I too felt the kid was rightly inspired and handed him a dollar bill along with a sincere *"Teshekurederem,"* thanking him in Turkish. Nesrin rattled off some fluent Turkish to the startled bugger, like, "Okay. Thank you. Now, goodbye."

Rachel, Nesrin and I talked about how we got out of Cyprus. But, as was typical when coming from afar like this and meeting up with those of the group, Britta and I were never really offered time to unwind and relax. The train ride from London had been bumpy and crowded. When we purchased our tickets—not first-class of course—it didn't mean we had a seat to sit back in and enjoy the scenery along the way. *Nope. Sorry.* We needed to change trains a few times with all our belongings and hoped to find a seat on the right train. So it would have been nice to head to a nice hot shower right now.

The four of us enjoyed a delicious Turkish restaurant meal together, but then Rachel, on her typically hurried schedule, dragged everyone across town to Taxim Square to spend some time with Father Matteo, our close priest-friend of Istanbul's Catholic church.

Finally, by late afternoon, we made it back to the Sultan Ahmet area where the cluster of group members resided—not in an apartment or home now, but in dirt-cheap-yet-comfortable, quite clean hotel rooms, where we shared a bathroom with other young travelers. Only four of the group lived here, including Rachel and Nesrin, and I knew the other two, who had also come here from Cyprus: Chris, my precious Cyprus, litnessing partner with his still-glowing smile; and the still-strange chick, Doris—the girl who might get a cramp in her leg in the middle of the night. I wondered if she ever found someone to tend to that "problem."

I loved seeing Chris and hashing over good ole times in Cyprus, "out on the limb" so often together, pounding the streets for Cyprus pounds in a hundred cities and towns. He was a bit too energetic and forward thinking in his spiritual life, though, to spend much time on . . . the past. I had walked back into the vortex of Sultan Ahmet, to now live in a hotel almost directly behind the cursed Pudding Shop.

Why did I choose to leave the comfort and stability of the London mansions, with regular meals, beautiful sisters and sexy, angelic-looking British women strutting the streets in their mini-skirts, only to return to the confusion of a place like Istanbul? That strange, driving force for challenge and adventure perhaps. Or was there something magical about the East that had even drawn Alexander the Great? Despite its difficulties, the third-world had a certain simplicity and human warmth and was laid-back and easier-going than Western societies. There was less stress here, no constant competition to keep up with everyone else. People spent more time enjoying life in these lands, than daily speeding through it.

Still, questions arose in my mind. *Why am I here, basically on the "front lines" again, with almost no money, no real home and still pioneering Turkey?*

Then, "sweet" Rachel informed me, "Wayne. Now that you're here, I need you to take over as shepherd. At least until Aaron comes. I'm going to Tehran with Doris."

Oh, joy. Just what I wanted. Tehran was my intended destination. Instead I'm left here to mill around the same locale of my arrest and, basically, against the advice of the U.S. consul who recommended I "*leave* Turkey, and don't look back." But in this life of faith and self-denial, it was my duty to . . . accept the calling, be thankful and . . .

praise God. And if it became too unbearable, I could throw it onto Him. Then, if it *was* His work and He *was* using me, *He* would give me the supernatural grace to accept the calling and, sort of, do the work through me.

It was a bombshell, but it didn't keep me from thoroughly enjoying the fabulous, however-crude, hotel *bed* that night.

The following day I awoke to the horror of being stuck again in Istanbul. But a myriad of responsibilities soon gobbled it up. Right away I visited old contacts, like hotel "patrones" (managers), updated myself on the current situation in Turkey and went across town to Taxim Square to see Father Matteo again. Once back in the Sultan Ahmet area, I found that Aaron had just arrived via a magic bus from London. *With* Aaron was a short, chubby, blue-eyed, natural-blond, bespectacled British girl by the name of Vivian.

Now why did Aaron return to the Middle East again? He probably didn't know himself. But here we all were—Rachel, Doris, Chris, me and now Aaron—hanging out here again.

At only 19 years old, Vivian was . . . bubbly. She played guitar and sang well also. So, what did this young inspirationalist do to show her excitement for being in a new land? *Yep.* She broke out her guitar and played some beautiful, godly songs to a small group of world travelers in the lobby of our Bahar Hotel. (The guy on the phone yesterday was wrong, *dammit.* Rose and the others did indeed still live here at the Bahar.) Then, before I could advise against it, Vivian and Aaron—also a newcomer to Istanbul and Turkey itself— had somehow wandered over to the dusty, grassless-but-tree-shaded park directly across the street from "Misery's" Pudding Shop. There, in the open air, under the trees, she started playing her guitar to some people, as if she was in the middle of Hyde Park, London. *Oh brother.*

Within minutes, she had drawn a crowd of nearly one hundred people, mostly curious male Turks who were not one bit interested in any of the deep, spiritual content of her songs. The guys were more interested in her rather shapely, fair-skinned, young body and in any of the other "free" Western females gathered within the crowd. And so the jeering began and the shoving and grumbling until there was a total mess of unruly people.

I was cringing somewhere on the edge of the crowd, taking no part with Vivian and Aaron. Finally, led by what insight I had about Turkey and my now-anointed leadership of the group, I signaled them to abandon their well-intended show of "guitar love," confirming what they themselves had sensed. Yes, both Vivian and Aaron had begun their serenade this afternoon with good intentions of imparting a little spiritual love—totally unaware of what the impact would be here in Istanbul. I knew, and it upset me. Unruly crowds? *No thank you*. Jesus Himself never tolerated them—not down in the valleys and cities anyway. He sensed the spirits of such crowds, went through the midst of them, and so passed by. Crowds to whom He willingly preached and ministered were usually those He invited up into the mountains—people who hungered spiritually enough to pay the price of hiking up there to see Him. Not just to be "entertained," like probably 98 percent of those gathered here for Vivian and Aaron. I made a move up to the two, made eye contact with them and gestured for them to pack up the guitar, slip away and say goodbye. *Allahsmallahdik* in Turkish.

At least they didn't hand out any literature. Since the time Sam and I were busted, litnessing remained off limits. Instead, we talked one-on-one to people.

Aaron had arrived, but he and Vivian would go tomorrow to Athens, Greece, for some kind of business. This same day I put Rachel and Doris on the 5:47 p.m. train to Tehran with a supply of cheeses, crackers, wine (a great bonus for a train trip) and jugs of water. I don't know why they took the train or why I didn't dissuade them from it. They could have taken a magic bus like Aaron and Vivian just arrived on. As it was, the train, somewhere in Eastern Turkey the next day, struck and killed a hapless soul on the tracks. They arrived a day late.

In the following days, Nesrin and I searched for rental apartments near Sultan Ahmet, but found nothing. Instead, the five of us, Britta, Chris, Nesrin, Adam—a 20-year-old Lebanese guy who recently joined us—and I, remained in two rooms of the Bahar Hotel. Guys in one room, girls in another.

On the third day of my return here to Istanbul, while walking down the stairs to the Bahar's small lobby, I came face-to-face with the same plainclothes cop who arrested me 16 months ago. The creepy cop stood behind the reception desk, nonchalantly rapping with the manager, looking like any other, clean-cut Turk in his normal plain clothes. He and I made eye contact. Apparently, the cop was not quite sharp enough, luckily, to place me, even though his mind *may* have—in nanoseconds—attempted it. But *I* knew immediately who the hell *I* saw, processed it instantaneously, looked away and continued my stride down the stairs past him.

I took it as a bad omen. *Oh no! Can't dig it at all.* I was still wounded from the ordeal the cop had put me through. I never intended to return or hang out here. So seeing "Harry" didn't help my paranoia at all.

Not to worry. Just keep litnessing to a minimum. Pass out literature only to select individuals. No obvious propagandizing. Walk circumspectly in this city. Underground, basically.

I fared all right, though, accepting my calling to lead the little flock here, imparting—instead of paranoia—the practicality of carefulness.

Aaron and Vivian returned after eight days in Greece, and, the next day, the seven of us moved into a room with seven beds, the arrangement proving economical and family-like.

With contentment, I relinquished Istanbul to Aaron who'd been commissioned for the job. Besides, he had the *desire* to be here. I didn't.

We hit it off well together, as always. Although serious about his job, Aaron knew how to have a good time. *God bless him.* I proposed traveling to the exotic Princes' Islands, just a quick ferry ride away, and he jumped on the idea. So, at the end of the next day, a Saturday, five of us, but without Aaron and Nesrin, packed sleeping bags and belongings, bought food and were on the 45-minute ferry ride out of Istanbul. We arrived at one of the nine islands by sunset.

As soon as we walked into town with our backpacks, guitar and "Western" written all over us, two young Greek guys came up to us. For some reason, Turks, Greeks and Armenians lived on this particular island, despite the animosity usually found among these three nationalities. I spoke some Greek to the two islanders and they loved it. They insisted we follow them up a quaint, shady road lined with small, brick homes whose walls and iron gates were lushly overhung with pink bougainvillea and assorted red, purple and yellow island flowers. The Greek guys showed us a vacant home perched at the top of this small mountain. The house looked across the Sea of Marmara to the lights of Istanbul, shimmering in the distance. Whoever's house this was, the five of us would roll out our sleeping bags and sleep comfortably and warmly tonight and the next night on its balcony. I considered it a small miracle—this instant, free lodging.

The next day the Greeks led us to a perfect beach on the other side of the island where we all swam in the Sea of Marmara. It was still warm enough in October. They showed us how to gather live, black-shelled mussels from under the shoreline rocks. We cooked them on an open fire. *Mouthwatering.*

In the early evening, back at the little, port town of the island, Vivian played guitar and sang, for probably half an hour with no hassles, to a crowd of at least 50 Turks, Greeks and Armenians. Demetrios, the owner of a Greek restaurant in town, observing it all, then graciously fed the five of us—for free.

That night, on the balcony of the vacant home, Vivian played some songs to the two Greek guys, and one of the Greek guys played his bazooka—that typical Greek instrument.

The following morning we hiked to the other side of another mountain to a calm bay, where we spent the day writing letters and reading—a "free day" out in the open fresh air. I wrote my beloved parents and reread a letter Aaron had brought me from Sheila—the girl, now living in Italy, who might, just *might*, be a possible mate for me. She'd sent a rather large six-by-eight-inch photo of her whole, clothed body, her face beaming and smiling—a definite uplift for me, out here "in the field."

We split the island that day on the 6:15 p.m. ferry back to Istanbul, after a warm goodbye to Nikos, one of the Greek friends. I will always remember my walk to the ferry on the wooden dock. Looking down, I found the water so clean and clear that I could actually see sea grass swaying on the white sandy bottom, at least 12 feet deep. Nature's simple beauty spoke to my soul, not far from the pollution of man-made Istanbul.

On the ferry ride back, while leaning on the wooden rail of the lower deck, I peered down into the spray of water the boat was making. Vivian came to my side. "Wayne. Guess what? You and I are supposed to go to Tehran together as soon as possible."

"What?" I asked.

"Yes," she continued, with her pretty little smile. "That's why Aaron didn't come with us to the island. He and Nesrin are checking out the best way for us to get there."

"Oh, that's great news, Vivian!" I don't know why she waited so long to reveal this to me, but it certainly encouraged me. *Yes. Oh, my*

God. I'm ready. I beamed, already floating on inspiration from the Princes' Island.

When we reached "home" to Aaron and Nesrin, Aaron confirmed that, yes, Vivian and I were to leave *tomorrow* for Iran. He'd found two magic buses going there. Another jerky move? *Whatever.* I was ready spiritually.

The next day, Vivian and I packed and headed for the magic buses to Tehran. Fortunately, neither one was leaving today as planned. *Good.* The delay allowed me to apply for a visa at the Iranian embassy. Vivian had secured hers days earlier from Greece. She and I then spent two hours in the covered market, buying food and water jugs for the three-day journey.

The two magic buses destined for Tehran sat parked at Sultan Ahmet. One was a fancy, air-conditioned, tourist-type bus, with plush, high-backed, burgundy-velvet seats. The other was simply a bus. A green bus. It looked like a child had designed it, plain and almost ugly. The seats looked like those on a school bus—bench seats, only up to the top of the rider's back, with a metal rail on top. It must at one time have been a European city bus.

So which one did we decide upon? The ugly one, of course. But not without consideration. Oh yes, the "tour bus" appealed to the eyes, no contest. But the driver was cocky, and his bus was missing something spiritually, even to the unspiritual. Whereas, the plain bus had a good "spirit" to it despite its homeliness and lack of amenities. And the British driver of the plain bus, Nigel, was humble, cool, and knew routes east. He already had nearly a full load of satisfied passengers who had been with him from the origination point of Amsterdam.

Vivian and I prayed over our decision. Neither of us wanted to be on the wrong bus all the way to Tehran. She, more spiritual than I, prayed for and received an astounding verse from the Bible that practically said, "Take the green, homely bus," Proverbs 16.19: "Better it is to be of an humble spirit with the lowly, than to divide the spoil with the proud."

The following morning, Vivian and I bought some more food—cheese and biscuits—I picked up my visa from the Embassy of Iran at 12 noon, and we boarded the bus. We paid Nigel the sum of $22 each to Tehran. Aaron and Nesrin saw us off, and the bus pulled out of Sultan Ahmet at 3 p.m., October 16, 1974, heading farther east.

PART TWO

Istanbul to Kabul . . .

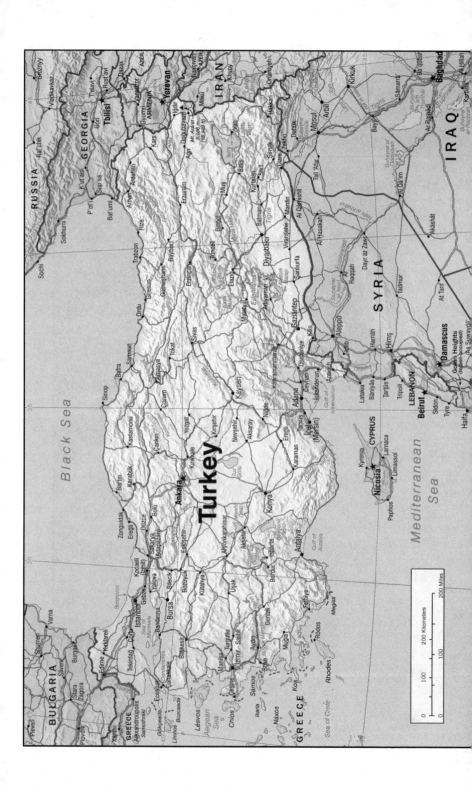

Chapter 13
∽ *Mount Ararat* ∽

VIVIAN AND I took up a green vinyl bench seat on the left side of the bus, near the back and over the rear wheels. This would be our niche all the way to Tehran. We put her backpack on the floor and my carry-on bag under the seat in front of me.

I looked around at those aboard. "Looks like a great mix of people, doesn't it?" I said to Vivian.

"Yeah!" she responded, bright-eyed and ready to talk to them all. (Quite a sweetheart, this one, Vivian, I realized.) The passengers seemed to be mostly Europeans and in their twenties. I noticed some Japanese, too.

Soon after the bus door closed, the music started. Not loud, but fantastic. The owner/driver, Nigel, had installed the sound system with speakers throughout and provided most of the tapes—The Beatles; Rolling Stones; Bob Dylan; Van Morrison; Crosby, Stills, Nash & Young; Creedence Clearwater Revival; Carole King; Jackson Browne; James Taylor; Cat Stevens; The Moody Blues; Jimi Hendrix; The Doors; Don McClean; other soft rock, blues and some classical. Some passengers offered up *their* favorite cassettes also as the bus made its musical way east, out of Istanbul, like an enclosed, "out-of-the-Turkish-world" capsule.

The first miles of the trip, Vivian and I made friends with those in front of us, behind us and across the aisle. Eventually, the three-quarters-full busload of people—33 or so—mingled like a big, happy family going on an outing or picnic. What a difference from taking a Turkish train or bus.

Nigel, 36 years old—with his slim, attractive, long-haired, blond German girlfriend as his navigator, also in her thirties—knew the route well. They knew how far they could push their passengers and how far to the next best roadside restaurant. Restaurant owners along the route remembered Nigel and his foxy girlfriend and bestowed meals and special favors on him for bringing in a busload of hungry, paying travelers. These restaurants served those delightful Turkish meals—half a loaf of fresh-baked bread placed alongside a hot, white ceramic bowl of fresh-cooked vegetables or white beans swimming in their own thick stew among chunks of tender lamb, all to be soaked up by the soft, dense, somewhere-between-white-and-whole-wheat bread—followed by a steaming-hot glass of that strong, red-amber black tea. So filling and at a ridiculously cheap price. But don't ever forget . . . Turkish yogurt. Practically a meal in itself with bread, it comes as a large, thick, white glob on a ceramic plate (not in those plastic cups with fakey fruit at the bottom to stir up into it). Usually made from sheep's milk, it tastes like yogurt should no doubt taste— creamy, real, and with a character of its own.

These taverns—some open 24 hours a day—along Turkey's main highways served great selections of hot food to volumes of hungry travelers. Those unable to decipher the crude menus could always walk over to the glassed-in stretch of steaming-hot, stainless-steel trays of food (like cafeterias in America), point to appealing ones and badger the cook with his frugal pocketbook: "How much?" A waiter would then bring the choices to the table. The restaurants were huge rooms of plain, metal tables with Formica tabletops and pipe-metal chairs with Naugahyde seat cushions set under bright, unromantic fluorescent lights. No regard for ambience. The intention was to feed the traveler well and send him on his way.

The restrooms all had plenty of toilets and sinks in a row—like at rest areas along U.S. highways—and were kept quite clean. Equipped for truckers and busloads of travelers to relieve themselves, wash up, freshen up, wake up and hit the road.

At 1:15 in the morning, we reached the capital city, Ankara, about 250 miles east of Istanbul. Parking outside some hotel known to Nigel, everyone stretched out to sleep inside the bus—somehow or another— on seats, between seats, on the floor, in the aisle, on each other, wherever. As Vivian and I lay down for sleep—she on the seat, me on the floor— she prayed, "Lord, please help everyone get a good night's sleep."

The next morning, we overheard nearly everyone exclaiming how they'd slept wonderfully, curled up in crevices and corners throughout the bus. Blessed by God's Spirit?

In the group, we always tried to bring good cheer, a word fitly spoken or at least a smile to people. And so it was when Vivian and I entered Turkish restaurants along the route—the Turks so receptive to any kindness shown them, especially from Westerners, and particularly from blond Western *girls*.

This morning, here in drab Ankara, we brightened the day of Mehmet, the humble Turkish owner of a restaurant near the bus. The guy loved that I spoke some Turkish, especially when I mentioned Allah. So— along with some loving looks from Vivian—Mehmet, on his own accord, served the two of us a full breakfast of boiled eggs, cheese, bread and tea, for free. We had enough money to get to Tehran, but if a generous Turk wanted to help us out with a free meal along the way, we'd take it.

The bus pulled out at 11 a.m. and at 12:30 stopped for lunch at a restaurant where Vivian and I again befriended two Turkish waiters. Besides my normal conversing with them and expounding on the love of God, Vivian, who tended to "mother" or "grandmother" men anyway, insisted on bandaging the cut finger of one of the waiters. He flipped out, of course, at this simple care and insisted on "paying" Vivian and me with some Turkish yogurt, tea and special Turkish candy. A bit of love went a long way out here in the middle of Turkey.

Nigel then made good time, not stopping until 8:30 that evening for a warm, tavern dinner. This busload of people was like a whole society. Some highly educated, some dropouts, some rich, some poor, some professionals, some unskilled. Some had credit cards and some wouldn't obtain credit for the next 10 years or more. So, at these stops, some ate extravagantly—spreads of the costliest entrées— while others scrimped on soups, beans, bread or even their own grocery-bought cheeses, crackers and bread. Vivian and I were way down on the ladder but cruised along happily, nonetheless. Aaron's wise insistence back in Istanbul of spending two hours shopping for take-along foodstuffs had definitely paid off. Nigel and Heidi, his lady, always ate well—as driver and navigator should—whether they bought it themselves or were treated by the tavern owners or even grateful, well-off passengers.

Several more miles east brought the bus to the fairly large town of Erzincan, about one hundred miles west of the large city of Erzurum. The majority of travelers remained on the bus, parked outside a hotel. Everyone stretched out for another, cozy, good night's sleep. But Nigel and Heidi, along with some of the more well-off, and two or three couples who understandably had to rent private rooms for intimacy, slept in the hotel. Most of the travelers, as far as eating and sleeping, conserved their money. They had to since most of them would be traveling as far as India, Nepal or Thailand and back. Without endless credit, they would have to be frugal, even though probably none ever read and deciphered the great verse from Proverbs 6.11: "So shall thy poverty come as one that travelleth . . ." *So true.*

Traveling through Turkey in the middle of October like this was still fairly safe from snowstorms. But traveling east in this amazing country, we gradually ascended onto its eastern plateau, several hundred feet above sea level. The air became cooler and thinner.

The farther we traveled east into Turkey, the farther we traveled from civilization. It became another world. Turkey itself is wild. But Eastern Turkey is wild and *remote.*

Somewhere past the last significant city of Erzurum, after changing a flat tire at 3 p.m., we stopped in a small village for a break. Nearly all disembarked to stretch their legs or to purchase pastries and foodstuffs. The town was miserable. Seemed like there was no real rule here, certainly not with the mischievous kids. Scoundrels. Here was our busload of travelers pulling up with money in our pockets to spend, and these kids heckled and even threw rocks at the lot of us. *Damn it.* Adult villagers didn't even acknowledge the scene. *Get me out of here.* What a relief to get back on the "civilized-world" bus!

Another phenomenon out in this desolation was the Turkish sheep dogs. *Wow.* Vicious creatures. More than once, one of these canines would come racing full-speed out of nowhere, snarling and growling right at—inches away from—the very tires of this huge bus clipping along at 20, 30, 40 miles an hour. *Man. They were strong and mean.* Even within the protection of the metal bus, they scared me— realizing what they could do to me if they got me. Looking down at their rage through my window, I envisaged what I would like to do some day out here: securely attach a perfect-size piece of *burlap* to the hubcap or wheel rim of my vehicle. Then drive, at just the right speed, through an area inhabited by these crazed dogs. The burlap extends a few inches, flaps with the revolution of the wheel, and the dog—in its fit of evil yapping at the tires—yaps his teeth right into the burlap and . . . that's it. No more barking.

As we continued, mountains and rolling hills appeared—beautiful, though treeless. Only now, they were bathed in a stunning orange by the setting sun behind us. At twilight, we reached a group of dusty, brown hills and began a tricky trek over them. Tricky because the road was narrow and partially unpaved, with washouts, potholes and almost no guard rails. No one spoke, or moved about much on this stretch of the trip. Instead, everyone sat tight and prayed, or hoped, we wouldn't become a casualty at the bottom of one of the steep ravines.

Peering down at valleys below, I saw carcasses of huge tractor trailer trucks that had fallen prey to this crumpled road. Even if the drivers survived, their cargo was fair game to the first inhabitants lucky enough to happen upon it—looted, nothing remaining.

Truckers knew the dangers of this route, which would grow increasingly treacherous with the coming heavy snow and ice—not to mention the *bandits* in these hills. But the money was worth the gamble. Companies paid big bucks to deliver their valuable wares from Europe through this risky stretch of Eastern Turkey to the wealthy Iranians.

Nigel expertly maneuvered the bus through the scary curves, ascending/descending, accelerating/braking, leaning and rocking, until finally reaching a flattened stretch of road on the other side of these wicked hills. Little Vivian wasn't feeling too great though from the action required to conquer these rough mountain miles. But she never complained much either, *bless her heart . . . and stomach.*

The bus finally stopped at 11 p.m. in front of Nigel's intended destination for the night—the lone Hotel Kent, at the edge of the town of Dogubayazit, just 22 miles from the Iranian border. *What a relief!* Nigel knew the owner of this hotel and arrangements were made for everyone who didn't need a room—or couldn't afford one—to sleep on the floor of the carpeted lobby. *Now we're talking.* Nice and homey. Everyone appreciated a break from the bus, especially with the night quite cold now on top of this eastern plateau.

It was too dark to see last night, but I knew well where we all were sleeping—at the foot of the mountains of Ararat! The huge windows of the hotel lobby faced them—the two, predominant, snow-capped peaks of the mountains of Ararat, where, according to Genesis 8.4 in the Bible, rested Noah's ark. I imagined that the eight people—Noah, his wife, his three sons and his sons' wives, the only humans who survived the flood, being inside the ark—walked down these very mountains right outside this hotel, bred abundantly, particularly the three sons and their wives, and began to replenish the earth. In other words, all of us in the world today came from and are related to Noah?

As well, male and female of every living thing of the earth, all flesh, fowl, cattle and every creeping thing, also came down out of the ark and multiplied abundantly to fill the earth with the animals, birds and bugs we have today. All of them replenished the earth, starting at the foot of these mountains and possibly only five thousand years ago.

Mount Ararat from Hotel Kent

But where did *Noah* come from? Monkeys? Apes? Neanderthal men? Hominids? Hell no! Not if Charles Darwin's theory of origin is discounted and the Creation is instead believed.

And if Creation is believed, it can be determined approximately *when* the first human beings, Adam and Eve—looking exactly like we do today, not hairy and ape-like—were created. By knowing the historical fact of when the Jewish nation built their temple in Jerusalem, then referring to the genealogies of the Bible and adding the years from Adam and Eve until that temple was built, then simply adding *that* sum to today's date, the result is the astonishing number of only about seven thousand years as the age of the earth and man. As opposed to the zeros that evolutionists keep adding to the millions of years of the age of the earth.

As for scientific research that mountains appear to be millions of years old, well, they may indeed have been ageless, "God-years" old when God established them on the earth, by His hand, in six days, seven thousand years ago, appearing today to be millions of years old.

So, God created man and woman (Adam and Eve) in the garden of Eden—now Iraq?—and told them to be fruitful and multiply and replenish the earth. They then had children, who had children, until Noah was born of Lamech. And these people in the years from Adam until Noah must truly have erred and become spoiled and horrible—horrible enough for their Creator to destroy them all with a flood.

Now the flood and Noah are what concerned me this October morning, waking up out here on this plateau. I washed in the hotel's bathroom, ordered tea for Vivian and myself and, to better set the whole scene of Noah, opened my small, three-inch-by-five-inch Oxford Bible to the book of Genesis to read Chapters 6 through 9. By Chapter 6 in this first book of the Bible, God had created the earth and Adam and Eve; Adam and Eve had fallen in the Garden; their first son Cain had killed their second son Abel; and from them were begotten generation after generation of sons and daughters. Basically, the chapters read like this:

> And God saw that the wickedness of man was great in the earth, and that every imagination of the thoughts of his heart was only evil continually. And it repented the Lord that he had made man on the earth, and it grieved him at his heart.

Imagine: God was *sorry* He had made man.

> God then spoke to Noah, whom He had seen as just and righteous, and instructed him to make the ark from gopher wood: three hundred cubits long, fifty cubits wide, and thirty cubits high. And into the ark, Noah would bring himself, his three sons, his wife, and his sons' wives, and every living thing of all flesh, two of every sort, male and female to keep them alive with him in the ark—and enough food for all.
>
> God then brought a flood of waters upon the earth when all the fountains of the great deep were broken up, and the windows of heaven were opened. And it rained upon the earth forty days and forty nights. And all the high hills, that were under the heaven, were covered; and the mountains were

covered. And all flesh died that moved upon the earth, both of fowl, and of cattle and of beast, and of every creeping thing that creepeth upon the earth, and every man. All in whose nostrils was the breath of life, of all that was in the dry land, died. And Noah only remained alive, and they that were with him in the ark. And the waters then prevailed on the earth 150 days.

And God remembered Noah and every living thing that was with him in the ark: and God made a wind to pass over the earth, and the waters assuaged. The fountains also of the deep and the windows of heaven were stopped, and the rain from heaven was restrained; and the waters returned from off the earth continually. And after the end of the 150 days the waters were abated, and the ark rested . . . upon the mountains of Ararat.

Finally, after more than seven months the earth was dried. God then told Noah to go forth of the ark with his wife, his sons and his sons' wives and to bring every beast, every creeping thing, and every fowl after their kinds that they all may breed abundantly in the earth—to be fruitful and multiply, and replenish the earth.

And Noah went forth, and his sons, and his wife, and his sons' wives with him, and every beast, every creeping thing, and every fowl, and whatsoever creepeth upon the earth, after their kinds, went forth out of the ark.

God then made a covenant with Noah, with everyone that would come after him, and with every living creature with Noah, that the waters would never again become a flood to destroy the earth and all flesh.

No wonder we're all so sexually motivated—coming first from Adam and Eve who were to fill the earth with people, and then from Noah's sons and their wives who had this same God-created sexual drive to fill the world once again of people. Not to mention the animals and all living creatures, reproducing all day long.

People in the days before and around the flood, according to the Bible and Torah, often lived to be 900 years old or more. Some theologians and scientists believe this longevity may have been attributable to the atmosphere surrounding the earth being more protective against the *sun's* burning rays—before the flood, that is. Adam lived 930 years and Noah lived 950 years before they died. The earth certainly must have been an ideal environment, with ideal climate for a person to even *want* to live so long.

With any possibility of it all being true, I couldn't help but be in awe, waking up on this ground today. Most of the passengers of the bus, even, were familiar with the legend of Noah's ark, regardless of their backgrounds, as they gazed in varying degrees of wonder and amazement across the barren, dusty plains leading to the magnificent snow-capped peaks of Ararat.

I walked over to the Turkish owner/manager standing behind the reception desk and asked him, slowly in English with some Turkish thrown in, "What about the boat on the mountain?"

"There is no boat on the mountain," the man replied.

Oh boy. Get outta here. I felt he knew there was a boat up there. And it belonged to Noah too, damn it! Granted, he hadn't seen it, and neither had anyone else of the predominantly Christian expeditions that had based right out of his hotel in search of it.

Attempts to locate the ark have thus far been unsuccessful. Which doesn't mean it's not there . . . totally encased and preserved in ice within the glacier on the north side of the larger peak. It's simply too mysterious out here in practically no man's land, a land officially belonging to Turkey but fought over and claimed to this day by a nation of people who have no nation as yet—the Kurds, one of Turkey's worst thorns in the flesh.

The peaks themselves are only about 12 miles from the border of Iran and maybe 25 miles from the U.S.S.R. border. In fact, one definite obstacle to locating the ark has been Turkey's agreement with the U.S.S.R. to strictly forbid anyone—especially Westerners—from venturing up the peak and spying deep into Russia from its summit. Thus, Turkey has disallowed most expeditions up Ararat.

Adding to the intrigue too, regarding the ark, is the belief that the Jews must reach it and measure it, in order to find out what a cubit is so they can then properly rebuild their temple, as in Ezra 6.3. "Let the house be builded . . . the height thereof threescore cubits, and the breadth thereof threescore cubits."

The bus pulled away from the Kent Hotel at 10 a.m. and headed eastward along the desolate last 22 miles of road leading to Iran. Not far down the road, maybe 12 miles from the border of Iran, Nigel pulled over and stopped the bus on the left shoulder of the road. He'd stopped here on previous trips for the benefit of those with cameras to snap photos of the two, snowy peaks of the mountains of Ararat, glistening in the sun now on this clear October morning. Actually, Nigel was taking a risk here, since photographing Ararat was frowned upon, if not illegal. But there was no one in sight for miles. Of course the few Japanese aboard took great advantage of this photo stop with their superb outfit of cameras.

Stopping for photos proved to be a godsend for the near-tragic event seconds away. On a small bluff a short distance ahead, on the right side of the road, people were watching—four young boys. While out shepherding or doing nothing in this wilderness, they'd spotted our foreign bus and came running to the side of the road. Nigel, having traveled through these parts, and with his warm heart anyway, had stashed little boxes of *matches* beneath the dashboard of his bus—a much appreciated free gift for such kids along his route.

The boys, about 8 to 14 years old, likely made this a regular event—spotting magic, foreign buses and then running to intercept them for any free handouts. So there the boys stood, making the obvious gestures of striking invisible matches on invisible matchboxes, entreating the bus for these instant fire starters.

Nigel and Heidi noticed the boys and their pantomime in the distance, so Heidi grabbed a bunch of the matchboxes from under the dash to hand to Nigel, since there was no window to open on the right side of the bus where she was sitting. Pulling away from the photo shoot, still on the left shoulder of the road, the huge bus slowly picked up speed. Approaching the small bluff where the boys stood and before crossing *back* into the right lane heading east, Nigel tossed several of the boxes of matches out his window onto the left shoulder of the road.

Sure enough, one of the boys, a bit of greed overtaking him, decided not to *wait* until the 13-ton mass of metal—now moving at 25 miles an hour or so—passed. Instead, he ran right in front of the bus, and *almost* made it . . . but didn't.

Before Nigel could even slam on the brakes to begin stopping the hulk of metal, he had struck the boy with the left side of the front bumper. The kid literally went flying through the air and landed in a gully below and off the road. I actually saw something in the corner of my eye, flying through the air, but didn't know what it was. Vivian was showing me how to best put lotion on the dry skin of my face.

The bus stopped. The passengers had no idea what had occurred. Up front, Heidi was freaking out and crying. Turned out she was worried more for Nigel than the kid. After all, she knew the seriousness of striking and killing a Turkish citizen while driving as a foreigner in Turkey. It could mean a long prison term, thousands of dollars in payment to the victim's family, or both.

"Please, Nigel! Please! Keep driving," she pleaded, tears streaming down her face. We hadn't seen any vehicle since leaving town, nor any people out in this isolated stretch of land. The other three kids vanished after witnessing the scene.

Nigel looked down, slumped over the huge steering wheel of the bus. He contemplated the situation. Heidi, in hysterics, begged him to drive on, until he said, "No. I can't."

He *knew* he couldn't leave this kid out here to die, witnesses or not, girlfriend or not. He had too much conscience. Passengers who had seen it happen likely also had mixed feelings about leaving the scene or attending to the kid.

One of the girls up front, a Swedish nurse, was adamant about administering first aid to the boy. "Let me out! Let me out! I have to help him!" she insisted. Her professional concern soon made everyone realize . . . there *were* no choices here. She and four guys ran to the kid's side, assessed his injuries and brought him inside the bus where they wrapped him in blankets for shock.

By this time, everyone knew we'd hit a kid, and there was silence. The kid was alive. He had some kind of head injury. Nothing else was known. Nigel kept his wits, and knowing there was a Turkish Army base farther ahead—closer than the town of Dogubayazit—headed there for assistance.

This Army base was the last, eastern-most military post of the Turkish government before reaching the border with Iran. Delighted to see our foreign "hippie" bus enter their camp, the Turkish soldiers greeted us warmly. But when the bus door opened, the soldiers discovered it was a solemn arrival. They saw Heidi in tears and then focused on the wrapped-up Turkish boy in the Swedish girl's lap. The soldiers spoke only Turkish, so, except for hand gestures, there was not much verbal communication.

Turning to the passengers, Nigel asked, "Does anybody speak any Turkish?"

No one else responded, so I raised my hand and arose from my seat, while saying, "I speak a little."

A little, for sure, but it helped. At least the soldiers loved hearing Allah in my broken sentences, while details of the accident seemed to be understood. But there was nothing easy here. The first soldiers summoned their superiors who had to show off some in front of the Western girls. Division arose between these Turks on how to treat . . . and judge . . . the driver. No longer wallowing in the raptures of Noah and the origins of man here at the foothills of Mount Ararat, we had instead become entangled in the contentions and laws of man.

In a critical part of Turkey, this was a significant and organized army base dealing with the Kurds, who wanted this area. Turkey's military carried a lot of weight anywhere in this land, often policing parts of the country under martial law.

The officers treated the boy with further first aid and then transported him to the hospital back in Dogubayazit. But the busload of us spent the next four hours parked at the base while "red tape" reports were made out. Fortunately, helpful, English-speaking officers arrived. They sensed Nigel's humble spirit and believed his story. Nevertheless, certain laws existed concerning injuring or killing Turkish citizens with a vehicle.

We finally departed the base. Nigel still drove the bus but with two soldiers aboard and escorted by military vehicles. Basically, Nigel would be under house arrest until the boy's condition was known. The bus returned to the scene of the mishap as requested by the officer in charge. There, greeting the small convoy, stood the same three friends of the boy who was struck—no doubt wondering if their mate was dead or not. The three boys told the exact same story as Nigel and even showed the officers the boxes of matches they had later retrieved from the side of the road. In fact, the little matches likely had a large impact on touching the hearts of the military guys—that a Westerner would go out of his way and stock up on these little gifts in order to please kids along his way.

The convoy drove to the hospital in Dogubayazit where three officers entered to follow up on the boy's condition. Nigel drove the bus back to the Hotel Kent where we were left to fend for ourselves, while he was taken to some military barracks—kind of a comfortable, makeshift jail—and kept under guard. I accompanied Nigel to the soldiers' place as translator and took this chance to comfort and encourage him. "This might be a good time to get serious with God," I suggested.

"Yeah, that's for sure," he responded, looking so forlorn.

Humble anyway and now broken and desperate from the ordeal, Nigel soaked up any and all words of faith that afternoon. His main concern was the boy, but on top of that, he felt responsible for now stranding his busload of travelers out here in "wild land." It would take a miracle to resolve the situation. He and I prayed together for this miracle. I then departed back to the bus and hotel, leaving Nigel with some pamphlets to read that might encourage his faith.

The miracle came this same night. When two of the girls returned from a visit to the hospital, one of them announced to us all, "The kid is sitting up in his father's arms right now with a smile on his face. There's nothing seriously wrong with him!"

I awakened early the following morning, having to split quick to the toilet with a bad stomach. The cooks of this hotel obviously hadn't boiled the water long enough when making the tea others and I drank the night before. Now rather than sitting around and *talking* about our predicament all day, nearly the whole busload of us walked over to see how Nigel was doing.

The mass of 25 or 30 foreigners, mostly Westerners, outside the army barracks in this funky little town was tantamount to a protest. While concerned about being stuck out here with no driver, we knew he was innocent and deserved no ill treatment or confinement.

Guys and girls from the bus hung out in the street, smoking, joking, cavorting and generally disrupting the status quo of the town. These strangers—dressed in wild clothes, some even in shorts, guys with hair to the middle of their backs and sexy girls with bare arms hanging on their boyfriends—were definitely perturbing to the townsfolk.

At 12:30 p.m. we all returned to the Hotel Kent, where Nigel had now been taken. Surely God was on the throne, and prayer and action change things. Amazingly, the boy had suffered only a small cut on his head and some bruises. After a night of observation in the small hospital, he had recovered from the shock of it all and was released some time that morning.

Meanwhile, Nigel, with the support of the Turkish Army, had negotiated to pay a mere 25 Turkish lira ($1.75!) to the boy's father—for the father's one-night stay at the hotel.

Nigel was set free. And without hesitation, before anyone changed his or her mind, before an American-type lawyer arrived from out of nowhere to instigate a law suit for millions of dollars, we all loaded up and were on the road by 2 p.m. the same afternoon.

We slowly drove the 22 miles to the Iranian border at Bazargan—no stopping for photos of Ararat this time—and after a trouble-free hour of passport and visa checks, we entered Iran, October 20, 1974.

No one felt more relieved to get out of Turkey this day though, than Nigel!

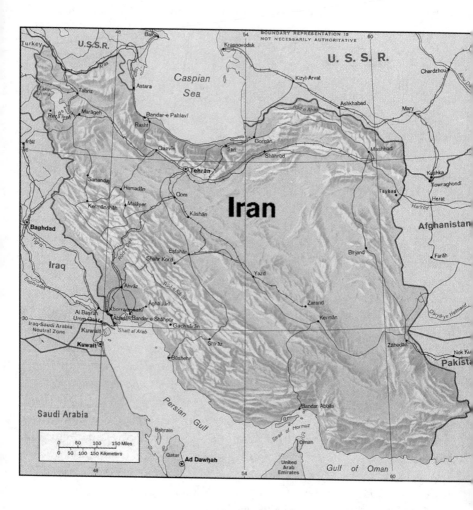

Chapter 14

∽ *Tehran* ∽

ABOUT 25 MILES inside this extreme northwest corner of Iran, with Turkey behind us, Nigel pulled into a crummy town for a meal. Later that night we stopped for a break and snacks in another small town. At this stop, Vivian and I discovered Northwest Iran was similar to Eastern Turkey—remote and wild.

It was about 9 p.m. when she and I wandered away from the bus and entered a small grocery store for some yogurt. Four Iranian guys in their late teens or early twenties, out cruising the town, followed us into the store, attracted by Vivian's blond hair. She wore a tight, pink, knitted, short-sleeved, low-cut blouse covering her shapely, decent-size breasts. Her whole chest sort of naturally, unintentionally, stuck out as she walked. Well, unable to control himself, one of the Iranian guys reached out and grabbed one of Vivian's plump breasts, right there inside the shop.

Whack! Without hesitation, without considering any consequences, Vivian hauled off and slapped the dude fully, right in the face! *Fantastic.*

The guy was shocked. "You bitch!" he must have said in Iranian. He was so humiliated he nearly struck little Vivian right back. Fortunately, his buddies grabbed hold of him. I, small of stature and build, was no contest for any of these guys—they knew it and I knew it. So there remained no retribution for little Vivian. I imparted a look of disgust at the perpetrator, that's about all. She and I eased past the guys, walked out of the shop and found our way back to the bus.

The young males obviously weren't accustomed to seeing much female flesh walking around the streets of their far-flung town this late at night, especially fair-skinned, natural blondes just turning 20 years old. Oh well, the Iranian yogurt in the flat plastic cup was cheap—10 Iranian rials (15 cents!)—and delightful.

At this stop, Nigel informed us, "To make up for lost time, I'll be driving through the night until we reach Tehran."

So we sprawled out to sleep in the best ways we knew by now, voyaging through these lands inside our green capsule.

This was no tour bus, so when we reached Tehran the following morning around 9 a.m., no announcements were made. What amazed me though, as I gazed out the window at the Tehran streets this sunny Monday morning, were the cops. They were dressed in perfectly fitting dark blue uniforms and equipped with the latest paraphernalia—walkie-talkies, handcuffs, ammunition and holstered pistols. Some had submachine guns slung over their shoulders. There was money here, and these guys were here to protect *it* and the status quo.

Nigel made his way through the crowded streets to the Amir Kabir Hotel. This was the "Sultan Ahmet" of Tehran, where all magic buses arrived and departed; where world travelers, hippies, freaks, Hare Krishnas, you name it, freely mingled and felt companionship in the otherwise intolerant streets of this city. A large bulletin board hung inside the lobby of the Amir Kabir where travelers posted messages to other travelers.

The hotel stood on a busy street between the good part of town and the southerly, poorer side of town. *Why is the south side of a city so often the poorer side?* Unlike the trees, parks and shimmering waters of the Bosphorus found at Istanbul's Sultan Ahmet, nothing pleasant surrounded the Amir Kabir hotel. Here, travelers took care of business—banking, mailing letters, obtaining visas for other countries—and moved on.

World travelers delight in one thing—whether on a quest for the truth, admiring nature or just having wanderlust—and that was the *food* of each land. Iran could keep them busy, too, with fabulous rice dishes, vegetable stews, desserts and even unique methods of cooking just eggs.

But Vivian and I had friends with an apartment here who were expecting us. So we said goodbye to those we'd met on this four-day journey and took a taxi to the address given us back in Istanbul. Two days later we returned to the Amir Kabir for a last farewell to Nigel and Heidi—both of them changed from the Eastern Turkey ordeal.

"Thanks for all you did for me back in Turkey," Nigel said.

"I didn't do much, but God bless and keep you guys."

The bus then pulled off to its next destination of Kabul, Afghanistan.

Greeting Vivian and me at the Tehran apartment, located a bit farther north and west from the Amir Kabir and in a fair part of the city, was veteran Middle Easterner and old cohort . . . Patrick. "Welcome to Tehran!" he said and hugged us both.

"Thanks, Patrick. This is Vivian," I said, as she demurely extended her hand to him.

Was Patrick glad to see me? Probably not. He didn't need his new domain here in Tehran threatened by me or anyone else. He still hadn't married his old girlfriend, Samantha, who loved him and wanted him as her husband. I think he still had visions of landing a Middle Eastern beauty as his wife.

The apartment was huge, new and clean with four bedrooms and two bathrooms on the basement floor of a new, five-story apartment building. Things were looking up.

About two dozen of the Tehran group resided in either this apartment or the "Office," several blocks away, where lived Rachel, Doris, William and his wife, Cindy, and their daughter, Sophia, and other "*office*-ers." In less than six months, the handful here had a sizeable bank account and knew embassy consuls and wealthy Iranians. But, most of all, they had a constant flow of friendly Iranians visiting the basement-floor apartment.

The source of the prosperity came from passing out our same letter-size pieces of literature—translated into *Farsi*—up and down the streets of this wealthy country, in exchange for Iranian rials and tomans. And, as everywhere, one person always outshone everyone else and brought in the most funds. Here, it was Joshua, an American guy in his early twenties standing nearly seven feet tall in size-thirteen shoes—the "Chris" of Tehran.

So, if someone didn't have a vision to get the literature out here, he soon learned to. Sure, idealistically, we passed the papers out to encourage people's faith in the One True God. But we also accepted as much compensation as folks were willing to give. And the Iranians were extremely generous when asked for a "donation" in return for the printings, handing over as much as 500 rials ($7.00) per pamphlet. Many were truly interested and received enlightenment from the words of faith. Others may have been curious about anything from the West. In any case, they responded regularly to the invitation on the back of the pamphlets—"*For more information, please write to P.O. Box 2825.*" We received one to nine responses *daily* in the mail from interested Iranians. And many came in person to our basement floor apartment, including beautiful, Iranian girls—to the delight of the other guys and me.

I spent considerable time selling pamphlets in Tehran. As in Cyprus, or anywhere, it was the best way to get to know a country and its people— pounding the streets, meeting and talking to them face to face.

Tehran is the capital and largest city of Iran. Out of the 29 million people living in Iran at this time, 3.8 million lived in Tehran. Set in approximately the central north part of this large 636,300-square-mile country, this enormous city stretched for miles in all directions.

It is a mountain city set at 3,800 feet above sea level along the southern slopes of the Elburz Mountains. The majestic peaks to the north, towering over the city, inspired me. There's just something spiritual and enlightening about mountains. And now, here in November, snow began to collect on their peaks. *Beautiful.*

Even though Tehran is 1,300 miles farther east from Istanbul, pretty much in the middle of nowhere and isolated from the Western world, its modernization amazed me. Shiny, brand new Mercedes-Benzes, Cadillacs and other fancy cars cruised streets lined with luxurious clothing and jewelry stores; attractive coffee shops throughout the city offered arrays of Persian and French pastries served with cappuccino, at classy, cozy settings; and Japanese, Thai, Italian and other foreign restaurants served their cuisines everywhere. Obvious wealth oozed here at the end of 1974. No wonder, since Iran was one of the largest crude oil producers in the world.

Recent rulers spent lavishly on Tehran. There were well-attended discotheques and nightclubs; theatres showing Western films; a large indoor ice-skating rink on the west side; and a huge, three-floor amusement center on the east side, containing a roller-skating rink on one floor, bowling alleys on another and games on another. Someone had also tastefully set soothing, tree-shaded parks throughout the city.

Tehran was not Europe or the West though. Rather, interspersed among fancy boutiques, eateries and theatres stood typical Middle Eastern vegetable stalls, tailors, public baths, barbers, tea shops, workers' restaurants and street vendors. Though "newly rich," traditional Iran was never lost.

We always traveled in Tehran by taxi, reasonable and necessary in such a vast city. The cabs themselves were Pakans, not a bad-looking compact sedan, made here in Iran, painted all orange and similar in appearance to a Russian-made or Japanese-made car. Nothing fancy, but they did the job.

Now, hailing down a cab here didn't make it our personal taxi. The drivers kept the cabs full to their capacity of five passengers as much as possible. It was accepted that the driver stop to stuff in more riders along the way. Not just economical, it was downright essential to do this in Tehran's bumper-to-bumper traffic. The influx of wealth had brought an influx of cars and commerce to this city, choking it. Stories abounded of taxicabs driving onto sidewalks and around light posts to get around a jam.

I actually saw tensions from the traffic cause drivers to get out of their cars and get into fistfights in the middle of the street, leaving pools of blood before it was over. *Scary.* Luckily they didn't have guns, like in America.

Another form of travel to experience in Tehran—maybe only once— was the dark green, double-decker city buses. Recommended only for their cheapness, these buses chugged off from their stops so crammed full of passengers not even standing room remained. They proved that plenty of poor existed here in Tehran.

There was something strange about the air. Dry and somewhat thin, it must also have been unclean. The mountains, though beautiful, surrounded Tehran in such a way they trapped the exhaust from so many cars, often leaving a brown cloud of pollution hovering over the city.

It was normal to find a small cut in the hand one day and the next day have a thin red line slowly traveling from it toward the heart. *Blood poisoning?* I flipped when one first appeared on my arm, originating from a small cut on my finger, yet no one seemed too alarmed. With a good washing of the wound, and some antiseptic, along with the body's own immunity, the line traveled no farther and soon disappeared.

But an illness I developed after being here just over one month did *not* subside nor disappear. It began at the end of November with severe fatigue, fever, loss of appetite and general sickness like a bad, bad cold. After three days of trying to shake it, it crept up on me even worse. On a visit to the bathroom, I knew I was seriously ill. Standing over our shiny, white, Middle Eastern "hole-in-the-floor" toilet to pee, I let forth a bizarre stream of deep-orange, apricot-colored urine! Weird enough. Then I went totally dizzy, bounced off the white-tiled wall around the commode and collapsed to the floor. I managed to keep from passing out, somehow got my pants up and staggered, barely, to the bathroom door.

"Help me. Somebody help me," I moaned. I couldn't even stand up.

Who heard my plea and ran to my aid? "Mother" Vivian, *God bless her*. She actually physically held me up and guided me—a mass of weak, sick flesh—back to my bed.

This same day, Patrick returned from a trip to Istanbul. He too, sick as a dog while traveling on the train, now stumbled toward the solace of his bed. But someone looked into Patrick's eyes. The whites were yellow. Patrick and I both had hepatitis.

We'd all heard hepatitis was extremely contagious. Now we knew it. Both of us had apparently been infected with the virus by simply using the bathroom at the other apartment where Cindy—just getting over the disease—lived. She figured she likely got it from some contaminated Tehran vegetable not washed well enough. Although progressive and wealthy, Iran lacked strict health standards. Doctors later told us outbreaks of hepatitis could be traced to the use of human waste as fertilizer on some Iranian vegetable farms. *Gross.* And it could spread quickly, especially with communal living. Patrick and I therefore would be isolated in a hospital before anyone else became infected.

William loaded us two germ carriers into the two back seats of our German Ford van and headed for the closest hospital, somewhere on the west side of Tehran. But, with no rooms or beds available there, doctors directed us to Firoozabadi Hospital way down on the southern, poor side of the city.

Comprised of one-story and two-story buildings, the hospital itself spread through soothing gardens and large shade trees, making it a haven from the dusty streets of South Tehran.

Here in 1974, Iranians admired and respected Westerners, so it was a good time to be an American. But that's not why hospital staff warmly received Patrick and me and led us to hospital beds—with no mention of money whatsoever. In Iran, just as in many third-world countries, medical and hospital expenses were entirely *free*. Free to *anyone* living in the country and in need of health care—Iranians and foreigners alike. Even medications. All subsidized by the government. *Amazing.*

Patrick and I ended up with a private room with two beds and a sink. At 6:30 p.m., an hour after snuggling between the perfectly clean sheets of our beds, an Iranian doctor came in, examined us and diagnosed a mild case of viral hepatitis. Like other medical personnel we'd thus far met, this doctor suspected us of contracting our hepatitis through intravenous drug use—sharing needles. Consequently, he examined our arms for track marks. He found none of course. Sure, drug users from foreign countries passed through Iran, but I felt these doctors didn't want to admit this horrible liver disease was attributable to substandard health conditions found within their own country—specifically unclean, contaminated foodstuffs.

Word traveled fast that two American guys had been admitted to the hospital, because at 8 a.m. the following morning, Patrick and I were awakened by six young female Iranian nurses giggling and staring at us. An embarrassing, but inspiring wake-up call.

The care in the hospital was extraordinary. Staff took periodic blood samples, gave us plenty of vitamins, and proficient Iranian doctors examined us regularly. And the food was delicious. At midday and then again in the evening the kitchen served us each a plateful of steaming white rice with either skewered lamb kebab and grilled tomatoes, or a boiled, half of a chicken, along with a small, packaged blob of real butter to melt into the hot rice, if desired—the lamb with rice called *chelokebab* and the chicken with rice, *chelomorg*, both typical Iranian dishes.

Following the harmonious rice-dish meals would enter the *"chai"* guy to serve another of Iran's traditions—boiling hot tea in a clear glass about the size of a "rocks" glass, with no handle and sitting on a saucer. Sugar came in a separate little bowl, unlike in Turkey where it sat on the saucer. The Iranians often poured some of the tea from the glass into the saucer. This helped cool the steaming hot liquid, and they would then sip it from the saucer—almost an art.

The sugar in the separate bowl sometimes came as manufactured cubes, but not always. Most chai arrived with *gant*—hard, compressed, broken chunks of solid sugar chipped off some large "mother rock." The pieces of sugar were not to be dropped *into* the tea either—there's not usually a spoon provided anyway. Instead, the sugar piece is placed inside the mouth, and the tea is then sipped over it, thereby sweetening the tea in the mouth—also an art.

Doctors told us to expect at least a 10-day stay in the hospital, which was fine with us since we were so exhausted and sick. Hepatitis is not a common cold, we soon discovered. It's a disease of fatigue and weakness. We had to lie down. I became tired just sitting up in bed.

Poor Patrick. Five hours after arriving via the tiring train from Istanbul, he is "thrown out" of the apartment and sent with me to this South-Tehran hospital. But Patrick, always a good sport, wanted what was best for the Work.

He and I made good company and had some great laughs together in our hospital room. Patrick was a natural clown. Forced into this helpless, humbling state and not having to prove himself a leader, he became himself—an ingenious joker.

As for the flirty nurses, they were always a welcome sight at eight o'clock in the morning. Then there was the "pill lady." She came on the scene the third day, bursting into the room, flicking the lights on at six o'clock in the morning to administer certain vitamins to us. "Come on! Let's go! Get up! It's time for your vitamins," she shouted. That's what we determined she said anyway, in her fast Farsi, as we squinted through our eyelids at her. We had the same rude awakening the next day but were now enthralled with the snow falling outside our second-story window. It was December 5, 1974. We arranged with the doctor that same day though, to kindly move the 6 a.m. pill lady reveilles to 7 or 8 a.m.

We weren't sure if it was a symptom of the hepatitis, food, pills or all three, but the flatulence we produced was phenomenal. We blamed the chicken. After all, for every meal of chelokebab (grilled lamb), we were served probably three chelomorg (chicken and rice) dinners. We seemed to let loose simultaneously too because the room would fill up with the same, distinctive smell every time. "Damn chickens running around in here again, aren't they?" Patrick would say. Hopefully a nurse or a cleaner wouldn't enter the room when full of these wild "chickens."

At the foot of our beds, near the window, an aluminum, oil-burning furnace kept the room comfortably warm on the cold December nights. In the middle of every night, a faithful, young kid kept it fueled.

The head nurse, a decent-looking girl in her late twenties, became a close friend during our stay, providing us with everything from biscuits and furniture to an always spotlessly clean room. She eventually asked us for our address, so she and another nurse could come and visit.

The nurses were amazing. Different groups would come into our room at different hours of the day to talk and giggle. Patrick and I stumbled along in Farsi while the nurses stumbled along in English. They seemed comforted that we always smiled, consistently spoke of *Hoda* (God) and were interested in their souls, not just their bodies. Nevertheless, a physical attraction did exist between us in our twenties and these girls in their teens and twenties. *Goodness.* I had to work at staying spiritual when they came in to change the sheets, naturally flirting like they did the whole time. And then, there was something sensual about it when one of them would come to the side of my bed with her tray of vials and syringes, roll up my sleeve and hold my arm in her smooth, delicate hands to prick my finger or vein for a regular blood sample. I would just study her dark eyes and lashes.

But I could never forget the hepatitis. It was a chore just to walk down the hall to the bathroom—since there was no private toilet in our room. And once there, even if I thought I was normal, I was reminded of the disease when I saw what came out of my body in the form of urine and feces. The urine remained apricot-colored, while the feces became *pure white.* Apparently the disease causes the liver to be too sick to excrete bile so the feces have no color, while more bile goes through the kidney, making the urine darker.

After a two-week hospital stay, a doctor, on December 15, reluctantly released Patrick and me, mostly at the insistence of Patrick who was gung-ho to "get back to work." Although a mild case, it was still hepatitis—a serious disease that permanently damages, to some degree, the liver it attacks. The doctor knew this, recommending we remain in the hospital to recuperate a while longer and warning us to take it easy and continue resting in bed at home. Now when we asked the doctor if we could drink alcoholic beverages, he said, "Stay away from alcohol for one year."

"What did he say? One *month* . . . ?"

The sincere, professional concern toward us amazed me in that it meant no benefit or financial profit to either the doctors or the hospital.

The doctor wrote us a prescription and gave us each a note stating we'd had hepatitis. We took addresses of nurse-friends, the cook served us one last delicious meal, and we thanked everyone for the fine care given us. At 12:30 p.m. we walked out of Firoozabadi Hospital and caught a taxi home.

Chapter 15
— The Lady Farideh —

"WHAT'S THE STORY with these women?" I asked Joshua, who'd been here in Tehran a while. "They're beautiful!"

"I know," he replied. "They're friendly too."

The good looks of the Iranian people are legendary. It's believed that when Alexander the Great of the Grecian empire conquered Persia in 331 BC and saw the beauty of the Persian women, he encouraged his soldiers to marry them. Thus the dark-haired, dark-eyed but fair-skinned, beautiful people. The Iranian babies are exceptionally cute, nearly all having big, round, dark eyes with long eyelashes and light skin.

The Iranian women brightened the streets here with their long hair flowing around white faces and looking from dark eyes through long, black eyelashes and beneath nicely trimmed eyebrows. And it seemed every one had a perfect derrière, enhanced by tight jeans, slacks or dresses.

These women had money for expensive perfumes and cosmetics and knew how to properly adorn themselves. They looked elegant even in blue jeans. They applied their make-up tastefully, allowing their natural beauty to take precedence.

No wonder husbands, brothers and parents attempted to cover these women up with *chadors*—a black cloth draping the whole body from head to toe. But those women and girls forced to wear the chadors would often let them drift open for peeks at miniskirts or whatever else underneath. *Goodness.* Frustration among the menfolk of this country—like beating one another up in the streets every now and then—might well have been attributable to their *seeing* these beauties everywhere but not being able to *touch* them. Usually, men and women remained virgins until marriage.

Now if invited into an Iranian home with unmarried Iranian girls present, we found it not uncommon for one of them to enter into a provocative Persian dance. It was in their blood, perhaps a carryover from the days when girls used to dance before princes and kings in courtyards of Persian palaces.

"Dance, Parveen," her mother might say. And Parveen would arise, shy and embarrassed. A sister would quickly fetch a sash or long piece of cloth to tie around Parveen's hips for effect, accentuating her curves, outlined already by the tight jeans she wore. And once the music started, that was it. She began to dance, not a belly dance, but a smooth, Middle Eastern dance, extremely sexy and artistic.

We were often invited into Iranian homes. But the Persian dance was not necessarily initiated, particularly if parents were present, unless one of *our* girls was along. In fact, the Persian girls danced as much for the visiting girls as the guys. We had a sister with us whenever possible in Iran, and not just for the dance. Girls make a difference anywhere. They break the ice, magically.

The physical beauty of the Iranian girls was not their only attribute. They were natural homemakers. I learned this when I met Farideh, the 18-year-old aunt of a close Iranian friend of ours. (Now, how she was the *aunt* of this guy, Abbas—who was in his twenties—and how *her* 38-year-old mother was *his grandmother*, is for a genealogist to figure out.) Still in her last year of high school, the girl was beautiful. She had dark, layered hair well past her shoulders and a perfect little body. But again, it wasn't just a physical attraction—I saw countless pretty girls on these streets—that struck me the day Abbas took me to the small, two-story apartment where she lived with her mother, older sister and two brothers. It was how she humbly served her mother.

The Iranians are known for their hospitality, and if they didn't invite guests for *lunch*, they made sure to welcome them with sweets and hot Iranian tea. "Farideh, please, can you make us tea?" her mother asked.

"*Bali*," Farideh said to her mother and went off to make the tea. She soon returned and gracefully served the tea with proficiency to me and the six others in the room. The scene triggered a love in me for this girl. She fulfilled some kind of idealized virtue I imagined the girl of my dreams might possess.

Farideh's nephew Abbas had sort of moved in with us. He was from a well-to-do family, but we had found him living in the streets—a dropout and outcast from his home. A black sheep. We cleaned him up, cared for him and fed him physically and spiritually until he pretty much became one of us. With purpose and direction in his life, he made amends with his family. But he had always confided in his grandmother and his two aunts, Farideh and Shireen. Shireen was Farideh's older sister, a trim and lovely 23-year-old, single secretary. Abbas thought it great, having Westerners as friends and loved introducing us to his relatives.

Abbas was close to Farideh—I sometimes wondered just *how* close—and he was thrilled when a love grew between her and me. He took me two or three times a week to her distant, North Tehran home, making sure I saw her as much as possible. She spoke and wrote English well, so we communicated satisfactorily on our brief visits. Physically we matched, but would she forsake everything, join our mission and become my wife?

Besides being physically attracted to her, I made every effort to woo and win Farideh's delicate, sad soul. Her father had divorced her mother and left them years earlier, affecting her negatively. Like so many in this country—and world—she lacked love and care. Still, I kept it spiritual, perhaps more spiritual than even *she* had hoped.

In fact, after having been with Farideh on several occasions during the past month, encouraging the girl's relationship and faith with the One True God, Abbas confronted me with an astounding notion. He told me that in order to fully reach his aunts and "bring them into the fold"—Patrick and others had been ministering spiritual things unto lovely sister Shireen as well—we might have to minister unto both girls' . . . *sexual* needs! *Uh oh.*

"No. Come on, Abbas," I replied.

"Yes. I think they need it to bring them further in," Abbas said.

This suggestion, from an actual Iranian and one who knew these girls, shocked me right off my cloud as a would-be pure and saintly minister. *Is it possible that in loving the soul of this fine woman I have been totally insensitive to her physical need or desire for sex? Quite possible.* The Children of God group here didn't consider using sex in reaching hungry hearts and souls. Yet the Iranian girls may have been experimenting with sex far more than we naïve Westerners realized. And when Abbas mentioned sexual needs, did he mean actual sexual intercourse with these girls? Or did he mean just kissing and petting? In countries like Iran, with its requirement that the girl be a virgin when married, some young women are *so* sexually motivated they resort to other "avenues" in order to satisfy their desire for sex. Was that the case here? I didn't know, but it wouldn't have been much of a sacrifice for me to oblige—in *some* way—the lady Farideh.

But my love affair with Farideh and with the country of Iran would soon be interrupted. Bryan was in town, and again my name came up to fill a gap somewhere. This time . . . Kabul, Afghanistan.

Typical for me. As soon as I adjusted to a place or became good at something . . . I uprooted myself. Here I was falling in love with a most beautiful girl who, according to Abbas, was falling equally in love with me. After three months, I was *into* this city, its people and the Work itself. Even the litnessing wasn't bad. Generous donations from the Iranians allowed litnessers to purchase fabulous chelokebab lunches while out, with plenty of funds left over to support both the Iran Work and that of other countries. A prosperous, high standard of living here. Comfortable. That's why I hesitated to accept the Kabul assignment . . . but my *spirit* finally did. Instead of taking the comfortable, easy route, I still looked for the challenge—new territory—wondering if it really was greener on the other side of the hill.

Currently heading the Kabul colony was Andrew, the guitarist and old friend of mine. Andrew was now needed in Tehran to form and head a rock music group in this progressive city.

So after contemplating the assignment, praying for a supernatural burden for it (one of the ways I had learned to test whether something was God's will) and getting over the initial shock of the request, I accepted the new position—whether there was much choice in the matter or not—as head of the Kabul colony in place of Andrew. Hopefully, Andrew would be pleased with the change—thus far knowing nothing about it.

"This Kabul assignment is only temporary," Bryan said. "You're doing too well here in Iran. We need you to come back."

"Sounds good to me," I said.

I went up to North Tehran to say goodbye to Farideh.

"I have to go to Kabul, Afghanistan," I told her. "But I'll be back."

Looking up at me from sad eyes, she said, "Please come back, Wayne."

"Do you have a photo?" I asked.

She went to her room and brought back a little, black-and-white photo of herself and handed it to me. On the back she had written: *to dear Wayne, from Farideh.*

I asked her to write down her address on a piece of paper, in English and Farsi. "I'll write to you," I promised. I secured a one-month visa from the Afghanistan embassy and reserved a one-way seat on a magic bus from the Amir Kabir Hotel to Kabul for $15.00.

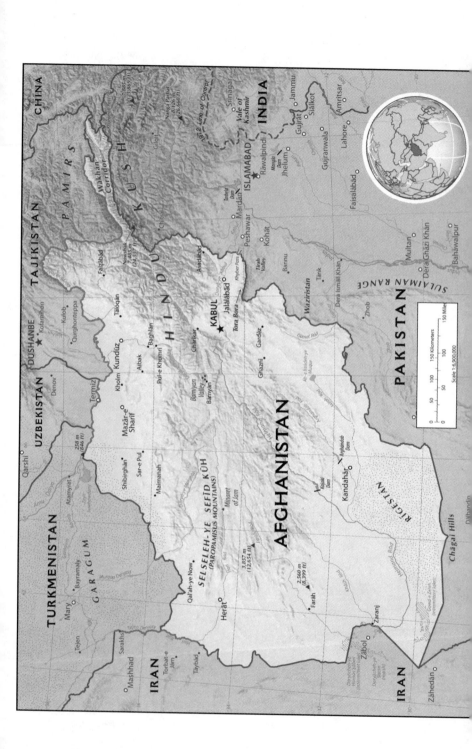

Chapter 16
∽ *A Magic Bus to Kabul* ∽

"WAKE UP, WAYNE!" Vivian shouted from the doorway of the single-guys' room. "You're going to miss your bus!"

God bless her. Again. It was 7 a.m. I'd overslept and barely made it, driven by two brothers on this snowy morning of February 6, 1975, to the Amir Kabir Hotel where the magic bus waited, held up just for me. The bus, simple but sound—like Nigel's that Vivian and I took from Istanbul—pulled off at 7:45 a.m. with 30-or-so travelers aboard, again mostly young and from all parts of the globe.

We headed northeastward in fairly heavy snow toward the Caspian Sea into the Elburz Mountains and past the magnificent peak of Mount Damavand (18,400 feet), in full view from the road. The Iranians were snow skiers, I noticed, as the bus passed quite a plush looking ski resort at the foot of Mount Damavand.

The route took us to within about 11 miles of the Caspian Sea, and then we headed eastward along rushing rivers and through mountains and picturesque, snow-covered valleys as we paralleled the border of Russia by about 80 miles.

Roadside stops were similar to those in Turkey except a bit wilder and less hospitable. The selection of food was of course different, with the prevalent dishes being the familiar piles of steaming white rice topped with melted butter, served with kebab meat or chicken—chelokebab and chelomorg. There were other foods at the stops, although not as many selections as those in Turkey. In my frugality I purchased only bread and tea at the stops, along with maybe some yogurt and Gouda cheese.

The bus traveled through the night, stopping only briefly at these rest and tea stops until we reached the major city of Mashhad at 8:30 the following morning. Situated in the far, northeastern corner of Iran—at a 550-mile journey from Tehran—Mashhad was reverenced as a religious city, the site of one of the country's most significant mosques. Although remote, Mashhad, like all of Iran, had modern conveniences and was organized and clean. Again, there was money in this country and it showed—even way out here.

Francis, the bus driver, knew the route and parked the bus at the Camp Mashhad Hotel on the outskirts of the city. He called it the "Visa Hotel" since we would remain here until those needing visas for Afghanistan got them. It was another busload of some great people—a lot of Italians, French and Americans.

It was Friday, the Muslim holy day, so the Afghanistan consulate was closed. Everyone spent the day resting and hanging around. I went back and forth to the edge of town with different people, assisting them with the language in purchasing foodstuffs, tea and meals. I had learned enough Farsi back in Tehran from friends, in taxis and on the streets to haggle with the money, as well as to open the hearts of Iranians with key words and phrases praising *Hoda*.

I learned a major lesson this day, though. One of the Italian guys, Roberto, whom I'd met and talked to on the bus, remained quite ill in his room. Everyone else was out and about. And I, on trips I'd made to town with others, failed to ask sick Roberto if he needed anything, or better yet, to thoughtfully bring him some juice or *something*. I was too busy with words when I could have touched Roberto's heart with a simple, cheap bottle of juice. He would have listened to anything I might have said from then on. A sample, not a sermon. Nevertheless, he and I remained good friends on the trip.

Refueling the Magic Bus

I was one of the few who didn't rent a room in the hotel, but an Italian couple who'd been touched by my message—or something right I'd done—invited me to sleep on the floor in their room that night, which I did, gratefully.

At 8:10 the next morning, Francis drove into Mashhad and found the Afghan consulate. By 11:15, everyone needing a visa for Afghanistan had one. The bus returned to the hotel and gathered the rest of us. We were on the road by 12 noon. Traveling southeastward, we reached the Iran-Afghanistan border by 4 p.m., where it took an hour to clear Iranian customs.

Customs? To *leave* a country? For what?

Driving three miles farther, through the typical no man's land separating countries, brought us to another world—Afghanistan. The border station itself indicated this, as border stations can. They pretty much reflect the economic conditions of a country, its type of government and the overall spirit of its people. Are the walls broken up, or are they cleaned and painted? Do the uniforms of the police and immigration officers look sharp and fit them well, or are they tattered and sloppy?

This border station needed financial assistance. Thus, when officials here discovered certain visas and vaccination certificates out of order with the bus, it took expert finagling by Francis and our two other drivers to acquire clear passage into the country. The three of them walked a dusty, dirt path with the officers in charge to a separate wooden building where they must have struck a deal over tea. Hilarious really. Totally under the table. The drivers and the officials even returned from their meeting, smiling and laughing. The spirit here, even with the Afghan police, was laid-back and non-oppressive. This was not an ordinary country.

But . . . those arriving at this border without immunizations up to date—smallpox and cholera—could expect to receive the vaccines right then with a dull hypodermic needle in a dark, back room of the border house. Two guys and a girl from the bus had to do just that.

After two hours, everyone had their passports stamped, and the bus rolled into Afghanistan. I didn't understand why, but a sense of relief and joy seemed to permeate the entire bus. Everyone, except maybe me and a few others, knew what arriving on this soil meant—some of the best and cheapest hashish in the world and the freedom to smoke it. A mecca of hashish smoking. Grown and produced here, it came in the form of oil, tar or the common, compressed blocks. Sure, there was hash in Iran and Turkey. But travelers were in deep trouble if caught possessing it *there*. Not so here. Hash and opium were two of Afghanistan's main cash crops, and they weren't ashamed to admit it. Rugged and remote, this land pretty much ruled itself. The government had probably said to the West, "Yeah. Right. Sure. We'll, uh, put controls on the drugs here . . ." Well, it wasn't 100% rampantly legal. Maybe only 95%.

The smokers on the bus knew all this. They'd been holding their breath through the last two countries and were now ready to let loose and . . . breathe deep!

As night fell, excitement and good spirits filled the bus for the 80 miles it took to reach the first major city of Herat. Arriving at 8:30 that evening, we checked into a hotel designated by Francis. That was another characteristic of this country, known by world travelers—the dirt-cheap cost of living. Hotels, food and nearly anything. Even I would get a bed tonight in a room with five others—for 50 cents!

Everyone ate well right there in the hotel—anything from eggs and bread to full-course, American-style meals of meat, potatoes and vegetables. But *eating* was hardly on the agenda tonight. *Smoking* was!

Anyone in the market for hash bought it soon after arrival right at the hotel, like the food. "Look at this thing!" Roberto said to me, pulling something from his top shirt pocket. He showed me the chunk he'd purchased. It was about half-an-inch thick and nearly the size of the Marlboro cigarette box he carried it in. I saw a few of the slabs people had, each weighing a few ounces and bought at some ridiculous price that if sold in America at street value, could have brought several hundred dollars in profit.

But these chunks were meant to be smoked right now. It was amusing. The hotel rooms became virtual hash dens. Here sat young people from America, Europe, Australia or wherever, accustomed to *illegally* purchasing small pieces of hash at maybe $10 a gram, conserving the heck out of it while possessing and smoking it in paranoia. Tonight, in contrast, they held several-ounce *blocks* of hash at not a lot more than $10 apiece and sat on a cloud of total freedom to carry it around in their front shirt pockets or in their hands, like a set of keys or something. And they could legally smoke it in their hotel rooms, all night long.

Hash pipes passed nonstop around the rooms, generously replenished by everyone's stash. So much smoke filled the small room I could hardly see the person across from me. It was too funny. These people were in hash heaven.

No stranger to dope smoking, I sat side-by-side against a wall of the room with everyone. But when the pipes came my way, I kindly . . . *regretfully?* . . . passed them on. No sense stumbling any lambs I'd spoken with on the journey from Tehran. I should be the example of a changed person to them. So, I played some guitar and chatted with them as they all toked up.

The bus wouldn't be leaving Herat until 4 the next afternoon, so when morning came, I checked out the environs. It didn't take long to realize how unaffected by outside influences was this distant land. Nearly the only evidence we were living in the 1970s was the presence of cars and trucks. Everything else remained as it must have been for hundreds of years—unpaved side streets bustling with the clang of blacksmiths and silversmiths; leather shops and carpet shops; open-air meat, fish and vegetable markets; the clomping of horses pulling carriages; donkeys and sheep walking around; whiffs of bread baked fresh in brick ovens; and the exact number of simple, crude tea shops necessary to get everyone through the day. Backward and poor, yet organized and fairly neat, with no visible beggars.

But the most striking aspect was the *people*. When I first set eyes on them, my mouth dropped open. Mostly men walked the streets, dressed similarly in pajama-like, earth-tone baggy pants, matching long-sleeved shirts with shirttails extending well past the buttocks, pocketed vests over their shirts and sandals on their feet. A brimless wool cap or a cloth wrapped into a turban covered every head. Such attire alone indicated we weren't in Turkey, Iran or any other country thus far traveled. But most astonishing were their *faces*—an amazing mixture of Turkish, Chinese, Mongolian, Persian, even Greek. Descendants of Ghengis Khan, Alexander the Great and whomever else. They had tanned skin and slanted eyes, and many had full, long, dark-black beards. Now beards grown by Western men are usually curly. Not these beards. They were remarkably straight. Long, thick, black and straight. Had I forgotten I crossed the border yesterday to another land, just the faces in the streets would have reminded me. They were fit too, these guys, strong and rugged. No wonder, being *mountain men*. Mountains covered nearly four-fifths of this country. Invaders, historically, never really conquered these people, except for a second attempt in 1879 by the British, who subsequently evacuated the country a year later.

The bus pulled off on schedule at 4 p.m. from the "hash-den" hotel. The same joyous atmosphere filled it. Everyone had enjoyed a good night's rest, plenty of food and good strolls through Herat. We were ready to conquer more miles. I was reminded of the beauty of these magic buses—the drivers were their own bosses, no strict schedule to keep, take it easy, enjoy life, get there in one piece.

Kabul lies straight east from Herat, but the main and best highway leads southward around the southwesternmost foothills of the giant Hindu Kush mountains and partly through the country's barren, western desert area. I was in awe looking out upon this vast land. So dry and harsh, hardly habitable.

Those at the back of the bus where I sat weren't concerned with the scenery outside. Since leaving Herat, they'd been too busy loading and passing around their hash pipes, getting high. Now they were pleading with me to join them.

"Here, Wayne. Have some," two or three of them offered.

"No, thanks, really," I said.

"Come on. Join us."

Finally I did. I smoked some. They knew by now I'd had a spiritual experience and was a changed person. It was just as important, I decided, to become one with them at the back of the bus. They loved it. It showed I wasn't too straight, or a cop or something.

Oddly, I only got a small buzz off it, after some heavy hacking, my lungs unaccustomed to inhaling *any* kind of smoke. After all, it had been over three years since I'd smoked resins of the same plant—the same day that I had met the girl in Orlando, Florida, who led me to this new, revolutionary way of life, following Jesus.

It wasn't a big deal to be high on hash out here in this desolate land. In fact it might have been quite normal. After observing mile after mile of this unforgiving scenery, it struck me the hash likely made life here more bearable—hardships and difficulties forgotten by the high of the drug. Perhaps it was just part of life with these people. No wonder it was so readily available.

Uninhabitable as the land seemed, families of nomads lived all along the route. The colorful dresses of the women caught my eye from miles away. Handmade with bright reds, purples, yellows and other colors, these dresses fit the women snuggly around their breasts down to their small waists and flowed outward from their waists to about their ankles. Not only attractive, the bright colors stood out vividly against the dusty landscape, naturally preventing these women from being struck by passing vehicles.

Caravans of nomads and their tent cities in the distance became the rule rather than the exception. Indeed, the size of the population of Afghanistan is hardly known since most of the people are nomads and farmers. Of the roughly estimated population of 15 million people, only about 18% lived in cities.

Noticeable about the nomads was their physiques. Not a fat one among them—they'd have never kept up. Each was perfectly proportioned— the women thin, trim and sexy; the men strong, lean and mean. They were naturally so, out here in this wilderness, constantly walking, and with diets of fresh, whole grain breads, goats' milk, cheeses and other wholesome foods. They probably had few diseases too, breathing nothing but fresh air all day long.

The ride was a bit rough on the imperfect, though decent, hilly roads, but the camaraderie, talking, guitar playing, singing and the hash!— although *I* didn't pursue it anymore—made it bearable and interesting.

At the southernmost part of the road to Kabul lies the city of Kandahar, about 350 miles from Herat. Located where the foothills to the Hindu Kush Mountains and Afghanistan's desert meet, at a latitude of about 32 degrees north, Kandahar provides the last chance during winter to see warmth. Travelers who get stuck in Afghanistan during the winter often head for Kandahar to stay warm and even sunbathe. We passed through this town around midnight, Francis stopping only briefly on the trip for tea, toilet runs and to change drivers.

From Kandahar, the road to the capital city of Kabul leads northeastward, along the Tarnak River and straight into the mountains. Sure enough, being February and the bus gradually ascending, the snows began along with the cold. I really had no idea what to expect of this land, its geography or its climate. I hadn't studied it. As usual, I'd been dumped into it. But that kept it a fresh surprise.

So it was all new to me, like our first stop for tea way up in the mountains, in the middle of the night, snow everywhere and deep. Fabulous too, this tea shop. Like a movie. Out here in the middle of nowhere in these quiet mountains. This was an Afghan road stop—so different from those in Turkey and Iran.

The place resembled a cave inside—dimly lit, low ceilings and crude, irregular walls of stone and mud bricks. To reach the tea room, we had to stoop down through an archway while pushing aside a hanging curtain. Inside was a fairly large, cozy room comfortably warmed by a metal wood-burning stove in the center. The beautiful, old Afghan carpets overlapped each other on the floor, naturally worn, their mostly burgundy colors nicely faded from being trodden on over the years by countless travelers. Customers sat on the floor upon hand-woven, cotton-stuffed, woolen pillows, which were also placed along the walls to lean against. Tea was served on low, wooden tables.

The owner knew Francis and greeted him like a long-lost friend, serving up anything he wanted, on-the-house. "Francis! How are you? It's been a long time. Sit down. What do you want?"

The owner and his waiters were so humble and friendly. They refreshed us, adding to the enchantment of this roadside inn.

Most on the bus ordered hot tea, while some thirstier passengers ordered . . . Coca-Colas. Yep, the real thing, served up ice-cold in their famous, little bottles. After all, we weren't in the middle of some remote African or New Guinea jungle. Although landlocked and isolated, Afghanistan is a crossroads between East and West. Silk and other traders had passed through this land and probably this same route for centuries. So it was no wonder that Coca-Cola was here tonight.

Now, how was tea served in *this* land? In its own Afghan way of course. First, a choice: *green* tea or *black* tea. (We must have been close to China with *green* tea an option.) The black tea was the same as that in Iran or Turkey, or as Lipton in America. But here, each person received their *own*, little, porcelain teapot holding a measured cup-or-so of brewed tea. Each pot arrived on a "private" tray along with a clear, shot-like glass, a small bowl of sugar and a spoon. Drinking tea here was obviously serious.

Back on the bus, coldness gradually crept in as we headed northward, steeper into the mountains. Other than a great bunch of people aboard, there weren't many perks on this bus—like heaters that worked. Sleep became difficult as we shivered under coats and blankets on the uncomfortable, city-bus-style seats. A lot of passengers seemed to be catching colds too, with the drastic changes in temperature and altitude. Francis pushed on through the night, though, stopping only for leaks and to switch drivers.

At 11 the next morning we approached what looked like a rather large village. These magic buses weren't normal touring coaches with some multi-lingual guide up front describing through a microphone, sites, landmarks and destinations along the way. Instead, after a night of little sleep, shivering, ears stopped up and fighting colds, those of us awake gazed blankly out the windows, hardly knowing the time, the day, much less where we'd reached. Nor was anyone saying a word, after 19 hours on this bus.

Again, not knowing what to expect of this country, I was quite amazed when I looked out my window and saw a crude fire station whose sign revealed in English and Farsi the name of this large village: Kabul! The sign read:

Kabul Fire House No. 5.

PART THREE

KABUL TO ATHENS...

Chapter 17
~ *Chicken Street* ~

THE BUS PULLED up to the Mustafa Hotel—Kabul's focal point of world travelers, like the Amir Kabir Hotel in Tehran. Almost fancy, the Mustafa Hotel was the "Hilton" of world traveler hotels here in Kabul. But $2.00 a night for a private room with two beds made it a bit costly. Many on the bus already had names of cheaper hotels and headed for them.

Parked out front of the Mustafa Hotel was a *real* one of those plush, guided tour buses loading up what looked like . . . actual tourists. Yep, cameras around their necks, happy-go-lucky, neatly-dressed youngish folks of various nationalities just passing through, enjoying these far-flung lands—in splendor and comfort. For some reason, they looked out of place.

I phoned my mates. Immediately, Adam, the Lebanese guy from Istanbul, came to greet me. "Wayne! You made it. How are you? Welcome to Kabul! It's good to see you," he said. We hugged.

"I'm good. How are you, Adam? It's good to see you too. You look good," I said. He really was looking strong and energized. He was in his realm in this sort-of-Middle-East, almost-Arab country.

I introduced Adam to some of those I'd met on the bus during the four-day journey from Tehran. He suggested I invite them to our home that evening.

Exhausted but happy to be in Kabul, all of us from the bus went our separate ways. Adam insisted on carrying the heavier of my two bags—the light-blue, American Tourister carry-on my sweet mom gave me back in London. I carried my small briefcase. No more backpacks. I hated them, especially the ones with frames that nearly every world traveler had, as if they expected to camp out along the way from London to New Delhi. These large packs, to *me* anyway, were an awkward, impractical hassle for anything except for what they were originally intended, such as hiking, camping and trekking . . . for hours, days or weeks at a time. They were *not* intended for city life, or to be hauled on and off city buses, or ferries, trains and planes. Their frames and straps were famous for jabbing and snagging other luggage; they never fit properly in overhead luggage compartments; and the whole combination of frame and stuffed packs were notorious for knocking into people, especially when backpackers hoisted them on and off their backs. It was a frequent occurrence to see a traveler clambering onto a crowded city bus with one packed full on his back, its frame jutting up over his head, while innocent commuters in their own country tried to avoid getting banged into by this monstrous outgrowth on this foreign idiot. If lucky, the locals might only get struck by the extra pair of shoes or hiking boots *dangling* from the contraption!

Unless a traveler intended on trekking into the Himalayas, or climbing Everest, a normal suitcase or carry-on bag proved more practical for checking into hotel rooms—where most world travelers "camped."

The five-minute walk to the house was along Chicken Street—the bustling, main street of world travelers in Kabul. Several blocks long, the quaint street was lined with carpet shops; clothing and jewelry shops; tea, coffee and vegetable shops; and bakeries, restaurants and small hotels. The entire street was charming, enhanced by the absence of automobiles.

But what amazed me was the solid *ice* covering the streets and walks. Without exaggeration it must have been one foot thick in places. Apparently the melting/freezing process of the winter snows, along with little or no plowing or clearing, had created a coating of ice that *covered* Kabul.

The house was located on a residential side street at one end of and just off Chicken Street. It was a single family home, enclosed by a white-stucco, seven-foot-high mud/brick wall for privacy—like most houses in Kabul. Single level, with a small front and back yard, three bedrooms, a full bath with two toilets, living room, dining room, kitchen and small office. The home was spacious, more than adequate and a deal at fifty-five dollars a month.

Members of the group had come and gone through the home since the Work started here five months ago, leaving now three guys and one girl—American Andrew, Lebanese Adam, and Kenny and Diane, both Australian. They all knew I was coming, but not that I was taking over the Work here. At six thousand feet above sea level out here in the middle of nowhere, they were excited to see me—or *anyone*—from the "other world."

They greeted me warmly. Andrew not home, Adam introduced me to Australian Diane. Tall, well proportioned and attractive—despite having no makeup on—Diane had found what she'd been searching for in her travels and joined the group right here in Kabul, three months earlier. Kenny, a "good ole boy" Australian, lay sick in bed, but managed to lift himself onto his elbow long enough to welcome me. Although not at all fat, Kenny met the criterion of dedicated Australian beer drinkers of being able, while standing erect, to support a can of beer on *top* of his self-extended beer belly, which he would one day demonstrate to me. The five of us were single and in our early or mid twenties.

The furniture, though sparse, was uniquely Afghani. Especially the rope beds. Instead of metal springs and mattresses, as in the West, these beds were made of thick, hemp ropes, strung crisscross, ever-so tightly— tight enough to firmly hold a full-grown adult—between a frame of solid, lathe-worked wooden timbers. Entirely natural, indigenous materials. The beds—one a bunk bed—some rope chairs and wooden tables were custom-made here in Kabul for practically nothing.

Andrew arrived at 1 p.m. He had expected to see me one of these days but was unaware of any details. The last we'd seen each other was back in Athens, Greece, 14 months ago. Being contemporaries with similar 1960's backgrounds and comparable spiritually, we wholeheartedly embraced one another.

"Wayne! So good to see you, man!"

"Yeah. You too. Last time was back in Greece, I think."

Soon after I settled into the new home, Andrew led me to my sleeping quarters—the bunk bed above his. From my briefcase, I pulled out the sealed letter I'd brought from Tehran and handed it to him.

"What's this?" Andrew asked.

"It's a letter from Bryan." I knew the contents, but told him nothing. The letter would say it better.

Andrew's reaction upon reading the letter was a lot like mine back in Tehran a few days ago when *I* received *my* request to come to Kabul—flustered. Like me, just when Andrew was getting into the place, digging it even, he gets uprooted. I had said to myself, *Man! I thought I was doing pretty good here, fulfilling my duties, progressing, being a blessing. But no. I've got to forget it all, stop everything, throw cold water on this place and my work here, switch gears entirely and move?*

But it took only a little time for me to get over the initial shock of *my* transfer and be grateful that I was needed at *all* to fill a position somewhere, anywhere.

As for Andrew, he was a musician first and *then* a leader. He sang and played the guitar too well to be encumbered with management, although he led others most capably. Still, I easily sensed he loved this place and didn't want to leave it, even though his new assignment of playing music in comfortable Tehran had plenty of its own merits.

Andrew accepted his Tehran calling—he *had* to—but wasn't going to abandon his "child" (the Kabul Work he'd thus far grown and nurtured) without leaving it in assuredly good hands. Thus, I couldn't have had a better breaking-in to this unique new field.

It snowed nonstop my first three days in Kabul as Andrew began transferring responsibilities to me. First, he oriented me to Kabul itself. We walked the icy streets across the center of town to the bazaar area, snapping photos of one another—mostly of Andrew for his last, cherished memories of this place and its people. We walked through the clanging, open-air tin market and across the Kabul River to our main link to the outside world—our P.O. Box at the "Post and Telegraph" office. Amazing as it was, mail arrived and was sent out from Kabul timely and untampered. Though primitive here, it was still the jet age and Kabul, too, had a functioning international airport.

Kabul tin market

Andrew showed me the bank he used, the best restaurants for cheap Afghani rice dishes; various outside kebab shops where guys used woven straw fans to keep the coals of their hibachi grills hot all day and night; fish markets for trout caught fresh out of the rushing, snow-melted rivers and other haunts he'd relished—like pastry and tea shops—while out running errands. Spiritual mission or not, if a person didn't partake of such pleasurable attributes of the land, he would have cheated himself of wonderful memories.

The author (R) with Afghans at a Kabul bazaar

On one jaunt, Andrew introduced me to the old Afghan owner of a small grocery store near the home. The pleasant old man with his white, cotton beanie on his head, didn't speak English, but Andrew and I conversed sufficiently with him in Farsi. Andrew and the others had a "credit account" with the guy whereby if they didn't have money—which was often—the guy let them "purchase" what they needed on credit. He simply wrote down the amount in his ledger and when money came in, a payment was made or the balance paid off, normal practice in these countries. I had such accounts in Greece and Turkey. Even if we had enough money, it was a good idea to create such an account with a shop or restaurant in case of unforeseen rough times. The merchants benefited—even though they charged no interest—because we "bought" our needs or meals exclusively from them.

At night, with snow falling here in February, Kabul became like a Christmas fairy tale. After 9 p.m. total peace and quiet settled across the city. Such solitude, such comfort. Then, adding to the serenity of the night's stillness in this capital city that was more like a large village, came pleasant whiffs of burning firewood—the predominant fuel used here for cooking and heating.

It was cold, but not bitterly cold. Although sitting six thousand feet above sea level on a plateau, the city was sheltered by tremendous stretches of steep, snow-covered mountains rising in the distance. Like in Tehran, the mountains inspired me.

The snows fell gently though steadily upon this town. Yet, while quietness settled soon after dark over Kabul, Chicken Street remained alive with foreign travelers well into the night. They didn't party in the streets, but mingled, rather, by "restaurant/hotel-hopping"—visiting on foot the numerous, inexpensive restaurants and cheap hotels up and down, on and off Chicken Street. Each restaurant had its own ambience and menu, and every hotel a unique lobby with adjoining restaurant and smoking/tea room. So the travelers traipsed from place to place until they found a comfortable setting with compatible people. Of course a lot depended upon the owners or managers of a place and how congenial they were to travelers.

Afghanistan was not a "normal" country nor Kabul an ordinary capital city, and the Kabul Work was not our normal ministry. We strictly directed our efforts here toward the world travelers, to get them in touch, if possible, with their One, True God. We mingled with them, basically. But we didn't just mingle and talk with these travelers. We *served* them. The first day I arrived, February 10, 1975, three of the French people I'd met on the bus from Tehran came to the house that night; nearly 20 people from the bus came two nights later; and almost every night we had visitors. They came because it was a real house—warm and cozy; they came for genuine home-cooked meals, often helping with the cooking and provisions; they came for the music; and they came because we were different and spoke of the Spirit. Some stayed, some left, some returned, some nearly joined us.

Dinner at the house with world travelers

Why were all these travelers out here in the middle of Asia? They were the same ones who were in Istanbul—searching for the truth and hoping to find it in perhaps the "spiritual" religions of India. And Kabul was on the main, overland route to India.

But Kabul wasn't just a stop on the Europe-India route, like Istanbul or Tehran. It was a heavenly place to savor—peace, quiet, freedom; cheap hotels; abundant hash and drugs; and, believe it or not, a lot of people hunkered down here for . . . the food. Complete dinners based largely on American-style menus, but at dirt-cheap prices—steak (often, choice camel neck meat), potatoes and fresh vegetables. But it was the *desserts* that were famous here—apple, cherry and pumpkin pie; chocolate cake; cheesecake; chocolate chip cookies; oatmeal cookies . . . just about any typical American dessert imaginable, all tasting as good, if not better, than back in the States, baked with the unadulterated flour from wholesome strains of Afghani wheat. (It *had* to be wholesome to grow in *this* rugged land!) Sure, the travelers sought spiritual enlightenment—not so easily found in most churches of their lands—but the food and drugs were a definite lure.

I saw all this in my first two or three days here. I had stumbled into a secluded, mountain hamlet, independent from the rest of the world, yet with anything available from Wrigley's Spearmint gum to Sony TVs. Anything. It was the jet age, after all.

If we didn't have visitors at our house at night, we sought them out—in the streets, hotels, restaurants. This was common practice anywhere I had been in the group, but doing so in Kabul was more like a dream.

Whether I had come or not, Andrew still had commitments to play guitar at certain places at night. So, on my second night here, he took me along to show me this "meat" of the Work.

Now just walking up and down Chicken Street in the quiet stillness of the night was enchanting—through falling snow among travelers from all over the world, many of them clothed in their newly purchased, hand-embroidered, long (usually past the knees) leather and wool Afghan coats and knee-high, Afghan leather boots. And experiencing an evening up in these mountains, in the back tea room of one of these travelers' hangouts—like this night at Ali's Restaurant and The Steak House—listening to Andrew sing and play his soothing guitar to a captive audience of 25-or-so people, set Kabul far apart from any other place. The rooms themselves were relaxing, with hand-woven, woolen Afghan carpets spread everywhere; large woven pillows for sitting on and leaning against; low, hand-carved wooden tables here and there; and one or two wood-burning stoves in the middle of it all. The stoves not only kept the room comfortably warm from the winter cold outside, but they were constructed with a chamber that boiled water used for the steaming hot tea served along with snacks and full meals throughout the night.

The owners and managers loved having Andrew in their establishments. His playing attracted good-paying customers. These hoteliers and restaurateurs didn't pay him, but treated him well, serving him anything he wanted from their kitchens.

Andrew's reward though was the appreciation from the crowd. Out in this remoteness, he played their endless requests for Beatles, Dylan, Hendrix, Don McClean, James Taylor, Eagles and other artists they loved. He put these souls—most of them stoned anyway—into a state of nostalgia. He also played spiritual songs of love and salvation, written by the Children of God and intended to reach the hungriest of hearts. The ambience of the settings was alluring, but we had to remember our purpose—to somehow express to these folks that God did truly love them.

Andrew continued to relinquish the Kabul Work to me by introducing me to foreign contacts and benefactors around town. He was close friends with a German businessman and the guy's wife and child; a group of Americans, including Peace Corps workers who met every Friday night at someone's home for a Catholic mass and potluck dinner; a German Methodist preacher; and other friends. He also introduced me to the consuls of the American, Swiss, German, Italian and French embassies, all of whom knew our work with the "world traveler community," as they put it.

"How did we exist financially?" One source was the Work in Tehran. I used to wire money to Kabul from banks when I had been there, though not a set amount, nor on a regular basis. And as in Turkey, we could *never* depend on distributing and selling literature in Afghanistan— especially to the Afghans. Not only was proselytizing forbidden here, but it was against the law for an Afghan to even *visit* the home of a Westerner or to have a Westerner inside his home. This was not a religious prohibition, but rather a dumb hangover that past rulers had concocted to assure independence and "non-pollution" of the Afghans. As if they couldn't *benefit* from outside influence? The government probably knew our group was here, but had adopted an attitude long ago with Westerners: "You don't bother us, and we won't bother you." They may have even thought we were some kind of intermediaries of the foreign embassies.

We quite nearly *were* intermediaries for the foreign embassies. Which is why embassies, especially the German and Swiss, donated money to us from time to time. It amazed me how concerned embassies were for their world traveler citizens. After all, it is the responsibility of *any* foreign embassy—caring or not, concerned or not—to assist its own citizens in a foreign land, or catch hell from someone back home if they don't. Besides that, a certain understanding existed among non-Afghans that we were all "in this together" out here in this untamed land. It was noticeable, though, which embassies cared more for their own. The German and Swiss sat at the top, and the U.S. and others, well, not *too* far behind.

The embassies knew we had a home off Chicken Street and that we mingled with and were in close contact with the travelers. So, if travelers ran into trouble, the embassies learned to count on us as their hands and feet to assist their own citizens—an excellent alliance since we wanted to be a sample and not a just a sermon to others. The embassies had the funds and wanted to help but couldn't always be physically close to their traveling citizens.

Travelers fell into trouble out here, too—*jail*-type trouble. *Yep*, drugs. Hashish, usually. It was inevitable. It was too cheap, too high quality and too plentiful. So much money could be made from it back in America, Europe or Australia . . . if someone could transport it there.

It was fine to freely smoke it in the country—but don't try to smuggle it out. It was not that easy, especially through the airport where most people were caught. Apparently there was a price on the head of smugglers—perhaps from the West—for a local to take advantage of. Sure enough, the Afghan that sold it to a person, or custom-made the boots for him, with the hash, hash oil or opium neatly hidden in the heels, would be the very one that rats out and cashes in on the smuggler.

Well, we rendered a significant service in Kabul . . . bringing food, money, blankets, coal for heating and cooking, mail and words of comfort to travelers unfortunate enough to have been busted and put in jail here. And, we helped get them the heck *out* of jail.

Amazing about our "jail ministry" was how world travelers who had *not* been busted latched onto this ministry with us. I think it was a vague, unexplainable comradeship that dopers and drug users had. When they discovered some of "their own kind" stuck in jail here, they wanted to help out.

Besides mentioning our jail visits during conversations with travelers, we posted notices on various hotel bulletin boards, describing the visits and asking if people would like to donate money, food or other supplies to those in jail—or just come along. We visited the jail at least once a week, sometimes with travelers along, with a basket of donated food, money and other items.

When I arrived, only two foreigners were in jail—an American guy named Ryan and a Swiss guy named Claude. Both had been caught at the airport on different dates, attempting to "export" hashish from the country. It was a fear hanging over every partaker traveling in these lands—getting stuck in some dingy, third-world jail, like the cell these guys shared. Ryan and Claude, transferred from the main holding cell, now sat in a small cubicle in a row of cells similar to rental storage units in the States, only these were made of brown, mud bricks fitted with bars in front.

Ryan and Claude loved the visits. As well, it pleased the U.S. and Swiss consuls to have a regular line of communication with the prisoners, while making every attempt—along with girlfriends, parents, relatives, friends and legislators back home—to set the two free. But I sensed, on more than one visit, that the two didn't seem that eager to *be* set free! Why?

Chapter 18
∞ The Kabul Work ∞

As with anything exceptional and wonderful, it seems there's always a price to pay. So it was with Kabul. Though serene, remote, cheap and free, it was *hell* on the body to live here.

First there was altitude sickness. All newcomers experienced it to some degree, depending upon their health and how acclimated they were to living six thousand feet above sea level. Symptoms included headaches, exhaustion, chills, loss of appetite and nausea.

Then there was the cold and snow in winter. Clean and beautiful, the snow, but its accumulation on our roof and in deep five-foot drifts around our house kept us fighting for warmth. It snowed so steadily that if the landlord hadn't regularly sent his servants to the house to shovel it off the roof—flat as it was—it would surely have collapsed. For heat, one wood-burning, aluminum stove standing in the living room and center of the house kept the place sufficiently warm. The only running hot water was the bathroom shower, a shower I would never forget. Although its large, metal container of water looked like any other hot water heater, the water inside was heated by a *wood* fire— like the living room stove. So if we wanted a hot shower, we had to build a successful wood fire inside a little cove beneath the container of water. It was pretty neat, having a crackling fire in the bathroom while taking a shower. The fire also kept the whole bathroom quite warm. Australian Kenny was a master at building a fire in there. Amazingly, the construction of the house of natural, one-foot-or-so-thick, mud brick walls, kept the home considerably well insulated from the cold.

The altitude, the persistent coldness and perhaps the lingering effects of hepatitis, left me debilitated for two weeks or more after arrival. As hard as I tried to function and flow with the others, I remained bedridden off-and-on with severe headaches, no appetite and bouts of flu-like symptoms.

Although many who came here never wanted to leave its peaceful solitude, nothing was easy here. Fresh fruits and vegetables were generally so contaminated not even soaking them in typical sterilizing agents could make them safely edible. A saying by foreigners was, "If you can't peel it, don't eat it." So we didn't eat much lettuce; and who likes *grapes* enough to peel every one?

Why was the food contaminated? First of all, except for the snow in winter, this was arid land. Dusty. And with no public toilets around, if nature called, some locals used the closest field or vacant lot—whether it be a lot between houses or buildings, or in the open countryside. Squat and leave it—right there on the surface, in the open air. The men's shirttails, extending well past the buttocks, completely covered their private parts as they squatted down to do their business. Some say that's why their shirttails are so long. *That's fine, but how about covering it up?*

Nope. They weren't educated that way, unfortunately. Instead, there the piles sat on the surface of the earth. And when the dust blew, it might settle upon the excrement, gather microbes awhile and be blown about again, this time settling on the fruits, vegetables and other foods sold in the open air. Flies could also do the contaminating after landing on the surface-sitting poop. Consuming local foodstuffs, then, resulted in anything from mild stomach ailments treatable with EnteroViaform or tetracycline to more serious illnesses—amoebic dysentery, hepatitis, tetanus, cholera, typhoid fever—or even death.

Even one of the two toilets in our bathroom was nothing but an indoor outhouse, the exterior and "collecting" portion of which led right onto the street out front. To use it—when the normal, Western-type commode was occupied—we would climb up about two feet off the floor into this square wooden box built into the wall and do it, squatting style through a hole, where it landed in an enclosure recessed into the front outside wall of the house and on the same ground level as the street. This was not the shabby side of town either—the president of Afghanistan, Mohammed Daoud Khan, lived with his family in their palace two blocks away.

At least we had an understanding among us that anyone having to use *this* toilet must immediately cover their doings with sand, dirt, snow—anything. Fortunately, some guy—perhaps hired by the city—came by regularly to collect the street-side accumulations.

But the worst culprit for disease and misery was the *water*. "Don't drink the water!" It was the first thing we were warned about in Afghanistan. The tap water contained vigorous amoebas. So vigorous were they that if we didn't boil the water continuously for a full, clocked, *five* minutes or more, it wouldn't kill them. Consequently, a lot of people—especially travelers and foreigners—unknowingly consumed live amoebas in the hot tea they drank, assuming, since it was *boiled* and hot, it was safe. And, to boil water for a *full* five minutes meant consuming more fuel—wood, gas, electricity—which became expensive. Economically therefore, restaurants and hotels didn't concern themselves with the "five-minute boiling rule," so people took their chances—even with steaming hot tea. Unless they had a glass at *our* house. Even the higher-class Mustafa Hotel was pinpointed for "tainted" tea.

Thank goodness for the samovar—a metal urn that sat upon a heat source such as charcoal, a wood fire or a gas stove. Sometimes it boiled all day long, sterilizing the water within itself for tea. At its bottom was a spigot, and on top a small platform held a porcelain teapot of concentrated tea steeping continuously just under the boiling point, extracting the essences of the tea. Concentrated tea from the porcelain teapot was poured into a tea glass, the glass then placed under the spigot of the samovar, and the boiling water added according to the strength desired.

The samovar

The samovar was not just an attractive ornament in such a country of tea-indulgent people, but a useful appliance efficiently providing a sterile supply of boiled water at the turn of a spigot. Restaurants, tea shops and even private homes used them. If not an actual samovar, stoves (wood-burning, gas, or other) used the same technique by keeping a pot of water steadily boiling, with a small teapot of concentrated tea placed on top of it or elsewhere on the stove at perfect steeping temperature.

How could water be such a threat, especially in a place surrounded by so much fresh snow? Because decrepit, underground water pipes ran along ancient sewer pipes. *Yep*, and who knows what seeped into the drinking water along the way? It seemed the Afghans spent more time fighting wars than concentrating on repairs of their own water and sewer systems. Consequently, if these hapless people weren't fighting human invaders or their own government, they still spent their pathetic lives fighting damned amoebas and other invading microorganisms *within* their bodies until their early, untimely deaths.

Australian Diane, therefore, demonstrated the safest way to brush my teeth—with the fresh-fallen snow in the front courtyard of our home. That's how risky the tap water was—we couldn't even brush our teeth with it!

Andrew finally caught a local, "non-magic" Afghan bus to Tehran at 5:10 p.m. on a Saturday evening, February 22, 1975—12 days after I had arrived—leaving me in charge of the Kabul Work.

"Have a good trip," I said, as Andrew boarded his bus. "Enjoy Tehran."

"Thanks," Andrew said. "Take good care of Kabul. You'll love it here."

A sinking feeling came over me as I watched this former head of the Work depart—that feeling a person can get when suddenly he is responsible for all decisions, schedules, the welfare of his team and the success of the operations. Soon though, a subtle, sort of supernatural inspiration overtook me and made me "grab the bull by the horns" to lead the way. Someone had to, and I was the current choice, like it or not.

But I remained frail into the next week with headaches, stomach problems and downright exhaustion while my body fought to adjust to Kabul's cold, harsh environment. I ran the Work from my bed, delegating responsibilities to the others, who humbly, willingly carried on as required.

Diane, Kenny and Adam were a precious, little flock who understood my plight. They'd been through it themselves and were still experiencing bouts of odd illnesses from time to time.

Soon after Andrew left, Diane, a new disciple herself, won a young Australian girl to the fold. "Winning a disciple" was the crowning achievement of the Work. The bonus and proof the Work was alive and worth following. It was like catching a piece of ripe fruit as it fell off the tree of life—finding souls who had searched for purpose in their lives and then providing them with a real, albeit sacrificial, means to fill that void and live that life.

Linda, the new disciple, was a bold girl in her early twenties. Back in Australia, she, like many in the group, was a misfit. Discontented with the status quo, she spent months at a time living alone in her own tent along beaches throughout Australia—searching for fulfillment. Not finding it, she set out on a world-traveling tour that led her here. Finally, at the end of February 1975, fellow Aussie, Diane, struck just the right chord in Linda's life one winter's night in the lobby of a Kabul "hippie" hotel. The girl ceased her searching and wanderings and joined up with us then and there. On February 28 she asked, "Can I move in and start my two-week trial period?"

"Yes, we'd love to have you," I said. The two-week, trial period was a policy we had, to assure any newcomer liked us, and vice versa.

She was petite and attractive with long, usually braided, sun-bleached blondish hair nearly to her waist, and she had a perfect body—sculpted from all the walking, trekking, surfing and exercising she'd always done. A natural, outdoors-type girl—fit, strong and lean—with long skirts, trekker boots and a snow-tanned face. Truly, she could easily have passed as a Nepalese Sherpa girl.

A welcome and much needed addition to the family, Linda was a testimony to travelers since she had already taken to the extreme what many of them set out to do in "finding themselves and inner peace." She had lived alone in a tent back in Australia on *her* quest to find herself. Diane brightened up too, having another sister move in.

Lebanese Adam stayed busy with the many French-speaking travelers, concentrating particularly on some of the beautiful French girls around. One such girl in particular, Geneve, visited the home often and sometimes spent the night. She quite nearly joined us. How Adam kept it all spiritual and his hands off *her* was a miracle. She could have graced the cover of a glamour magazine, but like many travelers, had become stranded in Kabul with no money. *Such a beauty, out here alone with no money.*

It's not that she and other travelers lost or wasted their money. No. Instead of carrying too much cash with them, travelers would send a telegram or message back home for funds to be wired to a certain bank at their next major destination, say Kabul. Problem was, it was said these tricky third-world countries would receive the wired-in funds and . . . use them, especially U.S. dollars. They'd loan it out and collect interest on it for a while—a week, two weeks . . . then finally say to the beneficiary, "Your money is here."

Fortunately, once a person checked into a hotel, anyone stranded could pretty much stay there day-to-day until their money arrived because the hotel held their passports. This was common policy among hotels anywhere out here. As soon as guests checked in, the management took their passports and put them in a safe. That way guests couldn't leave without paying their bills. People were *nothing* in a foreign country without a passport, nor could they leave that country without one. Friends and respective embassies assisted stranded travelers with cash for food and other needs.

As for French beauty Geneve, her money never seemed to arrive, and she never did join up with us. Somehow, she was able to remain at a nearby hotel. She was a "sheep" and absorbed the spiritual food we offered, but I wondered if she had other needs we never helped her with. Romantic needs. But here in 1975, we concentrated more on people's *souls* than on anything else.

In whatever manner Geneve worked out her own lodging and needs, she continued to visit us, as did five, ten or more visitors nearly every day. The house must have been like a base of stability for these far-flung youths, somewhat like a loving parent's home—organized, with warmth, coziness, good home-cooked meals and love. But it grew increasingly difficult for the five of us to properly minister to so many wandering souls, especially because, usually, at least *one* of us was taken ill with some weird Kabul headache or stomach ailment. I asked Tehran for more personnel.

Now not just anyone qualified for the Kabul post. It required people who could relate with the sort of hippie travelers, and at the same time didn't mind roughing it out here in Afghanistan's remoteness. It meant communicating with and being a role model to people, as opposed to passing out literature to them all day long. All this made the Kabul Work a sought-after one—especially by people tired of litnessing and ready instead to concentrate on *talking* with people one-on-one.

The first laborers sent were the humble and precious married couple, Ray and Judy, the same Ray and Judy I knew back in Istanbul. The two had married somewhere along the way and, after visiting their folks back in the U.S., had flown all the way here to Kabul. But they arrived with almost zero money. Not a problem with me, but a *big* problem with the Kabul government. After all, the Afghan government had laws and visa stipulations.

It just didn't make sense that an educated, newlywed couple could fly all the way to Afghanistan, have almost no money on them and expect to walk right into the country. When they went through the normal customs/visa/entry ordeal at the airport, authorities asked them, "How much money do you have?"

Ray told them the truth. "Fifty dollars."

Apparently the two of them were under the impression that since they could afford an airplane ticket, the Afghans would welcome them into the country.

Well, not only did the customs/visa guys refuse to grant them visas, but they also stamped *exit* visas in their passports which meant Ray and Judy had about three days to leave the country. The two were then transferred to a crude police station where Ray phoned me.

"Wayne! This is Ray. Judy and I just arrived on a flight from the States. But they're holding us at the police station. They won't give us entry visas 'cause we don't have any money."

"I'll be right there," I said.

Still new at my role as head of the Work, and wanting to be the dedicated, ready-to-die-for-the-troops, sacrificial leader, I dropped everything and went to their "rescue."

Once there, like long-lost friends, the three of us hugged one another in front of the police.

"Andy! It's good to see you," I said. I then turned to serious and scared Judy. "Judy! God bless you! What's going on?"

"It's like I said on the phone," Ray replied. "When they asked us how much money we had, like an idiot, I told them the truth, fifty dollars. Now they won't let us go."

I then took on the role of "savior" to my friends, even speaking some Farsi to the police in an effort to intercede for the two. But by the time I arrived on the scene, Ray and Judy and their "persona non grata" status had fallen into the jurisdiction of lower-ranking officials who had, no doubt, been instructed by the original, higher-up-and-now-off-work authorities to, "Not let those people out of your sight until it's decided what to do with them."

The Afghan police were clearly upset and didn't buy my attempts to take these two broke Americans under my care and "ride off with them into the sunset." In fact, my unwise dive into the middle of this "house arrest" irritated these underling authorities. Looking at me, one of them said, "Who the hell are *you*?" In their nervousness, they ended up arresting *me* along with the two. *What a scene.*

Near the end of the day, I called my U.S. consular friend, Bruce Beardsley. He came with *genuine* authority and convinced the police to release *me* from the ridiculous situation.

I learned a quick lesson that day. How stupid it was to walk into a trap and get "captured"—especially as the "General" responsible for the rest of the troops. But I remained with my friends until the cops decided where to put them for the night. Fortunately, they weren't jailed. Instead, it was decided they could stay at a hotel. With their passports seized, and a pitiable soldier assigned to them, Ray and Judy were escorted like prisoners to the Mustafa Hotel where I checked them into a good room. The pitiable soldier then stood guard with a rifle outside their door.

At 8:30 the next morning, Consul Beardsley called. "Wayne. I'm real sorry but I can't help Ray and Judy. Once they've had exit visas stamped into their passports, there's nothing I can do."

So the two caught a bus eastward two days later to Peshawar, Pakistan—the closest destination for a visa renewal—and returned to Kabul for ten days with some kind of visitor's visa, before heading back to Tehran and out of Afghanistan for good. Two humble people, well chosen and much needed for the Work here. A shame they weren't better briefed about Afghan visas.

Visas. They can be a constant cloud over a visiting foreigner, especially when the visitor overstays that visa. As for Afghanistan, most people could easily enough obtain a one-month visa and pass through the country. But if someone wished to stay a while longer, there were certain tricks they could use.

I called the tricks "The three Cs"—cash, clothes, camera. "Do you have money?" is the first question authorities might ask. It is wise, therefore, to have plenty of it to flash around, preferably in the form of personal travelers cheques, but if not, cash. As anywhere, money talks, and Afghan officials could and often would ask to actually *see* the money. Afghanistan was poor enough without having foreigners with no money bumming around.

We weren't bumming off the land but never had much money either. So, before venturing to the visa station, we borrowed cash from a friend for the day, at least 11,000 Afghanis ($200). We stuffed it right in our pockets, in case an officer asked us to prove we weren't complete bums.

As broke as we were though, no one would know it, seeing us walk in for a visa extension, because of the second trick: clothes. A lot depended upon how we dressed. Even with no money to our name, we could make a good first impression by *looking* neat and dressing sharply. No coat and tie, but something nice. What Samuel wrote in the Old Testament a few thousand years ago remains true today: "For man looketh on the outward appearance, but the Lord looketh on the heart" (1 Samuel 16.7). The "bum effect" again. Why should a host country grant a visa extension to bums, or bummy-*looking* people, if it didn't have to? Unless the bums had plenty of money—money to spend on the country. Buy its products. Drop some good hard cash into the economy while here.

If we felt we had to further impress authorities that we were risk-free for a visa extension, we might use the third trick: a camera. Sling an expensive camera nonchalantly around the neck. Borrow one if necessary. Not only did it make us look like we had some money, but also like we were actual, money-spending, picture-taking tourists. Even out here, nothing succeeds like success. The "camera effect" is not to say the Afghans are ignorant because they're not, *or* that they rarely see cameras. There were innumerable, excellent, 35mm Russian-made SLR cameras for sale throughout Kabul at the average reasonable price of about 1500 Afs ($27). It was simply added assurance—along with the cash and clothes—to dispel any notion that we might be a drag on their system.

I received a one-month extension after my first month, and another one-month extension after that. Of course, besides the above tricks, I had "recommendation letters" from the U.S. embassy. But once extensions were exhausted, we then, like in other countries, had to leave across the border, obtain a new visa outside the country and re-enter.

Chapter 19
⟶ *The Amazing Afghans* ⟵

I DOUBT A Westerner, after a stint in Afghanistan, could continue life without a constant recall of vivid details about this strange land and its people. Just the name "Afghanistan" paints a picture in *my* mind of the far-off, almost imaginary land that it is.

It is unique and untouchable, as history has proven. Unique because its people and past rulers desired to be unique. Untouchable because it's so rugged—and hell to live in—for anyone who doesn't have ownership rights here, like its citizens. Who else could have that driving ambition to survive off such sparsely arable patches of soil through year after year of severe weather? Only the nationals themselves who love their land and have determined to make the best of it. They are mountain people, tough and steadfast like their mountains, unconquered and independent.

Just the Afghans walking in the streets were impressive—robust, Caucasoid mixes of every surrounding territory's army of invaders and would-be conquerors. Then, to see them work, endure the cold and even eat was a phenomenon.

In the middle of winter, with snow and ice covering the streets, I looked down at the Afghans' feet—even of young children—and saw many of them actually had no socks on, no problem, just some kind of slip-on shoes. Apparently they had acclimated themselves to the severe weather from infancy. I doubt the word "pamper" is in their vocabulary.

I had to stop in order to believe my own eyes, as I observed men and even boys, as though they were oxen, pulling wooden carts piled with steel. Walking down the middle of the streets, they wouldn't be wearing steel-toed, leather work boots either. No. They'd be clad in sandals, slip-on shoes or possibly a crummy, $1.50 pair of *plastic* shoes—with or without socks. And like the nomads, there were no overweight Afghans anywhere.

What the heck did they eat? It seemed like practically nothing. Really. Nothing but bread and tea, all day long. They *must* have had more, but in my observation day after day, it appeared their staple diet was indeed bread and tea. It might warrant a study on whether or not the whole-grain flat bread (*naan*) was able to provide them with enough essential nutrients to enable them to work like horses. It would certainly show the fairness of God, that in this harsh land, the grains here could produce kernels so exceptional as to be an entirely substantial food source in themselves.

Afghans pulling steel

This normal, flat Afghani bread, baked fresh in clay ovens, was delicious, but eating its raw wholesomeness day after day became intense for us. That's when we would walk across town and buy, when available, a loaf of *white* Afghani bread. We had to endure the crowds fighting for it outside a portable, blue, wooden shack where it was sold, but eating it was a luxury after the whole wheat stuff. Like eating healthy cake.

A significant crop grown in Afghanistan besides wheat was grapes. Surprisingly, wine was officially produced, bottled and sold in stores here. In fact, if drinking alcohol wasn't so religiously frowned upon in the country, it's believed Afghanistan might well produce some of the finest wines in the world. Apparently the climate, terrain and soil in certain parts of the country proved ideal for growing various types and strains of grapes, tons of which were farmed and exported yearly.

The Afghans ate meat—often in the form of succulent lamb kebabs cooked over charcoal grills—but it may have been a bit costly for the ordinary person to indulge in regularly. Instead, a lot of Afghani dishes were appetizing vegetarian piles of steamed rice at incomprehensibly cheap prices. I remember frequenting certain working-class restaurants in Kabul where three of us would fill ourselves each with a pile of rice interlaced with slivers of cooked carrots, raisins and almonds, with bread on the side and tea for . . . *one* U.S. dollar (56 Afghanis)—the total bill for three hungry adults. Thirty-three cents each!

Sometimes we ate at the hippie/traveler/tourist restaurants, with names like The Steak House, Alice's Restaurant, Cable Hogue and The Mercedes Café. Here, for a little over twice the price, we could sit down to huge, U.S.-restaurant-like, full-course meals of meat (liver, beef, lamb, camel neck) or fresh river trout, potatoes with gravy, vegetables, bread and dessert—for about 70 cents U.S. per person.

The ambience of these tourist restaurants bustling with jubilant travelers, was a world apart from the drab, more serious atmosphere of the Afghan restaurants. On Chicken Street easygoing travelers splurged on cheap food, cheap drugs, cheap wares. After filling themselves on a plateful of well-prepared food, followed by an exotic dessert and tea or coffee—served by a humble Afghan waiter—many then retired to the "smoking lounge" of some tourist hotel. There they sat at low-slung tables on cushiony pillows, where they passed smoldering pipes of potent, inexpensive Afghani hashish well into the night, smoking themselves to oblivion, until they could no longer raise their arms to pass the pipe. Besides the plenteous food, Kabul was hash paradise. It wasn't uncommon to enter one of these lounges after everyone was gone, or the next day, and see a chunk of hash—two grams or more maybe—just sitting next to an ashtray, left behind. A chunk worth an easy 20 or 30 bucks back in the States.

A whole Afghan society existed, though, outside the Chicken Street scene, struggling to function normally despite ever-present political uncertainties. Not all Afghans were poor. By the looks of numerous impressive villas on the outskirts of Kabul, plenty of Afghans had money.

Not many foreign travelers encountered life outside Chicken Street. Most just passed through the country. Although it was against the law for an Afghan to invite foreigners into their homes and associate with them, some wealthy, open-minded Afghans disregarded this.

One such family hired me to teach guitar to their 12-year-old son, on the boy's electric guitar, for an hour once a week, at 200 Afghanis (about $4) per lesson—decent money in this land. The boy's attractive mother would pick me up at our house in her black Mercedes and drive me to their plush home outside the city with a swimming pool in the back yard. After a lesson, I would converse over tea and cake with her and her husband—in English of course—on the couple's frustrations with the country. "We've never trusted our government very much," the husband said. "It's so unstable." They were so intelligent and hospitable, but I sensed paranoia creeping in on them about having me, a Westerner, in their home. Besides, my ability to teach the guitar was limited, so the lessons lasted only a month.

Something else, strangely enough, existed in Kabul—a discotheque. *Yep.* It was the 70s, and third-world countries called for them. So Kabul had to have one. The only one in town, it was like any other disco—a loud, smoky, "meat market" of jet-setters. One of the girls and I were invited as guests on two occasions by the lead guitarist of the Afghan rock group commissioned to play there. The group was decent and the discotheque not bad at all, as far as discos go, catering to foreign diplomats, embassy personnel, other expatriates and westernized Afghans.

Regardless of the Mercedes-Benzes, the villas, swimming pools and discos, Afghanistan was still Afghanistan. For instance, it was not uncommon to see sheep, goats and horses grazing in open grassy fields in the middle of plush neighborhoods.

As for *horses*, the name "Afghanistan" is said to have come from the word "avghan," meaning horseman or cavalier. Another sight that impressed me while walking through Kabul was the sudden appearance of an Afghan horseman, or two or three, galloping up to me, perched atop stout, little Afghan horses.

Except for leather riding boots, the horsemen dressed normally, yet smartly, in typical Afghani attire, while adornment of their steeds was given obvious precedence with colorful, hand-woven woolen tassels dangling from the leather saddle and bridle. Both horse and rider harmonized, blending into the spirit of this land. They could not have looked more regal, yet these guys were not trying in the least to be showy. They and their horses were simply majestic, coming klip-klop, klip-klop out of nowhere, then vanishing, klippity-klop, klippity-klop away.

Then there were the Afghan *girls*. Just strolling the streets, usually outside the tourist areas, I couldn't help but notice them. They walked in packs and were trim and beautiful—a healthy mixture of Greeks, Turks, Persians, Russians, Chinese and Indians. *Goodness.*

Their mothers may have been veiled or covered with burqas from head to toe, but these young things were dressed to *attract*, much like the Iranian girls, wearing fashionable attire and tight, creased jeans. It was the jet age after all, and there were plenty of current fashion magazines to emulate, even in Kabul. So, like other girls worldwide in their late teens, early twenties, they were "hunting." It was nature.

They were too uniquely beautiful not to record on film, so I took my camera, and with some risk, snapped photos of them throughout Kabul. Oh, they were sexy, no doubt about it, and because they knew a Westerner would never touch or trouble them, they smiled boldly, with sparkling eyes, right into the camera. A real ray of light out here, like friendly women in any country.

Diplomats, foreign businessmen and professionals from all over the world intermingled throughout the wealthy suburbs of Kabul. And one thing that bonded them together—the Christians anyway— was their faith and respective places of worship. The Germans had a large congregation, whose pastor, the precious Mr. Karwehl, was a dear friend of ours who frequently assisted us with donations of cash money.

The Italians held a well-attended Catholic mass in a chapel right next to the Italian embassy. Their priest, Father Panagati, was also a close friend. He, in conjunction with the Italian embassy, compensated us regularly for our assistance to Italian nationals in Kabul.

Father Panagati had lived in Kabul quite awhile and was entirely hip to life here, often sharing with me much insight about this strange land. He asked me one day, "Wayne. Did you notice how nice the roads and highways are here in Afghanistan?"

"Yes, come to think of it," I responded. "I guess they are."

"Well," the Father said, "they were all made by the Russians at just the right widths and strengths to fit their tanks, in case they ever need them."

He went on to say that despite its fierce struggle for independence, Afghanistan was leaning more and more toward the communism of the Russians—like so many poor countries have in the past—that it was only a matter of time before the country fell that way.

Every Friday night, Father Panagati presided over a Catholic-like folk mass held at different homes of a small group consisting of American Peace Corps workers, embassy people and various professionals.

We were included as part of this group since those holding and participating in the mass respected our Bible-based work with the world travelers. I attended the gathering nearly every week, along with one or two from the house. It was a good break, mingling with "established" people of the community, but more than anything, it was a *luxury* since it also included an enjoyable potluck dinner and usually good Afghani wine. The four to eight couples attending would each contribute a plate of food for the meal—everyone except us! It was understood among the folk mass members that we were generally a poor lot, living day-to-day, sacrificially assisting young travelers in need, and therefore we weren't really expected to bring a dish to the gathering. Or *were* we? Looking back, I realized it was a real oversight, a real negligence on my part, to *never*, during my time in Kabul, make, bake, buy or contribute one plate of food to the gathering. It must have irritated others at the mass. I mean, Diane and Linda used to make some good homemade yogurt at the home—even during the winter, in the warmth of the sun—which could have been brought. Something. Anything. The widow's mite, for God's sake!

Now the largest and probably the last church to be built in Kabul was the aptly named Community Christian Church. Understandably ecumenical, it served the diverse community of believers from Russia, Europe, Armenia, America or wherever. We were friends with the pastor, Mr. Griffin, who also donated money to us.

The Community Church building itself looked like a lot of churches in the world except for one thing—it had no steeple. The Afghans, without warning, bulldozed it right down to the ground as soon as it was built. Why? Why not? The steeple was built to stick so high into the sky that anyone approaching Kabul's flat plateau, from any direction, could see it.

The Christians were fortunate to rebuild and keep the church but without the steeple. The incident lived on and was considered by some as a test of their faith . . . or even, persecution for righteousness' sake?

But the bulldozing was really a physical manifestation of the Afghan outlook toward outsiders—"Don't mess with us, and we won't mess with you. Don't try to change us. Keep to yourselves or get out."

Chapter 20
∽ *Easy to Get Sick* ∽

WHEN THE SNOW and ice finally melted from the streets of Kabul in April and May, the city was transformed from an enchanted winter-wonderland to a delightful, cool and sunny springtime haven. This new, pleasant climate in the city, with snow-capped mountains in the distance, lured travelers from countries like India and Pakistan whose weather was becoming increasingly hot and uncomfortable. Kabul had a history of allurement. As Mary Louise Clifford wrote in her book, *The Land and People of Afghanistan*:

> All lands from India traded in Kabul, finding every kind of fruit and nuts. The city was loved as far back as 1504 by its then ruler Zahir-ud-Din Muhammed Babur for its climate and scenery.

Somewhere, out of the harsh landscape of Afghanistan here in spring, a variety of superb fruits and vegetables appeared. On several Chicken Street corners, street vendors popped up with the latest in electric juicers. *Yep*, the Afghans knew how to "make a buck" off the tourist/travelers, especially those conscious of healthy natural foods. Someone had raised enough capital to invest in these brand-new fruit and vegetable juicers and to sell carrot juice at some ridiculously cheap Afghan price—bunches of fresh, peeled carrots stuffed into this machine to bring forth a glassful of pure carrot juice, so fresh it gave me a health rush when I drank it.

Fresh water flowed into Afghanistan's valleys from the melting snow of so many mountains—enough water to irrigate as much land and crops as humanly possible. During summer, we sometimes escaped just outside the city to refreshing lakes or rivers for a picnic or swim.

So many travelers began streaming into Kabul it became expedient for us to create an information leaflet for them. So we filled the back and front of a small piece of paper with visa information, drug-smuggling warnings, laws of the land—like it being illegal to wear shorts in public for girls *or* guys—locations and prices of recommended hotels and restaurants, and most importantly, food and water warnings. We made up a name for our house—"The Travelers' Open Door" (the TOD House)—and produced a map to it along with the sheet in case anyone needed to come by for firsthand help. We handed out the papers and distributed them in hotels. The U.S. embassy, along with German preacher, Mr. Karwehl, liked the leaflet and map enough to print and mimeograph them for us for free.

After all, despite Kabul's beckoning of cheap rates and wares, delightful climate and serenity, it was *not* heaven on earth. It was too easy to get and remain sick here for an extended time. People traveled around India and notoriously unsanitary Nepal and never became sick . . . until they came to Kabul. Kabul's idyllic, high-altitude setting amidst mountains topped with fresh, heavenly snow gave a false sense of purity and cleanliness. Thus, the information sheet.

Kabul is where I learned the *value* of medicine, particularly antibiotics. In a land like this they could save the mortal flesh from destruction.

I quickly learned which medicines worked for which ailments— mainly stomach problems since it was difficult to avoid them and still eat here. Some of the medicines described on our paper were Lomotil, an anti-diarrheal to stop the runs; Mexaform; EnteroViaform; tetracyline—excellent, all-around antibiotics capable of killing microscopic demons and putting a person back on the path with the living—and on up to more potent drugs to kill amoebas, which none of the aforementioned medicines was capable of doing. Anyone could purchase these medicines over the counter from pharmacies here with no prescription, no $25 doctor's visit as required in the States.

I knew Kabul stomach ailments firsthand. I had the runs and horrible stomach problems nearly the whole time I lived here, even though I had tried many of the above medicines. Finally, after noticing blood in my stools one day, I was referred to a German woman doctor who immediately diagnosed me with amoebic dysentery. She prescribed a miracle drug for me whose name (because of its effectiveness) I would never forget: Milibis, an intestinal amoebicide. It contained about 3% arsenic, which, by this time I was glad to ingest. Anything to kill these goddamned microscopic invaders inside me. I could actually *feel* the arsenic poisoning me when I took the medicine, but what the heck. The doctor also instructed me to take vitamin B-complex tablets along with the Milibis.

After taking an eight-day course of the Milibis, I had the first formed stool I'd had in probably four months! As I say to this day, "You can never appreciate hard shit until you don't have it for days, weeks or months straight." And to think my suffering and dragging could have been eradicated with a ten-minute doctor visit and one eight-day prescription of medicine. How much more could I have accomplished, if I'd been in good health the whole time? I was too unaccustomed to taking any sort of medicine, even aspirin, before coming here to the East. "Why suffer?" I now say. "Enjoy life. Take drugs (medicine)."

Now, where did I get the amoebas? I was too cautious, along with the others, to get them from the water. We *always* boiled it sufficiently. Besides, no one else in the house got it. Then I remembered buying and eating, back in the beginning of March, a small bag of sweet Afghan mulberries, which I bought off the open cart of a street vendor. It was soon after I took over the Work (became the "CEO") and had a little extra money. I ate them all myself. I justified it. I was the head and deserved "a little more" than the others.

Consuming mulberries from an Afghan street vendor was something I did before I'd been educated and warned about airborne food contaminants. The luscious, cheap fruits and vegetables abounding in the markets here were just too tempting for someone who hadn't been sufficiently warned: "If you can't peel it, don't eat it." Even then, if I hadn't become ghastly ill, I might have forgotten the warning.

We took our information sheet seriously. We didn't wish ailments *we* had suffered upon anyone else. We had all dealt with various Kabul illnesses in our months here and knew how unsanitary this town could be.

For instance, how can heads of lettuce stay crisp and appealing? Splash or soak them in water, right? Well, if I hadn't seen it with my own eyes one spring day, almost directly in front of the presidential palace, I may not have believed it. A guy selling heads of lettuce from his wooden cart was fishing them out of a canal-like ditch of water he'd thrown them into to get them crisp, and was putting them back on his cart, to take them downtown for sale. Tossed salad anyone?

We became virtual doctors and nurses to sick travelers in Kabul. Besides public health education on the leaflets, we went directly to hotel rooms, bringing food, vitamins and medicine to those too ill to get out of bed. Word traveled quickly that the "TOD House" was a reliable source of assistance to stranded, ill or needy travelers, free of charge.

A German guy traveling through Afghanistan in a large, recreational vehicle, who'd learned of the TOD House through the German embassy, had an oversupply of gamma globulin—a fairly new drug that increased the body's immunity against diseases such as hepatitis and tetanus—and was anxious to donate it to the right source. The German consular introduced him to me. Recalling the misery of *my* hepatitis, I readily accepted the medicine, even though it was in liquid form for injection only.

Sure enough, two travelers—a Swedish guy and an American girl, both exposed to friends with hepatitis and about to travel on—had soon learned of the free gamma globulin and were directed to the TOD House. They were in need of as much boost and prevention against the disease as possible. I immediately handed vials of the medicine to the two, who went to an Afghan clinic to have it administered to them.

The clinic, unaware of the source of the medicine, declined to inject them with it. The two returned to the house, still desperately wanting the medicine, and asked my advice.

Realizing the benefits gamma globulin could have on disease-exposed bodies about to be subjected to overland journey, I offered to inject them with the medicine. Back in the States, before my conversion, I had learned how to use needles from a friend. He was close friends with an ophthalmologist who had given him an expensive glass syringe that sat in purple velvet inside its own wooden box. We dabbled in injecting ourselves with vitamin B-complex and other "medicines"—nothing habit forming, but we did get into the "thrill of the needle" for a while.

I led the two to the quaint, back office of the house. The room had become what looked like a small Afghan museum. Exotic, hand-woven Afghan carpets covered the floor, even overlapping one another, while neatly placed, hand-crafted brass and copper trays, swords and Afghan artwork lined the walls. It all belonged to a guy from Belgium I'd met a few days earlier. The guy, Doug, was in Kabul purchasing these Afghan wares and artifacts for export to Europe. He jumped at an arrangement to reside temporarily at our home and store his expensive purchases here—as opposed to some not-so-secure hotel room.

The instant, office "clinic" had a luxurious, entrancing appeal as we stepped a few inches down onto the plush thickness of the mostly burgundy and dark red carpets. Good thing, because our two patients needed as much comforting reassurance as possible, even if it *was* just ambience.

The German guy who donated the gamma globulin also supplied me with sealed, sterile, disposable syringes and needles. But the needles were thick, heavy-gauge suckers, and I—way out of practice anyway—was unable to find a vein in the poor Swedish guy's arm. So I injected the medicine into his triceps muscle instead.

"Whoa!" the girl said, as she observed me jabbing around with the big needle. "I think I'll take mine in the butt, if you don't mind." She wasn't about to try the vein entrance.

"Sure," I said, understanding. She was beautiful, of course—a typically robust American girl in her early twenties.

At the desk in the room, I prepared her dose with a new syringe and needle from their packages. I came around behind her and she nonchalantly pulled down the right side of her cotton, ankle-length skirt from over her perfect butt, revealing burgundy bikini panties underneath.

"I guess bend over and lean on the desk," I told her.

She bent over leaning on her elbows on the desk, after reaching back with her right hand to pull down the right side of her panties, so as to expose her right cheek. I then, as professionally as possible, injected her butt with the preventive medicine. "Okay," I said, and she pulled her panties and skirt back up.

"Thanks so much!" they both kept saying. "We really appreciate it."

The girl hung around the house the rest of the afternoon. She might have been curious as to what we were all about. But—being American—she was probably waiting around to make sure no weird reaction resulted from the injection.

Meanwhile, with all the work and travelers in need, the house was often down to as few as three people carrying the load. Then, early in the morning of March 27, Kenny and I awoke to find that Lebanese Adam had vanished, leaving behind only a heartfelt note of goodbye to us all. In the note he mentioned he needed to go see his parents in Lebanon.

"We have to find him!" I said. So, Diane, Kenny and I immediately went out to locate him, console him, at least hug him one more time. We went from hotel to hotel, restaurant to restaurant. But we never saw him again.

Three days later, on March 30, Diane hooked up with Ray and Judy and departed with them to Tehran. It was hard to see Diane leave. Such a far-out woman, such a blessing, always smiling. But she'd been in Kabul long enough and was thrilled to move on.

Then, at the end of April, Linda sat down with me and expressed her desire to leave the group. "Wayne. I don't know how to say this really. But I want to leave," she said, hardly looking me in the eyes. "I just want to pursue my artwork. Is that okay?"

"Of course it is. It's up to you if you want to stay or leave," I said. "You miss Diane a lot I'll bet, don't you?"

"Yes. But that's not why, really. I've been thinking about it for a while," she said, still looking down. She parted congenially on April 26 at 5 p.m. Another great girl. We saw her two days later and she gave us 30 British pounds (£30)—well over one month's rent—from money she'd just received from Australia. I walked around town with her the next afternoon before she treated the now three of us in Kabul to a full dinner at the Steak House off Chicken Street. God *bless* her.

Fortunately, Joshua—the two-meter-tall American guy—had arrived from Tehran to be a part of the Kabul team. Back in Tehran he'd been hounded and threatened by so many Iranian secret police for his relentless distribution of literature, he barely escaped arrest and deportation from Iran. He was ready anyway to turn in his stacks of literature in favor of a more personal approach to reaching souls.

Another guy, Max, arrived May 3. British, with dark hair and dark eyes, he could have passed for a Middle Easterner. He'd also been in Tehran awhile. He was a jovial person who adapted well to any situation and was thrilled to be in Kabul among flipped-out hippie types like himself.

Groups of two or three passing through Kabul on their way to or from India, would also help out with the Work for a week or two before traveling on.

Chapter 21
∽ *Peshawar, Pakistan* ∽

By May 8, 1975, I had been in Afghanistan for three months, having acquired two extra months out of the original, one-month visitor visa. But now I had to make the visa trip to Peshawar, Pakistan—the closest place to Kabul for a new, one-month visa. Although these visa trips were like a mini-vacation, the best thing about going to Pakistan was *returning* to Kabul.

Fortunately for me, my dear friend, the German preacher Martin Karwehl, had business in Peshawar at precisely the time I needed to be there. I wasn't sure he wanted me to tag along with him and his brunette wife, the lovely Brigitte, but when I called him he said, "Yes! You come with us!"

Martin picked me up promptly in his VW minibus at 7:30 in the morning May 7, and the three of us headed east out of Kabul. We followed the Kabul River, now raging with the melted snows of winter.

"Have you ever been on this road before, Wayne?" Brigitte asked me.

"No. This is my first time."

"Oh! The scenery is beautiful! We'll be going through the Kabul Gorge," she said. "It's scary, but beautiful."

Peering down from the road, I saw in the distance, established along the banks of the river, picturesque scenes of Afghan mud villages nestled in lush green crops, tall columnar trees lining the roads. The Afghans, hard workers as they were, loved their land and had tapped the natural, freshwater resources, converting the otherwise barren, mountain landscape into these verdant oases.

In any other country, such a scene of greenery might not have been so remarkable. But these green oases contrasted so vividly against the harsh, rocky background I couldn't help but revere them.

We reached the border station at 1 p.m., and apparently Karwehl had passed through here so often he knew nearly all the officers and workers present. "*Salaam, salaam,*" he said to many, shaking their hands. Besides being such a cool and friendly guy, he had probably pressed several Afghanis into these guys' palms on previous trips in order to process him through with no hassles. We sailed through in less than an hour—record time, considering we had a vehicle that the Afghans didn't know if we stole or not.

From the border station, we descended into the mysterious . . . Khyber Pass—an awesome stretch of road zigzagging through menacing cliffs that separated Afghanistan and Pakistan. We stopped for photos, and it amazed me to reflect on the history of this place through which conquering armies and famous people had passed. I didn't have to be a history scholar to know it. The Pass just echoed it. Except for some caravan tracks and a road from Kandahar in the South that led to Quetta in Pakistan, the Khyber Pass was really the only significant road that connected Afghanistan to Pakistan and places east. Therefore, on this day—like most days—the Pass was busy with camel caravans, trucks, buses and cars making the precarious few miles of two-lane road.

Khyber Pass

But there was another astonishing phenomenon to me that day: the American-made, 1953-or-so-model, antique Chevrolet cars making the journey. If I hadn't seen them myself, I might not have believed each car was hauling approximately 20 fee-paying locals—crammed inside, hanging out the windows, standing on the bumpers and piled on its roof, trunk and hood—up and down, back and forth through the Pass. Fantastic! A real testament to Chevrolets. It could have made a great advertisement for General Motors.

Once through the Pass, Peshawar was only about 25 miles farther. About five times lower in altitude than Kabul, the city sat in a lush, almost-tropical river basin.

At 2:30 in the afternoon, we pulled up to the plush villa of the Karwehls' wealthy friends on the outskirts of Peshawar. We all had tea together. Then Karwehl, having business elsewhere in Pakistan, dropped me at the recommended Greens Hotel in town.

"I am sorry. We are full," the guy behind the wooden reception counter said.

A young kid standing next to me beckoned. "Not to worry. Follow me." The kid then led me to the nearby Taj Hotel where, for eight rupies ($1.06) a night, I rented a private room with not-necessarily-clean sheets and a shared bathroom down the hall.

Back in Kabul, Kenny and others who'd already made this Peshawar visa jaunt, had given me advice. "You'll stay at the Greens Hotel, or near it," they said. "Be wary of the food; don't drink the water; eat at the Jans Hotel." The decent Jans, just up the street, had a dining room of white-cloth-covered tables where I ate dinner that night at the fairly high price of six and a half rupees.

Not intending to remain in Pakistan any longer than to secure a visa, I was at the Afghan embassy by 9:30 the following morning after coffee and toast at the Jans Hotel. I applied with photos and a form. "Your visa will be ready in the afternoon," the clerk told me.

I then hired a horse and carriage—driven by a guy named Babba—to show me around Peshawar until my visa was ready.

But the next business was to make sure I could get *out* of this country on time, so Babba took me to the bus station where I purchased a one-way ticket to Kabul for the following day at 23 rupees. A ticket in hand was priority—before I ran out of money or before all seats were sold.

I was also on a mission to purchase a pair of *Peshawri chepalis*—special leather sandals—for Hadji, the Afghan proprietor of the Friends Hotel in Kabul. It seemed every Afghan and Pakistani guy wore these sandals or an imitation of them. They were made of two large pieces of leather overlapping each other at the toes with a strap around the heel and were supposedly better made here in Peshawar. Of course Babba knew the best stores for such sandals—at the Old City bazaar—so he directed his horse there.

Oh Lord. This was a taste of hell, this bazaar. Up until now, the only delightful aspect of this city was the grass and shady trees on its main and side streets. All else was pretty much drab, broken-down buildings. The bazaar/marketplace was a scene of overwhelming confusion. In its streets, lined with every type of vendor, walked throngs of people in front of cars, trucks, horse carriages, donkey carts and bicycles. The drivers didn't care if they hit someone or not. Drivers here had the attitude: "It's *his* fault if he walks in front of me." It was a miracle more people weren't maimed or killed. Even the bicyclists were a menace, weaving full speed through the crowds with complete disregard for anyone. *Disgusting really.* Narrow misses everywhere. A total mess. No rhyme or reason for anything, including the backdrop of dust and dirt, ugly jumbled storefronts and crumbling buildings—all built on a whim with no standards or codes.

Peshawar market

Eastern *souks* (markets) are generally chaotic, but a certain miserable characteristic set this Pakistani market apart from any other souk—the *noise.* And it wasn't the bellowing of vendors hawking their wares either, which can be obnoxious, but bearable. No. Not even *they* could compete with the greasy, three-wheeled, two-cycle-engine-powered, falling-apart, rickshaw-like scooters puttering all over the city. A-*reen*-nee-nee-nee, a *reen*-nee-nee-nee, all day long, dominating the streets with their noise. Pakistanis used these vehicles as pick-up trucks and everything else, but a good many of them were taxis with a crummy, little, half-enclosed compartment mounted behind the driver, that could, with considerable cramming, hold three adults.

As if a person couldn't already hear these rattletraps coming, the drivers of these scooters kept their thumbs on the high-pitched, cheap-sounding buzzer/beepers mounted on the bicycle-like handlebars of the contraptions. In fact, the whole marketplace and town resounded with a constant, unabated honking of horns, buzzing of beepers and ringing of bicycle bells. Even the *horse* carriages used an unpleasant air horn to add to the cacophony.

The people seemed oblivious to the confusion, most of them knowing nothing different their whole lives anyway. They probably figured this was just part of the misery of life on earth.

Anyway, somewhere in the middle of the bazaar, I bought a pair of Peshawri chepalis for Hadji and a pair for myself at 55 rupees ($7.30) each. Babba then showed me around some gold stores, gem stores and other fairly interesting shops in this hubbub market. But none of the products appeared to have much quality, not even the carpets.

One phenomenon of handiwork stood out though: the repair of porcelain teapots—undoubtedly a vessel of priority in their lives. The Pakistanis felt their teapots "must live on," broken or not. They pieced broken ones back together, somehow with tiny wires. Not just spouts, but the whole teapot. It had to be some hidden technique and secret—an art—how they could restore these pots and continue brewing and serving steaming hot tea in them *without leaking*. But my goodness, couldn't they have just made another one? Was this country so poor they had to spend time wiring their teapots back together? These works of art amazed, but also troubled me. How could they allot so much time to broken teapots?

Babba and I finally left the bazaar and headed for the Peshawar Art Museum to wait in the shade until returning to the Afghanistan embassy where I was granted a new one-month visa.

Babba then dropped me at my hotel at about 12:30 p.m. "Fifteen rupees," he said. Actually, I thought he was ripping me off, considering a

155-mile bus trip all the way to Kabul was only 23 rupees. But, $2 for a three-hour horse-and-carriage tour of a town? Not bad.

After a shower, I shopped at some nearby bookstores and bought some quick gifts for those back in Kabul, just before all shops began closing for the afternoon—like the siesta time of the Mediterranean. It was at this time, about 1:30 p.m., when I about flipped. Inside some shops, with half-closed metal latticed gates, I saw shop owners firing up their hookahs—water pipe/hubbly bubblies. Openly smoking hashish, unhidden, was apparently normal and accepted here. Was it the same syndrome as in Afghanistan—the hash cushioning the harshness of life? Or, was regularly imbibing it partly to blame for not improving their lives?

Citizens smoking hash in public was only a big deal to Westerners like *me*. Here, it was an age-old custom. But it wasn't just hash they were enjoying. Inside the bowls of the pipes sat smoldering sweet tobacco. They sprinkled bits of hashish into the tobacco while special, glowing coals, strategically placed around the perfect mixture, kept it all alight. As the person inhaled, the smoke was somewhat cooled by the water below. And Western hippies thought *they* knew how to smoke dope.

I wandered across the street from these shops to the one beautiful area of this town—its main street mall of grass and shady trees, a short distance from my hotel. There, I sat down and drank a cold Coke—a somewhat expensive yet safe way to quench one's thirst in such countries. Business accomplished, I had the rest of the day to absorb this place.

Lying on the grass of the mall, on this pleasantly cool afternoon with some other Westerners, I met and talked with two French guys, Bernard and Jean-Paul.

Then came Beshir, a rickshaw taxi driver. It wasn't clear if he wanted to sell a taxi ride to me, practice his English or just be friendly, but I was genial to him nonetheless. I also quickly learned more about hashish smoking.

Here at siesta time, mid-afternoon, it was time for Beshir to toke up—right here in the middle of the mall. His method was strange to me. First, he pinched off a small piece of hash (the amount he intended to smoke) from a larger chunk of the stuff, put this small piece in the palm of one hand and closed his hand tightly around it. After awhile, body heat from his closed palm caused the resins holding the hashish together to loosen up. So, when he opened his hand, the original small piece of hash had crumbled into flakes.

He then took a normal filtered cigarette—a Winston—twisted a bit of tobacco out of it into the hash flakes and mixed it all together. Then he *re*-loaded the hash-laced tobacco back into the cigarette by putting the filtered end in his mouth and sucking up the mixture out of his palm into the cigarette, then twisted its end to keep it all in.

He lit it, toked on it and handed it to me. I kindly refused. Inhaling the tobacco alone would have wiped me out. And I wasn't about to stand out in the open, toking up on *dope* with some strange Pakistani taxi driver. No. I just enjoyed observing the guy's masterful technique of preparing his hash cigarette. *Damn though.* I now wondered how many of these guys I saw smoking everywhere had hash in their cigarettes. *Uh-oh. The two-cycle, three-wheeled scooters. Don't tell me those driving them are stoned.* Oh well, this is Pakistan, where two of the primary crops are opium and cannabis.

Nevertheless, the two French guys and I accepted Beshir's offer to drive us around the city. "For free. No money," Beshir said.

Sure.

But the two French guys said, "Okay. Cool." They may have figured, *This guy's stoned and wants to give us a free ride.*

So the three of us tortured ourselves by accepting this guy's offer to weave us through the unpalatable streets of the Old City in his loud taxi. Driving around in this rattletrap, I viewed what may have been the worst part of this place yet—scores, if not hundreds of Pakistani *guys* hanging around in the afternoon together, idle, dressed similarly in solid, drab-colored baggy pants and shirttails to their knees, all of them doing nothing, just hanging around talking and gawking. And not *one girl* in sight.

Girl? I might not have seen the whole face of any Pakistani woman here whatsoever, much less any other part of her. The few that were out at *all* were covered head-to-toe.

Enough of this place. I asked Beshir to drop us at some semblance of civilization—the Jans Hotel—for a safe-to-eat dinner. *Ah-h.* White tablecloths in an organized dining room. *Thank you, Lord.* But not before Beshir griped and moaned about getting paid for his "free" services. I gave him five rupees, with some disgust.

. . .

Perhaps there are better places in Pakistan than Peshawar, but this town certainly did not appeal to me. I could only describe Pakistan as the end of the world, into which all other countries drop off.

And I wasn't *out* of it yet. Out the window of the bus back to Kabul on the following day, I had to face, near the border, young kids—some looking 15 or 16 years old—brandishing large rifles. Who they were and why they were out there with guns didn't make any sense to me. Apparently they were from the village we were passing through. All I remember is looking through my window at the back of the bus, now stopped at the edge of this town, and there stood a kid, maybe 17 years old, in normal Pakistani clothes, staring at me with the meanest look on his face for no reason, while holding a large rifle across his chest. Turns out, areas like this one along the border between Afghanistan and Pakistan are ruled by seven independent tribes who are basically outside direct administration by any government because they maintain their independence by direct force of arms. *Great.*

Once past this no man's land of rifle-toting menaces, and after two hours at the border station, my jaunt to Pakistan was complete. I was back in "my land." The best thing about taking a visa trip to Pakistan— knowing I could return to Kabul.

As for the Peshawri chepalis, they ended up being the most uncomfortable shoes I had ever worn. Their stiff leather dug into my flesh and *never* became comfortable from breaking in. Then, after a few weeks of suffering with them, they broke. Can anything good come out of Pakistan? Probably only the drugs.

Chapter 22
∽ *Leaving Afghanistan* ∽

So MUCH FOR a vacation. There were countless travelers to assist in summertime Kabul. And no one forgot those in jail. Besides, the jail ministry was our bread and butter—something society could grasp as a reason for our existence—even if only a fraction of what we did.

Fortunately, few travelers ended up in the Kabul jail and, perhaps due to us persistently bothering jail officials with our regular visits, along with the relentless pursuit of embassies to have their citizens released, those busted were actually being set free. Claude, released on March 14, headed straight for the TOD House and nearly joined us but instead, on advice from his consul, returned home to Switzerland.

Before Claude's release, an Italian guy, Antonio, was jailed on March 2—not for drugs, surprisingly. No, this guy was as odd as the reason for his arrest. Living in the Mustafa Hotel with another guy, Antonio had suspected his roommate of stealing five dollars from him and started a brawl in the room, whereby the hotel's management summoned the police. Once in the room, the police discovered that Antonio had about ten thousand dollars on him that he had not declared when he entered Afghanistan, which was highly illegal. They arrested him and eventually put him in the cell with American Ryan. A month later in April he beat the heck out of poor Ryan, totally freaking him out. He was a brawny nutcase, Antonio.

Another young Italian guy was jailed on June 5 for smoking dope and sleeping in a public park. Also quite a character, this guy faked being deaf and dumb, hoping for sympathy from the Afghans—or to drive them nuts trying to deal with him. We discovered him by chance in the main holding cell of the jail, standing apart from any foreigners. We had to write notes back and forth to him because he never let up on his deaf act. Sure enough, with intervention by the Italian embassy, both he and crazy Antonio were freed on June 9, the "deaf" guy paying a fine of 500 Afs ($9) and Antonio forfeiting most of the $10,000 for his freedom!

Then a young Canadian girl was arrested June 20—caught at the airport with 350 grams of hashish. Her French-Canadian boyfriend, Laurent, unable to contact any embassy for help on a Friday, was led to the TOD House. The guy appeared at our door in hysterics. "My girlfriend! She's been caught at the airport with drugs. They took her to jail! What can I do?" He was in tears.

"Calm down. Calm down. Come in," I said. "We'll get to her. We'll go to the embassy tomorrow. They're closed today. She'll be okay. Sit down."

We really had to calm this guy down and assure him, he was *so* freaked out and worried about his girlfriend. *God bless him.*

Early the next morning, without further ado, I picked Laurent up at his hotel, and we were at the British embassy (Canada's represented embassy) by 8:45 a.m. There, we immediately met with the consul, Mr. McCulloch, who was entirely hip and helpful with the girl's plight, assuring Laurent everything possible would be done to free her. "What's her name? We'll do everything we can to get her out," McCulloch said.

Laurent and I then went to visit the girl at the Kabul Women's prison. There, a huge, thick, arch-shape wooden door opened to a dusty courtyard where she stood, while Afghan guards and women prisoners crudely held her by her arms, several feet away from us. It was bad enough to see the reaction of *guys* when they were put in such jails, but the fright in this girl's face broke our hearts. She wasn't just crying, she was shaking with fear—desperate and forlorn after only a night inside. She obviously hadn't bargained on being *caught* transporting hashish out of the country.

God only knows how the male officers ran this jail, but from the looks of the place and the expression on the Canadian girl's face, it was no convent. Laurent and I tried to comfort her in the few seconds we had together, until the huge wooden door shut on her, leaving her there alone, tears streaming down her white cheeks.

Meanwhile, American Ryan languished alone in his cell. But as we learned months later, Ryan was not exactly "alone." He had a "companion" so much a part of him, that despite his acting how tough it was within the cell, he hardly had the incentive to leave: unbeknownst to those visiting him, Ryan was junked out on heroin! *Yep.* With funds from family and friends back in the States, steadily distributed to him by the embassy and the TOD House, he kept himself supplied with the freshest, purest Afghan heroin and opium money could buy, readily available within Kabul's prison system. Like any other junkie, with such a steady pipeline to the stuff, not much else mattered.

I heard later that when Ryan finally did get out of jail, he joined our group in India—perhaps feeling indebted to us for our many loyal visits—but he *still* chased heroin, so had to leave.

Besides striving to release their citizens from prison, foreign embassies in Kabul were prudent in keeping problem ones out of jail in the first place. For such cases, the TOD House became most helpful. The two of us—embassies and TOD House—"scratched each other's backs." The embassies gave us money and political backing while we served as their hands and feet.

That's how we struck a rapport with the French embassy—by handling Jacques, a French orphan beyond their capability. This guy had been in and out of prison in Pakistan for vagrancy and other charges. Vagrancy? In Pakistan? Imagine. And now, here in Afghanistan, he was drifting into the same predicament. Kind of an embarrassment to the French embassy. Yet he was their responsibility. So, like other embassies here, they assisted him, provided for him and did just about all they could.

At just a short walk from the French embassy, our home was exactly what they needed to keep Jacques alive and out of jail. The French consul called me one day and arranged to have Jacques move in with us June 9, under French embassy sponsorship. They gave me money and asked that I dole it out to the guy daily, or as he needed it. Otherwise, as the embassy knew from experience, such people would squander a lump sum of money, mostly on drugs.

"We can't give him money and put him on a bus back to France, either," the consul said. "We are quite sure he would get off somewhere along the way and spend the money until it runs out. And flights out of Kabul are not only expensive," he added, "but there are no non-stop flights all the way to France. We are afraid he would get off at the first airport stop, spend all his money again and end up back in prison."

Jacques owed some kind of hotel bills or fines in Kabul, and sure enough, the day after he'd moved into the TOD House, Afghan police came looking for him to take him away. But Jacques and I both said, "No way. No can do. Not today!" While Jacques physically resisted the forces, I quickly phoned the French embassy. They immediately sent a consul to the house, who resolved the situation and aborted the arrest. The authority of an embassy!

We tried to help Jacques, even spiritually, but the guy was a tough case. No doubt abused by authorities of the many prisons he'd been in, he rebelled at any signs of rules at our house. We instructed him not to drink the water, but he didn't care. He drank it anyway, straight from the faucet. *Oh my God.* He got so pathetically sick with wrenching stomach pains, vomiting and diarrhea. Yet he continued to drink it. The guy was such an extreme case of self-neglect, he had almost become numb to hardship and pain.

The embassy regularly sent over a psychiatrist to check on the guy. Of course the psychiatrist soon discovered how Jacques treated his illnesses and pain when he ran across a box of packaged syringes Jacques kept for injecting himself with Valium and narcotics—substances readily available over the counter in Kabul. Jacques was also adept at warming hashish in his hand and loading it into cigarettes like the Pakistanis.

Pakistanis? Not two days after Jacques had moved into the house, a young British couple knocked on our outside door for help. I could tell they were not bums, but they looked distressed.

"We need help," the girl said, teary-eyed. "Can we come in?"

"Yes, come in," I said. They stepped into the courtyard, and I closed the wooden door behind them. "What's wrong?" I asked.

"We've just come from India, through Pakistan," the girl said, crying now. "We were sleeping in our tent outside of Rawalpindi and five Pakistani men came in and raped us. Both of us."

"They took all our money, too," the boyfriend added.

"Oh, man!" I said. "Let's go in and sit down." They were so young and precious, had survived it and now needed, basically, some tender loving care. "Do you want to stay with us for a while?"

"Sure. If you don't mind," the girl answered. Fortunately, dear and valuable Swedish Britta, who had accompanied me on the train from London to Istanbul nine months before, was temporarily in Kabul at this time, on her way to India. Between bouts of Kabul illnesses, Britta was her typical, bubbly well of spring water, tirelessly ministering to anyone coming through our door—like this young couple—or out in the streets to those who never found our place.

The couple moved in for three days until their money came in, wired from their parents. The girl nearly joined us.

As for Jacques, he actually began helping out—cooking, gardening and cleaning. Despite the rules and religious flavor in the house, he knew darn well it beat prison—he didn't need a psychiatrist to tell him that—so he cooperated pretty well, even though he still used Valium and anything else he could get his hands on.

In the midst of our workload, humor showed its oft-comforting face ... this time in the form of a Swiss guy named Vincent—a problem case of the Swiss embassy. The guy just sort of appeared one day.

It was Monday, June 16, and I had gone to the Swiss embassy, for funds. But the main thing on Consular Doerig's mind this day was Vincent. Doerig received word that Vincent might have "surfaced" in Kabul and so began explaining the lad's history to me. Twenty-one years old and from a wealthy family back in Bern, Switzerland, the guy had managed to swindle Swiss embassies in countries neighboring Afghanistan. He took them for hundreds of dollars—promising to pay them back, but only getting deeper into debt with them—barely escaping arrest by local authorities wherever he went. But now it was over for him. He had an outstanding Kabul hotel bill, his visa had expired, and he was again out of money. The embassy, now wise to him, waited for him to knock on their door.

After explaining all this, Mr. Doerig said, "Please, if you run across this guy Vincent, let us know."

"Did you say, Vincent?" I replied. "He's at our house even as we speak."

Vincent knew the embassy was on to him so had knocked instead on the TOD House door. When I returned from the embassy, there he was at our home, talking with Britta, who was faithfully ministering to him like any other soul in need.

"Hi! How's it going, Vincent?" I asked him.

"Fine," he said, already expecting something was up.

"I just came from the Swiss embassy," I told him. "They're kinda looking for you."

"Yeah, I know. I owe them some money."

I telephoned Mr. Doerig to let him know Vincent was still at our home.

"Do you think you could come to the embassy tomorrow, Wayne?" he asked.

"Sure," I said. "What time is good?"

"How about ten in the morning?"

"That would be fine. I'll see you then."

At the embassy the next day, Mr. Doerig asked me, "Do you think Vincent could stay at your home for a while? Until we can work things out with him?"

The Swiss embassy and Mr. Doerig had always been helpful to us. I was thrilled to now be able to help *them* out. "Of course, Mr. Doerig," I said. "I'd be glad to have him stay with us."

Vincent had made it to our house just in time, too, with Kabul authorities right on his tail for local debts he'd incurred. Like the French embassy had done with Jacques, the Swiss embassy paid off Vincent's debts, then gave *me* money to dole out to him for his daily needs.

A real character, Vincent—extremely wise and interesting, but, it turned out . . . another junkie in trouble. It was too easy to be a junkie out here with so much cheap, freshly grown opium around. And if someone needed a fix in the vein, it was just as easy to buy vials of Valium or similar narcotics at any pharmacy, right over the counter.

We at the TOD House were pretty naïve about heroin, and Vincent was clever enough to hide his habit from us for quite a while. But when Jacques and he—cohorts together—ran out of drugs, it was another story. Vincent would nag me until I finally gave him money, used most assuredly to fetch some more.

Vincent was also a great actor—good enough to finagle various Swiss consuls out of so much money! One day, he even smashed a box of 20 or more vials of good Valium right in front of me in a staged demonstration of his false disinterest in the drugs, as if he was kicking the habit or something. *Right.*

He got a good dose of some badly needed religion, though, while under the TOD House roof. Like Jacques, he actually tried to help out around the place, cooperating quite well with us. Apparently, Vincent's parents in Switzerland, concerned for his well-being, were expediting his safe return home. But Vincent had a notion he was wanted by the Swiss government on drug charges. "I'm afraid if I go back, they're going to put me in jail," he told me. He knew he didn't have other options though.

It was about this time—June 24, 1975—that I received a letter from Tehran requesting I return there. No one remained in Kabul too long anyway, and by July 8, I would have to renew my visa for the fifth time—*if* the authorities granted me a new one at all. So, I consented in a letter to Patrick to return to Tehran. Australian Kenny, who had extended his visa here about to the maximum, had left for Tehran the prior week.

A married couple, already in Kabul since June 14, had been well chosen by someone in Tehran to take over the Kabul Work. The guy, Louis, was Swiss and his wife, Fiona, British. Two days after their arrival, I announced them as codirectors of the Work. Now, I would slowly relinquish the Work to them.

Louis was in his realm here in Afghanistan. Before joining the group he'd lived on his own somewhere in North Africa selling and trading in . . . camels! He herded them from one desert market to another, actually making a profit on them. I observed Louis' adaptability first-hand when one day I took him to the Kabul marketplace where the guy bartered Afghans down to practically nothing for their wares. Then, on the way home from the market, Louis bargained with a young street peddler of hand-woven woolen socks, scarves and outerwear until the kid sold him a fine pair of woolen socks at something like 400% less than the original asking price. I felt sorry for the peddler kid, but was also amazed, after living here five months, that such fine woven ware could be bought for so little and the kid could still make money on it.

Summertime was also when *scorpions* appeared in Kabul. Huge ones! And they fascinated Louis. Kenny, before he left, had discovered them scratching their way up our outside screens and would awaken Louis in the middle of the night—the only time the arachnids appeared. The two of them observed the creatures crawling around the front concrete patio and up the screens and sides of the house and then killed them.

As for Louis' British wife, she was an adept guitarist and a smiling inspiration to all. On top of that, they had an eight-year-old son who added more of a family atmosphere to the home, as only a young child could.

I did *not* want to leave Kabul. It was too idyllic and the work here particularly rewarding. But it was time to go, so I began transferring responsibilities to Louis. I introduced him to every embassy consul, every friend, every benefactor and every hotel, restaurant and store proprietor I knew.

"Don't ever forget the Canadian girl in jail," I emphasized.

"We'll visit her often, Wayne. Don't worry. Besides, the British will get her out."

As for the markets and amenities of Kabul, it wasn't necessary to show these to Louis. This guy would find them himself, no problem, and surely discover more about this land than I would ever see.

Five months wasn't nearly enough to know Kabul. I learned that my last week here. I'd lived my time here among tourists with money on the *good* side of town. Then one morning, I made a wrong turn across town into the alley of a really poor section. Every city has them, although in Afghanistan, nobody begged or even indicated they were poor. Afghans had too much dignity. And they didn't tolerate *not* working. The dirt street of tattered mud huts I'd walked into was an inappropriate area for a Westerner. For the first time in my months here, I felt extremely intimidated. Nearly every dark eye on that street followed me with antagonism until I found my way out.

But it was a young street peddler selling cigarettes and chewing gum who revealed to me how poor some people were in Kabul. I had seen these young kids with portable stores slung over their shoulders, selling cigarettes, chewing gum and other stuff, but they never begged or even pushed their wares on us too much. Then, while strolling about the tourist area with Louis one day, I saw a world traveler accidentally drop and spill a small bag of fresh, Afghan bakery cookies in the middle of Chicken Street. He picked up the bag of what was left in it and walked off—leaving any cookies that had spilled in the street. The peddler kid saw it happen and quickly grabbed every cookie to eat, crumbs and all. He wasn't starving—no one starves in Afghanistan— but the fresh-baked Afghan tourist pastries were a *luxury* his poverty couldn't afford, and he wasn't about to let them go to waste in the middle of the street. It made me understand why there was contempt from certain Afghans toward foreigners.

My last days in this fabulous city were fast approaching. I'd given my all here. At the house, those whom I had led actually seemed sad to see me go. But an unexpected reward came when U.S. Consul Bruce Beardsley came to the house at 8:30 one morning to say goodbye to me.

"Wayne, I wanted to come by and personally thank you, once again, for the work you've done here," he said, "and to wish you a great future."

"How about some tea?" I asked. He came in for tea and chatted with all of us for a while. "Bruce, *you* have been so unbelievably helpful to us," I told him. "I can't thank you enough."

I said heartfelt goodbyes to Reverend Karwehl, Father Panigati, Consul Korth of the German embassy, a good Peace Corps worker friend named Ken and every other supporter and friend to whom I'd become close while here. When I went to the Swiss embassy to say goodbye to the precious Mr. Doerig and told him I'd be moving to Tehran, he nearly flipped.

"Tehran?" he asked excitedly, his eyes widening.

"Yes," I said, "the group has asked me to return there."

"Wayne. There is a direct flight from Tehran to Switzerland that the embassy wanted to put Vincent on," he explained, "but we didn't know how to get him to Tehran without him flaking off somewhere along the way. Is there any chance you could take him with you? We will pay your way."

"Of course I can take him with me, Mr. Doerig. I'd be glad to," I said, pleased again to recompense him and the Swiss embassy for the unwavering assistance they'd given the TOD House.

On Wednesday, July 2, our visas secured, Vincent and I walked to the Swiss embassy, where Mr. Doerig explained everything to Vincent in German and then handed me 4,500 Afs (about $81) for all bus fares and expenses. "Two thousand are for you alone, Wayne," he said.

We purchased two bus tickets for early the next morning to Herat, at 200 Afs ($3.60) apiece and returned to the house to pack. I had now transferred the Work to Louis, including his link to the outside world—the P.O. Box.

At the house, Doug—the artifacts exporter from Belgium—handed me a wad of about $150 as a gift to take with me to Tehran. But, without Doug knowing, I gave all of it to the Kabul home, knowing they needed it more than I. I also gave my Olympus camera to Louis because the group wanted more photos from Kabul for their worldwide newsletter. I later regretted giving this fine little camera to the clown when I learned it was later stolen. *Oh well.* We all hugged, prayed and said final goodbyes that night, but I felt heartsick leaving the "child," the Kabul Work, I'd inherited from Andrew five months back.

Vincent and I boarded an Afghani bus at 5:30 a.m., July 3, 1975, taking up one of the bench seats on the left side near the back, and headed out of Kabul. Vincent was in great spirits despite the early hour. "Look," he said.

"What's that?" I asked.

"It's opium," he said. In his palm he held five, small, tar-like opium balls, each about half-an-inch in diameter. He smiled. "These should keep me going for a while."

Lucky for Vincent he'd be feeling no pain. This bus was hell—the wrong choice of buses for sure. The atmosphere was "down home" Afghani—packed full of Afghans screaming and arguing with each other; a few live chickens, sheep and goats aboard; huge burlap sacks of grain and rice piled in the center aisle. And at 12 noon after lunch, we picked up two pathetic, chained and shackled prisoners. The guards basically dumped them in the aisle.

I didn't know the make of the bus—Russian maybe—but it was old, with cracked red vinyl seats. A real clunker.

We reached the southern city of Kandahar at 2:15 p.m., changed to a worse bus and at 4:30 p.m. headed toward Herat. Not far into the trip, the bus stopped alongside the road, in the middle of nowhere, for the sunset prayer. There were no other vehicles anywhere, and the driver turned the engine off.

The stop was also a break for everyone, so I wandered off alone into the vast wilderness to take a leak. Typical Afghani scenery—flat, brown and dusty, with barren, rocky hills in the distance, except that now the setting sun had turned it all a radiant orange, while the crisp, unpolluted air of the night sky began to slowly darken and sparkle with stars. So calm and quiet in the desolation, it was LOUD! The *Spirit* was loud—*God's* Spirit—throbbing and pulsating in the untouched stillness, practically audibly *humming* in my ears. Evident! Alive!

The two prisoners—faithful observers of prayer times or not—became adamant with their guards to join in with everyone else in prayer, on rugs on the ground outside the bus. It might earn them some leniency. They must have done something pretty bad because, besides the fear on their faces, I could tell one of them was feigning slight insanity, no doubt for pity. Continuing our journey, I felt it freaky and pitiful seeing them shackled and thrown in the aisle like animals.

I spent much of that night on the bus, listening to Vincent, talking to him, trying to love and feed his soul. He seemed to thirst for words of faith, but whether or not they sank into him through the haze of opium, I don't know.

We both drifted in and out of sleep, bouncing up and down in our plastic seats, until the bus finally reached its destination of Herat, the closest large city to Iran, at 6:30 in the morning, 25 hours on this crowded, clunky bus.

Vincent and I checked into the Mohmand Hotel, ate some breakfast, showered and slept most of that day. At 6 in the evening we strolled around laid-back Herat, ate some cheap, tasty rice and meat and just savoured our last hours in this unique land neither of us would likely ever see again.

A mistake I made in my five months here and even in my last hours in Herat was not purchasing any Afghan handiwork, article of clothing, souvenir, trinket, gift for a loved one or any other reminder of this great country. There were even beautiful silver rings the Afghans made that I liked. The rings were like wedding bands but with colorful, semi-precious stones inlaid around them. They were cheap and unique, but I declined purchasing even *one* of these for myself, or as a gift. How could I be so *tight?* I think I just hated bargaining or getting ripped off. But, then again, I wasn't out here for collectibles, nor did I have extra money for much, nor did I really care. I was still on a spiritual mission—perhaps taking it *too* seriously though.

Tangible treasures or not, I was leaving this land with respect for it, a love for it and with a wealth of memories from it. I could easily describe Afghanistan in one word—*fascinating.*

The following morning, July 5, we bought minibus tickets, left Herat at 7:40 a.m. and arrived at the Afghanistan border two-and-a-half hours later. There, it took us two hours to process through customs and change our Afghani money to Iranian rials (100 Afs equal to 120 rials) before finally leaving Afghanistan and traveling the three miles to the Iranian border.

The border station of Iran. *Oh Lord.* This is where a person could be standing around, waiting for processing, when some Iranian cop, customs or narcotics agent, or whoever the heck he might be, could appear out of nowhere and put his open hand right on the person's *heart*, to detect in that instance through his devious expertise, if the heart is beating wildly in anxiety and fear—like it would be if smuggling drugs! *Shit.* One of them did it to me so fast this day I didn't realize until later what had happened. I guess he came from my left side, I don't know. All I know is he suddenly had his hand on my heart. *Bastard.* Disgusting really, that these officials could be so disrespectful of a person's inner body. Another world, another country, where again, its border station reflects its character. Compared to the struggling Afghans, the Iranians were a bit haughty with their wealth, their regime rather fascist. No one messed with these guys at the border. No one played games with them, bribed them, fooled them or struck deals with them. With the Shah as their dictator, they were chumming with and compelled to gratify the West—particularly the United States—by visibly controlling the flow of drugs in and out of Iran.

As a foreigner, world traveler or hippie type, it was best not even to *think* of transporting any of Afghanistan's inexpensive, high-quality dope into this place. Guards were ready for anyone dumb enough to try and were experts at finding it. Besides, Iran grew so much of its own opium and hashish, it didn't need any competition from Afghanistan or Pakistan.

Inside the station sat a morbid display, like a small museum, that I couldn't avoid seeing. It featured photos of unsuspecting travelers they'd busted for drugs right on these grounds. The people stood in front of their confiscated contraband alongside these same, proud, Iranian officers. Typical drug-bust scenes intended to strike the fears, horrors and consequences of smuggling drugs through these parts. The pictures even exhibited the actual tires they had cut open and found stuffed with hash oil and such. And who knows? Some of these busts may have been a result of that quick, heart-check method. *Gross.*

Vincent, far too wise to chance carrying even his personal stash of opium balls into Iran, had consumed the last of it back in Afghanistan— enough to get him through the border, or so he hoped. He hadn't counted on the Iranians also being astute to proper inoculation requirements. So when they discovered he had no record of being vaccinated against cholera, they informed him he would have to remain in quarantine at the nearby hospital . . . for 24 hours.

Oh Lord. He freaked right then and there. Even though he was still high on what he'd eaten a few hours earlier, he knew he was OUT and would need more soon—much sooner than 24 hours. Anticipation alone of withdrawal caused him to skitz.

Not a tall guy, but wiry, lean and mean, Vincent was capable of becoming downright ornery and not one to take much gruff from anyone—especially someone trying to stand between him and his dope. He lashed out, verbally anyway, at the authorities and their demands to hold him. He was furious, screaming in a last-ditch attempt to get the Iranians to overturn their decision. To no avail, of course.

Somehow, I had separated from Vincent in the border processing since the small, light tan medical building was across the road from where I'd been. When I stepped outside, I *heard* Vincent making a ruckus. "No! You can't keep me! I'm not staying here! Forget it!" he screamed at them repeatedly.

I rushed to him and luckily calmed him down before the Iranians lost it with *him*.

Vincent knew he was doomed but kept grumbling anyway. Finally at 4 p.m., he, a few other foreigners and I climbed into the back of a covered, flatbed truck provided by the border station and headed for the hospital—all quite organized and efficient.

It was a sad ride, and when we arrived, Vincent looked at me as if I were a close family member to whom he had to say goodbye before going off to jail to accept his punishment, sagging and defeated—like it was the end of the world for him.

"Don't worry about it, Vincent," I said. "I'll see you tomorrow." But I didn't really know the *magnitude* of being physically addicted to a drug and going "cold turkey."

The truck transported the rest of us—mostly partners of "quarantine people"—to an area of cheap hotels in the nearby town of Taybad. But the hotels looked so seedy I soon found my way to the nicest hotel of the town, the Taybad Inn. There I met the manager of the place, Ebrahim, and I explained to him the work I had with travelers. The guy then provided me with dinner and an air-conditioned room—for free.

The following day I walked to the hospital, which happened to be near the Taybad Inn, to find "the Vincent," expecting the worst. Instead, he came up to me excited. "Hi, Wayne!" he said, smiling and looking rather chipper.

"Good morning, Vince. How are you?"

"I'm good. I'm good."

Strange, I thought. He took me by the arm to walk me around the hospital grounds.

"Sorry for making such a scene at the border," Vincent began. "But you know, I was out of stuff and just freaked. Well, I started going cold turkey sometime in the night, and the Iranian doctors knew it right away. What do you think they did?" Unable to conceal any longer what had transpired since the two of us had separated, he continued. "You won't believe it. They told me not to tell anyone, but I'm telling you. Two of them took me outside to that guard station over there and smoked opium with me into the night—enough to keep me going until now!"

This is definitely not America.

The hospital cleared Vincent and gave him his passport and the two of us walked quickly to the Taybad Inn. I introduced Vincent to Ebrahim who clearly saw I wasn't joking about my work with travelers. "Ebrahim," I said, "thank you so much for everything—the nice room, the food. He and I will be going to Tehran now. God bless you!"

Vincent and I caught the 1 p.m. bus to the city of Mashhad. Any bus was better than the last one we took from Kabul. We sat back and enjoyed the ride, Vincent still feeling victorious with the outcome of his quarantining.

Now Vincent, as far back as Herat, had planned to breeze through the border, reach Mashhad in plenty of time before his next fix and buy his drugs from pharmacies there. He'd lived in Iran a few months ago and remembered freely purchasing Valium and barbiturates from pharmacies. He knew, or *thought* he knew, he could easily meet his needs. What he *didn't* know was how fast Iran was Westernizing and changing. Laws had quickly settled across the land, forbidding pharmacies to sell habit-forming drugs over the counter.

He couldn't believe they weren't selling him anything. When the third place refused him, he became frantic and intolerant. But in his persistence and dire need, he dragged me from one pharmacy to another through the streets of Mashhad until, after five or six attempts, he finally bought some Valium, ate it and immediately calmed down.

Traveling with Vincent revealed something quite shocking to me about heroin and addiction: no matter what qualities people have, how intelligent they are, what potential they have, if addicted to heroin (or another narcotic drug) they *are that drug.* Because if they don't have it, they can't function. A real waste of a human being, especially one with such potential as this guy, Vincent.

Vincent satisfied, I looked up an American cohort of mine at the Koroush Hotel. The guy, one of the brethren, was living out of the hotel with his wife and child, trying to establish an outreach in this far-flung

Iranian holy city. *Good luck.* I said hello, goodbye, and Vincent and I caught the 7 p.m. bus to Tehran.

We traveled through the night without much stopping and awoke at dawn to clouds overhead—a soothing rarity in these lands during summer—and magnificent scenery of mountains, valleys, rivers and greenery. This was the same route, through Iran's northern Elburz Mountains, I had traveled in the opposite direction on my way to Kabul exactly five months earlier, when this landscape was equally beautiful covered in snow.

After a stop at 9 a.m. near Sari, close to the Caspian Sea, we continued on through solid mountainous beauty until reaching Tehran at 2:30 in the afternoon.

Gross. The horrible shock of a bustling big city again after five months in the peace and quiet of Kabul. There are advantages to a big city, maybe, but *serenity* is not one of them.

I remembered something good about this city, though: chelokebab, that steaming hot white rice with melted butter in the middle and grilled lamb on the side, along with an ice-cold bottle of real Coca-Cola. Many restaurants served this flavorsome plate, and we headed for one immediately in the Naderi area.

Following our meal, we walked to the Swiss embassy to meet Vice Consul Fred Jenny. A long hallway led to Mr. Jenny's office, and when Vincent and I were summoned in, the consul nearly flipped. He could not believe I had actually brought the *real Vincent.* For all his Swiss composure, the consul was unable to conceal his utter surprise and amazement. This extremely difficult case of theirs was now standing before him, in the flesh, alive and on schedule.

"Gentlemen! Gentlemen!" He stood up from behind his desk and came forth directly to shake our hands in sincere gratitude. "Sit down. Sit down." Tea was ordered, and Mr. Jenny discussed the flight Vincent would be taking early the next morning back to Switzerland. Mr. Jenny was another cool, far-out guy, much like Mr. Doerig back in Kabul. We parted genially.

But all was not well. Vincent had barely survived the meeting with the consul. He was long *out* of the small amount of Valium he'd been sold back in Mashhad and was flipping out, once again. He thought he could easily meet his needs from the Iranian pharmacies, especially with so many here in Tehran. But it seemed these pharmacies were even *more* reluctant to sell to him—since this was the capital where the decree not to sell to people like Vincent had originated.

Vincent became furious. He finally caused such a scene that one pharmacy consented to sell him enough Valium just to shut him up and get rid of him.

With Vincent still in my care, I took him to the Amir Kabir Hotel at about 5:30 that evening where we both would sleep the night. *I* would anyway. Vincent, without me knowing, spent a good part of the night out at a doctor's office. As he explained to me the next morning, the few tablets of Valium he had bought and eaten had worn off quickly, so he found a private doctor open who actually shot him up with drugs, for a fee, like any other patient with a disease or illness. The doctor also wrote him a prescription for another dose or two, enough to get him to Switzerland.

Poor Vincent. Although his addictive needs were met, he remained very sick and weak when he and I walked from the hotel at the ungodly hour of 5:30 a.m. on Tuesday morning, July 8, 1975, and caught a taxi to the Swiss embassy. It was not necessary that I remain with Vincent any longer, once I delivered him to Mr. Jenny's care. But in the cab, Vincent insisted I accompany him and the consular to the airport.

"Please, Wayne, come with me to the airport. I need you!"

"I will. I will. Don't worry," I said.

We met up with Mr. Jenny, and the three of us, chauffeured in an embassy sedan, reached the Tehran airport in plenty of time for Vincent's flight.

At boarding time, Mr. Jenny handed Vincent his ticket, said some official, though kind words to him and gave him a farewell handshake. Vincent looked at me before walking through the gate and said, "Thanks for everything." He then reached forth and *hugged* me. My heart about sank. Vincent had been a difficult case. He knew it, and I knew it. And *everyone* knew it was a bit of a miracle he was there at all, safe and boarding a plane home. But memories of any hard times I had gone through with him vanished and didn't matter. It was all *more* than worth it for that grateful hug.

It continued to break my heart to see him standing there weak and helpless, not sure if he would face jail time back in Switzerland—nor caring much at this point either.

Tears welled up in both our eyes as we faced one another in one last handshake. I hugged him while saying a prayer over him, "Thank You, Lord. Bless and keep Vincent, Lord. And keep him in Your care. In Jesus' name, Amen."

"Amen," Vincent chimed in softly.

He then ambled down the enclosed corridor to his plane without looking back.

Chapter 23
∽ *A Tehran Kiss* ∽

WHAT A DIFFERENCE a country can make. Iran—especially Tehran—was now such a contrast to me after Kabul. Was it money—having it versus not having it—that so drastically distinguished Iran from Afghanistan?

After all, that's what inspired me to come East again: the group here had money in the bank ($10,000). Comfort and security. *Who wants to struggle for a living if you don't have to?*

Tehran was too crowded, though. Traffic jams everywhere. The pace was fast, with materialism invading the minds and hearts of the Iranians. They needed to return more to the basics, like before the oil boom. Iran's youths knew it more than anyone and responded well to us, their contemporaries, pushing simple faith in God.

We weren't ashamed, though, to ask for rials and tomans in exchange for words of faith. The Iranians—and not just young people—generously donated hundreds of rials, right in the streets, for our literature.

But by the time I returned here in July 1975, super litnessers like tall Joshua and others had burned out the main streets, inundating the Tehranians with literature. We were now being harassed by religious sorts and chased by police. Tactics would have to change if we wanted to continue distributing the words, meet people and still receive enough donations to survive.

So we left the streets and went house-to-wealthy-house in the northern, more well-to-do areas of Tehran. It wasn't exactly door-to-door, but rather gate-to-gate, since every house was secured from the streets by walls and iron gates equipped with electric-buzzer doorbells and working intercoms. Apartment buildings had locked security doors at their ground-level main entrances and intercoms to each apartment.

Buzz, buzz on the doorbell. "Hello! Do you speak English?" we said clearly over the intercoms.

"Yes, just a minute." And they came to the gate.

There the Iranians saw two, smiling, unobtrusive Westerners, usually a guy and a girl. (*Got* to have a *girl* if at all possible!) Then, standing at the security gate, we quickly explained our social work in as much Farsi as possible—like singing in hospitals and getting young people off drugs—

handed them an appropriate piece of literature through the gate, asked for a donation in return, ready to go on our way.

Rarely did any Iranian home turn us away or deny us a donation. Instead, the Iranians often cordially invited us into their homes. Iranians were hospitable, and they were extremely open to Westerners—especially at this opulent time. After all, Iran (Persia) sat pretty much by itself out east here in its affluence, set apart from its poorer neighbors of Turkey, Southern Russia, Afghanistan, Pakistan and even Iraq, which was oil-rich but backward.

Many homes were nearly palaces, two or three stories high, elaborately furnished and full of Persian, handwoven carpets so intricate and expensive they seemed to pulsate with life. Shimmering in the backyards of some homes were not just little kidney-shaped pools, but ones long enough to do good laps in.

Still, we were interested in the souls of men, so we conversed with our hosts about God as much as possible over tea and sweets. We talked with many great people and became close friends with some—mostly young women, for some reason. Donations were decent, but didn't quite match "blitzkriegging" the streets.

Then we discovered something more lucrative—offices, hundreds of them scattered throughout this bustling, wealthy capital. Teams of two, usually a guy and girl, dressed nicely and headed out during morning business hours to Tehran's finest, high-rise office complexes. Sure, we wanted to meet people and get the message out, but we headed to these offices predominantly for *living* expenses. And we got it, too.

We used the one advantage we had—our "ticket" of being from the West—to even get *near* high rollers of these companies. "May we see the manager, please?" was about all it took for the secretary out front—the hatchet person—to escort us right into the plush office of a company manager, owner or chairman. Then, in all politeness, we introduced ourselves, described our work, handed the guy a piece of literature, or perhaps a photo magazine of our worldwide work, and asked him if he would like to assist us with a donation.

More often than not, these guys didn't mind being disrupted from their busy schedules to chat with us—especially when one of us was a female—generously order us hot tea, coffee or a cold drink, and then hand over a few hundred rials cash ($50 to $100 generally), right then and there. Like other Iranians, they seemed to *value* what we had to say and were surprised and impressed to hear us speak of God. Who else was speaking of Him these days, the pursuit of money dominating so much?

Apart from all this up-scale begging, we made a living one more way here in Tehran. Two or three of our musicians had a decent contract to play guitars and sing—mostly our own songs—nearly every night at an Italian-style pizzeria called the Wine Cellar, off Pahlavi Avenue, the main avenue running north and south on the west side of the city. The gig brought good, steady income that we all, as usual, shared—one purse. "And all that believed were together, and had all things common; and sold their possessions and goods, and parted them to all men, as every man had need" (Acts 2.44, 45). True communism, but with God.

Also, to conserve our cash, two of us—usually myself and another, sometimes a girl, would head down early every Thursday morning to Tehran's huge produce market on the south side of the city. Buyers and sellers there haggled over the best prices for any type of food in bulk while trucks and taxis, competing to transport it, lined and packed the streets. It was hectic, but worth the torment, especially when we received crates and bags full of fresh vegetables, fruits and grains all for free, donated by generous merchants. Again, trying to make the world a better place, we asked without embarrassment for a little help in return from people who could afford it. And with 20-or-so of us now spread throughout Tehran, we appreciated the free food supplement to our uncertain cash income.

Besides the produce market, various merchants donated wood, paint, meat products, office supplies and even a freezer and stove—like companies did for charities in the U.S. and Europe. Bob—my companion from London to Rome back in December of 1972, who now lived in Tehran with his pregnant, Italian wife, expertly coordinated the provisioning, while I assisted him.

At the end of a hot day in August, Bob and I sat down together in a small café off Koroush-e-Kabir Street to have a cold beer. An older gentleman who appeared to be an American sat at a table near us, looking rather lonely. Bold-and-outgoing Bob struck up a conversation with the guy. (Not many Americans hung around drinking in restaurants here, so it was obvious we should meet one another.)

"Hi," Bob said. "Where are you from?"

"I'm from America," the guy said.

"I thought so. My name's Bob." He extended his hand.

"Hi. I'm Wayne," I said, waving to the guy from the other side of Bob.
"I'm Mike. Nice to meet you both."

The guy brightened up. "What are you guys doing here in Iran?"

"We live here," Bob said. "We do social work, visit hospitals and pass
out literature about God in the streets. We live by faith, actually."

I could see Mike's eyes immediately well up in tears, but he didn't say
anything. "How about another beer," he said, "on me."

We chatted with him awhile, exchanged phone numbers, and the guy
ended up becoming one of our closest friends and benefactors in Tehran.
He was an architect, living here with his German wife and their 13-year-
old son.

At our next meeting with him, he told us how he nearly cried to
hear Bob and me talking about God in the middle of Tehran. "It was a
breath of fresh air and a comfort to my heart," he said.

From then on, at least two of us met with Mike once or twice a month,
usually on a Wednesday afternoon or evening (the equivalent in Iran
of Friday-after-work in the States) at the Pizzaland Restaurant off
Koroush-e-Kabir Street. We ordered pizza and red wine, the wine an
understood part of the ritual since Mike loved to drink with friends. *Oh
well. Sometimes we just had to sacrifice in this business, become all things to all
men, that we might win some . . . and get half drunk with the guy.*

Such a great guy, Mike. He loved words of faith and always paid for
the meals and drinks. He usually handed us an envelope with an Iranian
bill or two inside worth anywhere from $70 to over $200 each time we
met—money that went a long way in Iran, where, except for rent, one
could live very cheaply.

Here in Tehran, I remained pretty much out among the populace, hitting
the streets, houses and offices with the literature, getting donations in
return—much like I did in Cyprus.

One day, after being in the streets all day, passing out literature
with one of the girl/nannies, and Rachel's baby pooping all over the
place in a stroller, I telephoned in to the main apartment. A group
member told me not to come home. The Iranian landlord, living next
door in his attached, similar, two-floor, condominium-like home, was
reneging on the rental agreement. He wanted his son to move into
the place, so, in various devious schemes to physically encourage us
to vacate the place, he (or someone) had now resorted to *slashing* all

four tires of our car. Meanwhile, periodically, the landlord's wretched wife, for her part, would wait until the laundry dried that we had hung out on our clothesline. Then, standing on a chair, she'd take her water hose and soak down our laundry over the wall separating the two homes. *Great.* What had been an excellent townhouse, in a good Northeast-Tehran neighborhood, at a decent price—something quite difficult to find in Tehran—had become a small battle zone.

Eventually we moved out, but not before police were called and one of our short, Italian-American leaders stood also on a chair one night in front of some famous Iranian movie-star friends we had over, threw water directly into the jabbering face of the landlord who, noticing we had guests, was purposely screaming out false accusations for our guests to hear. If it wasn't for some of us holding back the Italian, I don't know what he might have done to that landlord. *God help us all.*

Fortunately for me, when I made the call that evening, I had already become good friends with an Iranian family who lived a bit farther north from the apartment. Someone in the group had met one of the sons, Jafar, an excellent guitarist in his early twenties. Jafar had three sisters, and whenever I visited the house, I often found myself sitting down and talking with the youngest, 17-year-old Rana.

When I called Rana and explained my situation in mostly slow English and some Farsi, and asked if Sue (the girl/nanny) and I could stay with them, precious Rana asked her family and said over the phone warmly and excitedly, "Of course you can!" That night turned into a month because girls of the group and I would sleep there off and on, whenever we had landlord or housing problems.

Rana's family bestowed true Iranian hospitality on us without hesitation and seemed to enjoy our company. We usually ate breakfast with them, remained out all day and returned at 9 or 10 in the evening to sleep.

Although the family lived in a decent neighborhood, they had little money. Their old and outdated, two-story house had no running water and an outhouse as a toilet; showers had to be taken at a nearby public bath. As modern and progressive as Iran was, apparently many such fine old homes were still being lived in with no plumbing. As for this family, the father's aging mother resided nearby in a large, newer, fancier home, and they anticipated that when she died, they could move into it, instead of upgrading the old house.

Like many homes here of large families who couldn't afford a house with separate bedrooms for everyone, a large, open room with closets around it served as a huge living room during the day. At night the family transformed the room into sleeping quarters for the women or men. Fairly thin, but adequately comfortable, one-person, cotton-stuffed *mattresses* stacked along the walls, used as couches during the day, were laid out on the thickly carpeted floor for beds at night. Upstairs in Rana's house were the men's quarters—also a large room with mattresses neatly stacked along the walls during the day and laid out on the floor for beds at night. Next to this large upstairs room, the parents had their own separate bedroom. *Thank God.*

Rana was a typical Iranian girl—sweet, feminine, naturally sexy and domestic. Mother's little helper. She was like my original Iranian heartthrob, Farideh, though not quite as beautiful.

As for Farideh, she had sort of fizzled out, even though I saw her a few times when I returned from Kabul. I had written her some letters from Kabul, but she was a bit too dedicated to her family to follow on with me.

But an attraction grew between Rana and me that we both were careful not to make too obvious in front of others, especially there in the house. Rana and her open-minded mother were close to one another, so her mom surely sensed the affection. Rana was the biggest influence on keeping the home open to us all.

Rana was cute, with her short, black hair, dark eyes, light skin and well-defined body, but it was probably more her domestic womanliness inadvertently stealing my heart. I remember walking into the kitchen and seeing her working with her mother over a large round aluminum tray of uncooked rice, separating tiny rocks, rice chaff and other natural imperfections found in the huge burlap bags full of bulk rice they, and most Iranians, purchased. The thing was . . . she didn't do it grudgingly; she just naturally accepted it as part of her duties to her family. In fact, she kinda *ran* the family along with Mom. Anyway, it stood out to me, as an American, knowing teenage girls back in the States would never *happily* sit in the kitchen with their mothers preparing rice to be cooked for the family—not city girls anyway. At the same time, Rana excelled in her progressive Iranian high school, avidly learned English and remained . . . contemporarily glamorous.

Nothing much ever physically happened between Rana and me—these things just didn't happen too easily here—except for one evening when she and I were out alone away from the house. We did sneak an innocent but real kiss on the lips—no big deal, but so cool . . . and probably her first. It was time. We had to. We liked each other too much. Walking along in the dark, no one on the streets, we stopped and faced each other. She had obviously seen movies where the woman's head falls to one side, her eyes close and her lips part, because she did just that when I met her lips with mine. We kissed passionately. We just weren't afraid, despite the complexities of Tehran, to express in those few seconds the love we had for one another. *It was delicious.*

I bought her things from time to time with what little money I had. One day I gave her a pair of highly prized, faded U.S. blue jeans, hoping she might try them on in front of me. She was thrilled when I handed them to her. "Oh! Thank you, Wayne!" She then hardly hesitated before dropping her slacks to try them on. But, with one of her sisters present in the room, I instead looked the other way. *Oh well,* it was rewarding enough when she modeled them for me. "How do they look?" she asked. They clung tightly to her shapely body as she turned around in them. It got worse from there, too. Whether she did it consciously or not, or whether she was "ripening" uncontrollably, it wasn't uncommon for her to sit around from time to time in those same tight jeans, slouched in chairs with her legs spread wide-open in front of me. *Oh Lord.*

There wasn't much threat from me, though—Rana's mom even knew I was practically celibate in my service to God and reaching souls. I used to share scripture with Mom, who even asked one day that I pray for her healing, which I did. I shared spiritual things with the family and simultaneously partook of their physical, carnal things, as Apostle Paul wrote to the Corinthians: "If we have sown unto you spiritual things, is it a great thing if we shall reap your carnal things?" 1 Corinthians 9.11.

Rana's father was a likeable guy, but he wasn't around that much. About the only times I ever saw him were in the kitchen where the guy would be cleaning his specially made, nearly-two-foot-long . . . opium pipe! Generously, he would ask if I wished to join him in smoking some opium. *Amazing. This was definitely not Kansas, or Orlando.* I declined, of course, much to the relief of Rana, her mother and any other kids present. They all seemed a bit embarrassed at the old man's habit and hoped he wouldn't corrupt me with the drug. But in Iran it was understood and even *legal* for anyone over age 50 to freely buy and smoke opium—grown and produced here and one of Iran's exports. *Yep.* I often smelled its distinguishable aroma coming out of windows while walking the streets of Tehran.

I also smelled hashish smoke in Tehran. But it usually came from guys in their twenties who used that similar Eastern method of mixing the hash with the tobacco in their cigarettes. It looked like they were smoking normal cigarettes as they walked down the streets . . . unless the wind blew it my way.

I came across actual marijuana plants growing out of small patches of soil alongside streets right in the city. Perhaps they were only hemp plants. I never did clip and dry any of their leaves to determine their THC content, but for sure, they were cannabis sativa plants, some seven feet tall and higher!

As for Rana's brother Jafar, one of our American girls fell in love with the guy for a while and moved right in with him.

Chapter 24
⚮ *Trabzon, Turkey* ⚮

To RENEW OUR Iranian visas, we headed for Turkey, to the city of Trabzon, a small seaport on the Black Sea of Northeastern Turkey. There, an Iranian consular friend, knowing our social work, granted us one-year, multiple-reentry visas. That meant we didn't have to leave Iran every three months to get another visa. And we could leave and re-enter the country anytime we wanted within that year.

It was an exceptional visa to have, even though it took nearly a week, sometimes more, to make the nearly two-thousand-mile roundtrip, overland journey to obtain it. Just reaching the border of Turkey at Bazargan from Tehran took 16 hours by car or bus. Then it took a day from Bazargan to Trabzon, and at least a day in Trabzon to get the visa before returning to Tehran.

I made my first trip *alone* in the beginning of October with hardly any money, as usual—about enough for bus fare to Trabzon, a cheap hotel room once there and food along the way. Nothing for the return trip. All by faith: "... the just shall live by his faith" (Habakkuk 2.4). I'd have to find my way back to Tehran. God would provide. Funds or not, the scenery through the countryside enchanted me, *especially* through the lush, green mountains near Trabzon, not to mention two passes by Mount Ararat.

Fortunately I knew enough Turkish to provision food from some local merchants, thereby keeping enough money to rent my own, little room at the Yayla Hotel in Trabzon at 10 Turkish lira (60 cents) a night. Good thing too, because the day I arrived was the first day of the major, three-day holiday of Bayram, and the Iranian embassy was closed. *Bad planning.* Amazingly though, a worker at the embassy put me on the phone with the consul who said, "Don't worry. Meet me at the embassy tomorrow morning at 11:30, and you'll have a visa."

Trabzon was quaint and small, with the typical, relaxed atmosphere of a seaside town. In the middle of the city, away from the shoreline, was a large, European-like square of open-air restaurants in front of at least one fairly fancy hotel. I could tell there was money in this town, no doubt due to the shipping and trading done through its port.

Noticeable also in Trabzon was the mix of people. Unlike most Turks, many of these people had blond hair and blue eyes—people whose ancestors had obviously intermarried with Russians. Trabzon was the closest seaport city to Russia.

Sure enough, the Iranian consul arrived at the embassy at 11:30 the next morning—the second day of Bayram—met and talked with me and stamped a one-year visa in my passport. While there, two Venezuelan guys my age were also trying to get visas to Iran but were being refused. I made friends with them, and they drove me from the embassy to a parking spot on the Black Sea for the Volkswagen minibus they were traveling in. The bus belonged to a Swiss guy who was so sick he could hardly move and whose stunningly beautiful, blond, Swiss girlfriend was now falling for one of the Venezuelan guys, Carlos. Also traveling in the bus was the other Venezuelan guy's sister, Rita. They had all reached Trabzon by ferryboat from Istanbul in hopes of obtaining visas to continue on to Iran and points farther east. Turned out these two guys were on the lam from the mandatory Venezuelan military induction and were *hoping* the Iranian consulate way out here in Trabzon was too far-flung to have received updated bulletins—bulletins from Venezuela, requesting the two be refused passage anywhere.

They offered to take me back to Tehran, where they also were headed—*if* the two could get visas, of course. So I hung around with them while the embassy remained closed for another, third day of Bayram.

The two, Carlos and Enrique, were hilarious and so cool—carefree and jovial, despite their predicament. Here in conservative Turkey, in this small town, it didn't phase them to jump around and play like friendly kittens running and pushing one another and even staging a fake fight—right in the main square—rolling around on the ground, jumping over railings after each other and generally disrupting the entire place. The Turks looked at them like they were nuts, until I, though laughing, advised them to stop. Turkey was not a country to goof off in.

That evening, I sat down with Carlos in the open air of the main square over dinner and tea and got serious with the guy about God, Jesus and the world. Carlos was precious and receptive, receiving the words like a child until he finally, humbly, prayed with me right there at our little table to receive Jesus in his heart! A real highlight of the day. Somewhere in the world after this, Carlos may well have looked back on this night and realized, "You never know where you might find God knocking on the door to your heart—even on the shores of the Black Sea, in wild Eastern Turkey."

I returned to the embassy with Carlos and Enrique the day after Bayram, now my fourth day here in Trabzon. I thought maybe I could influence someone there. But the two guys were still denied visas.

Back in town the same day, I met up with Majid, the male secretary of the Iranian consul, along with an Australian traveler named Ralph, and the three of us had a lunch of fresh fish at the apartment of a Turkish friend I had met earlier. At the apartment, Majid said to me, "You know, there is a way for your friends to have visas to Iran."

"Really?"

"Yes," Majid said. "The girl. The Swiss one. Someone at the embassy has seen her and said, 'If they will share her, I will give them visas.'"

Oh brother. Amazing what could go on in these guys' minds. I don't know, maybe such arrangements are sometimes entertained throughout the world. Who knows? I passed it on to the Venezuelans who shared my disgust.

As for me getting back to Tehran, the Australian guy Ralph was heading alone in his car to Iran that evening and was pleased to take me along. I said goodbye to the Venezuelans and Swiss, to the consul by phone and to Turkish friends I'd met, grabbed my bag at the hotel, bought some fresh bread and food and left Trabzon at 7 p.m. with Ralph.

We slept in the car outside a small village at 11:30 that night and were on the road at 8 the following morning, headed for Erzurum and the border. Ralph was set up to cook *inside* the car, so we didn't spend much time in villages along the way. Good thing, too. Ralph also had learned firsthand what it meant to walk around as a stranger/foreigner in small Turkish towns—confrontation with "freak-demon" Turkish kids. *Damn. What's the story here?* The same scoundrel-type kids who were heckling and throwing rocks at Patrick and me at the extreme *other* end of this country (at the Greek border), were here at the *Eastern* end doing the same thing! *Shit.* From one end of this country to the other. Was it the rampant male superiority syndrome? Or, did parents let their boys— especially the oldest—do whatever they wanted?

We made good time until Erzurum, but after that, the road became increasingly rough, with potholes everywhere. Roads of Eastern Turkey are notorious for their bad condition, and, sure enough, Ralph's car had a blowout just 30 miles shy of the Iranian border. We fixed the tire, but we still wouldn't reach the border because night was falling and three miles up ahead the Turkish Army stopped us and directed us to pull off the road and park for the night, along with every other car, bus and truck passing this way. The reason? No one travels through this area at night, here at the foothills of Mount Ararat, because of . . . bandits from the hills. *Yep.* It was easier for the Turkish Army to keep travelers safe and under their watch in these wild parts than to try to control raiders coming out of nowhere in the dark to rob unsuspecting motorists.

Did these marauders come on horses, or what? I wondered. Whoever they were, it was serious enough for every truck and bus to comply, with no complaints. In fact, a community atmosphere instantly permeated what became a field of vehicles parked along the road for the night in this cozy little safe haven provided by the military, here at the foothills of . . . The Mountain.

At daybreak, we all continued our journeys toward Dogubayazit and the Iran border. And once again I was elated when we passed by Ararat. Thus far in the car, I had already gently wooed Ralph to words from the Bible. In my diary last night concerning Ralph, I wrote: "There is a spiritual man and he needs spiritual food." Today, as we drove past Ararat, I read to him the appropriate section of the Book of Genesis— Chapters 6 through 9—about the Ark entombed in ice on the other side. *I* believed it anyway.

Unfortunately, we had to stop in Dogubayazit to look for a tube for Ralph's blown tire. This crummy town of unfriendly people loafing around in their tea shops, along with the classic, obnoxious kids, hadn't improved since I was stuck here a year ago with the magic bus from Istanbul on my way to Iran. Dogubayazit? *No.* I would name this town *Doggyville.*

At the Turkey/Iran border, customs guys checked Ralph's car engine number before we breezed on into Iran. We reached the large city of Tabriz at 8 in the evening, stuffed ourselves with chelokebab and slept one more night in the car on the outskirts here. The following day we traveled through the pleasant green meadows, valleys and hills of Northwestern Iran until stopping in Tehran at 8:30 p.m.

Five days after arriving from my Trabzon trip, who calls me? The crazy Venezuelans. They had *somehow* been granted visas and were in Tehran, so the three of them—Carlos, Enrique and Rita—came to visit us in our Northeast Tehran home for some good songs and sharing of hearts, minds and the love of God!

Then, three months after my ten-day Trabzon visa trip, I took another one. This one was to escort Benjamin, an American guy and one of the leaders of the Tehran group.

Our consular friend in Trabzon stamped a good visa in Benjamin's passport, and then, since we'd used up nearly all our money, we tried for three hours to *hitchhike* out of Trabzon, to no avail. But I had finally become *adept* at something—traveling quickly, keeping the move on and getting *out* of a place. It meant meeting bus schedules, asking if any seats were available on the next one, buying it *now* and . . . being on time. Though Eastern Turkey might seem primitive, their buses departed *promptly.* Don't miss the bus. Get *out* of there. This was particularly expedient in small Turkish towns. *Nobody* wants to get stuck overnight in one of these. Keep moving!

So, from our hitchhiking spot, we went straight back to town to the hotel where Altaf, a young Pakistani guy, was staying. We had befriended him at the embassy, and we knew he was headed by bus for Tehran.

"Altaf. We need to borrow money from you to get to Tehran," I said. "We'll pay you back in Tehran."

"Okay," he said. "We'll travel together."

We stayed in a room next to his for the night, and the following morning, the three of us caught a 7 a.m. bus out of Trabzon.

It was January, so snow and ice covered nearly the entire route from Trabzon to Tehran. But the shocker for *chilling* cold for me was at the Erzurum bus depot. I think it was the coldest I'd ever been in my life when the three of us had to walk across its parking lot of *solid* ice in driving wind and snow that stung our bare faces until we reached and boarded our next bus. Bitter cold! Then, the only seating available for the three of us on the bus to Dogubayazit was the long bench seat at the extreme back of the bus where the right rear, back door opened every now and then to load and unload passengers along the way—the door that let the icy air gush right in on us every time.

Arriving in Tehran, we set Altaf up in the Amir Kabir Hotel, went and fetched 1600 rials ($23) from our brethren and fully paid him back that night. *God bless him.* Now *that* was a miracle—God touching the heart of a traveling Pakistani to loan money to two strange Americans.

Chapter 25
—∞ *Persian Girls* ∞—

TEHRAN HAD BECOME a decent place to live. Perhaps it was the combination of bars serving ice-cold, Iranian *obb-joe* ("wheat water" or beer); the abundant restaurants with cheap, flavorful food and good Iranian wine; the available fast food restaurants; and . . . the exotically beautiful Persian women everywhere. The high standard of living helped, too.

It amazed me, though, how Iran, like other countries out East here, provided for their poor, working-class citizens. There were no beggars, and no one starved in this country. Food staples and good hot meals were too cheap for anyone to go hungry. Like the Iranian bread. Wholesome whole wheat, flat, round and nearly two feet in diameter, it cost a ridiculous 10 cents or so, and one piece could fill an adult.

There was another flat bread—a rectangular one—about two feet by one foot, more puffy, about an inch thick, with ridges down the length of it. Made of refined white flour, it was more palatable so cost a bit more. Both breads were freshly baked in brick ovens of the numerous street-side bakeries. Inside the ovens, the bread sat on hot, natural little pebbles that often remained stuck on the bread when we bought it. I enjoyed dislodging and flicking these pebbles into the street whenever I walked home with the bread.

Then there was a working-class meal in Iran that could revitalize the hardest working laborer for a few measly rials, about 69 cents. It was called *obbgoosh*. Iranian friends introduced me to it, and I ate it every now and then, though it sat a bit heavy on my "Western" stomach. Served only at workers' restaurants, it arrived at the table in a fairly tall, metal chalice-like bowl along with a rod—like a mortar and pestle—to smash it all up. Consisting of boiled potatoes, carrots, other vegetables, some lamb meat and legumes, it came so piping hot that smashing it with the pestle helped dissipate some of the heat. It was gratifying, especially on a cold winter's day when we didn't have much money.

Mandatory to eat with the obbgoosh was a raw onion. Iranians *had* to have them. I remember when the country had an onion shortage once. It caused a national dilemma.

Another cheap place to patronize for the working class, or anyone, was the basic tea shop. Usually situated at street level, these shops served hundreds, if not thousands of glasses of steaming hot Iranian tea a day, along with plenty of that hard gant sugar. Nothing quite compared to this tea to recharge a person while out walking—or litnessing like we often were—in the streets of Tehran, especially during the cold of winter when it often snowed quite heavily. So warming. Something from God to keep us going.

The bread, the obbgoosh, the tea—were so cheap. They must have been subsidized by the government. Otherwise, it was unfathomable how shop owners could make any money on the pittance of coins they charged for these products, all the *same* price throughout the country.

Outside Tehran, wondrous natural beauty existed. Within minutes we could separate ourselves from Tehran's concrete and asphalt and go to the fresh clean air of majestic mountains and crystal clear rivers flowing through untouched valleys and meadows. God obviously knows our spirits need contact with His creation since some form of nature remains near any city.

I had a great experience with Rana in the middle of such nature northeast of Tehran. She and I went there in a car one sunny afternoon with her younger brother and some of his friends. After stopping, Rana and I became slightly separated from the others. It was one of the few times I was able to have her alone to myself, away from her home and family. That's when I led her to Jesus. We were sitting on some grass next to a beautiful stream, talking about God. I then took her hands in mine, we bowed our heads, and she repeated after me, "Jesus, please come into my heart. Forgive me of my sins. And give me eternal life. Amen."

It was magical. She looked up into my eyes and smiled. She then stood up and went to the stream, bent down to the water and said, "Should I wash my face with this water?"

"Yes. If you want," I said.

She lightly splashed her face with the water, as if baptizing herself.

But oppression hung over this land. Prosperity was here, yes, but it was overshadowed by the dictator of the country—the Shah. Women dressed fashionably in tight jeans and skirts, bars legally sold alcohol, there were discotheques and nightclubs—freedom, so to speak. But don't speak against the Shah. Those who did were jailed. Or worse. What could be expected from a guy who demanded his picture be displayed everywhere and who called himself the Shahanshah—The King of Kings?

The Iranians said nothing concerning the Shah—for or against him. When I asked them how they felt about the Shah, they'd put a forefinger to their lips and say, "Sh-sh-sh. I will say nothing, for or against. The walls have ears." Indeed, Savak—the Shah's secret police—insidiously infiltrated the entire country.

Near the end of my stay in Iran—spring of 1976—the Shah's influence seemed more overwhelming than ever. Driving through the country, I saw banners stretched across main roads, proclaiming his magnificence next to giant drawings and photos of the guy. Was this a sign of his insecurity due to an evident, underlying *un*popularity? How many people could continue to stand by and watch their sons and daughters disappear at the hands of this despot and continue to comply with hanging more of his photos in their homes, businesses and streets? A good sign that a ruler may soon fall—when he demands *more* acknowledgment and displays of himself.

Beating the streets of Tehran and other major cities—Isfahan, Shiraz and Tabriz—proved fairly successful for us. We reached souls and encouraged their faith in God. For some reason, girls and young women seemed most attracted to the words. They stopped on the streets for the literature, gave generous donations for it, responded to it through the mail and actually met with us in person.

A few Iranian guys became close friends and lived with us for a while, but nobody fully dropped out and joined us. Family ties here ran strong, and it would have been too much of a shame to "forsake all" and join up with our "band of Westerners."

Christian Armenian girls came closest to joining us. More free and radical than their Iranian counterparts, they voluntarily translated our literature and even distributed it along with us.

One Armenian girl, Sylva, came as close as anyone to joining us, and I became "responsible" for her spiritual growth. A 21-year-old attending college, she sort of joined us while continuing to live with her parents near our home. She said to me while the two of us were out alone together on a Thursday evening (the equivalent in the West of a Friday or Saturday weekend night), "Wayne, you know what *most* people do on Thursday nights here, don't you?"

Oh Lord. It did not even sink in to me until later, when I learned a little more about this hot little 21-year-old, that she might want to play around with me sexually. I totally missed her hint. How naïve could I be? Or, was it miraculous ignorance? Perhaps it was *God,* keeping me from marrying one of these women . . . out in this strange and distant land.

Then there was the decision I'd regret and wonder about for years. I was in a taxi with one of the sisters on Pahlavi Street, on our way to distribute literature when who hails down and joins us in the same cab? Farideh and Abbas! My heart somersaulted, and I'm pretty sure hers did too. Our flame rekindled in the close confines of the taxi.

"Becky, this is Farideh," I said. "Remember I told you about her?"

"Yes! Hi! How are you?" Becky said. "Wayne told me a lot about you."

"I am fine," Farideh said, as she looked down demurely.

Goodness, I loved that girl. And here she was again, sitting on the other side of Becky from me, in the back of this cab, so modest with her styled black hair flowing around her pretty face. Unpretentious, like so many third-world girls.

"Where are you guys going?" I asked Abbas, who was up front with the driver.

"We're going to a movie near Namazi Gardens," he said.

A good area for litnessing, we decided to go there with them.

Once there, Abbas, knowing how much Farideh and I cared for each other, *insisted* we go into the theatre with them.

"Wayne. Please! You have to come in with us," he pleaded. He then whispered to me, "Farideh really wants you to come. She told me to tell you."

I knew he was lying about that last part. He just had always wanted Farideh and me to hook up, for some reason.

I looked over at Becky whose face was now contorting through all this.

"What do you think, Becky?" I asked.

"We're supposed to be litnessing, Wayne," she replied.

"Okay." So I *declined* to go into the romantic theatre with this sexy Iranian girl where who knows what kind of touching or simple intimacy may have developed between us. I wouldn't dwell on it, but I'd never forget the dumb choice I made that day either. There were plenty of days to litness. What were the chances of running into this girl in the same cab in such a huge city and then being invited to sit next to her in a dark, air-conditioned theatre?

I never had been alone with Farideh at night. But a couple times my lips did meet with the lips of Sylva and of the precious Carine, another Armenian girl and near disciple. I *had* to kiss some of these girls—single like myself, nearly the same age, often working close together and attracted to each other. They'd have thought I was non-human, or at the least awfully weird if I hadn't responded to the invitation they sometimes made to their wet, waiting lips. *Somebody* had to do it. *Right, Wayne?*

I never led them on though. The only leading on I did with them was toward God's Spirit despite hints from some women for more. As it was, some of them fell by the wayside because it went no further than a kiss, and they wanted—*needed*—more.

We eventually nurtured a group of American high school girls toward the Light. Their dads were in Iran with oil companies or with military companies like Grumman, Boeing and Bell Helicopter. I met the first girl, Andrea, at the City Recreation Center (CRC), there on the east side of town, where she was sitting on a bar-type stool in extremely tight blue jeans with her legs spread open but with an unhappy expression on her face. I happened upon her at a time when she apparently needed some kind of love. From the way she was sitting that day, it may have been a small miracle that some lecher didn't beat me to her. I would learn weeks later that back in the States in her early teens, she'd already had an abortion. Whatever, she proved quite spiritually minded, readily absorbed God's love and sought to associate with us. Eventually, she influenced other American girls and their boyfriends as well. Her younger sister, Katherine, also in high school, gradually came around too, and good thing, because she, like a lot of American kids here, was unknowingly falling victim to the readily available Iranian heroin by "innocently"—she thought—smoking it. Many young Iranians smoked it, sometimes using the foil from their cigarette packs. They sprinkled the heroin powder along the channel formed by folding the foil long-ways into a "V," lighting it from underneath and inhaling its smoke—"chasing the dragon."

Looking back on my 14-month stay in Iran, I figured I knew what kept me here in the crowded metropolis of Tehran for so long—the beautiful

Persian *women*, just admiring them walking in the streets. They're probably what inspired all the guys, Iranian or not, to keep going here.

But it came time to leave this land, beautiful women or not. Despite distributing thousands of pieces of literature that *hopefully* stimulated the faith most Iranians already had in God, the work here was stagnating. Iran was a challenge. Family ties remained strong here, and young people had plenty of love and care right in their own homes. They would not consider dropping out and forsaking all.

We were also causing no small stir. Cops nabbed us off the streets and dragged us down to headquarters for questioning, releasing us, fortunately, because we were Westerners. It became difficult to get the words out. We gradually left to greener, riper fields.

I lucked out. The German Ford van we had on loan from Italy was registered in my name, and those in Italy needed it back. So I would drive it to Italy and then remain in Greece. *Yes.*

As usual, I had only a day or two's notice to uproot myself and move on. This time I didn't have a whole work to hand over to anyone, as in Kabul, but it was most disheartening to have only enough time to say my goodbyes over the telephone to the precious persons—mostly girls— to whom I'd come so close. I was able to see Mike, though, since two others and I already had an appointment to meet him at the Pizzaland Restaurant the day before I was to leave. At the meeting, I gave him an expensive, small Bible, and the three of us gave him a book on the prophecies of Daniel and a certificate as an honorary member of our group. Mike was "gold"—possibly the coolest person we met in all Tehran. When he learned of my plans to leave, Mike handed me $60 (a good chunk of money out here) and bought me a pizza and a bottle of wine for the trip before the two of us embraced for the last time and said goodbye. *God bless him.*

Lauren, an American girl of the group, would accompany me on the journey. She obtained an international driver's license from her expired U.S. license, but it was I who would drive the entire distance with *no* driver's license, since I had lost it back in the Cyprus war, along with my eyeglasses, which, though not critical, I usually used for driving.

Colony shepherd Benjamin and his wife, Becky, awoke early in the morning to pray for us. Benjamin handed me $146 for the trip to Athens, I fired up the van, and Lauren and I departed Tehran at 5:30 a.m., May 15, 1976.

The only thing tricky on the six-day trip to Athens for Lauren and me—two single adults in our mid-twenties driving alone together through the entire length of Turkey and a good part of Greece in our fine, empty, German-built Ford van—was our *libidos*. Opportunity for physical intimacy was there ... but it never happened. On the fourth day, though, I nearly stopped the van along the main highway somewhere between Ankara and Istanbul to wander off in broad daylight into the exceptionally beautiful landscape of pine trees, valleys and grazing cows, to have a *picnic* with Lauren. Possible scenarios ran through my mind, but the urge somehow passed, and I continued driving until we reached Istanbul at 8 p.m. When we discovered our brethren had since moved, we headed for the Sultan Ahmet area and parked the van in what would be the only legitimate place we'd parked for the last three nights—between two white lines in the paved parking lot across the street from the Pudding Shop, alongside other world-traveler vehicles. I fell asleep on the front seat as usual while Lauren took her place in the back.

In the wee hours of the next morning, I had unmistakable clues that Lauren had the same problem as I when I heard her in the back "helping herself out." *Oh, man. What were we supposed to do?*

Off we drove from Istanbul, arriving in Athens two nights later at midnight of our sixth day traveling. We'd made the journey without incident from either our sexual urges or *far* worse encounters, while sleeping in the van at night along rivers, farm roads, main roads and fields—a young American couple at night in the middle of nowhere, just *out* there—protected, for sure, by angels and prayer. "The angel of the Lord encampeth round about them that fear him, and delivereth them" (Psalm 34.7).

Chapter 26
⇜ *Quick Trip to Italy* ⇝

GREECE MUST BE one of the best places in the world for sex, fun and sun. The dry, sunny, Mediterranean climate alone—in summer anyway— attracts people from all over the world who, if they come to Greece, end up in Athens at some time or another. The country is a bargain, too—a lot of food, entertainment and good housing for the money.

Still on a mission, though, to "save the world," we were not here as tourists. We were here to *work* in Athens, or better yet, to "work Athens" with the literature and God's love—to reach as many people as possible, including Greeks.

So what did Lauren and I do the following morning after tele-phoning the base home of our arrival the night before? We went litnessing. A girl from the Athens colony came and accompanied us. *Oh, joy.* A "great" reception after traveling a few thousand miles from out East. No offer to shower, freshen up, unwind a little bit, get acquainted with the Athens Work. No. Plunge right into the streets by 12 noon. Bite the bullet, Wayne, and keep praising God. Sacrifice. Die to yourself. Follow orders like dumb sheep. Lauren and I did. And it wasn't too bad, either, along a street others had dubbed, "The Look of Love Street" near Syntagma Square, full of beautiful Greek and foreign women shopping.

Apparently litnessing was still the predominant means of support and method of getting the words out here in Greece. And with four million of Greece's total population of ten million living in Athens alone, there were always new faces to hand literature to.

This was one crowded city. Fortunately, I spoke some Greek—from my seven months in Cyprus. But *still* I was lousy at litnessing. Hopefully, I could be used here in some other capacity.

For now, I had to deliver the van to Italy. So, after three days of "working" the streets—but not before reuniting with some good old acquaintances like Aaron and Debbie, now married and with a child, Bob and his wife, and some others—I was glad to drive off westward toward the port city of Patres, Greece, along with a married, Canadian couple of the group needing a ride to that city. Given $100—about enough money to purchase one-way ferryboat tickets for myself and the van to Brindisi, Italy—I barely made it through customs in time to board the *Crysovalandou* ship by 9:30 that evening.

I enjoyed being alone. But it turned out to be a good thing I remained faithful to preach the Gospel to every creature wherever I was, because I did just that while sitting in the airline-type seats in the ship's upper lounge that night. There, I struck up a conversation with Angelo, an Italian, Marxist guy who'd been in Greece for a few weeks on a writing assignment. He was fairly receptive to the words, but the main thing on this guy's mind tonight, believe it or not, was *spaghetti*. A plate of real Italian spaghetti. Upset that during his time in Greece he was unable to find any *good* spaghetti, Angelo was now thrilled to be returning to his homeland of Italy for the *real* thing—natural noodles cooked "al dente" and topped with sauce that had simmered for several hours with genuine Italian herbs and spices. I was taken aback that the guy was entirely serious, but apparently it's no myth Italians love their spaghetti.

Angelo discovered that aboard the ship I had a van I was delivering to his same destination of Bari—a two-hour drive farther north from Brindisi, where the ship would dock. "Can I get a ride with you? To Bari?" he asked.

"Of course you can," I said, happy to oblige. We said goodnight, and I walked down to the deck below for a good, sound sleep in the van.

The boat stopped at the Greek island of Corfu sometime the following morning to load and unload passengers, made it pleasantly through the Strait of Otranto—between Albania and Italy—and arrived in Brindisi at 4 in the afternoon Italy time, two hours behind Greece. Angelo joined me at the van, and I started to drive it off the ship when an Italian policeman, looking over the papers of the van said, "*Aspetta. Aspetta. L'assicurazione e finito. Non e possibilay entrare Italia. Mi dispiace.*"

The insurance on the van had expired, and the policeman was not allowing the vehicle to even *leave* the ship. *Great.* And of course I had no money. *Well, it looks like I'm going to have to trust God. After all, He did get this van all the way here from Tehran. He can surely get it off this ship.*

And He did.

Hardly knowing me or if I would pay him back, Angelo said, "Don't worry. I will pay it." He stepped out of the van and walked down to the dock. There, he paid the Italian authorities 19,000 lira (about $35) for the minimum requirement of five days of insurance and brought the papers back to me. I showed them to the policeman, and he let us drive off the ship. We then headed northward to Bari along the lovely coastline of the Adriatic Sea. And sure enough, Angelo directed me to a restaurant he knew in Bari where he partook of his long-anticipated spaghetti, treating me to the same, and it *was* yummy. From there we drove to my friends who gratefully reimbursed Angelo 20,000 lira, and I drove him to the train station. The lesson I had learned on previous trips came alive once again today: when traveling, especially *alone*, try to make good friends with people. You might suddenly need them.

The following day I cleaned the van to spotlessness, actually had a good first experience at passing out literature at an Italian stoplight and was now in awe of the beauty of *Italian* girls. One day in Bari, Italy, and I had changed my opinion of "most beautiful women per capita in a country" from Iranian girls a few days ago to Italian girls today. These girls weren't even *trying* to be sexy and attractive—they were just naturally so—as they scurried, scantily but neatly clad through the city on foot or puttered through the streets on their own little motor scooters, oblivious and unconcerned that their miniskirts might be hiking themselves up, up, up their thighs nearly to their panties! *Oh, my Lord.* It was already getting tough here in Europe for me. In battles between the physical and the spiritual, the physical was winning more and more.

When two guys came from Rome to pick up the van, they were amazed to see it shiny and clean—especially after its stint in Iran. I signed the papers over to one of them and handed him the keys. My mission was accomplished on my second day in Bari. So I headed back to Athens, accompanied by Jeff, the head of the Bari Work, who was transferring to Athens for some reason. We caught the 5:30 p.m. train to Brindisi for the 19-hour boat ride, at 18,000 Italian lira (about $33) each, to Patres, Greece.

Aboard the ship, at Jeff's instigation, we passed literature out . . . to my dismay. I had not yet adjusted to the *unfettered* Italian litnessing attitude as opposed to the *circumspect* litnessing outlook necessary back in Tehran, and even Greece. I never liked "confined" litnessing—on buses, trains, boats, subways, planes—either. I hated being exposed like that. I felt, too, that passing Words of Faith to others was more a personal thing, almost spiritual lovemaking—to be done with finesse. Not only that, there was nowhere to run and escape from possible opposition. I mean, the following morning Jeff was up litnessing first thing, while I enjoyed breakfast and checked out the ship decks, the sun and passing Greek islands.

We arrived in Patres at 7:30 p.m. Greece time—two hours ahead— caught a plush tourist bus at 8:30 for 200 drachmas ($5.70) each, stopped for a lunch of skewered pork kebabs at the Corinth Canal and arrived in Athens at midnight for a good sound sleep in one of our coffeehouse homes.

I was back in Greece.

Chapter 27
— *Living in Plaka* —

IN SUMMER, FOREIGNERS flocked to Athens before dispersing to the beaches and islands of Greece. So, knowing the city well from pounding its streets daily, we assisted them with an "Athens Information" sheet, like the one we had in Kabul. Directed mostly toward travelers on tight budgets, it listed some of the best and cheapest restaurants and hotels in Athens, among other points of interest not found on normal tourist maps and brochures. We handed the small sheet of paper out for free; it broke the ice and helped us get to know some of the foreigners. To cover the cost of printing, two guys and I periodically collected donations from certain restaurant and hotel owners listed on the sheet. If places turned weird, we crossed them off.

Myself and a couple others of the 20 or more workers in the Athens group were chosen to live among the world travelers in the Plaka area of Athens, near the Acropolis, where hotels on the information paper were located. I liked this assignment. It meant freedom. Go as we pleased, no house rules, and it kept us in the midst of young people from all over the world.

Establishments listed on the information sheet were tried and proven—slept in or eaten in by us—before making the list. Some of the hotel/hostels were: Fotis House, World Inn, Jimmy's Student House, the International Student House, Kouros Guest House, the Students' Inn, Mary's Guest House, Fantis House and the Meeting House. Some of the traveler-friendly restaurants were: the 16th Century Restaurant; Pete's Pub; Happy Trumpet; the YMCA cafeteria; and Mary's, George's, Fritos', Diana's and Latif's restaurants.

The "houses" and "inns" were quite a bargain at about 45 drachmas ($1.95) a night. A guest didn't have a private room at that price, but he didn't complain either that he slept in one big room with everyone else. *Heck no.* Not when half those in there were *girls*, dressing and undressing nonchalantly, getting in and out of their beds wearing nothing but panties and T-shirts. It was quite a show, any time of day or night. If a girl had an eye for someone, she'd make sure to undress in front of him. *Good Lord.* For a little extra money, *inhibited* girls could rent a "Girls Only" room in most places.

For even *less* money than the *indoor* rooms, guests could sleep *outside*—still co-ed—on the flat roofs, walled of course. Skies over Athens in summer were clear enough to sleep under with little or no chance of rain.

It really was . . . the *life* here in Greece. We couldn't complain, even if we *were* practically penniless most of the time, selling literature in the streets to stay alive. *I* probably averaged about 250 drachmas ($7) a day in donations, which, with our lifestyle, was more than enough to comfortably live on around Plaka, send some of it in to home base and still enjoy the delicacies of Athens.

A typical day for me in Athens in summer of 1976 would be to wake up in a youth hostel (among half-dressed girls) and head to a small café with a partner for a breakfast of thick, Greek, sheep yogurt topped with pure, natural honey (*yaourti mai melli*)—served in a small, plastic container along with a cup of overly caffeinated Nescafé coffee. This normal sheep yogurt was superb, *or* we went for the thicker *fagay* yogurt that had gone through a process whereby most of the water is extracted from it—the *real* thing. We then hit the streets with the literature for two or three hours. I had good days and bad with it, but in Greece we learned to ease the strain of litnessing by rewarding ourselves, after a morning session of it, with a hot Greek lunch along with a cold bottle of Amstel beer—quite possibly one of the world's best commercially produced beers, brewed here under license from Holland. Then, like the Greeks, we rested in the afternoon, away from the heat and sun.

In the evening we went back out into the streets, now cooler and once again lively with Greeks, but not before "taking the edge off" with a glass or two of cold *Retsina* wine at any open-air tavern or café. After an hour or two of getting some words out and some drachmas in return, we'd mingle, meet and talk with any of the multitude of travelers or even young Greeks, usually in the Plaka area.

The Greeks, more than the travelers, supported us with their donations for the literature. And, with the group increasing in number all over Greece, we had to use different techniques to get the literature into the hands of the people and a donation in return—without totally burning out the small Greek population of 10 million people and getting run out of the country. One way was to "café litness." Two of us went out into the cool of the evenings, one with a guitar, and approached Greeks who were enjoying a favorite pastime—sitting at street-side, outdoor café-restaurants in the pleasant Greek night air, consuming little, grilled, pork or lamb kebabs skewered on short bamboo sticks along with continuous little plates of delectable Greek foods, while sipping on brandy, wine or beer and listening to Greek *bazooki* music. They were loosened up and in their realm at these cafés and were generally conducive to handing a few hundred drachmas to us "odd Western minstrels," as we sang songs in Greek to them and passed them pieces of literature.

Tactics would still have to change though for us to continue functioning here in Greece. And they did. We opened a discotheque the first week of July, 1976, on the edge of the night clubs of Plaka.

The place—a huge second floor of a building—was normally used only for a discotheque during the cooler, winter months. The Greek owner, like other disco owners in Athens who felt such lower floors were too hot during the summer, had transferred his club to the breezy open-aired roof on the floor above since it cost too much to run air conditioning in Greece. So, we rented this second floor for nearly nothing from the guy, put some fans in the windows, and it stayed pretty cool.

Located near the Acropolis, our disco was open to anyone but was directed more toward foreign, student/traveler types—like Americans, Europeans, Australians. More of a meeting place of entertainment than a disco, it served well our intended purpose: to offer somewhere foreign travelers could hang out at night. At a nominal cover charge that included the first drink, it stayed packed nearly every night. We offered a simple selection of drinks—Amstel beer, red and white Greek Domestica wine, and Cokes—all sold at nearly cost. The club wasn't there to make money off the travelers who had little anyway, but rather to, "knock on the door to their hearts."

Besides having tables and chairs throughout the place, we built a small stage next to a small dance floor for our own live band and upon which we performed skits "with a message" in front of our "captives-unawares." Our disco was a disguised *trap*, run and infiltrated by members of us who latched onto hungry souls with God's love, before the guests knew what had happened.

They loved it, though, these wandering souls from developed countries, entering into the dimly lit floor with "Tequila Sunrise," "One of These Nights" or "Lyin' Eyes" by the Eagles or other familiar tunes blaring wonderfully over the sound system between the band's sets. They could relate here, feeling more at home than in the Greek discos. Besides being clean and different, it was Western!

The club was a great diversion for *me* too, since I was getting tired of litnessing all day. There had to be another way to reach souls. I became one of the club's managers but was particularly in charge of its maintenance. I acted in some of the skits but felt totally out of place. What I did take pride in was keeping the place clean and well supplied with everything from drinks to toilet paper. As for the bathrooms, I was fastidious with them. My one chance in the world to have an establishment like this with bathrooms that remained spotlessly clean and never lacked paper towels, toilet paper or soap, damn it . . . unlike so many dumps. When the club had guests, I'd check on the men's room periodically and straighten it up and supply it myself, if need be. I assigned one of the girls to do the same throughout opening hours in the women's room.

Like the rest of the discos and nightclubs in Athens, ours sometimes remained open into the early morning hours. Greece in summer was a nightlife place where it wasn't uncommon to stay out until sunrise. Although Athens is a large capital city, I felt safe walking around at three, four, five o'clock in the morning.

I learned about nightlife in Plaka when I moved into the small home those of us who ran the disco found to rent near the club. Sitting above and overlooking the whole Plaka disco/nightclub scene, the cozy abode was one of several little homes clustered on the northeast slope of the actual Acropolis mountain, making up the village of Anafiotika. Any tourists approaching the Parthenon from Plaka followed a winding stone path right past our window. Made of mud bricks, whitewashed and trimmed with blue paint, the typically old, adobe-like, Greek home stayed quite cool in the summer heat. Flowing with the contour of the mountain, the house, though small—one bedroom, one bath, large living room, large porch—was two levels, connected to each other inside by neat little stone steps. The place was "home" to me, and it beat the "camping out" at the student houses I'd been doing for weeks.

But it was also where I learned to despise the sound of an electric piano/organ—those portable types, like they used down below our house in the Plaka restaurants and nightclubs. Whee-whee-whee they went with that tinny sound all night long, into the early morning hours. Eventually I learned to sleep with the background noise of Plaka, but to this day I do despise the sound of an electric keyboard. *Whee-whee-whee.*

Chapter 28
❧ *Sex, Fun and Sun* ❧

BY THE MIDDLE of July, I needed to get out of Athens for more than just a day, for a better taste of Greece. So three of us—Nick, a British guy of the group; Carol, a British girl who'd met someone on the streets with the literature three days earlier and was considering joining the group; and I—headed north for a vacation. One of those "out-on-the-limb" vacations—"by faith," with no money, only a guitar, some literature, swimsuits, sleeping bags and a change or two of clothes. Challenging, yes. But not necessarily the best way to take a vacation. Not that God couldn't supply, but He usually doesn't drop money from the sky.

Tallish and slim, in her early twenties, with blue eyes and dark wavy hair nearly to her waist, Carol was simply sexy and attractive. The three of us hitchhiked easily from Athens northward on the main E75 highway to the coastal town of Kamena Vourla, about one hundred miles away and not too far from the larger city of Lamia. Having a guitar along helped, even though *I* had to play it. I knew some songs in Greek and did "okay" when forced into it. Good enough for the three of us to get fed well that night from singing at restaurants and passing literature out. But not quite good enough for a hotel room. We drank some glasses of red wine at an outdoor café and ended up among small fishing boats on a little, slanted beach of tiny rocks where we stretched out our sleeping bags for a good night's sleep in the open air.

First thing in the morning, Carol and I went straight into the water, just steps away from our sleeping bags. This calm body of water was more of an inlet, rather than the open Aegean Sea. Across it, easily visible, stretched the long, extended island of Evia. *Perhaps we should go there.*

On our walk to buy food with what money we had left, we checked out the ferryboat to Evia. *Damn.* Eighty drachmas ($2.20) roundtrip, 45 one way. More than we could afford. *Man, I was a lousy guitarist, beggar and litnesser.* By this time Carol started losing it—out on the limb like this, with us bums. She questioned this whole vacation.

Then, after an unsuccessful hour or two of *kindly* trying to get some drachmas for the literature here in Kamena Vourla, I too grew disgusted with this town. As hard as I attempted to teach and show this new girl some faith, the people of this town weren't yielding or helping at all. Nick hadn't been in the group too long either, so it was up to me to lead the way. And I did. I led them right back to the dock, money be damned, to "get the hell outta Dodge!" The three of us *ran* to the ferryboat, but there it was, already churning its engines and pulling away.

I waved it back in earnest. The boatswain, still winding up the ropes, saw us and quickly told the captain, who immediately reversed his engines, returned to the dock and waited for the three of us to jump aboard. It was a small ferry, 40-footer maybe, with not many passengers today, Tuesday. Instead of inside seating, we chose one of the long, wooden benches on the boat's upper, open-air deck.

It wasn't until the boat was about a quarter of the way into its run across the bay that the same boatswain who'd let us on came around to collect fares from everyone.

"*Then ekoomay leftah*," I said to the guy, looking him right in the eyes. I'm pretty sure he sensed, before even asking us, that we had no money. But when I confirmed it, the expression on his face contorted in milliseconds between amazement and anger.

In place of a ticket or money, I handed him a piece of literature and explained our missionary work to him in Greek. The guy was not amused. He was Greek. In my opinion, the Greeks have never done well with money. They seek after it too much. Here they are with one of the most beautiful countries in the world—mountains, rivers, greenery, beaches, islands, crystal clear waters, a Mediterranean climate and land capable of growing nearly any type of fruit, vegetable or nut known to man—and yet they want *money*, too.

Mentioning O Theos to the guy was probably what kept him from throwing us overboard right then and there. He'd get over it. Maybe not today, but soon. And God forgive us.

We humbly disembarked on Evia at Ayios Georgios, grateful for the free ferry ride and happy to set foot on new territory. The short, seven-mile boat ride had landed us in another world, thickly shaded by a forest of pine trees spread along hills and valleys all the way down to the water's edge. "Can you smell that?" I said to Nick and Carol, as I sniffed the air.

"What?" Nick asked.

"The smell of pine," I said.

"Yeah! Yeah!" they both said.

Now noontime, the sun was baking out the sap of these trees, creating this refreshing scent, combined with a pleasant, salty sea breeze drifting through the air. *Invigorating already out here, money or no money.* Hardly a soul in sight, just total peace and quiet. On the edge of town, we swam in calm, clear water and then had a lunch of some bread, cheese and olives we'd brought along.

Walking along the only road, a paved road eastward, we came upon an isolated, Greek, seaside home. Family members sitting outside compelled us to come down off the road to join them. "*Katheestay, katheestay,*" they insisted, whereby I soon broke out the guitar and sang some songs in Greek—to their amazement. Nick and Carol sort of sang and clapped along. The family loved it. Not many strangers on foot passed by their home for them to entertain, and far fewer stopped to entertain *them*, like we oddball Westerners. They showered us with sweets and coffee.

Our goal today though was to find a good beach. "*Poo enay paralia kala?*" I asked them.

"*Ekee, ekee, akoma leega,*" they nearly all replied, pointing farther eastward.

There it was, not too far down the road from the house: a dream-like, private, secluded cove, wrapped with a white, sandy beach and surrounded by the same prolific, shady pines. We walked to the other side of the cove for the afternoon sun, noticing on the way, tucked into the woods, what appeared to be an expensive resort. *It must be nice. Maybe some day.*

The resort probably had its own private beach because the only people sharing this cove with us today were those of a small, glistening-white, French sailing yacht anchored a hundred yards out from where we stretched our towels for some swimming and sunbathing.

Nick and I were soon in for a show. The French yacht also had a ski boat with topless women skiing behind it around the cove all day long. *Goodness.* Had the skiers minded Nick and I watching them, they might have put their bikini tops back on. Instead, they dropped their tiny bikini *bottoms* too, and skied around butt naked. *Ahh. The fun and sun of Greece.*

The sun set, the cool of the evening crept in, and we still had food and water so we figured we'd sleep this night under the stars in this idyllic setting. But no. We were reminded that there is *no* perfect place on earth.

With no breeze tonight, "the curse" came to us in the form of *hungry mosquitoes*. We tried to sleep, but if we stuck our faces out of our sleeping bags to breathe . . . bzzz, they attacked us.

"Oh, I can't take this!" Carol said.

"You're right," I agreed, "we need to get outta here. We'll go back to that home." We packed up and headed toward the Greek house. Those monsters might have killed us if we hadn't left that beach.

When we reached the home at 10:30 that night, the Greeks, like most Greeks, were still wide awake. Our singing and talking about God earlier with the family had apparently imparted our trustworthiness because they welcomed us warmly, *God bless them*.

"*Poli kounoupi eki!*" we told them, concerning the many mosquitoes there.

No shit! the Greeks probably wanted to say. Instead they said, "*Nay, nay. Poli kounoupi ee neekta,*" echoing our words. "*Prepeena yeepto mai mas apopsay,*" they continued, insisting we stay the night with them.

They seemed happy to see us—*thank God*—and fed us lavishly right then and there, before leading us to our own private room for the night. *Rescued again, Wayne?*

Before drifting off to sleep, Carol and I talked. "I was raped," she said.

"What?" I asked, surprised.

"Yes," she continued, "a few months ago, back in England. I knew the guy, but still . . . he raped me. It was horrible."

"I'm so sorry," I said. It explained why she was a bit standoffish to me—even though back in Athens she didn't seem to mind if I saw her white panties beneath the nice, blue-jean miniskirt she often wore. We talked until we fell asleep.

Everyone awoke by 7:30 the next morning, the young children of the family eager to spend time with "the foreigners." So, after a Greek breakfast of olives, Feta cheese, bread and coffee, and hoping to be a blessing to our delightful hosts, we spent three wonderful hours with the kids doing what comes natural to Greeks—swimming. The kids led us to the clear, clean water at the shore straight down from the house, like any other kids of the world might take you to their backyard to play ball. There was an added luxury to the fun and sun of this swim, too—using the kids' masks and fins. A big deal to us beggars.

But it was time for us to end our little vacation and return to Athens. We bid farewell to this loving family, caught a ride to Ayios

Georgios and somehow came up with 35 drachmas each, for the half-hour ferry ride back to the mainland. *This* ferry went to Ayios Konstantinos—a straight run across the bay—more of a port city than goofy Kamena Vourla. From there we hitched a ride with a rich, young Greek guy from the nearby island of Skiathos and arrived in Athens by 4 p.m.

Returning to most big cities from a serene vacation in the countryside can be a real letdown. But Athens, and particularly Plaka—bustling with its turnover of travelers—wasn't too bad. I found it comforting actually to be back in Athens after being out in unfamiliar, practically uninhabited Ayios Georgios. Picture-perfect and naturally beautiful, but with no money and no potential to make any either. At least in Athens we had work with thousands, if not millions, of people who might buy our literature. We could survive here. It's what attracts people worldwide to metropolises—opportunities. A chance to survive.

Athens served up inexpensive Greek salads, souflakis and wines; we could shower and sleep for less than $2.00 a night in a student/traveler house; and, while maintaining this decent lifestyle selling literature to the throngs of people, we simultaneously reached lost souls in the streets.

I kept busy with the disco, not only helping run it, but nurturing some of the girls who latched onto the Message of Love found there— American, British, Canadian, Danish, Norwegian, Greek and other girls. *Somebody* had to do it. *Might as well be me. Man! There were benefits in this work.*

The disco "trap" worked well, but by the middle of August, we decided to close it. Besides neighbors hassling us for being too loud some nights, we figured if we were going to live in Greece, we should be reaching Greeks. Let them take over the Work here in their own country.

Going to movies at night was another bonus in Athens where theatres showed the latest feature films in English. Some of the movie houses were quite amazing. Certain of them had retractable roofs that opened in summer. We watched movies under the fresh air and stars, unless it rained, whereby they closed the roofs. Or, for a few measly drachmas, we sat in outdoor theatres on wooden chairs to catch a flick. That's how fantastic the weather was in Greece. Although sometimes hot during the day in summer, it was a dry heat, and nights were usually quite cool.

Still, the highlight of Greece is its islands and beaches. The country covers only 50,000 square miles—about the size of England or the state of Alabama—but it would take a lifetime to explore just the coastlines of mainland Greece and her islands with all their nooks, crannies, coves and beaches. And that's without even experiencing her *inland* beauty of mountains, valleys, rivers and quaint little towns.

Fortunately, I got a chance, after working hard enough in Athens all summer, to visit another island of this wonderful country before the cold weather set in. The first week of September 1976, a brother, Alberto—a manager and actor at the disco—and I, went to the island of Hydra for a spur-of-the-moment vacation.

Goodness. What a fabulous island, and so close to Athens. Again, it would have been great to have some money along, but what the heck, we both needed a break from the city. So we stuffed some canned foods and literature into our backpacks, had a smattering of drachmas and purchased two one-way tickets to Hydra on the 2 p.m. ferry from Piraeus.

After three or four quick stops at islands along the way, we reached Hydra in three and a half hours at 5:30 p.m. Nearly straight south from Piraeus and just off the easternmost peninsula of the Peloponnese, Hydra was a gem of an island, especially for its nearness to Athens. In less than four hours from Piraeus—on a slow, non-express ferryboat— we docked on this serene island with all the amenities of the civilized world, like restaurants, discos, hotels and shops, yet no cars were allowed. There were paved roads, but the only vehicle on the island was a small dump truck used to collect all the trash. How nice it was to walk in a city without the apprehension that a car, truck or bus might run us over. The place soothed us immediately, its quiet, little harbor dotted with simple to elegant shops, pleasant outdoor restaurants and cafés and a separate impressive stretch of moored, private luxury yachts off to the side.

The island had been recommended to Alberto and me by colleagues back in Athens, but we would have to discover the place for ourselves. We used up some of our drachmas for dinner and then wandered up and down charming, cobblestone streets and alleys of the main town here, also named Hydra. Before long, we came across two girls, one a Greek-American and the other, an American married to a Greek guy. They knew the island well.

"What do you normally do around here?" Alberto asked them.

"Well, tomorrow we'll be going out to a nearby island to swim . . . in the raw," Lisa, the married one, said. "My husband's coming and some others. You guys are welcome to come along, if you want."

"Uh, yeah, maybe," Alberto replied. "What time are you going?"

"We meet at 12 noon, down by the small fishing boat at the center of the harbor," Lisa said.

After that we met up with three British/Yorkshire girls our age with whom we spent the rest of the evening eating, drinking, talking. Women were everywhere here, obviously. "Where are you all staying?" we asked them, at the end of the night.

"Nowhere," one of them answered, "we don't have any reservations. Most places were already booked when we got here. We don't have much money anyway."

"Well, we have no place either," we told them.

"We figured we'd find somewhere in the surrounding hills to camp," Alberto said. "Care to join us?"

"Sure. Let's go," two of the girls said.

The five of us walked up the paved road northward out of town at midnight or so and before long rounded a large hill that left us completely out of sight of the harbor and town behind us. There, across a steep, rocky cove, a small house basked in the moonlight all by itself, with not a sign of life in it or anywhere else in the secluded hills.

We followed the road around the cove until we reached the house. "Wait here," Alberto said to the girls, who appeared apprehensive— pausing and huddling together. "Wayne and I'll go check it out."

Alberto and I cautiously approached the home, though it looked quite obviously vacant. It was a brand new, stone cottage sitting just off the road on this bluff, overlooking its own private rocky cove below, the sea and the Peloponnese mainland in the distance. After walking around the house to make certain there was no one inside, I returned to the girls. "Come on down, ladies," I told them. "There's nobody here."

No one was going to do any breaking and entering of any house on this pristine island, but fortunately the home had a long, walled, concrete balcony built onto its north side. Although narrow, the balcony had plenty of room for the five of us to stretch out our sleeping bags and make ourselves comfortable for the night, still in the open air, but sheltered and protected by the house—for free. Literally "on the house."

This must have been the only house for miles around because when we awoke the next morning, there still wasn't a person in sight anywhere. Having slept well, we all packed our bags and walked the paved road back to town for breakfast. By now, Alberto and I had struck up an inkling of a relationship with two of the girls, but when there are three girlfriends together like that, and one's left out, it's odd and hard to develop the relationship further.

"Well, I guess we'll see you guys later," Sharon, one of the girls, said. "Maybe we'll meet up in the evening somewhere."

"Yeah. Okay. See you later," I said.

The girls walked off and Alberto looked at me and said, "Are we really going to go swim naked with those people?"

It was a bit scary, but we decided we would. We met up with Lisa at the dock, right where she said she'd be at noon. On the trip would be Lisa and her Greek husband, Lisa's friend the Greek-American girl, another Greek girl and an American-Indian-looking, Charles Bronson-type guy—all of us somewhere in our twenties. The five of them had been on this excursion before so had already arranged with the same weathered, laid-back Greek fisherman to run us out in his skiff to the small island. We were asked to contribute to the roundtrip boat ride. Fortunately, we still had some money.

The boat was a typical little, wooden Greek fishing boat, like a long rowboat, painted blue and white, about 20 feet long, with a small Johnson outboard engine on the back. We all introduced ourselves and climbed into the boat. It puttered out of the harbor at 12:30. Once out of the port of Hydra, the fisherman stretched a nice canvas canopy over our heads for shade. We headed southwestward and reached the tiny barren island in about 20 minutes. The fisherman dropped us off at the west corner of the island. He knew we'd be swimming and sunbathing out here naked, but couldn't care less really. Sex and the human body were not strange in Greece, so it wasn't uncommon for people to be in such a state at certain beaches. He just went off fishing for the day and would return for us at the appointed time of 5:30 p.m.

With no sandy beaches, the island was nothing but an elongated mass of rock jutting up from the sea. A half-mile long by a quarter-mile wide and barren except for scraggly bushes all over it, the island had no sign of civilization except a professionally made cross on its highest point, probably established by the Greek government to denote it as a possession. No doubt every Greek island and islet had at least one such cross.

Alberto and I followed the five up to a smooth rock formation that stretched along a secluded cove of deep, transparent water lapping at the rocks 15 or more feet below. These people had evidently been to this exact spot before because they laid down their towels and belongings at what seemed like "reserved" positions on the ridge. It was not exactly a "family" outing either. The girls and the husband settled at one area, while Alberto and I followed Charles Bronson's hint to settle a few yards away with him.

Everyone undressed like it was nothing, including Alberto and me, as nonchalant as possible, hoping nobody realized it was our first time at this. I hoped no involuntary muscular embarrassments *arose*, which didn't, *thank God.* After all, these girls were no trolls. The three of them, in all honesty, were slim, trim and beautiful.

When not sunbathing, the seven of us spent the afternoon jumping and diving from the ridge into the cove of refreshing, deep water, swimming, snorkeling and talking—totally naked. The Greek girl and the Greek-American girl took masks, snorkels and fins, and with their perfect, naked bodies outstretched behind an air mattress they held with their hands, paddled around the whole island. What a scene for the birds above and fishes below!

The place was not a nudist island, per se. It was more of a secret island getaway where, if people disembarked on it, they took their clothes off— like another group of people who later arrived up the shore a ways. One of them—a tall, blond Scandinavian girl who knew the five—came to join us in diving into the cove, totally naked of course. Bronson gave her hell though for jumping into the cove with us when he noticed one of those little white strings hanging between her legs. *He* was the freak out here though, not her, so proud all day of the long, dangling member between his legs. *Jeeez. Weirdo.*

Vacation or not, naked or not, could not Alberto and I speak to others about God, if so led? Why not? Later in the day when I had become acclimated to naked women around and was confident nothing embarrassing might arise between my legs, I wandered down to the edge of the sea where the young Greek-American girl was swimming. I talked to the others but was mostly led to *her. Who wouldn't be?*

I helped her out of the water and onto the rocks, stood there face to face with this beauty—nothing on either of us but salt and drops of clean seawater—and spoke of the Creator. I doubt I would forget this encounter, two strangers of the opposite sex, totally naked on a Greek island, talking about God. It was all pretty natural. Different, but natural.

We all got dressed, gathered our things and awaited the fisherman, who appeared on time. Arriving back at civilization, the harbor of Hydra, Alberto and I sincerely thanked the group. "Thanks so much!" we told them all, particularly Lisa. "It was a great day out!" And we all went our separate ways.

After some bits and pieces to eat, Alberto and I returned to the little balconied house, exhilarated, but tired. The three British girls came later, on their own, comforted to see the two of us already there. For some reason, we didn't even mention any nude swimming—only that we'd had a great, full day in the sun and sea. And, like it or not, I got closer to the one girl through the night—some good deep kissing, anyway—as did Alberto with the other one at the other end of the balcony. "Two's company, three's a crowd" or not.

Leonard Cohen and his wife lived on the island—something Alberto and I already knew, especially since the guy sang about Jesus. We approached him the next day, September 5, as he sat in the very middle of an expanse of chairs at his favorite outdoor café, located at the center of the harbor and looking out upon it. We handed him two pieces of our literature—one about Don Quixote. He was friendly and thanked us. But we knew our brethren in Athens had already talked to him plenty, so we didn't bother him.

We met a black trombonist who played for some German band called "Ambrosia." He was sailing on a Russian cruise ship now docked at the harbor. We spent most of that day and the next—our second and third day on the island—swimming, sunning and diving off rocks and cliffs south of the harbor and town. We also continued meeting girls—from Canada, Germany and America—while still sharing evenings and then nights at the little house with the British girls, who, on our third day of knowing each other, left on an 11:30 a.m. ferry back to Athens.

The three girls left just in time too, before the weather changed. That night, a cold front blew in while Alberto and I were sleeping on the balcony for the fourth time. Winds became fierce, cold and downright scary. We needed to get *inside,* but all the windows were covered with locked shutters, and we still didn't want to break in. Maybe there was a key somewhere. Up until now, the weather was so ideal for sleeping outside on the balcony none of us even *considered* entering the cottage.

We made our way through the relentless wind to the front of the cottage. "Look!" Alberto said, holding a key he'd found under the front door mat, the first place he looked. *Oh*. So nice to get inside this house, the winds now howling and pounding on the shutters outside. With matches lit, we saw that the inside was just one large room with a concrete floor one step up from the entrance and so brand new the only furniture was one large wooden bed with no mattress. Whatever its décor, it was warm and cozy inside this refuge. We stretched our sleeping bags out on the bare bed and slept like refugees the rest of the night, not awakening until 1:15 the next afternoon.

It was time to end this island vacation and return to Athens, although by now we had no money for the ferry back, or even food. A restaurant friend, Nikolas, gave us coffees, and we attempted selling literature, but to no avail. "This isn't working," Alberto said. "Let's just start asking people for money." We did, and sure enough by 5:30 in the afternoon, we had plenty of money. We ate and purchased two tickets back to Piraeus on the 6:05 p.m. *Mania Express* ferryboat. Vacationing in Greece in September, is touch-and-go. The seas today, on September 7, 1976, were so rough and the waves so high from last night's storm the small ferryboat broke down for half an hour on the route back, finally reaching Piraeus at 8:20 p.m. with several seasick passengers. Regardless, Alberto's and my Hydra vacation would remain a great memory.

With the disco closed, and foreign students returning to semesters back home, it was mainly back in the streets with the Greeks and Greek literature. As much as I disliked litnessing, it kept me out in the streets meeting people, making friends, nurturing relationships.

That's how I met Elana, a local Athenian girl. She bought a piece of literature from me outside the shop where she worked on Metropolis Street near Syntagma Square. We talked some and dated after that. I ministered the gospel to her while she taught me a thing or two about the Acropolis—and not about its history either! She showed me firsthand what the Acropolis was used for at night. Tourists may have visited it during the day, but in good weather, young Athenians used it at night, an ideal place to go with a date, no money required. All around the

Acropolis mountain were parks, benches, rocks and stone walls where friends and lovers could sit. And then . . . there was the *southern* slope of the mountain, west of the old Theatre of Dionysus, where footpaths wound through a dense covering of bushes and low-growing trees. Serious lovers who needed more than just *sitting*, might venture here to lie down together, hidden off the paths late into the night in private little niches beneath the bushes and trees. Kind of a crude place to take a date, but Elana took me there one night . . . and I didn't mind one bit.

Sex, fun and sun. And sure enough, here in October 1976, I would leave it all—once again never settling down to a relationship, once again wandering off to other countries and work. The main manager of the disco, Paul, with whom I had become good friends through the summer, had selected me to accompany him and his wife to Egypt. Sounded good to *me*. We'd be the first to establish a work in that obscure land and would have to "go slow," maybe not litness too much, if at all. Perfect for me. And for the first year, the Work would be funded from headquarters in Switzerland.

And who was Paul's wife? Sheila—my old flame who I once thought might be my wife. When I lived in Tehran and she was living in Italy, I proposed to her in a letter but later learned she was already taken and had a child by Paul. They had their second a month back, here in Athens. The three of us had been in Athens all summer and even lived together in the small adobe-like Acropolis house for the past two months.

We all got visas, and their toddler, Teresa, a smallpox vaccine, but Paul and I would go alone to set things up, and Sheila and the two children would follow. I said good-bye to friends, especially Elana.

"I do love you, Elana," I told her. "I'll miss you." She had become close to our little family on the hill and used to come over and help me babysit. Another great acquaintance and blessing put in my path, *thank You, Lord*. At least this time I was able to hug and kiss this girl goodbye the day before I left, Thursday, October 7, 1976, when Paul and I took a 5:15 p.m. Olympic Airways flight at $38 each for one-way tickets to Cairo.

PART FOUR

ATHENS TO CAIRO

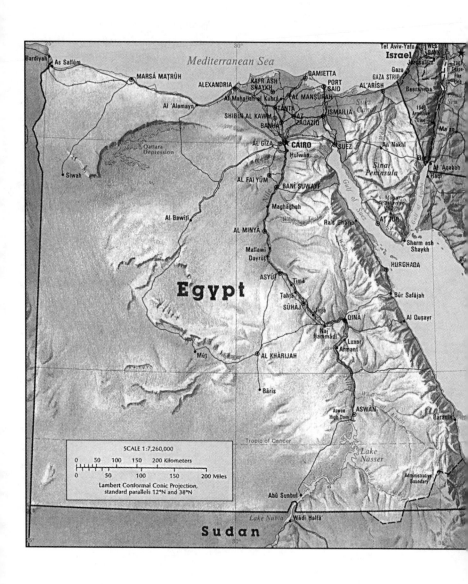

Chapter 29
∽ *Cairo and the Egyptian Desert* ∽

THE SHORT HOUR-AND-A-HALF flight toward the southeast from Athens landed Paul and me onto the strange continent of Africa— new to us both—and into the Arab Republic of Egypt at Cairo. Like Afghanistan, this place would not be a "normal" country, I felt. A simple glance at the Egypt Air logo verified this to me. We had dis- embarked the Greek airliner from the "civilized world" around 7 p.m. and were boarding an Egypt Air passenger bus to get to the terminal, when I saw the logo on the outside of the bus. It was the symbol of Horus—the stern-looking falcon bird of Egyptian mythology, with plumes trailing behind his head. He seemed to look at me in those split seconds and say, "Believe it. The land you have stepped upon is ancient and mysterious." Indeed, where civilization began.

Customs officials never checked our bags, but by law foreigners had to exchange a minimum of $150 to the local currency to even enter the country. So, at the rate of $1.00 equaling £.E. 0.672 (Egyptian pounds)—or, one pound costing almost $1.50 to buy—that gave us a little over 100 Egyptian pounds each.

Although we had an Egyptian contact to look up, no one met us at the airport, so we made our way through throngs of men in robes to the taxi stand where we chose a dark-blue Mercedes *Misr Taxi* at the agreed price of £.E. 3 ($4.50) to take us to the Viennoise Hotel in downtown Cairo. It was a three-star hotel, recommended by someone back in Athens, but was full except for one "special" room on the first floor at £.E. 6 ($9) a night. An assistant to the receptionist led us to the room. As he opened it, we saw desks, filing cabinets and telephones. The man quickly explained to us that, yes, during the day the room is used as an *office*—but with the two, cot-like single beds placed amid the furniture, it became a hotel room at night. "And besides," he said, "you're lucky. Tomorrow is Friday (the day off in the country) so no one will be using it all day." *Okay.* Who's going to complain on our first night in a new country with no alternative hotel choices right now? *I guess we can expect just about anything in this country.*

We'd eaten a pretty good meal on the Olympic Airways flight, so the first thing on the agenda—especially with a guy like Paul, who wasn't afraid to enjoy a good drink or two—was to visit the decent little bar of the hotel, where we could take up a bar stool each and welcome ourselves to The Arab Republic of Egypt. The bartender served us up some peanuts and popcorn to go along with our two, cold, Egyptian *Stella* beers—not a bad taste at all and the *size* of the bottle most impressive: a whole cold *liter* in a clear bottle.

Back when we checked in at the reception desk with the middle-aged brunette, she said to me, while eyeing my month-old beard, "Who has come here to us tonight, one of the prophets?"

At the bar now, I asked Paul, "Did you hear what that receptionist said to me?"

"I *know!*" Paul said. "What's the story? Do these people see things or what? It's like she knew we came here to preach!"

The best way to get the feel for a place is, of course, to walk its streets, which is what we did the following morning after a free breakfast from the hotel. We walked across a bridge to the other side of the Nile River and soon stumbled into one of Cairo's *poor* areas. *Whoa! Jeeez.* This place is *poor,* we soon saw, as we drifted down dirty, dusty side streets of bare-footed, rag-clad kids. Even a dead dog with rigor mortis set in was lying along a fairly main road, pretty well indicating an air of apathy here. Yet, a little farther walk led us to a nicely maintained public garden, dense with well-placed palm trees, shade trees, grass and flowers. The Nile River was the refreshing plus, though, flowing calmly through this overcrowded city of eleven million people—originally built for three million.

I swear, if it wasn't for attraction to the opposite sex in this world of ugly cities, I would have found life difficult to tolerate. Especially in cities like Cairo with its honking car horns, carbon monoxide billowing up from the exhausts of decrepit Fiats jammed in the streets, general frustration building on everyone's character. Add to that, endless merchants along every street, vying for the money in our pockets.

And these Egyptian merchants had an uncanny perception of who was *new* to Cairo. They could suck anyone in, no matter how clever.

Paul, I had come to learn, was a *very* clever talker and finagler. But was Paul ready for the merchants in this land? Out for another walk not far from our hotel, we were persuaded to enter an "essence" shop. These places specialized in concentrated oil scents in small glass vials that the sellers claimed were the actual bases of French colognes and perfumes, like Chanel and Christian Dior. "Yes, they *all* buy from Egypt," they'd say, "then mix them and add alcohol to them."

Fine. And they did smell pretty good. But how the heck did one of these "essence guys" persuade Paul to buy amber paste? The oily substance is supposedly derived from—

"Oh, yes indeed," the merchant had said, "it comes from crocodile vomit and is an aphrodisiac that you mix in hot tea."

We drank some later that night mixed in white porcelain cups of hot tea; it tasted horrible and produced no effect whatsoever. If we had each had a partner of the opposite sex to go along with it, well, it might *then* have had an effect. I doubt it though. But who could resist a small wad of it after the seller's professional spiel? Perhaps finaglers like Paul are the easiest kind to sell to.

Back at the hotel, we refreshed ourselves with another cold, one-liter Egyptian beer each and continued our exploration of downtown Cairo. Again not far from the hotel, we stumbled into what must have been nearly or mildly a "red-light" restaurant, or at least the wonderful-looking Egyptian waitresses there seemed willing to sell more than just food. *I mean, tight*-fitting jeans over near-perfect hips and butts. Both of us calmly tried to partake of what we originally came in here for—exotic food—but couldn't really resist gazing at some of these women's wares. Paul, while admiring the rear end of one of them as she walked to the kitchen, responded with the absolute perfect three words to describe these Egyptian women—"Built for breeding," he muttered, shaking his head.

The following day, we checked out of the Viennoise Hotel and took a taxi to Heliopolis—a pleasant suburb northeast of Cairo where our Egyptian contact, Sharif, lived with his American wife, Nancy. As instructed by Nancy over the phone yesterday, we checked into the Hotel Roxy, a rather funky, not more than three-star place, near the center of this little town of Heliopolis, or "Place of the Sun." Before long, Sharif's father—a wiry, rather distinguished, and obviously fun, rambunctious type—came to the Hotel Roxy to pick up Paul and me in a chauffeured, shiny, black Mercedes-Benz, not a late model, maybe 15 years old.

We rode in the Mercedes to finally meet Sharif at his home—a huge but older, second-floor apartment in a nice, upper-middle-class area of Heliopolis. Sharif lived in the apartment with Nancy, their new baby, Sharif's mother and father, Sharif's younger brother and his good-looking-but-strange, trying-to-keep-up-with-the-rich sister in her late twenties.

Sharif, 35, an ex-copilot of Egypt Air, had on trips to India met members of the Children of God and was now anxious to meet the two of us who had come to his land with similar godly intentions. We were warmly greeted by the family, all of whom were well educated and spoke English fluently, along with Sharif's precious American wife, Nancy, who was enthused to fellowship today with God-fearing fellow Americans like herself.

But the evening was spent with Sharif, who, after getting a feel for Paul and me over shish kebabs and tea and realizing he could trust us, that we weren't some weird religious fanatics or such and that we sincerely wanted to somehow be a blessing to Egypt, saw our potential as business partners—partners in any of his interminable, far-flung business prospects. Apparently he'd become *bored* (or *something*) with his Egypt Air job and had resorted to—like so many in this life—anything that smelled or hinted of a possible money-making business adventure, including hopping onto the video/filmmaking ideas Paul now mentioned. Filming that might possibly assist in relieving the country of illiteracy. Since changing careers, Sharif already had things planned. "I'm starting a skin diving resort," he said, "on the Red Sea, at a place called Hurghada, about 250 miles south of here. I've got a partner, an American skin diver. He'll be here in three weeks."

Sharif, business-obnoxious or not, was our "king" at this point, our only contact here—our benefactor and sponsor. And he did come through as a tremendous help setting us up by introducing us to Mona, two days later. She and her two beautiful sisters in their twenties along with their mother, had inherited real estate from their deceased father. Mona rented us a fine, seventh-floor, two-bedroom apartment in a good part of Heliopolis at the special price of £.E. 80 ($120) a month. The place wouldn't be ready for another ten days, so Mona set up Paul and me in a temporary flat for free—with one double bed full of bedbugs that viciously attacked Paul the first night, leaving him the following morning with not less than 30 itchy, horrible bites across his abdomen and back. As for me, I didn't get a single bite even though we slept side-by-side in this only bed of the apartment. Depends on the type of blood or skin apparently, and they didn't like *me, thank God.* In fact, back in Tehran I never got one bedbug bite while sleeping in the same room among friends who were continuously attacked by them. We moved right back to the Hotel Roxy.

To succeed as the first team sent to Egypt, Paul and I figured we'd better get to know the place as much as possible rather than bombard it with our own ideas and what *we* thought best for the people. We read books like *The White Nile,* by Alan Moorehead, and bought guide books and Arabic language books.

Well, no one comes to Egypt without visiting the Great Pyramids at Giza, where we headed ten days after touch down. Conserving our funds now, we started taking city buses and trams crammed full of people. So to reach Giza, we boarded a bus from the main, downtown line at Tahrir Square and headed southwest. Battling masses of people in the aisles was so distressing that, after several stops and starts, I nearly forgot why we had originally boarded the bus until it finally started emptying and we found seats. Then, with no forewarning . . . there it was, looming in the distance over rooftops and trees—the huge, Great Pyramid of Cheops! Like other wonders of the world, this Great Pyramid was just that, a *wonder—* "a cause of astonishment or surprise." A person can't really prepare for coming upon a wonder, approaching it for the first time. My mouth dropped when I gazed upon that massive structure. The bus continued, nearly empty now, straight toward it until reaching the end of the bus line, the end of the city of Cairo and the edge and start of solid desert.

From the bus, we walked up the paved road that led to the top of a plateau where sat this Pyramid of Cheops (or Khufu)—the world's largest stone edifice. In the distance were two smaller pyramids, the Sphinx to the side and extensive remains of temples everywhere. On the left side of the road going up, we noticed horse stables, camels and their drivers. Tourists were everywhere of course, along with any number of those large, fancy tour buses. And the predominant salesmen vying for our money today, were camel drivers. It looked too crowded to enter the Pyramid today—especially for extremely claustrophobic *me,* who would never make it too far inside a jam-packed pyramid—so we opted for a one-hour camel ride at a mere 80 *piastres* ($1.20) each. Now, one hour perched like a king upon this majestic desert animal, our eye level a good eight or nine feet above the ground, traipsing among ancient four-or-five-thousand-year-old ruins (from the beginning of civilization), was far too fascinating for us to stop riding so soon, especially when we were quickly learning to master these huge beasts.

The credit for our enchantment with these camels went to the 19-year-old camel driver, Hassan. The guy was a super salesman, an expert at getting tourists onto his camels. But he also felt a certain bond this day with Paul and me, knowing we weren't typical tourists. Before the one-hour camel ride was up, he had taught us not only how to stop the camel by pulling back on the reins, but how to make a certain *gurgling* sound with the back of our throats, causing the long-legged beast to sit down so we could dismount it. After a few attempts from us, the animal recognized the sound and knelt down onto its front legs. *Whoa.* While he was kneeling down, I thought I would go flying forward over his head. But he sat right down on his hind legs so we could then easily climb off, since our feet were now almost touching the ground.

To go for a camel ride, we mounted the sitting camel onto what was quite a comfortable saddle made of wood, leather and wool. Then, with a specific clicking sound we made with our tongues, the camels arose. The beasts went through the same elaborate bending-rocking process, now in reverse of how they sat down, lurching us heavily forward and then backward—enough to discourage many an observing tourist from even *attempting* a camel ride. With the camels now standing, we had to have a stick—provided to us by Hassan—to tap their butts in order to advance forward. Otherwise the animals just stood there.

Hassan explained all this to Paul and me in broken English he'd learned from tourists. He focused on Paul though because he knew Paul had the money, and he knew that out of the two of us, Paul was in charge. Besides, Hassan and Paul were both the same—both entrepreneurs, not afraid to go beyond the norm, off the beaten path, away from conventional tourist routes. Hassan may have been one of the few camel drivers at the Pyramids who ventured afield of the routine routes and took adventurous tourists beyond the Great

Pyramids plateau into the desert and on to other pyramids such as those at Saqqara, about eight miles to the south. And *that* would be our next adventure, starting tomorrow night. As for now, Paul had accepted an invitation to go later tonight to Hassan's home in Giza, the small village that abutted the Pyramids.

After a meal of roasted chicken at a restaurant back down the hill from the Pyramids, then back up the hill for photo shoots of the Sphinx before sunset, Paul and I hooked up again with Hassan at the feet of the Sphinx at the appointed time of 6 p.m. Of course we wouldn't *walk* to Hassan's house—we'd be riding our own camels there that Hassan already had saddled, ready and waiting for us. And off we rode, perched up high on them like nobles or something, through the barely-lit, somewhat-creepy-at-first nether world of rag-poor Giza villagers. Camels and horses really were the stately means of transport through these streets, and I felt as though I had money, looking down at those on foot quickly clearing the way for us. Mind you, Giza village was not a *slum* at all but rather a neatly kept town, although the mud-brick homes were crammed wall-to-mud-brick-wall like one, large, single-story condominium, separated only by dirt streets and alleys.

The 15-minute camel ride from the claws of the Sphinx brought us to the huge, eight-foot-high, wooden front door of Hassan's mud home. "*Eftah il bap*," Hassan said to a kid who'd been following us on the ground below. The kid unlatched and opened the giant door as requested. The three of us then rode right through the doorway on our camels into Hassan's home. *Yep. No kidding.* We had to duck down pretty good, but ride right in we did. *It was great.* There was no other practical choice really, since the alley was too small to accommodate parked camels, and it was too much to make these beasts go through all that rigmarole of rocking back and forth onto their knees to get us off their backs so *we* could *walk* into the house, and then make the poor things wobble back up on to their feet, lead them into the home and make them sit back down again inside.

After dismounting our camels, we met Hassan's beautiful, gypsy-like, 17-year-old wife, Sania. "This, my wife," Hassan said.

"Salaam," we both said.

"*Ahlan weh sahlan*," she said, coyly, welcoming us into her home with a pleasant smile. Her head and hair were covered with a black scarf, her body draped with the typical black *abaya*. She wore no makeup, but was naturally pretty and no doubt trim and fit under her coverings. She retreated off to the kitchen with the couple's two babies.

The home was totally open-air except for two, enclosed mud-brick buildings, one for the kitchen and the other across the yard and sitting on a small plateau for the bedroom/living room. Therefore, other than these two buildings, the home was basically a stables and farmyard, enclosed by fairly high walls that separated them from their neighbors and the dirt alleys outside.

The camels were "parked" in the "camels' corner" of the open courtyard of the home, near the entrance. In the opposite corner of the home from the camels stood a donkey inside its stall. And scattered everywhere were chickens and geese that made no mind of barging into either enclosed building—kitchen or bedroom—since both had no real doors on them.

"Sit down. Sit down," Hassan said. "We will eat soon."

Fast operator that he was, Hassan, in the two hours we'd been separated from him—back at the Pyramids before sunset—had organized and instructed his wife to buy and prepare for us a small dinner of costly camel meat.

"Look, look," he said. He had brought out a scrapbook with photos of other tourists he'd taken to Saqqara, with their handwritten comments and praises about Hassan and the journey. One photo was that of a young New Yorker in his twenties who had written comments that hinted of gay affection toward Hassan. *Uh-oh. Don't tell me this Hassan . . . and some other Egyptians . . . would oblige anyone for a dollar.*

Although the Saqqara trip wouldn't cost much, Hassan would make a decent lump sum of money by taking us there, as opposed to what he'd make in a day hustling tourists at the foot of the Pyramids for camel rides in competition with the several other camel drivers.

The camel meat served by Sania was somewhat tough but tasty, especially when so well complimented by savory *couscous*, the boiled, cracked wheat arranged around the meat. The delight of the night though, was the fresh, hot, Egyptian-style black tea she served. Each person's clear glass of tea—about the size of a "rocks" glass—was brewed with its own loose tea inside the glass, the leaves now settled to the bottom of each glass. Extremely sweet, the brew also had fresh mint leaves dropped inside for taste.

The surreal evening took place on a black wool rug on the sand, under the stars, with that charming Arab hospitality and a delicate woman. Even the sweet, quiet animals nearby were soothing.

By the time we departed Hassan's at 7:30 this evening, we had seen the Great Pyramids and Sphinx, nearly mastered camel riding, and savored the hospitality of peasant villagers in their simple home. And who to thank for all this? Paul—the leader of this two-man Egypt team. I would learn much from Paul. He wasn't afraid to take chances, venture outside the norm, follow his instincts, spend money. I find it strange, but true, that the follower (in this case, me) of a leader/commander will too often try to *douse* the flame of his leader's enthusiasm, his leader's eagerness to step out on a limb by faith. That's what I might have done concerning trusting this fast-talking, rather hard-sell camel driver, Hassan. And *that* is the lesson I learned this day at the Great Pyramids—"Do *not* mistrust someone (like Hassan) to the point of having *no* adventure." And now we were scheduled to embark on a further adventure with Hassan: the eight-mile journey to Saqqara. It would take a whole day there and back, so we arranged to spend tomorrow night in Hassan's home in order to head out early the following morning.

The next evening, now October 18, 1976, 11 days after arriving in Egypt, we returned to Giza by taxicab. There, after sunset, we attended the worthy, pertinent-to-the-Great-Pyramids-visit "Sound and Light Show," sitting in chairs outdoors at the feet of the Sphinx. The hour-long show began after dark with the lit-up Sphinx narrating an informative history of Egypt and the building of the Pyramids, while colored lights nicely splashed temple ruins and the three main pyramids in the distance. It was pretty good, but pretty cold on that October night.

After the show, we met up with Hassan and his humble friend and companion, Jamal, along with a camel for each of us. And on through the now-more-mysterious, darkened alleys of Giza village, we rode to the large, wooden front door of Hassan's home, proceeded through on our camels and "parked" them in the "camels' corner" just inside the entrance to the home.

We were welcomed to the home even more warmly tonight by Sania and some of her relatives, who treated us to dinner and that fabulous hot tea. We then headed to bed. Bed? There *was* no "bed" here tonight.

The one, enclosed bedroom-plus-sitting-room structure was occupied by Hassan's wife and their two babies. No way were two men going to be sleeping inside there anywhere near *her*. So, Hassan spread a large rug just outside the door of the building upon what was a sort of dirt plateau, fortunately *above* the level of the beasts-of-burden camels and donkey. There the three of us stretched out to sleep under the stars. Well, *tried* to sleep. The weather was cool and clear in the middle of October and blankets kept us fairly warm, but it was a horrible night on that hard ground, along with flies tormenting our uncovered faces all night, robbing us of sleep.

Flies! Daylight brought more of them. Thousands of them. Great, Egyptian "sticking" flies. They actually *attached* themselves to us. Infants and children—like Hassan's two little ones—normally had, with no exaggeration, as many as eight to ten individual, goddamned flies stuck to the corners of their eyes, eating the tears, secretions or whatever might ooze out of the eyeball and without *any resistance* from the child host. That is, these kids were so used to the flies they no longer batted them away. We, coming from the nearly sterile West, could not absorb this horror. What kinds of diseases, eye problems, perhaps sight loss, might result from these menacing scourges?

The only respite from this gloomy awakening was watching Hassan's silly-ass geese walking between and even *on* the three of us and having their morning breakfast—gulping down fly after fly right out of mid-air with amazing, neck-snapping action! *Fantastic. Eat 'em up ye geese.*

Sania—another inspiration to awaken to—prepared us some breakfast and tea, and by 7 a.m., Jamal showed up with a camel named Daisy for me, and a camel named Whiskey for Paul. And the four of us—Hassan, Jamal, Paul and I—started our journey south, toward Saqqara.

Looking at a topographical map of Egypt, one can quickly see that practically the only fertile green land found in this rather large, 386,100-square-mile country, is along either side of the Nile River. As far as humans have irrigated the land from the Nile, that is how far the lush vegetation extends. Then it abruptly stops and becomes solid desert.

After mounting the camels inside Hassan's home, we rode through acres of this fertile land full of vegetable crops and shady groves of huge date palms and indigenous trees. Peasant farmers and kids were actually *smiling* this morning going to work in the midst of it. A few crude diesel water pumps clattered away in the fields, but most water for irrigation was pumped along by water buffaloes walking in a continuous circle, yoked to some sort of ancient pumping method—no different than thousands of years ago when the pyramids were built.

The best route to the Saqqara Pyramids led to the west and then south through the desert. We reached the desert by clomping along a dirt road through the lush farms and groves, past bubbling irrigation ditches and peasant villages, with one of the Seven Wonders of the Ancient world—the Great Pyramids of Giza—sitting majestically on their plateau to our right, through the trees. It was a great way to start a morning. Half an hour in these soothing surroundings brought us to the Egyptian desert—also beautiful.

Hassan led the way with Jamal in the rear as the four of us plodded through desert trails familiar to Hassan and along a dirt road. Otherwise, we would have had to climb and descend good-size sand dunes of this beautifully mounded desert. Hassan knew well how to care for his camels, to not overtire them by leading them up and down these dunes. He referred to the camels as, "cheep a da desert," and that they were, ships of the desert, with their huge, flat, padded feet spreading out upon the sand with each step, on and on without any complaint of thirst, hour after hour. And, *Glory to God.* These animals could eat any vegetation along the way, no matter if it was a bush of thistles and thorns. I saw my camel bend its long neck down and munch into a complete *thorn* bush, no problem. Imagine the roofs of their mouths!

Riding in the saddle with the gait of the camel was absolutely comfortable. The *fun* though, was galloping and nearly *racing* with these creatures, which was easily learned, naturally acquired. With our mandatory stick, we tapped them on their rear ends, not too hard, and once Paul and I learned how easy it was to get these camels moving out across the desert, the two of us began *racing* each other on them, despite Hassan's disdain and preference to conserve the animals' energy for the day. It was just too damn fun though.

We reached the main Step Pyramids of Saqqara at 10 a.m. and followed Hassan to a huge canvas tent. "We will eat," Hassan said. We dismounted and entered the tent, the only restaurant in the area. Except for being a tent, inside it looked like a restaurant, its whole floor spread with neatly set tables and wooden chairs. We stuffed ourselves with flat bread, boiled fava beans swimming in olive oil, cheeses, all topped off with ice cold beers. This was the life out here now, our camels parked and fueling up outside on fresh alfalfa while we, inside the huge restaurant tent, consumed enough food and drink to get us through the rest of the day—in the midst of timeless buildings, pyramids and temples built nearly five thousand years ago during man's first civilization.

After this lunch, we mounted our camels and Hassan led us to the actual Step Pyramids of Saqqara and other popular tourist sites, ruins and underground temples. It seemed there were endless excavations, free of charge even. The underground temples, reached by steps and hallways from the desert floor, were particularly interesting with paintings and hieroglyphics still intact along their walls. Out here in the Western Desert (west of the Nile), it wasn't uncommon to see ancient, half-buried entrances only partially dug out, leading to who knows where or what and easy to fall into.

The four of us and our camels were nearly alone, site after site, with pyramid after ancient pyramid to ourselves. Paul and I were not that intrigued by the dead-stones-over-dead-bodies pyramids and other rubble, but traipsing around the desert on foot and camelback through all this history was pretty damn cool to us Westerners.

By early afternoon we headed back north toward Giza. Somewhere about halfway, we stopped at a small, white, cement guard shack, dismounted our camels, and the guard—a friend of Hassan's of course—prepared us some sweet black tea. We then stretched out next to the shaded side of the shack, and in the pleasant dry air of the desert, fell asleep for an hour. Nice.

We made good time after our break, Paul and I insisting on galloping every now and then, and ambled into the shady, green Nile belt just before sunset as farmers—many just kids—were returning at the end of a day's work in the gardens, *still smiling*. The farmers' camels were piled high with straw, alfalfa or any other harvested produce, along with donkeys and massive water buffaloes working these verdant valleys as the ancients had done. The weather in Egypt at this time of year was another plus for this day—sunny but dry, with the cool freshness of the Nile valley mixed in. Nearing Hassan's home, still perched upon our camels, the Great Pyramid of Cheops suddenly appeared to us through the tall trees and palms. Only now, it was magnificently silhouetted on the horizon by vibrant red, yellow and orange rays of the setting sun, shooting from behind and all around it.

This young finagler Hassan had successfully introduced Paul and me to . . . the desert—beautiful in its own right. That, and these wonderful "ships" that transported us over it in ease and comfort. It simply brought peace and contentment, the desert.

And Hassan's "Saqqara package" deal wasn't over yet. When we reached his home and parked our camels inside, the lovely Sania soon served us (we were so hungry now) a huge communal plate of couscous, camel meat and *bomyuz* (okra), followed by one, last, hot glass of freshly-brewed "gypsy" tea to end this fulfilling day.

Chapter 30
⊷ *The Egypt Work* ⊷

ON OCTOBER 22, 1976, two weeks after arriving in Cairo and living in funky hotels and the bedbug-infested apartment, Paul and I happily moved into our furnished, seventh-floor, $120-a-month Heliopolis apartment, thoroughly cleaned it and stocked it with food. Two days later, Paul's wife, Sheila, flew in from Greece with their two little girls, Teresa, 18 months old, and Debra, only 6 weeks.

Our little family now, with me the oddball single guy, would attempt to . . . "reach Egypt" with God's Love. *Right*. Well, we had good intentions, but no one changes this place too fast, if at all.

It was good to have a family here though—a mother and little kids. It was less threatening. Sheila herself was a bit of a fox, too—short, only slightly overweight, with a pretty, young-girl face enhanced by straight, silky, brownish blond hair flowing to the middle of her back, totally sexy and an honestly good mommy to her kids. Sharif and his family liked her and her inspirational smile. And the two little girls could open doors and hearts anywhere, as young children can do.

Not long after Sheila arrived, Sharif's prospective skin diving partner, Alex, and his wife, Connie, arrived from California . . . to get the famous Egyptian run around from Sharif. *Oh, my*. Month after month after month would pass with no real skin diving resort developments whatsoever. They undertook a few diving escapades to the Red Sea together, to keep the inspiration alive, but when it came right down to it, neither Alex nor Sharif had any money—capital—to scratch ground (or sand) on their business adventure dreams down in Hurghada.

As it was, Alex and Connie moved in with us three weeks after they touched down in Egypt. Alex was a great Jewish guy and Connie—a Gentile—was totally likeable, friendly, skin-diver-trim, not too tall, slightly freckly, with reddish blond hair, extremely cute and vibrant. She and Alex had recently married and were a close, loving couple; we all fared well together in the modest apartment.

When Alex and Connie flew in to Cairo, they came with two 19-year-old California girls whom they'd met on the airplane, Karen and Gayle.

The two girls were embarking on a touring adventure of the Middle East with Egypt their first stop. Gayle was Jewish, like Alex, and he, having been to Egypt before, insisted on taking them both "under his wings" upon arrival in this strange land.

Karen ended up marrying Sharif's younger brother, Nasser, while Gayle, the Jewish one—now also living with us in the apartment—eventually grasped our mission and joined us. Gayle was a hard one to sway, and neither Paul, Sheila nor I pressured her in the least, but let her run free until she could no longer deny the truth we spoke or the love we had for her soul. Her long, drawn-out reluctance before finally making the decision to forsake her worldly possessions and prospective adventures, made her a strong, sold-out member of our team. Looks-wise, she was tallish—maybe five feet six or eight inches—well proportioned, with tannish complexion, dark brown hair to her shoulders, quite cute, slightly freckled, with unmade-up face. She often wore skirts or dresses only to her knees in order to reveal her unmistakably beautiful . . . legs. *Lord.* She knew they were showpieces so would sit around the apartment expertly crossing and exposing them, up to her undies sometimes. *Jeeez.*

Besides being funded from headquarters in Switzerland, our "Egypt Work," headed by Paul, was getting off to a good start. Here, in our second month, we had already won a strong—and beautiful—disciple. Back on November 4, 1976, before a month had passed, I received a letter from an American friend of mine who used to live in Isfahan, Iran. The guy, Jack Reed, was a genius, a bit eccentric, and was making thousands of dollars on a contract he had with the Iranian military to service their F-15 jet fighter computers. He had been enthralled with our group back in Isfahan and particularly our insight into the endtime and Bible prophecy. That we were now establishing a team in Egypt, was too intriguing to him. Inside the letter was a $5,000 check to me for the Egypt Work. He actually sought us out, insisting we accept his donation. The check took a little longer than a month to clear through Cairo's Citibank, and once it did, the "leadership" in Greece—knowing about it—took nearly all of it. *Damn.*

Visiting the pyramids and the desert around them at Giza soon became a regular event whenever visitors (like Karen and Gayle) and friends of ours arrived. It meant contacting Hassan for camels on each visit, so the guy remained quite a valuable asset to the Work. One evening, after Paul, Gayle and I had spent the afternoon riding camels at the pyramids, kindhearted and open-minded Paul said to Hassan, "You and Jamal will come to our home tonight. *Momkin?*"

"Yes. Momkin," Hassan responded, readily accepting the invitation.

Wow. How fantastic, to pluck camel-driving villagers like Hassan and Jamal out of their habitats and abruptly place them in the modern world! The five of us crammed into a Peugeot station-wagon taxi. Soon, in the close quarters of the car, Hassan hit on Gayle, figuring, out of his instinctive male sex drive, that if this fair young thing was willing to sit next to him in this small car, in her extremely tight jeans, she must be fair game. No problem, Gayle was no dummy. She removed his hand from her thigh, and we drove on to our flat in Heliopolis where Hassan and Jamal met Sheila and the kids. We served and treated the two as honored guests.

In this attempt by Paul to bestow his appreciation on them as friends, the villagers hardly knew what the heck they were doing in our home, much less how to act. It became awkward, and contrasts in backgrounds and ways of life soon manifested themselves when Hassan took a banana from a bowl of fruit on the living room table, peeled it and, yes, threw the peel right on the living room floor without the slightest concern or hesitation! *It was great.* We city dwellers had to laugh, but we also had to tell him, "Hassan. You cannot throw it on the floor." After all, we had no domestic animals running around in the apartment to process such food remnants. The same thing happened with Hassan's *cigarette.* After smoking it and flicking its ashes everywhere, he threw the butt of it down and stamped it out on the tile floor. *Fantastic.* Nothing irregular to him. It was a *marvel* to us.

Two weeks later, on Christmas Day, 1976, Paul thought to take gifts to Hassan and Jamal. So we borrowed Sharif's U.S. Army-type Jeep, drove to Giza, and gave new, woven rugs to both camel drivers for their homes, along with some brand new pots and pans. The two were surprised and appreciative to get the gifts, but Hassan was, noticeably, not too impressed with such practical items—not when it *could* have been *money.*

I don't know who might succeed as a foreign businessman or entrepreneur in Egypt. This country could chew them up. We met two or three such businessmen who not only failed here, but eventually barely escaped with their lives. One was Frank Smith, an American guy in his sixties, from Miami. A widower, Frank had a rich, widow-lady friend his age who funneled money to him from Miami for his grandiose ventures, while he made his office and residence in a fancy, expensive suite at the Meridien Hotel on the Nile in Cairo. Paul—himself the entrepreneur-type—met Frank and remained loyal to him when he should have been alarmed as soon as he read the guy's business card. Besides "Real Estate Developer," he listed six to eight *other* titles for himself on that one little card.

We all befriended Frank, no doubt impressed by his swanky Meridien suite as an abode. Frank had visions of grandeur all over Egypt. For instance, being from Miami, he had real estate delusions of developing Egypt's practically untouched, white-sand Mediterranean coastline into a Miami Beach, starting about 13 miles westward from Alexandria, in a project he called, "VIP Africa/Middle East." *Oh brother*. And when he came across the likes of Paul, Sheila and me, he saw us as prospective partners to assist him in his ventures.

Then, on January 4, 1977, a single, divorced, American girl, Maggie, in her mid-twenties like the rest of us, arrived from the group in France to join the Egypt team. A *very* pretty, very classy redhead. *But Lord, she was so straight.* Yet she was cut out for what she came here to do—be a secretary for Frank in his fancy suite. Frank kept her busy and paid her, which gave us all some cash flow.

Maggie was another of those women of the group whom I didn't mesh with in the least bit. Neither of us was attracted to the other, really, so despite living in the close quarters of the small apartment, even sleeping in the same bedroom together, nothing even *remotely* sexual happened between us. Not that it did anyway, among members of the group at this time.

That was the extent of the Egypt team for four months until a single American guy came who was sort of an assistant to Paul, until Paul threw him out after a tenure of exactly two months. The guy, Greg, kept wanting to run the Egypt Work like Europe, maybe start litnessing in the streets, even. But Egypt was Paul's and my field and it wouldn't be run like other fields of the group, like it or not. Besides, Paul was known personally and respected by the hierarchy, in particular "Queen" Diane—wife of the Italian duke. Diane, now in Switzerland, communicated and counseled with Paul regularly through the mail, via telegrams and over the telephone concerning the Egypt Work.

Paul, Sheila, Maggie, Gayle and I were settling into Egypt for what we felt might *desirably* be a good long time. It was the first assignment, for some reason, where I felt I might remain indefinitely. The climate was pleasant, similar to California—sunny and dry, with mild summers and winters. Food, as everything else, was dirt cheap. We bought fresh, juicy oranges at 7¢ a kilo, lettuce at 5¢ a head and fresh mangoes at 7¢ a kilo! Then there was the fresh meat. Beef was so fresh and cheap we regularly bought the *filet* and cut it into steaks for grilling, or, had it minced into hamburger meat—filet hamburger meat!

Near the butcher, we'd pick out a *live*, healthy chicken—check to see if its eyes were bright and clear—from the "live chicken store." The guy would slit its neck and pluck its feathers right then and there in a sink at the back of the store, and we'd take it home, *still warm* from being alive minutes before, and roast it in the oven for a markedly fresh-tasting, delicious bird. If we had an urge for *bacon*, we'd buy the best, backstrap cuts of it, quite cheaply too, pork being consumed here only by foreigners and Coptic Christians. It was said that certain Copts made good money on pork products by going around town with their donkey carts collecting garbage at no charge, to raise their pigs on.

We found it the ideal frontier to apply new techniques in establishing a Work and reaching a country. We couldn't expect to just bombard these people with the literature like the group was doing in so many countries. We'd get thrown out or jailed for sure. So, in an attempt to better function here, Paul and I enrolled in the British Institute in Heliopolis to learn colloquial Arabic. The course was cheap at £.E. 23 ($35) for two hours, twice a week, for 11 weeks. It was good basics, but in actuality, we learned most of our Arabic from riding in taxis!

Without really striving to, we began hobnobbing with the rich—meeting them first through Sharif and his younger brother. We went to some classy, belly dance nightclubs—like that of the Oberoi Hotel near the Pyramids—discotheques, private clubs like the After Eight in downtown Cairo and numerous parties of the rich. Like in other third-world, developing countries, we had "the ticket," the main credential necessary for acceptance into the upper echelon of Cairo society—we were *Americans*. We partied with a Japanese chairman of Sony, with Mr. Oberoi of the hotels and with influential Egyptians. Of course, Sheila and Maggie—the females—were the main keys to opening doors . . . likeable, pretty and always cheerful.

It was, then, Paul, Sheila and Maggie who generally socialized with these people, while I, more often than not, ended up watching Paul and Sheila's kids at home. I didn't really mind it that much, "staying by the hearth." I just didn't care to beat the streets, stay out late and hassle with life. But, caring for kids is *the* hardest job in the world. I thought I was patient until I was commissioned so many times for . . . childcare. It was particularly difficult with two in diapers at the same time as were little Teresa and Debra. I learned to never expect a minute to myself as long as they were awake. So demanding they were, always needing food, attention, changing, entertaining and constant protection from harm.

Sometimes, young, "beautiful-legs Gayle" and I wound up watching the kids together. *Uh oh.* Now, when two young adults of the opposite sex are confined in the same enclosure (apartment, house, cottage, building, villa) together, if they have any sort of attraction toward one another, are not repulsed with each other, *it* is likely to happen. *It* did with Gayle and me. And it was a *fabulous*, mutual need and love we each provided the other—especially for *me*, since Gayle hadn't exactly been celibate during her weeks here in Egypt before joining up with us.

Chapter 31
— *Alexandria* —

I FELT GOOD in Egypt. And no matter who came here, Paul and I remained the two-man team in charge. Paul decided one day, "Wayne. Let's go up to Alexandria again. Maybe we'll open an outreach there." Alexandria, 130 miles north of Cairo, is Egypt's main port on the Mediterranean and its second largest city. Paul and I loved traveling up there on the train. At the Ramses Train Station we purchased first-class tickets at the student rate of £.E. 1.59 ($2.38) and then sat in huge, burgundy velvet, airline-type seats for the two-hour-or-so ride, while sipping on cold Stella beers the whole way. To prevent too much drunkenness or illness from the beer, we ordered plenty of side-plates of food ballast like boiled chickpeas, hummus, cooked beans and flat bread.

In Alexandria, we found decent, little hotels like the Minerva, Admiral or Philip at £.E. 2 ($3) a night. We scoped out the town on foot and in taxis, found great, reasonable restaurants and made friends with a local photographer named Helmi, who we stayed in contact with for advice on this multi-national port city.

Port cities, like Alexandria, are not typical cities of a country. They are infiltrated with a constant turnover of street-smart foreigners— merchant mariners off docked ships from every corner of the globe. And the only people slyer than these visiting sailors are the local chaps who prey on *any* visitors.

Having lived in Egypt nearly six months, Paul and I felt we had become wise in our dealings with Egyptians. But on this latest visit to Alexandria, the street-side money changers proved we were no match for them. Paul had already heard their pitches to passersby several times, "One dollar, point eight." They were offering, in Egyptian pounds, an exchange rate far better than the banks or established exchange companies. These guys, of course, had no office. They worked right on the streets, some just outside our favorite restaurant in a decent part of the city.

The rate was too good. Paul had to give it a try. Make a few extra pounds on $80 dollars. It was black marketing, so a money changer agreed to make the transaction down the street at *our* hotel, away from the crowds. They worked in pairs, these money changers, although *we* thought the guy was alone.

It was all very amazing. On the dimly-lit staircase of our hotel, Paul showed the guy his $80 dollars in twenty-dollar bills, which the guy held and counted. He then handed Paul the equivalent in Egyptian pounds, corresponding exactly to the exchange rate we had all agreed upon. Having already figured out the math of what we should receive in Egyptian pounds, Paul counted carefully the various denominations of genuine, non-counterfeit bills, and was satisfied, feeling slightly ahead of the game of life. Just then the ingenious "exchanger" gestured forth to Paul for the pounds. "Wait! Let me see," the guy said, as he took the wad from Paul and shuffled through it quickly, as if counting it, to make sure no one was being shortchanged. He then handed the money back to Paul who was happy to have the stack of bills *back* in his hands. The transaction, having taken place under the pressured rush of illegal expediency, was now completed. The Egyptian guy went his way outside, while Paul and I went the opposite way, up the stairs and to our room, somewhat amazed to have struck this little deal so fast off the streets. *Fantastic though.* On the *top* and *bottom* of the stack were large five-pound notes; and in between them were one-pound and smaller notes, rendering the stack worth only about . . . $23! *Wow.* On that last handling of the money, the skilled exchanger had expertly switched the full, $80-dollar-equivalent stack of pounds with *this* one—already made and in his pocket.

"Oh my *God*," Paul said. He was furious. We ran downstairs into the street, frantically searching for the exchanger, actually running up and down main streets, side streets and alleys. Only minutes had passed since the scam had occurred, and yet the exchanger had vanished like a cockroach.

"We have to find him!" Paul said. We'd find him. For sure. Alexandria wasn't that huge.

After exhausting our search on foot, we hired a horse and carriage for probably 30 minutes, in a last, desperate attempt to spot the guy on the street. But it was futile, and we only spent more money and time on the failed attempt to "*gyp*" an Egyptian—a *very* difficult feat. The guy was probably *watching* us as we rode in the horse and carriage. Luckily, it wasn't a great amount to lose, but it was a real shocker for us—plenty of money for *our* budget, gone in seconds. The lesson: never do deals in the dark—like our hotel staircase that was quite dark; and *nobody* needs street-side money changers!

Our purpose for coming to Alexandria this time was to establish another home. But it didn't happen inside Alexandria. Instead, Paul had brought me to Alexandria now, here at the end of March, to show me a beachside apartment west of the city that he and Sheila had found a week before. "Wayn-o!" he said. "You're gonna *love* it!" In fact, we were here today to sign a six-month lease with the Egyptian doctor-friend who owned the place and to pay him £.E. 160 ($240)—first and last months' rent. We settled the deal, got the keys and hired a taxi for the 30-minute ride to the coastal town of Hanoville, sort of the edge of where "Meridien" Smith, our American businessman friend back in Cairo, had high hopes of creating a Miami Beach.

Now, if the money exchanger rip-off wasn't enough, here at the end of our taxi ride to the beach, the driver began insisting on a fare above what his meter was reading. "*Ashra guinee*," he demanded. He wanted *ten* pounds, when his meter was reading *six* pounds.

Paul generously handed him seven pounds.

"*Leh! Leh!*" the driver responded, when he counted the money. "*Mish kefayah. Maku had hinee al hane. Shoof,*" he moaned, while sweeping a hand across desolate Hanoville, indicating that seven pounds wasn't enough, since there were no riders around the beach here at this time of year who could hire him for the return trip to Alexandria. He'd have to return empty.

"*Leh. Kefayah. Masalaama,*" Paul said, knowing he'd given the guy plenty. He started to walk off.

The taxi driver then grabbed six-feet-tall Paul by the arm.

Paul stopped, shook the guy's hand off him and shouted in his face, in English, five words I will never forget: "Don't *ever* touch me again!"

Shit! When is this taxi driver ever going to see Paul again to be able to touch him? Paul and the guy came extremely close to blows, but the driver lost and grumbled off.

Paul and I both cracked up about it later. "Don't ever *touch* me again?" I said to Paul with a question, repeating what he had said to the driver. "When the hell are you ever going to see that taxi driver again for him to touch you?"

"I know! I know!" Paul responded, as we both doubled over in laughter.

It wasn't exactly clear to me why Paul decided to rent this beach house for the summer months. We just all sort of agreed that yeah, we can probably reach a lot of the people who flock to the beach during the summer, by having a place right in the middle of them.

But when Paul led me up the one flight of nicely done, off-white, cement, outdoor stairs; opened the front door of the apartment; and led me inside, it didn't much matter what we *might* use it for. The place was exotic. The building itself was one whole ground floor apartment and then this one above it was two floors, like a townhouse, with a beautiful, inside, tiled staircase leading to the top floor. It was a bright, white, beachy home, spotlessly clean, fully furnished with sheets and towels even, a total of five bedrooms, two living rooms, two kitchens, two baths and its own wall-enclosed, flat rooftop for sunbathing. It also had two wrap-around, white cement balconies, one on each floor, looking onto the Mediterranean Sea, the water's edge less than two hundred yards away. We had to have it, especially at £.E. 80 ($120) a month. *Surely, God would bless it.* We needed the condo . . . for our spirits—an escape from bustling Cairo.

The flat would be our summer retreat, and, hopefully, some souls would be reached from it. The town of Hanoville itself looked to be just starting to get built up into a resort town that, until now, was scattered with low-rise apartments like this one, owned by wealthier Egyptians for *their* summer retreats and/or investment properties to rent out to Italians and other foreign contract workers. There was one decent hotel with a restaurant and a few shops around, but Hanoville, here in March, was quite nearly a ghost town with hardly a soul along the adjacent miles and miles of white sandy beach.

We used the flat well—from March 24, 1977, when we signed the lease, to October 13, 1977, when we moved out—a little over six months. I alone made eight roundtrips from Cairo to Hanoville to luxuriate at the place, either alone, with Paul, with Paul's wife, Sheila, and kids, or others. Paul and friends visited the place even more often.

Whenever Paul and I were there together, one of our pastimes was to bodysurf the usually good-size, three-, four-, even five-foot waves for hours and hours. But this vast, white-sand coastline with its lovely blue waters contained a nearly invisible killer: extremely dangerous undertows and riptides. *Lord.* How many hapless Egyptians had they swallowed? Paul, an excellent swimmer, and I, not *too* bad, experienced this treacherous phenomenon a few times, these tides and currents wickedly pulling us out toward open sea, until good-sized waves came along to overcome the "tow," and deliver us back onto the safety of the shore. It was, too often, an unsafe water's edge for children or inexperienced swimmers.

The beach was great though for sunning and strolling. We sometimes strolled along it to Agami, a well-established town on the same beach, about a mile farther east. Agami is where Egyptian girls and women hung out in bikinis during the summer. It was the "beach scene" again, naturally inducing people to feel freer than when living inland. Women not customarily that open in Cairo, took it off and exhibited their wonderful, bathing-suit-clad bodies along the beach. I even came across Egyptian girls I knew from Cairo and talked to them, trying to act like it was indeed natural and nothing extraordinary to now be seeing them with only a few square inches of material covering their private parts. *Jeeez!* Still, most did not seem promiscuous.

But there was an action I wondered about, that some of these sexy Egyptian girls did, whether in Cairo or here at the beach. A 19-year-old, Amina, whom I knew from Cairo, and who sometimes visited her wealthy dad in the villa right next to ours, did it to Paul and me. Clad in nothing but a *tiny* bikini and stretched out on a chaise lounge on her balcony, just below and across from ours, she looked up at us, stuck her tongue out and wiggled it suggestively right at us! *Lord.* She then put it right back in her mouth and looked away, like it was nothing. Back in Heliopolis once or twice, cute, usually affluent, teenaged girls had blatantly done it to me and other American guys I knew—from their cars or just walking on the street. *Why?* Would they have done anything if we'd responded? Or was it a complete tease? Probably just a tease and something these sexually overripe young women did without thinking. *They were hot though, let's face it.*

We were still pretty naïve Westerners, but it sure seemed easy to satisfy sexual needs here in Egypt, if need be. Whores, that is. But the trade was quite disguised, not like obvious hookers in the West. Here in Hanoville, probably the second day after Paul and I moved into the summer beach condo, the Egyptian *bowab* taking care of the place asked us, "You need maid? To clean?" And before we could hardly decline, and thinking the guy really *was* offering a maid to clean, we looked down from our balcony. There, from behind a building across the dirt road, appeared not one, but *two*, trim, attractive Egyptian women in their, say, late 20s, early 30s, with makeup on and knee-length skirts, coyly smiling up at us.

"Uh, not today. Thanks anyway. We will, uh, clean the place ourselves," we told the bowab.

In fact though, Paul and I had visited the villas of single American, British and other foreign men on work contracts, both here in Hanoville and back in Heliopolis, who indeed had maids to do the cleaning, cooking and a whole lot more—pretty Egyptian women about these guys' same age, looking so sexy it seemed apparent the women did a lot more than just clean these guys' homes! *Glory.* One guy introduced his "maid" by name, "This is Fatima, my maid," he said, with a smile and his arm around her waist.

On July 25, 1977, the beach home became a perfect base for Paul, two other guys and me to film a music festival at nearby Agami. Paul had learned about filming back in Italy from his Italian-screenwriter friend, Piero Tellini, had a good knack for moviemaking anyway and had now somehow secured this contract to professionally film the event, called "Sandstock," where over two thousand, mostly young people came to flirt, mingle and be entertained all night by live music, from rock n' roll to traditional Egyptian folk music. The main promoter of the festival, the Rothmans Cigarette Company, paid Paul several hundred dollars for four rolls of 16mm film he produced for them. Fortunately, Paul, a month before, had met and been working with a professional Egyptian cameraman from ABC News back in Cairo. The guy, Mahmoud Sayed, was the frequent, chosen cameraman for Anwar Sadat, president of Egypt. An expert with the 16mm camera, Mahmoud had become good friends with Paul and was ready for the moonlighting work of Sandstock. Paul, Mahmoud, another camera-man named Marc, a beautiful Egyptian girl in her late 20s named Nadia, and I drove up from Cairo in Marc's small station wagon with the cameras and equipment in the back.

As for the Egyptian beauty, Paul met her in the lobby of the Meridien Hotel in Cairo, where we had all rendezvoused for the trip to Agami. She'd been attracted to the filming equipment—and Paul—and when he discovered she was on her way to Alexandria, he generously offered her a ride with us, which she accepted. She spoke hardly any English but having lived in Italy for some time, spoke Italian fairly well, so Paul and I were able to communicate with her in the amount of Italian and Arabic we both knew, Paul speaking Italian quite well, actually.

Sandstock was a first for Egypt, and it went well, set up with floodlights, speakers and a large wooden bandstand just behind Agami's best beachfront hotel. At the beach like this, the open-minded, well-off Egyptians attending the event remained well behaved, thrilled that their country was found worthy of such a wild, all-night gathering.

Groups played on into the early morning hours, while Paul, the two cameramen and I worked nonstop filming it until about 4 a.m. And Nadia stuck right by us on the camera platforms all night, with her pretty Egyptian face and tight, revealing blue jeans—a film crew's typical female assistant. Quite a sweet girl really. I, not as busy as Paul and the two cameramen, conversed amicably with her throughout the concert, but when it all finished, she found her way to Paul—her original contact—and the two of them, for some reason, *walked* the mile home along the beach from Agami to Hanoville. She had earlier accepted Paul's invitation to stay with us, too, at the condo for the night. I helped pack up the gear and everyone met back at the Hanoville home, exhausted.

The cameramen took their showers first and fell off to sleep, leaving Paul, Nadia and me for ours. It was when Nadia went in to take her shower that Paul revealed what the girl had said to him in the middle of their walk on the beach. In simple Italian she had said, "*Mia pantaloni via thump, thump, thump.*" She was throbbing in her pants for sex! *Good Lord.*

Paul—not that he would oblige her anyway, being married and all—was now feverish and quickly fading into extreme ill health from the attack of some vicious virus.

When the girl walked out of that shower, my mouth dropped open. She was dressed in a short, black nightgown she'd brought in her small suitcase. Her black, shoulder-length hair was wet and combed back. Her face was exquisitely, though lightly, made up with eye shadow, eye liner, a bit of rouge, lipstick, the works. This woman knew how to freshen up and prepare herself. She was radiant, smiling and clearly . . . not intending to go to sleep. She smiled sweetly at me, as I happened to pass her in the hallway, but she was headed for Paul's room, not knowing that by this time the poor guy was practically bedridden. The lovely thing appeared before Paul, and he could hardly move. He called me into the room and said, "Wayne. Isn't she beautiful?"

"She surely is, Paul," I said.

"Please, Wayne, take her upstairs. I'm so sick I can't even move."

I smiled, "Yeah, okay."

She was despondent not having Paul and felt sorry for him being so sick. But when Paul instructed her in Italian to go and be with me, "*Perfavore, via con lui,*" she responded, hesitating slightly, but accepting it with, "*Si. Va bene.*" She rose up from the edge of Paul's bed, where she now sat, patted Paul's hand, said goodnight to him and walked over to me, the consolation prize.

I was no stranger to her. We knew each other quite well by now, since I had spoken to her kindly throughout the Sandstock night, something on which I would later reflect: women need and enjoy talking.

With her head down a bit but her eyes looking up, straight at me, she gave a slight smile of approval and acceptance to me, her new partner. I said goodnight to Paul, took the girl by the hand and led her down the hall, everyone else in the house fast asleep. By the time she and I had walked through the hallway and reached the staircase to the upper floor, it was as if there was never a Paul; that I was her date; that she was now mine for the night, or rather, morning.

There was a private little bedroom at the top of the stairs to the left, away from the rest of the home. It was almost like a room in a castle in that the only window was a narrow slit in the wall near the bed. I led her into the room, lit a candle and lay down with her on the small bed, she completely submitting to me with no hesitation. She was a blessing: warm, receptive, loving—hot actually—ready and totally yielding, with a body so clean she smelled of soap and perfume *everywhere*. It had been awhile since I had been with a woman—when Gayle left for Greece two months earlier—so I didn't perform too well, yet soon after it all, we both fell off into a satisfied, deep sleep.

This lady delighted in sex. Her whole intention for leaving Cairo yesterday and coming to Alexandria was to have and enjoy it. She later said she was married and that her husband didn't mind her traveling out like this, but that didn't seem too likely. She might have been a sort of whore, or perhaps a woman who simply loved sexual adventure and took money for it only as needed.

She was sound asleep when Paul knocked and opened the door to the room at eight o'clock in the morning. Standing at the entrance, he whispered loudly to me, in an almost upset tone, "Wayne! Get up!" He was adamant, standing there at the doorway, that I get out of the room from sleeping with this chick. The reason? There was a member of the group who lived in the condo—a precious and sweet American guy named Steve, who had come to Egypt only two months before. Paul was afraid the guy might "stumble"—spiritually—if he found one of the two "leaders" of the Egypt team (me) bedding down here with some strange bird. *Darn it, though.* I was *rock hard* when I woke up, so ready for a second act with this girl, only to be *robbed* of it by Paul like this. Nadia, when she later awakened—also with sexual muscles now stimulated for further indulgence—was most perplexed to find me *gone* from beside her. She felt "abandoned," spurned almost, unwanted at the least. I assured her how great the time was with her but that I had to care for Paul—still very sick and feverish—and see him off in the car to Cairo with the two cameramen.

Steve awoke late since he had performed songs on his guitar at Sandstock into the early morning hours. For what it was worth, no one except Paul had any idea anyone had slept with the girl. Turned out *Steve,* often left alone at the Hanoville condo, had been regularly "helping out" a wealthy, middle-aged Italian lady over in Alexandria. Good-looking, blond-haired, blue-eyed in his mid-20s, Steve resembled Tom Cruise. Quite a ladies' man.

I prepared some breakfast for Nadia and me, but the mystery of this girl continued. Thinking maybe she *was* some kind of hooker, I repeatedly asked her if she "needed" any money—for her travels, for taxi fare to Alexandria, anything, something. "*Non. Non. Niente. Khalas. Mish owaz hagga,*" she insisted, in a mix of Italian and Arabic, vehemently refusing any money whatsoever. It seemed she simply enjoyed the ride up from Cairo, the whole Sandstock event, the sex and being in the company of Westerners.

She had money and did have some kind of rendezvous in Alexandria, so I walked her over to Hanoville's main street to put her in a cab. While awaiting a cab, a small, white van of Italian guys—contract workers—happened by, amazed to see an American guy standing there in the middle of Hanoville with this beautiful, obviously Egyptian woman. They slid the van door open, and in typical, bubbly

Italian cheer and good humor, greeted us with, "*Ciao!*" wondering if we needed help or a ride.

Nadia, thrilled at the chance to use her Italian again, quickly became genial and considered accepting a ride with them. I became uneasy and protective of the little femme fatale who had just hours earlier brought me so much pleasure. I wasn't falling for her or anything but had developed enough care for her that I now felt responsible for her well-being. With a frown on my face, eyebrows lowered and with a slight shake of my head, I tried to express to her my apprehension of her accepting a ride with these chaps.

But heck, this chick could handle herself, and despite my recommending she take a cab instead to Alexandria, she told me in Arabic not to worry. "*Maalesh*," she said, kissed me on the cheek while squeezing my hand and climbed into the van of Italians. *Okay. Lord, help her please,* I prayed.

I saw her fleetingly two times after that in Cairo from a taxi, she and another girl both times hailing down a cab in the opposite direction. One of the times we even waved to each other. *Strange bird.* Maybe she "treated" foreigners and "charged" only Egyptians. Who knows? What I do know, is she treated *me* to one of the *nicest* mornings I ever had.

We all continued using and enjoying the lovely Hanoville beachside home, until moving out in October.

Chapter 32
⁓ *Egyptians* ⁓

BACK IN MAY, our landlady, Mona, wanted to raise the rent on our seventh-floor Heliopolis apartment. So, instead of staying, we found and moved across town to a nice, fully furnished ground floor of a private, brown-brick villa for £.E. 110 ($165) a month. The place sat off a dirt side road on about a quarter-acre of land. A privacy wall of rock and wrought iron surrounded the property. Large palm trees shaded the front yard, and on the tiled patio of the home, we often grilled our filet mignon steaks and hamburgers.

This was the life in Egypt really. We all came to love this cheap, fun land. But there were also challenges and idiosyncrasies to face and endure here. Like the telephone system, unreliable and nearly nonexistent in even middle-class areas as back at our seventh-floor apartment. In order to make a call over there, we had to use the phone at a nearby little grocery store, along with the neighbors. That telephone was one of those old, black, pulse-type ones with a circular dial on the front that you stuck your finger in and turned clockwise for each number. It was at this telephone one day that I learned a phenomenal characteristic of Egyptians—"*your* business is *their* business." I was trying to call Sharif. I dialed his number a couple times, but it was busy. So I stepped away from the telephone so the guy waiting behind me could use it. The guy took his turn, dialed a number, turned to me and said in English, "Your number is busy."

"What?" I replied, bewildered.

"Your number. It's still busy," the guy repeated.

Oh, Lord. In the seconds it had taken me to dial Sharif's number, the guy, unbeknownst to me, had *memorized* the number and dialed it himself. *Helping* me, you might say? *I don't think so.* It was more of an uncontrolled obsession to make *my* business, *his* business. *Damn it.*

That was one Egyptian trait. There were others. Like going to a men's room to pee, particularly in a bathroom with several urinals. One of the few suitable toilets I ever found to use in downtown Cairo—I never found any *public* toilets—was that of a classy restaurant, down some fancy steps from its main dining area. Here, in my first or second week in Egypt, I was confronted with a fairly hilarious phenomenon. After peeing in one of the urinals, I looked up to see someone approaching me on my left. It was the bathroom attendant guy, and he had his hand stretched forth with something in it. *Whoa. Wait a second. What the hell is that?* The guy was offering me a piece of tissue to wipe it off with. *Okay.*

"Uh . . . no thank you," I said to the guy, shaking my head. I was not aware that guys in these parts actually did sometimes wipe it off, after peeing. Of course the attendant expected a fee for the tissue.

That was my introduction to the extent some Egyptians would go, to provide the most ridiculous service for *boksheesh*—a tip.

One time I pulled up in someone's car at a rest stop alongside a highway, and as soon as I opened the door, out of nowhere a guy appeared in his *galabaya* (Egyptian robe) to roll my window up for me before I could do it myself. And expected payment for it! Another stratagem *really* bothered me. Whenever I walked into my own apartment complex, the live-in bowab emerged ahead of me. "*Itfudal,*" he'd say subserviently, as he *pushed* the *elevator* button for me, ultimately hoping for a tip. *Shit. I'd rather pay the guy a certain amount each month if he'd just stay away from that button and let me push it myself.*

But worse than any of these services was their *expert* reaction that the amount of money, if I did hand them any, was not enough. They'd look at the money, then look at me and, with a frown and a shake of the head, retort, "*Eh dah?*"

Another trait was, "*Kolo kwis*" or "*Leh, kwis*"—saying everything was good when it was not at *all* good. Like when I had two suits tailor-made. Tailoring, incidentally, was cheap here. I had two, three-piece, British wool suits made for $60 each. But the leh, kwis Egyptian characteristic nearly drove me nuts before the suits finally fit. The first suit required no less than five visits to the tailor to have it fitted correctly. And, Lord. Ahmed the tailor was so convincing. He'd look at it, *wrongly* hanging off me everywhere, and *still* say, "*Leh, kwis.*"

I learned to never take "no" for an answer in Egypt, either. I went to the post office one day to pick up an expensive, leather-bound diary my brother, Gary, had sent me from England. I took the receipt around back and handed it to the guy behind the counter. "No," the guy said, "the package hasn't arrived yet. Come back *bokra.*" I was pretty sure the package was there since I had the receipt to pick it up, so I insisted the guy go and at least look for it. And sure enough he got up, went to the back, found it and brought it to me. Of course this happened all the time. Enough to be a pattern.

Just mailing letters in Egypt inspired Paul to coin a phrase that probably applied to the whole country—"Every slave has a slave." Paul discovered it after giving his letters a few times to an Egyptian guy he knew to mail them for him and realized the letters were taking too long to reach their destinations. He confronted the guy who unashamedly responded that *he* didn't actually mail the letters. "I gave them to Mahmoud to mail," he said . . . who gave them to Ali to mail, who gave them to Hussein to mail. *Every slave had a slave.* Was it laziness? Or worse. Maybe they considered it below their dignity *not* to use others to get something done.

The Egyptians were uncannily perceptive though, unless it was just part of their your-business-is-my-business trait. Paul and I realized it after shopping several times together at Khan-el-Khalili—the main, huge souk of Cairo. We took visitors and new arrivals there for anything from handmade carpets and camel leatherware to precious gemstones, gold and jewelry, clothes and material, to foodstuffs, kebabs and tea, haircuts, anything. When Paul and I first used to go there, vendors and merchants approached us, pestered us and even followed us, knowing we were fresh, untouched newcomers. But after two or three visits, we realized we were never being bothered again. The Egyptians either remembered our faces or actually perceived by our walk and air of confidence that we were no longer tourists here. Amazing. We ended up walking alleys and streets like locals.

A woman had to be careful if she *looked* at a guy in Egypt, because if she gave any *hint* of interest in him, that's it; he'd pursue her to the limit. It happened once with Gayle when she eyed an Egyptian soldier aboard a train she and I were traveling on to Alexandria. Sure enough, when we disembarked in Alexandria and were ready to hail down a cab to Hanoville, the guy suddenly appeared right there next to us trying to get the *same* cab as Gayle—letting be damned any partner she might have had.

"Where are you going?" the soldier asked.

"Hanoville," Gayle said.

"Me too," he said. "Shall we share the same cab?"

"Oh, brother," I said to Gayle. "If you had told him you were going to the *moon*, he'd have said the same thing.

Gayle let the guy share the cab, but we both gave him such negative vibes he got out of the cab in the middle of nowhere, not even halfway to Hanoville. Who knows *where* his real destination was?

Some Kuwaiti girls I knew told me how they had one day simply glanced at two Egyptian guys at the train station in Alexandria, thought nothing of it and boarded the express train to Cairo—the one that doesn't even stop but just barrels on at high speed to the capital. Sure enough, and to the shock of the girls, the Egyptians had maddeningly driven their car at some horrendous speed, *beat* the train and arrived there at the Cairo station to greet the girls when they got off. *Damn it.* The girls were *so* disgusted to see these guys' faces there at the Cairo station they gave them the cold shoulder and went their way.

Taxis. I figured I lost years of my life using them, just through the fear caused from sitting in them as a passenger as we squeezed between cars and huge buses, sped around donkey carts, disregarded stop signs and traffic signals and, most of all, narrowly missed hapless pedestrians. The drivers were skilled but reckless. I often had to tell them to slow down. "*Bishwaysh, min fodlick.*" It seemed they liked to show off.

And it wasn't that people in the streets *didn't* get struck or that taxis didn't have accidents. Four or five different times, I saw individuals lying *dead* in the streets of Cairo, with newspapers placed over them until they could be carted off. And at least three different times, I saw the little, black-and-white Fiat taxis wrapped—totaled!—around trees or posts, with little or no hope of survivors.

There was not much regard on the streets here for human life. As far as the taxi drivers were concerned, if a person walked in front of their cab, it was *their* fault if they got hit. The drivers let them know it too, by honking their horns and screaming at the poor pedestrians to open their eyes and look. "*Met fetah!*" the driver would scream, as he sped through throngs of people.

After a while, Paul and I figured there was only one good way to get from point A to point B in this city: chauffeured in the back of a van with no windows so we couldn't look out into the nerve-racking street scene, thereby avoiding the etching away of years of our lives from worrying over the endless narrow misses on human life. It was madness to exist in these streets, especially as a Westerner, who knew better than to put his mind, body and nerves through such torture. Only the grace of God with the help of angels protects people in such cities.

As a walker in downtown Cairo, even if with money, there was almost no place to take refuge from the hectic, hot-in-summer streets. No place to get into some air conditioning to gather thoughts over a quick bite to eat, a cool drink or a cup of coffee. The city had not been well thought out. Business after business, store after store had just sprouted up as someone had the inkling and money to start something—until there was no more room to compensate for a small café, sandwich shop or pub that had never been built. It was horrible really. I had been stuck in the city enough times and walked enough of its streets in search of a place to relax, regroup or reorganize, to know that Cairo just didn't offer many cool places to "hang out." The best and almost only place to do so was inside the lush Nile Hilton at Cairo's Tahrir Square. As a foreigner, I could blend into this hotel's cool, air-conditioned lobby with its high, high ceiling and sit nonchalantly on one of the several available cushioned lounge chairs, bothered by no one. The hotel was opulent—typical Middle Eastern—with huge chandeliers, its floors and towering columns made of shiny rare marble. A large brass lantern dangled above a winding staircase to the second floor and appealing artwork hung everywhere. All this without spending any money—using the clean, classy restrooms and the working pay phones.

Often I saw bedraggled young Western tourists wander into this safe haven/oasis—this semblance of civilization—dazed and confused, noticeably worn out from walking the unforgiving streets of Cairo. The problem with *them*—they were too obvious, dressed sloppily, maybe carrying an ugly backpack, themselves knowing they didn't much mesh with this fancy hotel. They couldn't be mistaken for paying guests of the hotel or even potential patrons of its restaurants. Not like Paul and I who knew how to dress accordingly to fit into such a scene, remembering the verse, "man looketh on the outward appearance."

For a small fee, Paul and I sometimes used the gym in the basement of the hotel so we could sit in one of the sauna rooms and then jump into the cold little plunge pool in the middle of the saunas. Or we'd unwind together and with friends over a beer or two in the hotel's classy English-style pub that joined the main lobby; we had decent haircuts on the upper, first floor for a mere £.E 1.50 ($2.30); or we partook of one of the world's finest brick-oven pizzas at the hotel's Pizzeria Restaurant, complimented by a bottle of the decent, locally produced *Omar Khayam* red wine, held and served in its own little straw wine basket. We used the hotel, but didn't abuse it.

Every large city, as I learned in Tehran and Kabul, has an escape not far away to some sort of nature, to renew the spirit—even for a poor man. Here, it was the *desert*. I often forgot its benefits until Paul asked me to take visitors there from time to time. And when I did, I always felt renewed and cleansed, just being in God's nature, albeit the barren desert. I would find Hassan and have superb tea with him and other camel drivers on a slope of sand just below the Pyramids near the camel stables; ride camels around the Pyramids, ruins and on out into the desert; and sometimes stop in at Hassan's house where his lovely wife would greet us and serve us tea. Quite magical.

The author near the Pyramids at Giza

It wasn't just camels we rode and raced up and down sand dunes in the open desert beyond the Pyramids. Hassan could just as easily set us up with *horses*—fast, small, Arabian horses. If we had time, we'd ride them or camels a half-hour to Sahara City—not really a city but an open-air restaurant that sat on a small desert plateau a few miles southwest of the Pyramids. Like a little, modern oasis, it was difficult to sit there at Sahara City without imbibing a cold bottle of Stella with some peanuts, chips, cooked beans or other side-plate of food, at a table with umbrella in the open air, while gazing out across the desert at the ancient Pyramids in the distance. Sahara City could also be reached by car on a paved road from the Pyramids for this same enchanting setting, but without feeling like a desert cowboy at our saloon table—horse or camel waiting out front!

The horses were fast and fun but were more out of place in the desert compared to the amazing camels. In fact, when we mounted our horses after the stop at Sahara City and they were too hungry, we hardly had a choice on what direction to take because these steeds headed, without hesitation, straight back to the Pyramids. The first time it happened, I wondered what the heck was going on here, until Hassan explained it to me, and not before we reached the Pyramids. Unlike the camels that could eat scrubby desert bushes, these hungry horses instinctively raced toward the stables for their food. They galloped at their top speed so fast it was scary. We couldn't really stop them or slow them down. They could ruin a desert adventure with their uncontrollable bolt back to food and civilization. They weren't like camels, who were one with the desert, or even donkeys that sometimes came along on journeys to carry feed for the camels. One of these donkeys became untied from my camel once when I got separated from the others on a little caravan adventure. And there I was, in the middle of desert-nowhere, chasing a donkey on my camel, trying to catch him to no avail until Hassan appeared, racing up over a mound, and easily roped him back in. It had to look great though—this dumb American, alone, out in the desert chasing a wayward donkey with no success.

Anyone out at the Great Pyramids late at night could witness what these wonders of ancient civilization were now used for—lovers. People, mostly Egyptians, freely drove their cars right up to them—no barriers and not illegal to be there—climbed upon their stepped facades, made-out, loved and did whatever.

Besides using them for romance, people also climbed to the top of them, although this was illegal since too many had died when they were blown off in strong winds or simply lost their footing and tumbled down one of the four sides. Mind you, the stones of the Great Pyramids are about chest high and over the thousands of years have become crumbly and irregular.

After a year here in Egypt, almost none of our prospects to "reach the lost" had even remotely come to fruition, like producing and broadcasting video tapes to villages to help resolve illiteracy, establishing Montessori schools for Egyptian village kids and bringing a music group here.

Soon, headquarters in Switzerland informed Paul they would no longer support the "pioneering" of Egypt. The year was up; the stipend would stop. *Never mind.* Although he complained a bit, Paul wasn't too worried. He was already making money on various schemes, ones even related to his field of interest—photography and filming. Throughout Cairo, he and I snapped still photographs of existing advertisements, such as billboards of Kent and Marlboro cigarettes, for a competing cigarette company. And for the General Motors Corporation, Paul organized and directed advertising film clips of Nile River taxi boats that used GM engines and of trucks with GM engines passing in front of the Great Pyramids. On the GM works, he hired Mahmoud to do the camera work, while I was the "soundman"—using a portable cassette tape recorder. It brought in good money, and, along with Maggie's decent cash flow from her secretary work, we all lived comfortably in the ground-floor, Heliopolis villa.

The filming—that gave us a reason to even *be* in Egypt, while providing us money at the same time—led us to assisting in the videotaping of the Cairo Film Festival from September 27 to October 5, 1977, at the Cairo Sheraton Hotel on the Nile in Dokki. We weren't paid for it but agreed to do it as a good gesture for Egypt's Ministry of Information who sponsored it—influence that couldn't hurt.

The week was interesting, meeting film producers, directors and film stars like Ursula Andress, Michael York and the genuinely friendly and humble actor, Trevor Howard. But perhaps more interesting to me was discovering that this particular Sheraton was quite the clandestine meeting place for some folks. Our Egyptian cameraman-friend, Mahmoud, who commissioned us for the event, revealed this to us. "My own brother," he said, "is a regular, paid gigolo for Saudi Arabian women here. *And* men. They give him gold necklaces a lot." Whether or not it was true, who knows?

As it was, I met and lunched a couple times with a Palestinian woman and a gorgeous twenty-something girl she introduced as her daughter. I surmised later the mother was more than likely there at the Sheraton to pimp the girl out to prime, chosen clients at top rates. They had sort of invited me to their table, not knowing I was a poor American and naïve to their intents. I had no idea at the time they might be "working" there in the classy setting of the Sheraton. Instead, I only befriended them, ate with them and considered them souls hungry for spiritual love. Actually, here in fall of 1977, troubles in Palestine caused many such Palestinian women to flee to nearby countries, forced to fend for themselves.

Then there was the "Lady in Blue." I met her the second day of the festival—a Syrian girl in her early twenties, attired in an all-blue, form-fitting, knee-length dress. She checked into the Sheraton with her dad, a businessman with meetings here in Cairo. While her father conducted business, she strolled through the lobby looking beautiful—on the hunt, obviously, the way she strutted her tight blue dress all over the hotel. I noticed her between our videotaping; our eyes made contact several times, and I approached her—a humble, sweet, ripening 21-year-old Syrian girl. *Glory.*

I introduced her to Paul, and she accepted an invitation to attend the movie *Airport 77* with us right there at the Sheraton in a makeshift theatre with folding chairs set up for those working for and attending the film festival. The girl was so open, and, within hours during the next two days, she and I fell slightly in love after some rather deep talks in the lobby of the hotel, she speaking fluent English. These Arab girls liked to talk about love and yes, even sex, and I would generally get right to the point with them on it—never failing to acknowledge the Creator of it all. We came to know each other so well in that short time I came extremely close to suggesting we go to her room when it looked safe, *she* possibly pondering it as well. But in all reality, it was too risky. It would have no doubt meant at least some luscious little kisses though, with this fresh young thing. *Goodness.*

She said a sad goodbye to me on the third day, and in the coming months, we wrote letters back and forth, she picking up where we'd left off at the Sheraton, talking about sex, love, God and true friendship. Another love-starved little Arab girl. Perhaps I was destined to someday find one as my wife. *Nah.*

Near the end of the film festival, Paul left Mahmoud and me in charge while he flew down in a small plane to Hurghada to pursue skin-diving-resort prospects with Sharif. Also vying for the virgin paradise of Hurghada—with its year-round warm climate, clear waters of tropical fish and endless coral reefs—were Germans, Italians and others. Yet Sharif, supposedly, was one of only three people given permission for some reason to establish any kind of settlement at this still-undeveloped coastal Red Sea village, located near the mouth of the Gulf of Suez and the Gulf of Aqaba. Meanwhile, Paul, in his charismatic friendliness, became good friends with the governor of Hurghada.

But nothing materializes too easily or too quickly in Egypt, as devout U.S. skin divers Alex and Connie learned. After devoting nearly a year struggling with Sharif on Hurghada, losing money and getting nowhere, Alex and Connie finally gave up on the whole idea, packed up, said some tearful goodbyes to us all and returned to California.

In fact, if a foreigner could run a business here and still stay out of jail, he was doing all right—unlike some of the people we had befriended, like our Italian-American engineer friend who landed briefly in jail back on September 3 for reneging on some contract with an Egyptian. You just don't *gyp* an Egyptian. One had to know that. You don't pull anything over on them.

Then, a major turning point in our work came November 1977, when we met an American businessman named Sam Watson, *almost* more clever than the Egyptians. I wasn't exactly clear what he was up to here in Egypt—interested in starting a tractor factory or something for more food production—but he *seemed* to be successful.

Like Frank Smith, he had a room at the swanky Meridien Hotel, though not a fancy suite like Smith's. Maggie met him there while working for Smith. According to Watson, she literally saved his life one night when she knocked on his hotel room door. Due to troubles in his life, Watson was contemplating doing himself in with pills, and there she was, standing at the door looking pretty—"Like an angel," he later said. She prayed with him then and there in his hotel room, he had a spiritual experience with his Creator, and his life was changed forever. The two of them soon fell in love with each other and married, though he was several years her senior. Their union meant he actually became part of the group, although not a full-fledged, "dropped-out," "forsake-all" disciple.

Spiritually, he was a "babe" and so we, mostly Maggie, nourished him slowly, while at the same time, we treated him respectfully as the elder he was. He was what we called in this family, a "king"—a close friend who graciously bestowed riches or influences on us. He proved that our targeting the influential, or rich, with the message of God's Love (as opposed to just the common man in the street) was not totally off track.

Always dressed in sharp, black suits, Gucci shoes, and sporting a gold ring with four rather large diamonds glittering across it in a row . . . Watson *looked* successful whether he was or not. He spent money in Egypt though, besides for his Meridien Hotel room. Like the car he bought here—a rare, faded-red, antique 1937 Delahaye convertible— from some rich lady. He just drove up with it one day and took everyone (except me, who stayed home with the kids) for a picnic at the Al Faiyum Oasis for the day.

Savvy on estate auctions, he used to take Paul and me to them in Heliopolis, coming away once with a set of valuable chinaware at £.E. 40 and an old painting of David and Goliath at £.E. 100, which he stored at the house. Who knows what else he used to buy?

Two days before Thanksgiving 1977, and only three days after Maggie had knocked on his door, he showed up with his Egyptian driver, toting a brand new, much needed, £.E. 300 range-oven for our home—just in time to bake a succulent Egyptian turkey to celebrate Thanksgiving.

He bought Maggie a good-size, maybe two-carat diamond ring she flipped over. I guess she would, being a disciple in this family where most of us were lucky to have two or three changes of clothes and not a penny in any bank anywhere! He whisked her off to Paris, then Japan and London on different business trips. She was enthralled by the extravagance with him, but she did truly love him, too, and was most faithful to feed him with spiritual words and readings from the Bible as much and as often as possible.

He loved our little family and splurged on us, one time returning from a trip to the U.S. with a brand new $1,400 Nikon camera kit for Paul. On his trip with Maggie to Japan, he brought back an expensive Sony component sound system with large Pioneer speakers for the home, all worth several hundred dollars, that he had *somehow* passed through customs with no duty imposed on it—a difficult feat, since Egypt had a 200% duty on such electronics.

Chapter 33
⟶ *Layla* ⟵

I MET HER at the Hilton Pizzeria Restaurant on December 11, 1977. Watson liked to take us all out to dinner, although I often stayed home with the kids. Sheila was going to go this time, but for some reason, *God bless her,* she said, "No, Wayne. It's your turn to go. I'll stay with the kids." Four months back, on August 18, Sheila had given birth to a healthy baby boy, so she and Paul now had three kids.

Watson, Maggie, Paul, Paul's little girl, Teresa, and I headed downtown to the Nile Hilton Pizzeria in, strangely enough, a big, black Mercury Marquis automobile. Smith had shipped the car here from the States and, since he was now on business in Morocco, left the car for Watson to use.

It was about 8 p.m. so the restaurant was nearly filled up. But we found a table in a corner right next to a table of what appeared to be four, well-dressed Middle Eastern girls in their early 20s. I gave my order and got up from the table to make a phone call to an Egyptian girl I knew. When I returned, our Italian guitarist-friend, Antonio—hired to serenade the diners here and whom we knew from previous visits—was on break and sitting in my seat. As soon as I returned to the table and found my seat taken, Watson, the romantic and manipulator as he naturally was, insisted I take up the one empty chair at the table of four girls. Smiling warmly at the girls, while authoritatively gesturing with his outstretched hand at the empty seat, Watson asked them, "Please. Can our friend sit at your table?"

The girls, having already seen the situation develop with the guitarist in my seat, didn't hesitate to cordially respond to Watson's request. Looking to me two of them said, with slight accents, "Yes. Please. Sit down." I was a bit embarrassed but didn't have much choice.

"Thank you," I said, as I pulled the small wooden chair out and sat down. "Where are you all from?"

"We are from Kuwait," one said. "Do you know where that is?"

"Yes, of course I know," I said. "It's not far from here and it's full of oil." All of them smiled at this depiction of their country.

"What are you girls doing in Cairo?" I asked.

"We three are studying medicine at Cairo University," one answered. "And she," pointing to one of them, "is a petroleum engineer."

"Wow. That's great!" I responded.

"What are *you* doing in Cairo?" one asked. (They already figured we were Americans.)

"Well," I said, while pointing toward Paul, "he and I are doing some photography here right now; and he," I continued, nodding toward Watson, "is a businessman."

The four spoke English nearly fluently, especially the three studying medicine. And all were ladies—fashionably dressed in high heels with skirts and dresses to about their mid-calves. No scarves on their heads, just nicely styled black hair flowing around their faces.

By this time in my life, I had no problem speaking openly and feeling comfortable with such beauties, whatever their nationality. But I also, by this time in my travels, didn't expect to get too far with Arab girls, either sexually *or* spiritually. Nevertheless, I fared well with the four and enjoyed my pizza and a glass of red wine.

I sat straight across from the most beautiful one of the four who was also the most open, friendly and talkative. Her name was Layla. She soon wrote her phone number on a white, paper napkin and also took down mine. Still, I considered the meeting just another fruitless, Arab-girl encounter that would get nowhere.

The four girls were here on full scholarships paid by the Kuwait government. They lived in a dormitory across the Nile in Mohandeseen.

"Oh! It's getting late!" one of the girls said, looking at her watch. "We are supposed to be in our dorm by 9:30."

"We'll take you there, if you want," I said. "We have a big American car." I turned to Watson to confirm we could take them.

"Yes, yes," he said. "We'll take them home."

The girls looked at each other. "Okay," two of them said.

We all nine crammed into the Marquis, and, with Watson driving, the girls got home in time. The one girl, Layla, *seemed* to be interested in me, and even sat next to me in the back seat, but I didn't take it too seriously.

Now 27 years old, I was seeking more than idle, get-nowhere conversations with girls, so I didn't even call Layla. But two days later . . . *she* called *me*. Now *that* bold act, with that sweet voice on the other end of the phone, changed things.

"Hi! This is Layla. Remember me?"

"Yes! Sure! How are you?"

A few words went back and forth until she said, "Maybe we could meet again somewhere."

"Uh . . . yeah," I stammered, impacted a little further now by the boldness of this chick. *Glory.*

"But it will have to be after the New Year," she said, "because me and my friends—the ones you met—we will be in Kuwait, for our winter break."

"Okay. We'll get together when you come back."

"I'll be back January 10."

"Shall I call you then?" I asked.

"Yes, please. Do you still have my number?"

"Yes, I have it. I'll call you. Have a good time in Kuwait."

"Thank you. Bye."

"Bye-bye."

Christmas came and so did Annie, a Jewish-American girl I knew back in Iran and Afghanistan. Now drifting through Egypt, she'd been in and out of this family, and she and I hit it off well together for a rather loving Christmas. As for Christmas dinner this year at "the villa," Paul had thought ahead and purchased a *live*, 12-kilogram turkey on December 10. We fattened it up in the backyard until Christmas Day when the landlady's servants slaughtered it for us. Watson then baked it fresh, fat and juicy in the new oven—*so* delicious!

Then, on New Years, Gayle flew in from Greece on her way to Bombay and *that* flame was rekindled for the four days she stayed.

But I never forgot the guts of that dark-haired Arab beauty Layla, calling me like she did, or the sweetness of her voice over the phone. I was touched firstly by her apparent interest in me, but mostly I was totally impressed that she had taken the initiative to . . . *call me first!* With the holidays over and our visitors cleared, I telephoned Layla at her dorm on January 10, now 1978. On her first phone call to me, when she had said, maybe we could meet again, she actually meant she and her Kuwaiti girlfriends. So we did. I met up with Layla and two of the same girls two days later at the Hilton Pizzeria and sat at their table with them while they ate a late dinner. The four of us talked and got better acquainted this night, Layla still the outgoing, feisty one.

It was all delicate and slow with these maidens, and, after another phone call or two over the next month between Layla and me, I met with Layla and just *one* of the other girls, again at the Hilton, but in the lobby this time. It was at this meeting on February 16 that I realized Layla and I would pursue one another. She was beautiful, with long, stylishly layered black hair flowing around her face, her front and to the middle of her back. Light-skinned for an Arab girl, she had high cheek bones with a touch of rouge on them tonight, alluring dark eyes enhanced with eyeliner and a bit of mascara on the eyelashes, eyebrows perfectly plucked and shiny lipstick on her full lips. Though her button-down blouses and expensive flimsy skirts past her knees didn't reveal her body fully, she was obviously thin and trim, full-breasted and not too tall (lucky for me) even in her high heels.

Being late now, 9 p.m., we didn't have much time together, but it was long enough for Layla to express her interest in me—with her eyes. Her friend Aisha was seated to her left, there on the cushiony lounge chairs of the hotel lobby. I was on the same set of lounge chairs, but at a right angle to Layla, on her right side. In this arrangement, and without Aisha seeing, Layla gave me these totally sexy looks from her dark eyes, imparting to me without a word that she had a desire for me. And a slight one or two touches from her delicate hand on my thigh was a further hint. She was an uncontrollable flirt, this girl, and I didn't mind being on the receiving end of it. *Man!* She was some kind of sexy though.

She intended to express this to me on this night since she and the other girls would fly to Kuwait tomorrow for two weeks. She wanted her eyes to *remain* in my mind while she was gone. Well, that look from those eyes remains in my mind to this day.

During this time, Paul, Sheila and their oldest daughter, Teresa, flew down in a small plane to Hurghada for two weeks with Sharif, while I "held the fort," and went nuts watching the two little ones at the villa. Luckily, we now had a faithful, middle-aged, Egyptian maid named Zeenat who came two or three times a week to clean, and assisted me with the kids. Otherwise, two in diapers at the same time? Very difficult, especially for a guy.

The Kuwaiti girls returned as scheduled on March 3, and Layla phoned me the next day. It was *alive* between us. I phoned her back in a few days, and then she called on the morning of March 10 saying she would finally be coming over to our house this afternoon, alone even, via a dormitory chauffeur at 5:20 p.m. I met her and the chauffeur in the car at the corner and led them down the dirt road to the villa. Now, on the outside brick wall at the entrance to our villa, was a brass plaque engraved with the name of the owner of the property, *Mikhael Saleeb, M.D.*, the old Coptic Christian landlady's deceased husband. So, since Layla was a medical student, she might, on future visits, be able to convince her chauffeurs that she came here to the "doctor's residence" for . . . *medical* classes—*anatomy* classes perhaps?

She was a lady though, and dressed like one as usual again today as she stepped out of that car. She was not overly dressed but wore a fashionable skirt with coordinated blouse and high heels. Her long, straightish black hair was perfectly brushed; she wore modest makeup and had the most loving, cheerful smile across her face.

"You look so pretty today," I said.

"Thank you," she replied. "Is this your house?"

"Yes. Come in."

She turned to the driver, "*Saah sabah. Meshi?*" she said, reminding him of the time to pick her up.

The villa was not elaborate but very neat and cozy with plenty of class even for a Kuwaiti's standards. It had a living room, a large dining room, two bedrooms, one and a half bathrooms and a kitchen. The furniture was decent, with an antique, wooden dining table and chairs that easily sat eight. French doors in the dining room led to the small, tiled patio that looked out on the front garden. And the expensive Sony stereo system with its large speakers added a touch of extravagance.

Today, the villa was, somehow, empty. I sat her down in the living room, served her hot tea and we talked. *Oh, my God.* This was no joke. There was nothing fake here. No difficulty looking into one another's eyes or trying to come up with something to say. I asked her, "Do you have any brothers and sisters?" After that, words flowed between us with a warmth of mutual interest in what the other had been dealt from life until now—until being placed face to face on this couch. We talked about family, God, love, the world and a *little* about sex. She loved the Beatles so I inserted *Revolver* into the tape machine.

I really didn't know what to expect from this Middle Eastern beauty, coming to my home, alone like this. Was she experienced? Did she play around? Was she a virgin? Or, was she here in total "Arab-girl innocence"—naïve and unaware of the potential *lechery* of men and the risk of being alone with one in his home like this? I surmised she was the latter—innocent, reserved, a bit shy, a bit nervous, yet still happy to be in my company.

"This is for you," she said, and handed me a large, illustrated book on Kuwait and a fancy Parker pen—gift-bearing apparently an Arab tradition, *God bless her*. We looked through the Kuwait book together.

She had taken another risk coming alone to a guy's house like this: defying what others might think—even her own girlfriends, *if* she had even told them. I knew this about Middle Eastern girls, so I was particularly careful to make her feel comfortable and at ease. She deserved to know today that she had correctly judged me, from our previous meetings, to be a gentleman.

I soon learned that at 21 years old, she was a third-year medical student, loved Western music, was an avid fan of British and American TV and movies and seemed kinda thrilled to now be conversing with an actual American.

It was pretty stupid to ask people in this part of the world if they believe in God. They all do. But I asked her, just the same, "You do believe in God, don't you?"

She looked at me with eyes widened, almost in shock. "Of course I do. I love Him. He is first in my life, even before you!" she replied, smiling, but sticking it to me nonetheless.

It was obvious she was not a superficial believer. She was one of God's sheep. And it comforted her, I think, that I brought Him up at all here today.

I barely touched her, maybe a gentle grasp or two of her arm, and didn't sit too close to her. But I also didn't fail to show her affection—something I felt a single girl her age sorely needed. As fixed up, dressed up, coy and smiling as she was here today, I'd have been a fool not to express as much admiration to her as possible, without scaring her off. I *had* to respond, howbeit carefully, to the sexy looks she gave me that evening on the Hilton lounge chairs.

We spent an hour and a half alone together here today, and it may have been a key to our future. We had found much common ground, she knew she could trust me, and the physical attraction between us now pulsated in the spirit!

She too had planned to not overdo her first visit with me so had already arranged for the chauffeur to pick her up sharply at seven o'clock. He arrived on time and she left. It was Friday, her day off from classes, and before leaving, she said, "I'll come back next Friday at the same time. Okay?"

"I hope so. Bye-bye."

That week I traveled up to Alexandria with Paul and Watson for three days to search out possible rental apartments on the beach, at Agami this time, for the coming summer.

Returning to Cairo Thursday evening, I phoned Layla to confirm tomorrow's date. I must have played it gentle enough with her on her solitary visit last Friday, because she came alone again at 5:10 p.m., as planned. She came bearing gifts again, too, in her classiness—candy for the kids and a bottle of expensive French cologne for me.

This time Watson was there, the kids, Paul, Sheila, Maggie, everyone, which couldn't have been more comfort to this little morsel we had found—somehow—in the middle of complicated Cairo. Here now were my friends, giving her similar, respectful love—sincere concern for her *soul*, not just for her fleshly physical beauty. Each one talked to her and was interested in her. I left her alone with them for a while even, until she probably wondered where I, her sponsor, had gone.

Watson cooked two chickens and his specialty potato salad right then and there, and she stayed nearly three hours this time until 8 p.m. when she had arranged for a taxi to pick her up at the front gate. It was obvious she didn't want to leave quite so early, but elegantly departed.

She returned a week later with her girlfriend, Aisha. Layla was warmed up to us all and seemed proud to share with Aisha the homey atmosphere of the villa of godly foreigners and little children. I snapped photos of the two guests while an American girl of the group, Barbara, who'd flown in last night on her way to Sudan, served tea and chatted with them. The dark eyes of Layla though, had become extremely inviting by this visit, along with significant, yet subtle, flirtations from her, while both she and I were careful not to make it too obvious, or for Aisha to feel out of place. The two had dinner with us and were off at 8:45 to some late medical class.

Layla phoned me two days later. "Hi! I will come to see you day after tomorrow, Tuesday, if that's okay."

"Sure! I'll see you then."

She came alone by taxi at exactly 6:30 in the evening, as she had arranged. Why did she come *alone* today? I was well aware why. My heart, mind or God Himself had prepared me for what this creature needed. After all, this was the sixth time she and I had communed together and realized we desired each other. Physically, we matched well, with me at five feet eight inches, and she at about five feet two inches. Brunettes were especially attractive to me, maybe because I was sort of blondish and fair-skinned and nature seemed to encourage such a blending of features. But these Middle Eastern women just seemed hotter than most women, sexy, "built for breeding."

So, yes, I was prepared to carry things further with this girl today than just talking. In fact, I arranged things with Barbara, the American girl. "I might have to go into the other room with her," I said.

"Don't worry, Wayne," Barbara said. "I'll disappear with the kids."

Layla came in a chauffeured Mercedes exactly on time, looking like a beauty queen with her typical broad smile and a particularly warm sparkle in her eyes. I sat her down, served her tea and put on a Beatles tape, while she, natural woman as she was, talked sincerely and lovingly with the kids. Soon enough though, Barbara discreetly took the two children to another room to play, purposely leaving Layla and me alone in the living room. I had also arranged with Paul and Sheila, who were out anyway, to use their bedroom if necessary since it was a nicer bedroom than mine, and mine was now being used by Watson and Maggie as long as they were in town.

Layla's cheeks and whole face flushed pink when I took her by her smooth hand and invited her up from the couch. With a slight nod of my head toward the bedroom and a smile, I simply said, "Come."

There was no hesitation on her part, for she also knew it was time. So when I put my arm around her, led her to Paul and Sheila's bedroom and closed the door—though her heart may have been pounding—she was as ready as I to carry our attraction to each other in a kiss. I sat right next to her on the edge of the double bed, put my left arm around the back of her neck, my right hand to her cheek and gently kissed her wet lips. It was only for, maybe, ten seconds and I backed away from her, enough to look into her eyes and ask, "Was that okay?"

"Yes," she humbly responded, "that was my first time."

"What?" I asked, not sure I'd heard her correctly.

"You are the first person who has ever kissed me," she replied.

My head dropped down and away from her as if in mild shock. In split seconds my heart broke, in love for this girl, her humility. If I thought I *liked* her before, I may suddenly have loved her now. How many girls had played games with my head? American girls, of course. An American girl, for instance, would find it difficult to admit she'd never been kissed, especially at 21 years of age. She'd rather give the impression she was . . . experienced. Not this one. Here was a girl, bold and beautiful, who liked me and was honest enough to tell me no other guy had kissed her. She would not play games with my head. Three months ago in December she hadn't waited for *me* to call *her* but had called *me* instead; when she flew back to Kuwait, she informed me of the exact day she'd be back and came to the phone as soon as I called her; when she said she was coming over to my house . . . she *did*, and *exactly* on time, *every* time. She didn't play hard-to-get with me, probably never heard of such a game. She had made our relationship one of *truth* and *honesty* rather than games and deceit. And now our lips had finally met. All the loveliness I had seen in this girl until now had culminated in one ten-second kiss.

Tears came to my eyes, pondering all of this, though she didn't see them, the room having now darkened with the sunset.

"You really are beautiful," I said to her, referring now to her soul and to her as a person more than even her face.

No sense crying here though, or getting too deep. This ripe little thing needed genuine kissing, the kind she'd seen on TV, like *The Saint*, with Roger Moore, or in the movie, *Ryan's Daughter*.

I reached down and took off her heels and my own shoes, and she instinctively moved to the center of the bed and lay down, her hair billowing around her head and onto the pillow. I'd never been so close to her hair until now but noticed it had the most wonderful scent coming from it. For the Arabs, apparently, it wasn't enough to have just clean, shampooed hair. No. Today, she had splashed a concentrated oil essence called *razji* throughout it and had permeated it with the smoke of *bokhor*—an expensive incense, for added sex appeal. I lay down next to her and kissed her deeply on the lips and some on the neck while lightly touching her neck, arms, underarm, side, stomach and eventually— though reservedly—her thigh, yet nowhere near any vital zones, not today. She was a lady and deserved to be respected and treated gently as one. She had fallen into my lap, and I was now responsible for her introduction to love and intimacy—an introduction that would take some time.

After these few minutes of heated, though innocent, kisses and caresses, we talked, openly as usual, right there on the bed, like lovers. The anticipation between us of this first union of our lips and bodies had finally happened here on March 28, 1978, three and a half months since we first met at the Hilton Pizzeria and since she had lit this fire with her first telephone call to me.

We put our shoes on and returned to the living room, glued now and melting into each other. *Lord.* We seemed made for each other. Anyone looking at us right now must have seen us *glowing.*

The encounter had not scared her off because she came to the house the very next day, this time with one of the other original Kuwaiti girls. And the day after that with still another Kuwaiti girlfriend, university student, not one of the original three. Either the girls had urged Layla to show them the "house of foreigners," or Layla was obviously excited and radiant about it all in front of them, or both. On this second visit since "the kiss" though, Layla hinted to me that she wished to be *alone* with me. *My goodness*—I pondered later in the night after they'd left— *these humble, Arab girls. They're too much, Lord.*

From that day on, Layla always came *alone* to see and be with me. We were falling deeper in love, and by April 11, two weeks after that first kiss and after a couple more heated petting sessions together in my bedroom, Layla said to me over the telephone, "I love you and need you."

At any opportunity between her medical studies and exams, she'd come to the house, usually not more than three or four days between visits. Paul, Sheila and the others also talked and joked with her whenever she visited, before she and I drifted off to my room for hours at a time to talk and play around together. She required plenty of talk—like *all* women—but I also knew she was overripe for being at least kissed and touched all over. I always went slowly with her introduction to it all, but I also had the attitude that time was short, that a girl this age and as sensual as she, needed physical affection now and if *I* didn't give it to her, someone else might. In fact, after several of these love sessions, she confided in me exactly why she, an Arab girl, a Kuwaiti, would even *consider* meeting a guy, alone, at his house. Turned out that back in Kuwait, she had prospects of marrying a rich Kuwaiti guy her same age whom she'd been saving herself for until recently. Well, the guy asked her one day, "What do you do in Cairo when you're not studying?"

"I go to restaurants, like at the Hilton Hotel with my girlfriends, and we sometimes talk to Westerners there."

Soon after that, he asked her to return to Kuwait to study science or something at Kuwait University. (There was no medical university in Kuwait at the time.) She didn't buy that at all though—she wanted to pursue a medical degree—so the guy called it off with her. This did not devastate her. She knew she was pretty, still young and could find someone else. The spurning sort of angered her and set her free. Free to explore the world of men, now that this cute, rich character in Kuwait rejected her, or rather, failed to appreciate her for who she was. She was now ready to burn free and disregard her traditional Kuwaiti society. That, and she was an independent girl, with guts.

I likened her to a piece of fruit that had fully ripened on a tree and fallen right into my lap. Not only had she fallen off the tree, bounced out of someone's hand and landed on the ground, but I had picked up this lovely, unspoiled piece of fruit right from the ground.

Right now, she felt herself fortunate, if not blessed, to not only have been found on that ground, but found by *me*, realizing that in her state of retribution to events in Kuwait, she could well have been stumbled across by someone far less caring than I and put in a situation she might regret.

We went around Cairo together to movies and restaurants where I further observed the *class* this lady had, afforded to her by having money, Kuwaiti money. She and her girlfriends always dressed expensively, sponsored by the oil-rich Kuwait government. Money was obviously no problem for them. But it was little classy things Layla did that struck me. We sat for a meal together in the English pub of the Hilton, and the waiter brought a basket of assorted bread rolls to choose from. She didn't just take one in assumption they were all good. No. With her delicate little forefinger and thumb, she pinched one or two of them to see if they were indeed fresh enough to accept. She had obviously sat at enough restaurants, spending money, to know how to act in one and how to expect to be served.

At the end of April, Paul, Sheila, their three kids and I planned a visit to the States to see our respective families and friends. I had not seen

America for nearly six years since I'd left its shores back in August 1972, to undertake this "mission to reach the world with God's Love." And now I was *in love,* expressing both spiritual *and* physical love to a beautiful girl, an Arab girl, who'd landed in my arms on this journey, a journey that seemed to be coming to a close, or at least heading for a drastic change.

At eleven o'clock in the morning on April 27, 1978, Layla came to the villa to say goodbye to us as we departed to the States. We would take a 4 p.m. Scandinavian Airlines System flight to New York via Copenhagen. By now, Layla had come alone to the villa seven times to be gently wooed and sincerely loved by me. Yet only God and the wind knew she had even kissed me.

"Don't forget me, Wayne," she said.

"Oh, I won't," I assured her. "I'll be back in seven weeks."

"I will write to you," she said.

"Okay, good. I'll write to you, too." We hugged one more time, before her chauffeur came to pick her up.

It was great to spend time with my parents in Orlando, Florida, along with my sweet younger sister, Marianne, who lived in Orlando near Mom and Dad. I played some tennis with the folks, looked up an old girlfriend and took a Greyhound bus up to Northwest Florida where I spent five days with my dear friends, the Matthews. Sister Diane, husband Jack and their baby flew in for a pleasant nine days with us in Orlando. But I missed Layla.

After seven weeks in the States, I returned alone to the Cairo villa. Teresa—Paul and Sheila's daughter—was having too many health problems related to Egypt, so Sheila and kids decided to remain in America. Paul set them up in Colorado and would return to Cairo only briefly before going back to America to join them.

For three days after arriving in Cairo, I was unable to reach Layla due to telephones not working. It was madness. I finally got through to her and she came to the villa with her typically punctual knock on the door at 10 a.m., Tuesday, June 20. I opened the door.

"Hello, my dear," I said.

"Hi!" she said, with her beaming smile, and stepped inside. I closed the door, and she put her purse on the floor so we could squeeze and hug each other. We couldn't keep our hands off one another. We were so in love. Withdrawing from the hug, I held her by her waist with my hands and looked into her eyes. "I missed you so much."

"Me too," she said. "Did you get my letters?"

"Yes. They were beautiful. Thank you." She had written two loving letters to me in the States, to the one I had written to her, *God bless her.*

We sat down in the living room for a little while to talk and catch up. But we were soon off to the "room of love" to *play* with each other, as we always had—until nearly 5 p.m. today since we had the villa to ourselves. We then took a taxi downtown to "our" Hilton Pizzeria for dinner.

After dinner, we went up to the hotel room of an American photographer friend, Walter, whom I had recently met in the hotel lobby. I knocked on the door and Walter opened it.

"Hi, Wayne! How's it goin'?"

"Good," I said. "Walter, this is Layla."

"Hi. Nice to meet you. Come in."

We chatted awhile until Walter said, "How about some dinner?"

"We just ate," I said.

"Well, I'm starving. I'm going down to get something to eat," he said. "You two stay here if you want."

Walter closed the door, and there we were alone together in this romantic Hilton Hotel room, overlooking the Nile River shimmering in the nighttime lights of Cairo. And there stood my Arab princess, driving me crazy today in her extremely tight blue jeans—even though her white button blouse modestly covered her vital regions. And there was the well-made-up hotel bed in the middle of this darkened room. We stretched out upon it and kissed. (After all, we'd been away from the villa now for nearly *two* hours without caressing each other!) I lay on top of her, both of us fully dressed, and she spread her legs beneath me, not minding me gently rubbing against her. We kissed for several minutes but restrained ourselves from going any further. We had reacquainted ourselves well enough for the day. After straightening the bed, we left the room, and I took her by taxi to her dormitory.

Layla came to the villa as often as possible between her classes—every three or four days. Every time she came, I bought fresh roses and put them in a vase on a table near the entrance, roses being as cheap as 60 piastres (90 cents) a dozen here in Egypt.

Our sexual adventures were great, for hours at a time alone in the villa, and communication between us wonderful. We were, at the least now, boyfriend and girlfriend. Between visits we telephoned each other, finding it difficult to be apart for too long. We talked of marriage and sometimes nearly cried over the love deepening between us. At the end of one day, July 9, when Layla had been at the villa for over 10 hours, I continued thinking of her and wrote a note to myself in my diary— "Don't think she's *not* the one you've been waiting for. Perhaps you'd better not let *this* one slip through your fingers!"

Then, on July 18, 1978, a month since I had been back from the States, Layla came to the villa at 9:40 in the morning to say goodbye to me. She had come to the end of another summer term at Cairo University and had to return to Kuwait. Separating was horrible, but we shed no tears since we'd be seeing each other soon enough, when she would return to her classes in the fall.

"I hate leaving you," she said.

"I'll be fine," I said. "We'll see each other soon—in fall, when you come back."

We hugged once more and she was off. All we knew was that in the 14 or so times she had come to the villa alone to talk about the world with me, to be loved, kissed and touched pretty much all over by me, we had fallen deeply in love. We meshed in all ways. Yet, in my respect and love for this girl, I had not insisted on going any further than all these kisses and touches. She would return to her country today . . . still a virgin. As far as any prospective Kuwaiti husband knew, she had not been *touched* by anyone. She was pretty and available.

Chapter 34
∽ *The Letters* ∽

MY FUTURE IN Cairo was not clear, since Paul and Sheila would now be settling in America. I had returned alone to Cairo—sort of by request from Paul—to pay the rent on the villa and keep the Work alive. I had to come back anyway to the Lovely Layla. And now, after spending a good part of the past four weeks alone with her at the villa, both of us were floating on a cloud of love.

Over the next weeks though, since Layla left, I found myself out and about more in Cairo's crowded traffic and began to freak out. It must have been my recent visit to the United States, where everything is organized and runs smoothly that contrasted so vividly now with Egypt. Amazing really, how the human body adapts to its surroundings and environment. I had not seen the confusion so clearly for the nearly two years I'd lived in Cairo, but now it was hitting me in the face.

Paul and Watson returned to Cairo August 1 at three o'clock in the morning on an Egypt Air flight from London. The three of us sat and talked in the living room of the villa and, before long, Watson began bad-mouthing old Frank Smith.

"Man! Back in the States," Watson said, "I found that Smith was spreading all kinds of rumors about me, saying I was a flake and everything else. Have you seen him anywhere lately, Wayne?"

"Uh . . . yeah," I said. "He's sleeping in the back bedroom right now."

I had tried to avoid it a few days back but let the poor guy in and allowed him to sleep over some nights at the villa. I even read Bible passages to him that seemed to comfort him. Poor Smith was essentially being chased by Egyptian creditors; the Meridien threw him out when they discovered he couldn't pay his bills, and they kept his passport so he couldn't leave the country; and now the villa was a refuge no one knew about. And who *else* had to hide at the villa? *Yep*, Gino, our Italian-American engineer friend. He, too, ran to the villa more than once under pretty much the same circumstances. Egypt was swallowing them up.

Before it happened to anybody else, Paul and Watson decided to make a good, clean exit from this land. We hadn't made any shady deals, we just weren't getting anywhere. Egypt was only *slowly* swallowing us up, by wasting our time. The same, sudden revelation happened to Paul and Watson, as it had to me, when they got stuck in Cairo's jam-packed, horn-honking traffic in the August heat, in un-air-conditioned taxicabs, trying to get business done. It just wasn't worth it.

In the end, I realized remaining in a country like Egypt—as a Westerner who knew better—became nothing but a challenge to our flesh, our stamina . . . that *we* could do it. *We* could function here. *We* could tolerate every Ahmed, Hussein and Nasser trying to gyp us, swindle us, jack us around, sell us a half-full, propane gas bottle with a leaking valve and generally waste our time. It was just a "works" trip, where well-meaning people, striving to prove their spiritual worthiness, live in a broken-down country, showing they are strong and noble enough to endure the hardships. When, instead, God might be calling them to a more "comfortable" environment—perhaps even America— where they could ultimately be a spiritual blessing to more people.

Paul—ahead of the game as usual—already had prospective filming adventures developing in Colorado. Along with his Italian-film-producer friend Piero Tellini, he'd found a five-bedroom home to rent in the Rocky Mountains 35 miles outside of Denver in the hamlet of Evergreen, Colorado, and he was now asking me to join him. At the same time we would not abandon the Egypt Work we had founded, nor contacts we'd made. We would hand over the Work to an American guy and his Brazilian wife, members of the Children of God, who, for some reason, had a desire for Egypt.

In the five days Paul and Watson were here, the two of them packed up their belongings, finalized business dealings and said goodbye to friends. On August 6, they took separate flights out of Egypt. Watson went back to the States somewhere with Maggie, and Paul flew to Athens, Greece, to meet Carl and his wife, who were already recruited for the Egypt Work. Paul brought Carl right back five days later, and we both showed him around Cairo. Actually, I think Carl and his wife wanted to come to Egypt to escape the rampant, sexual promiscuity now spreading throughout the Children of God movement. Out here in Cairo, although still part of the group, we were pretty much isolated from the actual sexual sharing that had become "expected" among members of the group there in Athens, and indeed Europe and the rest of the world. Paul revealed all this to me as soon as he arrived from Athens.

"Wayne, you wouldn't believe it," he said. "It's like *all sex* now in the Family. Everybody 'sharing' with each other. It's crazy!"

Paul sold the Sony stereo system to a rich Egyptian friend for $1,650 and then flew off from Egypt on an 8:30 a.m. flight, August 13.

Carl was a humble, great chap, but I clashed once or twice with his feisty little Brazilian wife who arrived three weeks later with their baby boy on September 2. I could have stayed on in Cairo with Carl, continued my relationship here with Layla, but back on the steamy, hot day of August 7, after being stuck in Cairo's useless traffic, I sat down and wrote my Loving Layla a letter. In it I expressed my continued deep love for her and how I missed her, but also my discontent with Cairo:

August 7, 1978

Hello, my <u>Dearest</u> of Loves, Layla,

Goodness! What a <u>Honey</u> you are. I love you <u>so</u> much that it's beginning to hurt me to think of you and realize that I can't <u>see</u> you. <u>All</u> of our times together seemed to be so <u>strangely</u> beautiful and yet so real. I will never forget you.

Paul and Sam finally arrived August 1. Layla, they both <u>really</u> miss you and <u>truly</u> were sorry they didn't get to <u>see</u> you before you left for Kuwait.

They were <u>amazed</u> like <u>I</u> was at the completely <u>confusing</u> Cairo, traffic, taxis, etc.! And I <u>still</u> haven't adjusted to the <u>inefficiency</u> found here—remember I didn't see you for <u>three</u> days when I returned because of the telephones?

My Dear, I have pretty much decided to <u>return</u> to America to work on some films with Paul and the Italian guy. We just can't get enough <u>done</u> here in Egypt for now. Paul will return to America by August 15 when he is supposed to begin the film on the American Indians I told you about. And now <u>me</u>, Layla, <u>I</u> will remain here in Cairo it looks like <u>only</u> until sometime in September. In fact the reason I have chosen to remain <u>that</u> long is because I am at least <u>closer</u> to <u>you</u> now and I can write you whatever comes to <u>my</u> heart right away. I <u>still</u> feel strongly about all things I've ever told you and I know we <u>do</u> have a valuable thing between us my <u>Dear</u> and it is <u>no</u> mistake that we <u>are</u> continuing to love and *write each other. I told you, too, that I __am__ willing to __wait__ and see what can happen between us, but not __very__ long. There's a verse I opened to just the other day that said, "What __God__ has joined together, let not __man__ put asunder."—or, in other words don't let friends, family or __anyone__ keep us apart!*

I believe you __are__ strong, Layla, I've told you that and you will __have__ to be of course in making such a __drastic__ decision as __marriage__—especially to a foreigner, __me__! Yes, we __would__ make a nice couple I'm __sure__!

You know, I would almost remain in this place though for __you__, __if__ there were some possibilities of good, beneficial work for me. I've already said it sincerely __many__ times to you, though, that I __would__ marry you.

Honey, why couldn't you even get into a medical university in America, specifically __Colorado__ where I think there's a __very__ good one? Now! Or maybe even by January 1, 1979? __I__ would just as soon, though, have you for my __wife__, support you and take it from there, but it would be up to __you__.

I love you __dearly__ and for__ever__—you __know__ that!

> *Love, in __His__ Name,*
> *Wayne xxx!*

Three days later, again after being stuck in Cairo's taxis and traffic, I wrote her another letter, a bit heavier this time, on her coming to the U.S. to be my wife.

Actually, I was also tiring from my spiritual endeavor—of the past six and a half years—to "reach the world with God's Love." Like social work, it was most sacrificial, economically difficult and with few material rewards. It seemed there was a limit to how long I could continue in such a calling. I was ready to make a change, be an individual, make a living, maybe write a book or something. Even Paul said to me, "Wayne, I think you're going to blossom soon."

Meanwhile, over in Kuwait, Layla was being swamped by the Kuwaiti system and traditions during her summer break there, living with and caring for her aging father and mother. She pondered my last two letters for three days, cried and then wrote me back:

August 24, 1978

Dear Wayne,

Hello my love, how are you I miss you so much. Thank you for your two letters. I thank you more for your beautiful words. I read them so many times.

Wayne, just now I am looking in the flame of a candle and remembering the beautiful times we spent together with the flame of your candle! Oh Love!

Anyway, I thought of your last words three days and especially last night. I couldn't sleep until 6 o'clock in the morning. I cried too much!

From my heart darling I am telling you as I told you before I will be the happiest woman in this world if I become your wife and you are my husband. This is my wish from my heart, how a beautiful couple we will be and how beautiful children we will have together. But I must talk to you truly, Wayne, that I want to continue my studies. I am afraid of feeling sorry for not completing two more years. You say it is not a problem that I can continue in a Colorado university. It is not easy, Love, because I must have some exams before then and may be accepted or not. Secondly, it will cost much money because I am Kuwaiti. I know you will support me by your love first and your money secondly, but I don't want to be that kind of heavy wife on her husband. So I am strong, Love. I can stay in this horrible city and continue my studies. Please support me by some of your true love from your heart. Every time I read your last letters I feel those words "killing me softly" as that song said. I love you forever.

Second thing, it is not easy for a young girl to kill her old sick father by saying to him, "Dad, I love an American man and I want him to be my husband." He suffered too much and I can't bear him another load. I told you that Wayne before. Do you remember? But as you said, if God wants us together, no one can keep us apart.

I agree with you, both of us would never find another such Love, my Darling. I will never forget you. From deep of my heart you are the one that I want. Sometimes I forget

my world here, forget what I am, and just remember loving
you, Love, and imagine that you are my husband and live
in any part of the world, just me, you, and real Love, but the
truth wakes me up again.

Anyway, are you going to America for making good
films? I hope you can with God blessing you, Darling. But
don't forget me and write me always and I will, as we
promised. Tell me about everything. Even if you have a
girlfriend, I think I will feel happy for you and I will love
her too just because you love her. Ah! Yahalatic tehabel!

The important thing, Wayne, I want to talk to you about
is your staying in this horrible city of Cairo alone, Love,
this long for me. Please, please, for my sake don't wait until
I come back in October because I don't want your heart and
mine to be broken again. Am I coming in October to say
hello, then goodbye for how long? I don't think we are so
strong to meet then say goodbye, am I right?

And now I will say bye in another letter. You must write
to me as I will to you and hope we will meet any time, any
place, maybe in America for beginning our new life together
"Inshallah" I hope so!

> *Love you forever,*
> *Layla*

The letter wasn't clearly a "Dear John" letter, nor did I decipher it
as such. Instead, it was a subtle, sad, somewhat confused surrender to
strong Arab and particularly Kuwaiti family ties and her own devotion
to her parents. I knew the ties too well by now. As for completing her
degree in the States, she was right, that was too far flung.

I replied to this letter September 1, praising her for her decision to
remain virtually *suffering* in Cairo to complete her studies, and adding
that it was wise and unselfish of her to do so. I told her how my love had
grown for her; that I would be the happiest man on earth to have her
as my wife, but could be sensible and wait for the right time; and that I
could love no other as I loved her.

When she read *this* letter, that I *agreed* to her continuing her studies
in Cairo and that I understood her difficult situation, she cried, realizing
she *needed* this guy now. She wrote me back the same day she received
it, September 11:

September 11, 1978

Dear Wayne,

I found myself needing you too much, Wayne. I cried and I am looking for your arms to take me in between them to cry as much as I can (where are you, Love?)

So, I am asking you from the deepest of my heart to wait for my coming back to Cairo just one week before you go to America. . . .

I want to see you before you leave, sigh! O.K.? I will bear that moment and try to take some love from you to keep me warm nights and days after you go, Darling! And I will try to give you some of mine (Kwis)! I miss you so much, so please let me near your chest surrounding me by your arms for a while touching your sweet lips and your blond moustache. I like it, Oh! Hugs and kisses for my ever-loving, ever-lovable Wayne!

Layla

But I had already left Cairo on September 13 when her letter arrived, forwarded to me in Colorado by the new guy, Carl. Before I left, I had written her one more letter on September 7, informing her of my TWA reservation early Wednesday morning, September 13. In it I wrote how I imagined her coming to my front door *one* more time before leaving to America. Also how my friends and acquaintances in Cairo had asked, "What about Layla? Are you going to *leave* Layla?" Even the old landlady upstairs asked about her and spoke so many sincerely nice things about her. "She's so ladylike and kind," she said. Her daughter and one of her granddaughters even said to me, "Are you going to marry Layla?" Finally, in my letter, I reminded Layla: "*Please don't let man-made traditions come between the True Love we have so wonderfully found!*"

On September 17, the day after receiving this letter from me and learning I was now *gone* from Cairo, Layla wrote me at my new address in Colorado:

Hello Darling, how are you, Love? What can I say now after receiving your last letter telling me you will leave Cairo September 13. I received that letter Sept. 16.

Why didn't you wait until you hear my answer to your last letter? I cried as much as I can when I read your letter before the last one (September 1). So I sent you my letter asking you to stay and wait for me before you go so far away, Wayne.

Now I blame myself of all what has happened. Now it hurts too much, this is such a heavy load. I can't bear it. How can I go to Cairo now (without you)? I hoped you just waited for a week to read my answer. Why did you leave so early? . . .

How could you believe me? I will be crazy now. What shall I do? . . .

So please send me some of your love encouraging me in my life and my studying in Cairo. I never forget you, you are in my mind and your love in my heart. I love you. I hope you enjoy yourself in filming and enjoy your life with your friends. Be happy always. You can have a girlfriend, but she must be beautiful, no, ugly, in order not to steal you from me! I'm afraid now you may forget my love. If this happens you must tell me that, O.K. Darling? And if we are lovers we must be friends too, right Habeebi, *Darling?*

I love you more and more. You taught me many beautiful things, the most of them is the true love I have for you. I miss you. Just now I want to lay my head on your chest crying for a while then I will touch your lovely lips with a special kiss.

O.K., I hope God will bring us together one day. God bless you, Darling. I will pray for you. Enjoy your time, and your business. Be always happy and smile always. Say hello to all your friends and your parents and sisters if you call them. Be gentle to yourself. It is important for me. Hugs and kisses for ever-loving, ever-lovable Wayne.

Layla

She wrote me further letters to Colorado—how she missed and loved me, that her heart was for me, how she needed my help, that she hoped no other girl would take me from her, that she thought of me as her husband:

I don't know how can I bear our separation. I hope God helps us to be strong enough. I will send you some of my photos. I hope you like them (just not to forget my face).

I am still thinking of you as my husband, oh, am I gonna have this dream come true, please God can You help me. So I will wait to see what will God do!

Yes it's hard days and nights without you, Darling, and I love you.

She sent another letter, written three days later:

Nothing reached me from you since you left to America (22 days). Are you busy with films? Or maybe you forgot my love. I know there are many girls there. . . . Don't worry, I know being alone is difficult so enjoy your time, Darling, but please keep writing to me as I said to you before.

I love you, Darling. Do you love me? I always think of our marriage after I finish my studies. I still remember your beautiful words about taking me in between your arms (under your wings, oh!) in that big country and you are ready to marry me anytime, Darling. Day by day my Love grows and grows. Just now I want to be between your arms. I hope God will let us to meet again. . . .

She heard *nothing* from me for one month . . . two months . . . and figured she had lost me for good, taken by some girl in the U.S. She blamed herself and was nearly devastated, when she wrote, in her letter of October 31:

What's happened to you, are you all right, Darling? I have been worried about you too much, thinking of you always. Darling, please write to me. Don't let me down. I love you too much. I think you know the hard life here in Cairo. I can't bear it at all even without you. You are still the dearest man to my heart, Wayne. I need you so much, Darling. I waited all this time for your letter and I received nothing, just thinkings and doubts. . . .

You know something, all my friends say, if you have Mr. Wayne as your husband, you will be happy with him. This always makes me cry, Wayne. I will try to have you, Darling, just if you wait. But also you can enjoy your life, and I hope no other girl takes you from me. I don't know, but you must tell me that if it happens. . . .

I hope you send me a letter because I need your help even if you are so far away from me, Darling. Please write to me!

On November 25, I telephoned her at her dormitory. The receptionist answered it and rang the first floor where Layla lived. The housekeeper picked it up and went to find Layla.

"Hello?"

"Layla? This is Wayne."

"Wayne! How are you? Where have you been? I miss you! Why you didn't write to me? I've been so worried about you!"

"I wrote you two letters," I said.

"I never received anything from you. I thought you forgot about me."

"Oh, honey! I love you! I could *never* forget about you. I think of you *all the time!*"

"Me, too," she said. "I want to *see* you! How is everyone there? The kids? I miss them. But I miss *you*, Wayne!"

"Everyone is good. They ask about you all the time."

"How is your work?" she asked.

"It's okay," I answered. "How's your studying?"

"It's okay, but I wish you were *here* with me, Habeebi."

We talked for about eight minutes. I didn't have much money at the time for long distance calls. But those eight minutes renewed this little princess—by the same love I'd given her before, a love that had never died in the least but had only grown in our separation from each other. We were more in love than ever, though we were seven thousand miles apart. And although I had been settling in to fast-paced America (into a system of no mercy, where nothing is free and only hard work survives), I *had* faithfully written her a loving letter, mailed from Denver back on October 2, not long after I had left Egypt. For some strange reason, the letter didn't reach her until December 13. Over two months! And another letter of love on November 14.

She later said, when she heard my voice over the telephone, "I came back to life! I couldn't believe you called me! My life was empty without you. I was dead. I thought you forgot about me; that you had gone on with your life."

The call proved I was true to her, not playing games with her. This was the man she wanted to marry, despite any objections from others. After all, it was not normal for a Kuwaiti girl to marry a non-Kuwaiti man . . . and nearly *unheard of*, an American.

A week after the phone call, on December 3, she wrote to me:

> *I can't get you out of my mind . . . your love grows in my heart. I don't know how can I bear this life without you, so please come back to me. I want to see you as soon as possible. I decided to be your wife, just wait for me to continue my studies, O.K. Darling?*
>
> *You know something? I think I forgot how to kiss. So, doctor, please, I need revision and practical classes. Will you come back so I can have a course in love with you? Inshallah. This is a special request from deep of my heart, Darling!*

She soon wrote that she would come to Colorado to visit me for a month in the summer between her college terms, and . . . "give me everything." As she wrote in a letter at the end of March, 1979:

> *I really love you and I want to be with you forever. I'm gonna stay for one month.*
>
> *And about your Virgin Child . . . I thought about it and I love you so much and cherish you so that I will give you everything. I will be your wife and have your babies, God help us to do so.*

And she did, exactly as she promised. The little lady purchased a round-trip Pan Am ticket from Cairo to Denver, got a visa to the U.S. where she'd never been before and landed in Denver at eleven o'clock Friday night, June 22, 1979. Somehow information got crossed and I (idiot!) failed to meet her at the airport when she arrived, poor thing, all alone, first time ever in America. So she hired a cab for the 30-minute ride up into the mountains to Evergreen and arrived at my doorstep at 1:15 a.m.

Here in Evergreen, Paul, Sheila and I had found a choice condo to rent in the Hiwan Country Club community. It was 25 miles outside of Denver, and the taxi driver wasn't at all familiar with the area, so it still took Layla awhile to reach my door. Looking from my window, I saw her pull up in the taxi and ran outside to meet her.

"Hello, my dear!" I said. "You came!" shaking my head almost in disbelief that she was once again next to me in this world.

"Of course I did," she responded, with her same broad smile and full of love. "I said I would, didn't I?"

The taxi drove off, and we simply squeezed and hugged each other on the concrete walkway of the condominium complex. *How did I stay apart from this creature for so long? Nearly a year!*

I picked up her suitcase, and we made it into the condo. And as soon as I closed the door and put the suitcase down, we embraced and kissed each other like never before. Our love had become deeper and more spiritual through our letters for the past year, but we could never forget the *physical intimacy* we had enjoyed together. Indeed, right there, inside the entrance to my home, without realizing it, I was aroused when her body pressed next to me. *Looking* like she did right now didn't hurt either. For sure, she wasn't wearing *sweat pants* when she stepped out of that cab tonight! No sir. Minutes ago, when I saw her first high heel touch the ground from the back seat of that taxi, I knew—*she's back!* And there she stood, looking classy as ever in a flimsy, purple skirt just past her knees, a lavender button blouse, a bit of makeup and her black hair nicely brushed and flowing over her shoulders.

I had on a thin, light green, cotton Egyptian robe she had given me back in Cairo, and as I held her close to me now, my hardness pressed into her body. She later told me, "I will *never* forget you pressing into me through the thin material of your robe and my skirt!"

I sat her down in the living room and poured her a glass of Orzata—a non-alcoholic, almond-flavored drink she used to love when she came to our villa in Cairo. We had a lot to talk about but didn't get much past her trip. We also had the whole, three-floor, five-bedroom condo to ourselves now because Paul, Sheila and the kids were visiting Paul's parents down in Texas.

"Are you hungry?" I asked this sweetness of mine.

"No. I'll use the bathroom, though. Where is it?"

In this luxury condo, I had a cozy, private room here on the ground floor, with a large, full bathroom next to it. I showed her to the bathroom and took her glass to the kitchen.

She came from the bathroom still dressed and in her high heels. "So. Where is our room?" she asked, with a smile.

"There," I said, and she entered. I followed her in, and she turned around to meet me at the foot of the bed. Standing, she put her arms around me, and we began kissing deeply on the lips, picking up where we'd left off back in Cairo. I ran my hands around her back and down around her waist while still kissing, and pulled her close to me. Her breathing became heavy. She then backed away from me so she could unbutton her blouse. I took over unbuttoning it and removed it from her shoulders. She unfastened her skirt, let it drop to the floor and stepped out of it. The temperature was perfect here in the mountains in June and in the room, so she was not uncomfortable standing in her sexy black slip and bra—and still in her heels. She sat down at the foot of the bed, took off her heels and then lay back.

We had known each other for one and a half years and had become most intimate in the 14 times she visited me at the villa in Cairo; in the past year she had written 26 letters of love to me, and I had written 20 to her. She had decided to be my wife, and now it was time to become "one flesh."

I leaned down and kissed her with her lying back on the bed like this. I then, without removing her bra, kissed her breasts for a while before going farther down to kiss her tummy and sides. I slid her slip down a little ways and there they were—the same type of tiny bikini underwear she used to wear beneath her flimsy skirts in Cairo. I remembered commenting on them once back then, "Your panties are so nice and tiny."

"I know," she replied at the time. "My sister overheard a Kuwaiti guy say once, 'Girls' panties these days are so tiny they could fit in a matchbox.'"

Tonight, I pulled them down a bit and kissed her there. She was entirely bare of any hair there and everywhere—arms, legs, thighs, everywhere. "It's normal for Arab women," she later told me. "We usually wax it off." Indeed. Leaving nothing but buttery-smooth skin!

I returned her undies and slip like they were, helped her up and we went to the side of the bed. I pulled the covers back and removed my robe. She stepped out of her slip and we climbed between the clean, light blue sheets of my—*our*—bed.

"You are precious," I said. She just smiled back, from her flushed and pink face.

We kissed beneath the sheets as we'd done in the Cairo "room of love," removed the rest of our clothes and loved for quite awhile, until finally, *this* time, I gently and slowly entered her virgin flower. She gave a slight moan and then responded passionately with my movements until we climaxed together.

Oh, Lord.

We showered in the bathroom, returned back to bed, curled up in each other's arms and drifted off into the most contented deep sleep, having become one flesh, joined together now to face the world as a couple.

The setting of Evergreen couldn't have been much more romantic or ideal up here in the crisp clean Rocky Mountain fresh air, some 7,600 feet above sea level. The condo itself sat on the number one fairway of the rather exclusive Hiwan Country Club golf course, overlooking rolling hills, endless trees and the green grasses of the fairways. Paul, Sheila and the kids came back after a couple days, and we all got along just okay, not that great. After all, Layla and I spent a lot of time off alone together in bed. Heck, we hadn't seen each other in a year and weren't sure when we'd see each other again so made the best of our time while together.

Despite the unavoidable conflicts inherent to living with others like this, Layla and I had a fantastic one-month "honeymoon," as planned, and she flew back to Cairo, no longer a virgin. She then flew on to Kuwait, keeping it all a secret, and was asked for her hand in marriage several times by Kuwaiti guys who knew nothing about her other than she was Kuwaiti, pretty, young and studying medicine. If they only knew! She wrote, back in her letter of October 4:

> *The Kuwaiti men? They just see the girl one or two times and they ask for her hand. They don't know even what is in her mind. Do you know how many Kuwaiti men asked for my hand last summer? Seven. But I refused all of them because first I love you and my heart is reserved for you and I have hope to have you as my husband.*

Chapter 35
⇜ *Phone Calls, More Letters and a Song* ⇝

PAUL, SHEILA AND I blended back into normal life, and gradually disassociated ourselves from the Children of God. Paul's filming endeavors fizzled out, so I ended up waiting tables at restaurants in the winter and landscaping and greens keeping in the warmer weather, while Layla continued her studies in Cairo.

Then, recalling how it had snowed six inches in Evergreen on May 2, 1979, six inches again May 8 and 9 and four inches on May 31, I figured it was time to move to the warmer climate of Florida, where my folks lived. I said goodbye to Paul, Sheila and the kids November 3, 1979, and flew to Orlando, where I settled into a condominium owned by my dad and got a backbreaking job landscaping and maintaining the lakeside estate of a millionaire whom Dad knew at the community of Bay Hill, southwest of Orlando. "Picking weeds," I called it. Life in the "real world" had passed me by while I traveled for nearly seven years with the Children of God.

Never mind. I remember saying to Paul in the car one day back in Denver when we were struggling to make ends meet, "Yeah . . . but you know? I don't ever regret spending those years with the group. I mean, look at the places we were able to *visit* during those times and the souls we were able to reach." I had found the love of my life out there, too— and she had found a way to come visit me *again*, not long after my arrival in Florida. One of her sisters had moved to Tacoma, Washington, with her husband and their young daughter, while the husband completed a master's degree there. So, on December 1, 1979, at the end of her fall term in Cairo and a little over four months since she'd left me back in Colorado, she flew to Tacoma to stay a week with her sister, before flying back to my arms once again.

She had already met my parents back in Colorado when they came there to visit my dad's brother. She even performed an Arab dance for them all at the Evergreen condo. Mom and Dad grew to love her like their own daughter in the one month she stayed in Orlando.

And what did this loving woman bring to me this time? Underwear! Years later I still reflect on her thoughtfulness for such a gift. Not just *any* underwear. Egyptian "Jil" brand underwear—quite possibly the best undergarments in the world, made in Egypt of Egyptian cotton. Six pair of midway briefs—typically worn by Arab men—and six T-shirts. I asked a textile industrialist who was a neighbor and friend of my dad, "Mr. Johnson, why is Egyptian cotton so exceptional?"

"Because," he replied, "the fibers of Egyptian cotton are longer than other cotton."

She also brought me a fine gold ring made in Kuwait with an emerald set in it.

So, she and I had a "second honeymoon" of love, this time in the privacy of our *own* condominium, she gladly preparing meals for me and drawing hot baths for my sore back when I'd come home from my weed-picking. *What a woman.*

This second visit of passion brought us deeper in love, and before she left we determined that six months would now be the maximum length of time we could remain apart. It was getting too difficult to live without each other. It was torture. Yet she had come too far—nearly five years now—in attaining her degree, to give it all up. We would have to endure.

She flew off that January 8, 1980, back to Cairo. We hardly knew *where* the other had come from, *how* we had met, *how* we had fallen so deeply in love with each other. The sex helped. We meshed and matched in all ways, and now, since Colorado, we knew—*everything* fit.

But still, how would "East" and "West" finally end up? The world—mine, and especially *hers*—did not acquiesce to our relationship.

When she left, I continued to slave—landscape and pick weeds—in the gardens of the rich around my parents' home at $5.00 an hour. But I soon figured I'd better find a profession less backbreaking than lawn and garden care—one that wouldn't leave me depleted of energy when I'd come home to the vibrant young Arab maiden I'd haply found over in the desert of Egypt. One of the worst things about lawn care too, besides the physical exhaustion of it, was the *boredom* of it. So mundane, especially as I reminisced behind a lawnmower about my eventful seven years of spiritual endeavor and travel. It would be better to fight in some war for a good cause, I thought, than to waste my life away cutting grass.

My dad had money but wasn't too sure what I should do for my *re-entry* into the system, after preaching the gospel for seven years. The best thing he came up with was, "Try real estate." So I did. Heck, like any sales, it was a profession that required no formal education, no skill and hardly any knowledge. And if any place in America was booming, it was Orlando, with Disney here. I signed up for a real estate course and began studying for the fairly difficult Florida Real Estate exam.

Actually, real estate was the first "light" for me since my arrival in the United States a year and a half ago. A chance to use my mind and get out of the dirt and into the "white-collar" world. I was about to start a life with a wife, and, as the verse says, I wanted to please her. "But he that is married careth for the things that are of the world, how he may please his wife" (1 Corinthians 7.33).

As for Layla, besides advancing in her studies, she always thought ahead. So, not long after leaving me on January 8, she figured out how we could get together again—in Cairo this time, during the summer, four months later—and still study and attend classes. *Heck yes.* It was about time I came to *her* anyway, and she arranged it all. She rented a small flat and sent me a TWA roundtrip ticket. I arrived at 5 p.m. on May 14 at the Cairo airport where she lovingly awaited me. We contained ourselves at the airport okay and in the cab ride as much as possible until reaching the modest, yet private, little, furnished, one-bedroom, third-floor apartment she had rented for us in El-Dokki—a decent area across the Nile from downtown Cairo—where we got reacquainted once again. It was strange, but we actually did have to get *re*-acquainted. Such a shock to finally face and touch the one I loved so much and who I could only love through words in letters and phone calls for the past months.

She told her dormitory that her family was visiting from Kuwait so she'd be staying with them for the next month or so—while I was there. It was perhaps fortunate that no great job prospects, super company, signed contract or any other total job commitment had developed for me that could have prevented me from dropping everything and flying off to her arms—or she to mine—for a month at a time like we'd been doing. I guess I was still a gypsy, a traveler, making money here and there, but able to drop it all and move on when necessary.

Lord. It was great to be with her again. And Cairo's misery could hardly show itself through the happiness we had when together like this. Actually, I had previously never lived day to day near downtown Cairo. It ended up being rather charming, if not romantic. This middle-class area of El-Dokki was both pleasant and down-home Egypt at the same time. On strolls through the neighborhood near our place we'd buy fresh, charcoal-roasted corn-on-the-cob-in-the-husk off the wooden street cart of the cheerful, peasant "corn lady." Or, around the corner from her, the "peanut guy" sold hot, charcoal-roasted peanuts. He had a wooden cart with wooden wheels and a metal hibachi built into it that he roasted the nuts over. For each order, he'd curl a piece of newspaper into the shape of a cone and fill it with either shelled or in-the-shell peanuts at about 50 cents per cone.

We usually cooked our own meals in the flat. But we also ate out at some good restaurants across the Nile, like the one by the pool at the Meridien Hotel. But the greatest dinner was at the same Hilton Pizzeria restaurant where we'd met two and a half years before—the night we exchanged phone numbers on that white paper napkin. "Where did you come from?" I asked her again, as I had many times before while looking into her dark eyes. "What realm?"

I had to laugh one afternoon when we returned to our apartment by taxi from across town. Layla paid the driver the amount on his meter along with a decent tip. During the ride, the driver had discerned from his rearview mirror that she was from the rich Gulf. So, when she handed him the money, he looked at it and said, "*Besi kedda?*" complaining that it wasn't very much.

To which Layla replied, "*Mish eyezoo? Ermee fee shara.*" He took the money and drove off grumbling.

"What did you *say* to him?" I asked her.

"I said . . . if you don't want it, throw it on the ground." She'd lived in Egypt long enough to know how to function here.

She attended classes both day and night. But we found time to walk the promenade, like other lovers, along the soothing Nile River flowing just a couple blocks from our place. We were careful though, while out, not to flaunt our love in this Arab country, officially unmarried as we were.

We made a few jaunts to the main souk of Khan-el-Khalili to buy Egyptian robes for my family and friends. I also wanted some emeralds. Visitors could buy anything in this country and emeralds had somehow found their way here, over the years, probably from Colombia, South America. I bought four for a total of about $150. I also purchased some beautiful, semi-precious lapis lazuli stones for $55 that ended up being fake. Fortunately, I showed them to an Armenian jeweler who immediately said, "They're beautiful, but they're fake—made in Germany."

Amazingly, a few days later, I went back to the guy that sold them to me and he gave me a full refund. "Yes, they are made in Germany," he said. "You didn't ask me where they were from." I bought a princess-cut emerald and a half-karat ruby with the money.

Near the end of my visit, we took a taxi to the Mena House Oberoi—a luxury hotel that looked out at the Pyramids on the edge of Cairo at Giza. There, we sat for lunch at an outdoor table by the cool, clear waters of the hotel's swimming pool. "It's horrible we can't just stay together right now, like this," I said.

In the taxi on the way back, when we reached the bustle of Cairo, I bought Layla a necklace of freshly-cut jasmine flowers for a dollar, offered to us by a street vendor kid. "*It fuddal, it fuddal. Ashan il helawa!*" the kid kept saying to me through the back seat window, insisting I take a necklace for "the beautiful one" sitting next to me. She always loved the smell of jasmine, and these poor kids would hawk these string necklaces at intersections in the summer for just about any price someone was willing to pay.

Our little flat had a small stucco balcony overlooking a rectangular park of flowers and grass half a block away, and our eye level was just above the tops of large palm trees shading the side street below. Though not air-conditioned, the apartment remained quite cool except for some hot nights when we had to fully open the glass balcony doors to let the breeze in, *and* . . . a huge, flying cockroach—probably from the palm trees. *Gross.* It was still Egypt and a wonder to me why the heck someone didn't come up with a scheme to screen the windows and doors in this country. Not even *hospitals* had screens to keep mosquitoes, flies and bugs out.

This third and lovely honeymoon of ours lasted a whole month and a half until my plane took off back to Orlando at 6:30 a.m. on June 30. It was a "jet-age love" we had; we had originally met due to the age of jet airplanes; and we had now joined together again—two people with entirely different backgrounds, cultures and customs, who could unite in a matter of hours. No barriers, as long as there was money for the fare.

Parting was worse than ever this time, maybe because the visit had extended to a month and a half. "Can't you stay here with me?

Please!" she pleaded, knowing deep inside it wasn't likely. "I'll support you. Or maybe you can find some kind of work here. At least until I finish my studies. I'll be finished in six months. I hate being here without you."

I actually sought out a few leads for employment here in Egypt but nothing developed. "You *know* I wish I could, my dear," I told her. "I need to get back though and pursue that real estate stuff. Get my license. Start making some money for us."

She sounded sad in her letter of July 4—her first letter to me since I'd flown from Cairo:

> *Believe me, I missed you so much and my love started to grow since I saw you pass through your passport check at the airport. It was so bad seeing you go off in the bus. Then the aeroplane took off and it was as if it took my heart between my ribs!*

I had learned from a phone call to my dad two weeks back while in Cairo that I had failed my first attempt at the real estate exam. I'd have to attend a better course and take the test again. In the meantime, I survived by gardening and landscaping. I moved in with my folks and saved money, so started sending $100 bills in letters to Layla in Cairo, even though she hardly needed it. I wrote at the bottom of the letters:

ENCLOSED: one gift.

In the next phone call with her, I'd ask, "Did you receive the hundred dollars I sent?" She always had.

Thank God for *telephones* though, to keep a long distance relationship like ours alive. We called each other nearly every two weeks for at least five or ten minutes at a time. It was crucial, hearing the undying love in one another's voice. Just a few seconds of her comforting words over the phone—"I love you," "I miss you so much," "I can't live without you,"—could bring me out of the slumps and chase away the doubts, lies and torments of the devil in my own mind that she might be fading, losing interest, finding another lover.

Thank God for the mail, too! The same words of comfort came on paper to be read, pondered and reread to nourish the ole heart, often arriving when assurance was needed that our love was not just magical, but real—growing and alive. We knew that, "What therefore God hath joined together, let no man put asunder" (Mark 10.9). Not even we ourselves could stop it, it seemed, nor miles between, nor family, nor traditions, nor systems, nor governments, nor friends . . . nor religion. I knew this girl loved God as much as, if not more than any girl I had ever met—whether in the Children of God or out of it. She had a broken heart for the poor, beggars and downtrodden. She admired *my* strong faith as well. We believed, "If God be for us, who could be against us?" I wrote her a poem in June, 1980, on my visit with her in Cairo, while she was attending classes:

My Dear Honey

How you spend your time on the one you love!
He sees it and speaks to others of it.
You <u>rarely</u> put yourself first,
May God bless your heart and hands with many gifts from above.

God, rebuke the lies from any physical or spiritual foes
For the love that's always so strangely within our hearts,
Whether with one another or thousands of miles apart,
Must surely be from Your Hand.

My Hon, we'll be together somehow forever
If we'll trust each other and believe our Lord.
Perhaps it's in His plan to stay apart as yet to make us see
How much I really need to be in love with you and you with me.

Your lover loves your every part, your every hair.
He loves your love of putting on little smells, of seeing you in your little frills.
These many little things will always stay in his mind and heart,
To remind him of the one he loves and always will.

He may write a book someday that others will see
Who are looking for that love and lover,
To show them it's really, simply,
A matter of <u>honesty</u>!

No games involved, no competition either.
You're a woman who acts like one
And he's a man in need of one
Who knows <u>he</u> will do his part to keep you as a happy one!

Months passed, our love grew, and I finally passed and received my Florida real estate license on December 24, 1980. In Cairo, on January 12, 1981, Layla took her last medical exam after six years of study. She hopped a Pan Am flight two days later to come to me in Orlando, though still for only a visit. I'd been looking for an apartment to rent for the two of us when, abruptly, on December 29, Dad's renters of the condo—the same one Layla and I used a year before—called saying they had to move out, leaving it now *empty* and available for us. *Yes.* I cleaned it and fixed it up. Layla would stay a whole seven weeks this time, our *fourth* honeymoon, under the guise of another university trip, no one but her close friends knowing anything about me.

On January 27, two weeks after Layla had arrived, her best friend, Aisha telephoned Mom and Dad's house to inform us that Layla had successfully passed all her final exams and had earned her degree as a medical doctor! But, she *still* had to return to her parents in Kuwait and *somehow* tell them about her American lover. She would also begin her work as an intern to make enough money for the means and freedom to . . . leave Kuwait (*vanish*, if necessary).

She left for Kuwait on March 5, 1981, for a separation worse than ever. Mom and Dad, who loved her dearly and were proud to have a future daughter-in-law as a doctor, were also sad when she flew off.

Ten days after arriving in Kuwait, Layla began work as an intern at Al-Sabah Hospital, the main hospital of the country. The money was good, but she was troubled with how to break the news to her father about me. And would her father ever give his blessing on our marriage?

She tried to make it all look normal—returning home to pursue her career after completing her six years of study abroad. She had eight sisters and four brothers, and the older sisters, unaware of me, soon started pressuring her to get married. They came up with suitors for her—arranged marriages being normal in Kuwait—or knew of guys who had seen her once or twice and wanted to marry her. Keeping her secret, she told her sisters, "Not right now."

Then, when she needed a car to get to work, she rented one. *Uh-oh.* Kuwaitis don't rent cars. They buy them. The sisters and father were far too perplexed at this. It didn't make sense, why she would rent a car when they were all willing to help her buy a new one.

The sisters put two and two together and figured she was in love with someone, so pried it out of her. But they also assumed her lover was some Kuwaiti, since, at this time—1981—it was nearly unheard of for a Kuwaiti girl to marry a *non-Kuwaiti* man, or even another Arab. So when the sisters discovered that Layla's lover was a full-fledged *American*, they became enraged. One sister even physically attacked her, jumping on her stomach, until the other sisters restrained her. "We don't care about you. You can go to hell. We only care about our poor father's health."

This is what troubled poor Layla daily while in Kuwait, as she went to work, came home and tried to fit in. She didn't know *how* to tell her diabetic father without breaking his heart or causing him to go into a coma.

Layla might well have been one of the *closest* of the 13 children to her mother and father, attending to them constantly. While growing up, even in high school, she always remained home with them. When she visited from her Cairo studies, she stayed by their sides, making her father tea before he went off to his wholesale grocery store, both mornings and afternoons. The guy apparently was a dear old man, loaning much of his money out to others, and was loving and caring, though overprotective of his kids. He dearly loved Layla, and she dearly loved him.

But I had said something to Layla nearly three years before when we sat one night at dinner in the Pizzeria, soon after we began falling in love with each other and discussing marriage: "If you're going to be my wife, you have to love me the most." This I said referring mostly to the love she had for her father and mother—the words now remaining steadfast in her mind.

At that time, my words were heavy to bear and confused her because she *then* loved her father and mother more than me. But now, after three years, she realized she loved me more than anything or anyone, often saying in her letters that she would die for me, "*Amote allek.*"

Back in Orlando, I "hung" my real estate license with a reputable company (referred to by Dad) and struggled to sell real estate in one of the worst markets the profession had ever seen. With fixed-rate mortgages as high as 18%, not many people were buying. So, for cash flow, I continued to pick around in landscaping part time, since my salary in the real estate business was entirely by commission—sell nothing, make nothing.

But whatever my job, or hers, didn't really matter, for our love was not one based upon convenience and whether or not the other had adequate education, degrees or job qualifications. It was based upon our beliefs, trust and a physical, passionate attraction we had for each other. What we knew was that our love had stood over time and separation. There had been plenty of opportunity for us to fall *out* of love with each other, or for one of us to find another lover. It hadn't happened. She said in one of her letters from Kuwait, "I do love you, and I'll never give up and will fight until I win you at the end. I don't care for what they say or do, I will bear everything for the sake of my Wayne."

In Kuwait, alone with her love for me, she found herself surrounded by a society and culture that had become hostile to her. Why did she have to fight for the pure and honest love she had somehow found in this cold hard world?

My letters of love flowed to her, giving her strength and courage to fight for this love. These and the pertinent phone calls enabled us to hear the tone of longing and love in each other's voices. By the grace of God, too, there was a person in Kuwait who helped this Lady in Love stay safely in touch with her lover without anyone knowing. That person was Mohamed, one of her four brothers, a bit older than Layla and like unto an angel or at the least, a servant of God. Mohamed liked Westerners, and when he learned that Layla had fallen in love with an American guy, he fully encouraged her to pursue her love for me. In fact, it would have been quite difficult for me to keep in contact with Layla while she was in Kuwait if it hadn't been for Mohamed. He personally collected mail from the family's post office box and delivered every one of my stream of love letters to her. He also arranged phone calls between Layla and me, making sure no one inside the home knew when she was on the phone to me, *God bless him.*

There was a song, too, by Kenny Loggins—who wrote it for his dad for some reason—called, "This Is It." The lyrics gave Layla resolve. She and I had listened to it on recent honeymoons, and as she now listened to the song in Kuwait, the words came alive to her, piercing her:

This Is It

There've been times in my life
I've been wondering why
Still somehow I believed
We'd always survive.

Now I'm not so sure
You're waiting to hear
One good reason to try
But what more can I say?
What's left to provide?

You think that maybe it's over
Only if you want it to be.
Are you gonna wait for a sign, your miracle?
Stand up and fight!

This is it!
Make no mistake where you are;
This is it!
Your back's to the corner
This is it!
Don't be a fool anymore.
This is it!
The waiting is over.

No room to run, no way to hide
No time for wondering why
It's here, the moment is now
About to decide.

Let him believe or leave him behind
But keep me near in your heart
Know, whatever you do
I'm here by your side.

You said, that maybe it's over
Not if you don't want it to be
For once in your life, here's your miracle
Stand up and fight!

This is it!
Make no mistake where you are
This is it!
You're going no further
This is it!
Until it's over and done.

No one can tell you what you know
Who makes the choice of how it goes
It's not up to me this time
You know
Comes a day in every life.

This is it!
Make no mistake where you are
This is it!
You're going no further
This is it!
Until it's over and done
This is it!
One way or another
This is it!

No one can tell what the future knows
This is it!
Your back's to the corner
This is it!
You make the choice of how it goes
This is it!
The waiting is over
This is it!

No one can tell what the future knows
This is it!
You're going no further
This is it!
You make the choice of how it goes
One way or another.

Kenny Loggins

Finally, five months after returning to Kuwait, working as an intern, she told her father: "I'm in love with an American man, and I want to marry him."

Her words clarified to the old guy the uneasiness he had sensed in Layla. She, poor thing, expected a compassionate response from him. But he replied, "What? Are you going to marry an atheist? What will the people say?"

His words saddened her. Right then, the deep love and respect she'd had for her father all her life began to fade, as he became an obstacle to the man she loved so much and could not now live without.

Her father tried to talk her out of it. "Write him a letter and tell him I won't let you marry him," he said. But the soft-hearted guy soon saw in his dear daughter's weeping eyes just how sincerely in love she was and that nothing and no one could sway her from the love she'd found.

"I won't live if I don't marry him," she told her father.

He looked down, unable to respond.

She knew her father would never *outwardly* approve of the marriage. He couldn't. The whole family, particularly the three brothers, would torment and blame him if he even *remotely* agreed to it. She had already seen the trouble the old guy had gone through at the hands of her brothers over three of her sisters who had fallen in love with and married "unapproved" husbands—actual *Kuwaiti men*, but with Iraqi or other roots. To Layla's father, knowing a man before marrying him was not as important as having a husband *chosen* for her. It was the jet age though. It had taken nearly five months in Kuwait now for Layla to reach this point with her father, and he responded like *this*? The "atheist" comment didn't help much either. In fact, she had become fed up with a lot of stupid things in Kuwait. She'd seen the "other side"—beyond tiny Kuwait—and now longed to start her new, married life with me. "I am thirsty for your love," she wrote to me in her last letter.

As for her mother—*God bless her*—she knew all about me weeks before from the sisters and responded to them with, "This is in God's plan for her; this is her share in this life; what shall we do?"

Layla would give her father a week or so to ponder it and then, for *his* benefit, she would *leave* Kuwait—*vanish*—without telling him. That way, she figured, she would actually release the old man from all and any blame from the brothers or sisters who otherwise might say to him, "How could you agree to let her go and marry a Westerner, an American, an atheist?" This way they could only blame *her*.

It may have been the most difficult thing she ever did in her life—leaving her father without telling him. But she did it. She had already resigned from her job, collected her salary and any money from the bank, and on Tuesday morning, August 18, 1981—with two bags packed and her father at work—told only her sweet mother she was leaving. "Mama, I'm sorry," Layla said, tears running down her face. "I love him so much though. I have to go to him. Please, tell Babba I'm sorry. I love you, *Yooma*."

"God be with you," her mother said, troubled though, when she pondered it all. "What will I tell your father when he comes home from work?"

"I don't know, Mama," Layla replied, now sobbing. She held her mother close to her heart and kissed her one more time, not knowing when she might see her again.

Layla also knew that three of her brothers would be out of the country at this time, so would not be able to interfere with her "escape." Aisha then came to the house and picked her up, as if taking her to work. Instead, she drove her to the airport where Layla boarded her flight to London to rendezvous with me.

Although elated to be finally flying to my arms and to have escaped the Kuwait system, she sobbed continuously during most of the six-hour flight to London until finally, a young Kuwaiti guy asked her, "What's wrong? Are you okay?"

She was just *so* broken over leaving her mother and father and especially for not saying goodbye to her father, even though it was for *his* sake that she did not.

I met her—not messing up this time!—at London's Heathrow airport, a rendezvous we had planned weeks before. The reason I flew to London to meet Layla was because in Kuwait a few days before, the U.S. embassy there totally fouled up Layla's plan to fly straight to my arms in America, when, upon learning of Layla's intention to ultimately marry me, they refused to even grant her a tourist visa to enter America. So I phoned the immigration service in Florida, and, like every immigration service worldwide, they *guessed* at the silly laws and told me, "Yes, of course you can marry her in England and come right into America."

So, Layla and I were legally married in Guildford, Surrey, England, on Friday, August 28, 1981. My brother, Gary; his wife, Rebekah; and three of their five children attended the simple ceremony. The seven of us then celebrated with a lunch of fresh brook trout at an outside restaurant in the English countryside. Fortunately for Layla and me, Gary and his family—still with the Children of God, he and Rebekah now leaders of a good portion of the group in England—were living outside of London in a cozy little cottage near the village of Wormley in Surrey. There, Gary graciously provided us his main, upstairs bedroom because we two newlyweds would be stuck in England now for the next six months!

Yep, three days after our wedding, Layla and I took the train to the U.S. embassy at Grosvenor Square in London with our new marriage certificate in hand. We stood in line until finally meeting a consul who stoically told us, "No, she can't get a tourist visa and go into America as your wife. She'll have to apply for immigration, which can take months." *Damn.* Typical of the immigration service. The immigration official back in Florida had given me totally wrong information on being able to bring my new bride into America. She would have to go through the whole process—prove financial support or have someone back her financially (my dad did); provide a criminal-free record from 16 years of age from every country she'd lived in (*Oh, Lord, how long would such records take from her six years in Egypt?*); and, of course, a physical examination.

Still, we were on a cloud—together at last and legally married, man and wife, eating together at London restaurants with some of the money we had. Also, besides telephoning her parents immediately upon arrival in England, Layla communicated with them regularly, ensuring them of her happiness. Her father, too, lovingly accepted her marriage, forgave her for leaving, was only concerned that she was happy and safe, and offered to send her any money she needed. He wished she could return to Kuwait and live nearer to him, in an apartment with me, but that was not much of an option when one of the brothers said that he would *kill* us both.

Finally, on February 9, 1982, after five months of processing, Layla received her immigration visa to enter America. And it might have taken longer if my precious mother hadn't contacted her Florida State Senator, Mr. Lawton Chiles, to expedite Layla's immigration papers. The consular officer in London must have put Layla's and my application at the bottom of his stack of papers, surmising that the two of us had married there in England as a convenient way to get this Arab girl into the States.

We spent the next days helping Gary fix up the quaint stone cottage before we all moved out of it. The home, which sat on a half acre of land along an ideal Surrey country lane, had been donated rent-free to Gary and his family by a wealthy British couple who lived across the street. Now, Gary, Rebekah and their five kids were moving to Thailand to continue with the Children of God there, and Layla and I would fly to America.

In gratitude to the owners of the cottage, Gary wished to deliver it back to them in pristine condition. We repaired the gutters of the house; replaced the roof of the shed outback; restored, upgraded and painted parts of the home's interior; made all necessary repairs; and cleaned the place to spotlessness. When the owner, Mrs. Bailey, came to inspect the place, she nearly cried. "Look what you have done to my home! It's beautiful! Thank you. We will miss you."

On the last day of February 1982, Layla and I said a sad farewell to Gary and his family. He was heading east this time.

Ten years back I was wonderfully transformed by the love of God and set out to share that love with the world. I knew God's love a little, but no one can know the *depths* of His love. I tried to serve Him along with others of the Children of God and when that chapter of my life ended, He continued to love me. He put a woman—one who dearly loved Him—right in my path. To Him, it was irrelevant where she had come from. She loved God, she fell in love with me, and I fell in love with her. Wouldn't I have been a fool if I had put God in a box and said, "My way, my Christian way, is how God is and how He must be served" . . . and lost her?

Layla and I boarded a Pan Am jet from London, prayed a quick prayer, kissed at take-off and headed west.

Afterword

After 34 years, Layla and I are still married and in love. We do everything together since it was so difficult having to live thousands of miles apart in the early years of our romance. We have four, grown, loving children, who are our life. Layla continued in medicine, earned two postgraduate degrees in public health and now teaches medical subjects at a small college.

God? He is the same God for her and for me and for our children . . . and for everyone else, for that matter. Why have religions put a division between us all? Because so much of religions are man-made.

The Children of God? I could never have experienced so many wonderful places and countries if I had not joined this group. Nor would I have met so many souls along the way, who, hopefully, I was able to reach with a few words of love about our Great Creator. And I would not have met my dear wife, who bore me such wonderful children.

The leader of the group, Moses David, might have succumbed too much to sexual temptations, but he certainly started a movement of young people who worked hard to bring words of faith to any and all nationalities around the world. Moses David has passed on, but as far as I know, many individuals he inspired are still out there, somewhere.

Acknowledgments

This book exists because of my loving wife. She found it worthy and encouraged me to complete it. I thank her for her faith in me. Our four children were also an inspiration for me. "How's the book going?" they regularly inquired. A parent could not hope for more loving, caring children than these. God bless them.

In my struggles to find a publisher, I was most fortunate to happen upon Micki Cabaniss Eutsler of Grateful Steps. If there was ever a book publisher in the field because she enjoyed it more than making money from it, it is Micki. A natural, whole-hearted editor and publisher, she imparts a genuine dedication to her authors and their stories. She always amazed me how, while juggling so many responsibilities, she could entirely focus on just me and my book when meeting with her. Despite downfalls and hardships in such a difficult profession, she also remains a testimony of continuous, strong faith in God. God bless her.

Sincere thanks go to John Pierce for contributing his ingenious writing talents to so many parts of the book. His sincere love and devotion to the craft of writing is most impressive. Thank you, John, for your time, your ideas and suggestions.

Thanks to Cathy Mitchell for her time and copyediting expertise. Her corrections and comments were most valuable.

I am grateful how Cynthia Sterling, of Lee Shore Agency, professionally reviewed my original manuscript and then skillfully recommended how the book should finally be written. Her knowledge of writing cannot be taken lightly.

Thank you, Miriam, my oldest daughter, for your many computer searches, your perception of graphics and fonts, and mostly for your loving commitment to produce a cover that appealed to us both.

Thanks to my son-in-law, Mohamed Fakhro, for sharing his uncanny ability to navigate certain computer programs to edit and produce the maps of the book exactly how I wanted them. I will never understand how he so effortlessly adjusted them to my liking. *Mishkour wiyed*, Mohamed.

A special thanks to graphic designer Sachan Chandran for his proficient guidance and technical advice during the making of the cover.

Finally, thanks to all the relatives, friends and acquaintances through the years who were considerate enough to never say out loud: "You're still writing that book?" God bless them all.

Mostly though, thanks to God for allowing me to be considered one of His servants and representatives here on earth, and for always meeting my needs.

About the Author

Wayne Cox left the Children of God when he returned to America in 1978. He sold real estate in Florida, landscaped in Kuwait and worked as an avionics technician on private and commercial aircraft. He and his wife and children live in North Carolina.